The French
Generation of
1820

The French Generation of 1820

ALAN B. SPITZER

PRINCETON UNIVERSITY PRESS
PRINCETON, NEW JERSEY

Copyright © 1987 by Princeton University Press
Published by Princeton University Press, 41 William Street,
Princeton, New Jersey 08540
In the United Kingdom:
Princeton University Press, Guildford, Surrey

All Rights Reserved
Library of Congress Cataloging in Publication Data will be
found on the last printed page of this book
ISBN 0-691-05496-7

Publication of this book has been aided by a grant from the
Ira O. Wade Fund of Princeton University Press
This book has been composed in Linotron Granjon

Clothbound editions of Princeton University Press books
are printed on acid-free paper, and binding materials are
chosen for strength and durability. Paperbacks, although satisfactory
for personal collections, are not usually suitable for library rebinding

Printed in the United States of America by
Princeton University Press
Princeton, New Jersey

FOR MARY

It is up to us, *jeunes gens*, children of the century and of liberty, to speed the dawning of happiness among nations, to make the security of thrones coincide with the freedom of peoples; already, we have great tasks to perform.

Honoré de Balzac,
Sténie; ou, Les Erreurs philosophiques

Contents

Acknowledgments

This book, which was long in the making, owes a great deal to the support of individuals and institutions. Consistent with its commitment to the encouragement of faculty research, the University of Iowa granted precious leave time. I am also grateful for the support of the National Endowment for the Humanities, the John Simon Guggenheim Memorial Foundation, and the Institute for Advanced Study at Princeton.

Portions of the manuscript were read and helpfully criticized by Paul Mazgaj, Jill Harsin, Charles Hale, Keith Michael Baker, Jonathan Beecher, and Robert Darnton. The entire manuscript was meticulously read and criticized by my teacher, colleague, and friend, the late Laurence Lafore, whose pedagogical virtuosity and personal integrity have provided models for my entire scholarly career. His loss is deeply felt.

I wish to thank Edgar Newman, Debra Perry, and Jean-Jacques Goblot for bringing relevant materials to my attention. The communication of source materials by Myriam and Daniel Conte affords the opportunity to express my gratitude for over half a lifetime of friendship, which has greatly enriched the experience of a foreign scholar in France.

Professor Gregory A. Caldeira of the Department of Political Science at the University of Iowa gave generously of his time and expertise to make possible the construction of the sociograms in appendix B. The preparation of the manuscript owes a great deal to the impeccable typing of Eunice Prosser, to Marie-Pierre LeHir for undertaking the travail of the final draft, and to the impeccable copyediting of Alan Schroder. I am grateful for the advice of my wife, Mary Freeman Spitzer, whose ear for language saved me from many infelicities. The completion of this work owes more than I can here express to her patient and affectionate support.

Preface

> This penchant to reason from the identity
> of words to the identity of things and to ex-
> plain the past by analogies drawn from the
> present is the most fertile source of histori-
> cal prejudices.
> Théodore Jouffroy, *Le Globe* (11 June 1825)

This book has been written on the assumption that age differences sometimes matter. It reflects the influence of Karl Mannheim's seminal essay "The Problem of Generations," in which the social phenomenon of a generation is defined as "nothing more than a particular kind of identity of location, embracing related age groups embedded in a historical-social process."[1] Its emphasis on the historical-social location of a particular age group—a cohort—born between 1792 and 1803 is not intended to illustrate some general theory of generations but to illuminate the Restoration era by the light refracted through the collective experience of what I, and others, have called the generation of 1820.[2]

A certain number of people were born in France between 1792 and 1803, but it is not self-evident that they were historically significant because they were more or less coeval. It is difficult but not impossible to write the history of a subject whose existence is problematic. The evidence for the generation's existence is to be sought in forms of collective behavior, in networks of personal relationships, in shared assumptions that underlay an ideology

[1] Karl Mannheim, "The Problem of Generations," in *Essays in the Sociology of Knowledge* (London, 1959), 292.

[2] In my usage, "cohort" merely refers to a group of people born between certain dates. Following Mannheim, I will define a "generation" as an age group with a particular historical identity (which remains to be established). However, I will use the term interchangeably in the sense that the cohort born between 1792 and 1803 constitutes my generation of 1820. Some demographers disapprove of this, insisting on the distinction between an age cohort and a biological generation.

and attitudes that constitute a *mentalité*, in everything that comprised
a common response to contemporary experience distinguishing the cohort from its contemporaries.

This "evidence" is, of course, a composite of what I have selected
from surviving documents—from letters, published and unpublished
reminiscences, recorded expressions by members of the cohort, and
comments by their contemporaries, from the reproduction of their individual experiences in fiction and the recapitulation in secondary
sources, and from the recorded traces of collective acts in current accounts, police records, and other testimony. This procedure is based on
the assumptions that the documents were produced by people who actually existed and that reconstructions of their behavior can be evaluated according to objective criteria as more or less plausible. I hold
these convictions with the same faith that informs my belief that I am
mortal and that Hiroshima occurred.

This is not to say that the documents contain some discrete truth
universally accessible to reason. Each text is read in the light of a mitigated skepticism, a suspension of final judgment that is not equivalent
to a self-refuting relativism. The sources are available for public scrutiny and contrary interpretation. Common sense, and a venerable critical tradition, prescribe the caution with which one assays the testimony of memoirs, often artlessly self-serving; letters, authentic
versions of immediate contemporary communication but sometimes
written for effect; journalistic commentary, in which a critical and independent voice is also the vehicle for collective self-praise; obviously
tendentious depositions of embattled authorities and political police,
though valid sources for all that; and novels too, as it seems wasteful to
set aside insights of genius because they were cast in fictional form.
Some of what these heterogeneous documents tell us will be taken at
face value. Much is treated as "the evidence of witnesses in spite of
themselves."[3]

All of this is undertaken in the awareness that the past can only be
reconstructed in the language of the present. Ernest Renan once remarked that the complex works of Victor Cousin, philosophic guru of
the Restoration youth, could not be appreciated by foreigners, who

---

[3] Marc Bloch, *The Historian's Craft*, trans. Peter Putnam (New York, 1953), 61.

would miss the felicities savored by the French.[4] Not too many years
after Renan made that observation there would be few native speakers
of the French philosophic tongue who could imagine what had impelled anyone to appreciate Victor Cousin. It is far more difficult now
to reimagine that appeal through the distance of years and the filter of
a foreign tongue, or to recapture the shocking force of Victor Hugo's
experiments with the alexandrine, or to apprehend the revolutionary
attraction of forgotten mediocrities such as the poet Casimir Delavigne. On the other hand, the language of the 1820s neoliberalism that
advocated freedom of expression even for Jesuits is perfectly familiar
to a member of my cohort and my culture.

The imprint of time and place that seemed most to distance me from
the historical-social location of that nineteenth-century *jeunesse* is a
radical skepticism more profound even than the authentic personal despair that once drove young spirits to suicide. This has nothing to do
with a skepticism as to the possibilities of social progress defined in
terms of the general standard of living. We have reason to be far more
optimistic about public policies that might ameliorate the lives of the
most numerous and the most poor than were the most idealistic re-
formers of the Restoration era. Nor do I refer to the fact that history
has provided us with the possibility of catastrophes far beyond the
worst imaginings of political pessimists more than a century past.

The difference is intrinsic. I can describe but not reimagine the cast
of mind that forecast a universal ideology destined to transform culture
and regenerate the social order.[5] It is no longer possible to believe, or
even to conceive as intelligible, the proposition that history might pre-

---

[4] Ernest Renan, "M. Cousin," in *Essais de morale et de critique*, in *Oeuvres complètes*
(Paris, 1947), 2:58–59: "l'oeuvre si complexe de M. Cousin ne peut être bien appréciée
que par des lectures pénétrées du goût français; qu'un étranger n'y verrait pas mille
beautés qui nous charment, et qu'il y apercevrait bien des lacunes dont l'art prodigieux
du maître nous dérobe le sentiment."

[5] David Joravsky, "The Construction of the Stalinist Psyche," in Sheila Fitzpatrick,
ed., *Cultural Revolution in Russia, 1928–1931* (Bloomington, Ind., 1984), 128: "In our
century a rational, comprehensive world view has become intellectually impossible. To
put the matter more concretely, it has become impossible to keep the sciences of nature
and human nature integrated with humanistic and artistic visions, and with the ideological beliefs that hold together such groups as political parties and governments." For
a (rather qualified) opposing vision, see Martin Jay, *Marxism and Totality: The Adven-
tures of a Concept from Lukács to Habermas* (Berkeley, 1984), 536–37.

The French
Generation of
1820

CHAPTER 1

Introduction:
The Generation as a
Social Network

"... la génération, notion indispensable et illu-
soire"

Pierre Nora, *Les Lieux de mémoire*

The assumption that a cohort
coming of age in the Restoration's first decade did exist for history is one that has a long history. The generation has certainly
existed for historians of French literature and Restoration
France, who have celebrated a tight cluster of distinguished
birthdates.[1] Henri Peyre discerned an eloquence in the "mere
enumeration" of the names of the most brilliant generation to be
seen in France in many years, citing such figures as Augustin
Thierry (1795), Alfred de Vigny (1797), Adolphe Thiers (1797),
Jules Michelet (1798), Auguste Comte (1798), A. A. Cournot
(1801), Victor Hugo (1802), Pierre Leroux (1797), Eugène Delacroix (1798), and Honoré de Balzac (1799) in a long list of luminaries of the "glorious generation." I will add many more without precisely subscribing to Peyre's chronological boundaries.[2]

[1] See Paul Thureau-Dangin, "Une Génération nouvelle," chap. 3 of *Le Parti
libéral sous la Restauration* (Paris, 1888), 191–264; Sébastien Charléty, "L'Avènement d'une génération nouvelle," chap. 3 of *La Restauration*, vol. 4 of *Histoire
de France contemporaine*, ed. E. Lavisse (Paris, 1921), 197–228; Charles Bruneau,
"La Génération de 1820," chap. 1, book 2 of Ferdinand Brunot, ed., *Histoire de
la langue française des origines à nos jours* (Paris, 1968), 12:103–15; Albert Thibaudet, "La Génération de 1820," *Histoire de la littérature française*, part 2 (Paris,
1936), 105–292; Louis Liard, *L'Enseignement supérieur en France* (Paris, 1888–
94), 2:142–44, 162–65; Henri Peyre, *Les Générations littéraires* (Paris, 1948), 136–
38; F. A. Isambert, *De La Charbonnerie au saint-simonisme: Etude sur la jeunesse
de Buchez* (Paris, 1966), 56–69; André Billaz, *Les Ecrivains romantiques et Voltaire: Essai sur Voltaire et le romantisme en France* (Lille, 1974), 2:623–35; John M.
S. Allison, *Thiers and the French Monarchy* (Hamden, Conn., 1968), 1–3.

[2] Peyre, *Les Générations littéraires*, 136–37. Peyre's list includes those born

Recent works, notably the doctoral thesis of Robert Warren Brown and the immensely erudite, imaginative, and provocative *oeuvre* of the Balzac scholar Pierre Barbéris, have situated the cohort historically, in the spirit of Mannheim's contextual approach.[3] For Barbéris, the self-affirmation of a generational autonomy by this French *jeunesse* posed "a new problem that literature does not create but records at the beginning of the nineteenth century."[4]

There is no doubt that the generation existed in the perceptions of its contemporaries. It was widely believed during and after the Restoration that the most visible and articulate members of a group whose mean age was twenty-three or twenty-four in 1820 constituted a privileged cohort, set apart by its talents and its coherence from older and younger contemporaries. Most of the evidence for this identity refers to a predominantly male, middle class, educated minority of the cohort, but that minority was perceived as authentically representing all that was freshest, most promising, and specifically youthful in the contributions of its coevals. Speaking to the Chamber of Deputies in 1822, Benjamin Constant characterized the coming generation in terms that perfectly reflected its self-image: "Less frivolous than that of the Old Regime, less passionate than that of the Revolution, *la jeunesse actuelle* is distinguished by its thirst for knowledge, its love of scholarship, and its devotion to the truth." Lafayette, a venerated, and politically exploited, standard-bearer of young opponents of the Bourbon monarchy, eulogized them as "our youth, the hope of the century, better educated than we, enlightened by their own insights and the fruits of our experience, eschewing faction, repudiating prejudice, accessible only to pure motives and generous methods but demanding liberty with a natural and therefore irresistible passion."[5] The potentialities of

---

between 1795 and 1805. I would begin and end mine at earlier dates for reasons discussed below. I will follow Robert Wohl, *The Generation of 1914* (Cambridge, Mass., 1979) and Peyre in entering the birthdate in parentheses after the first citation of an individual in the text or the footnotes.

[3] Robert Brown, "The Generation of 1820 During the Bourbon Restoration in France: A Biographical and Intellectual Portrait of the First Wave, 1814–1824" (Ph.D. diss., Duke University, 1979); Pierre Barbéris, *Balzac Et Le Mal du siècle*, 2 vols. (Paris, 1970).

[4] Pierre Barbéris, *Le Monde de Balzac* (Paris, 1973), 485.

[5] *Archives parlementaires*, 2nd ser., 35:446, 28:154–55. See also Lafayette to James Monroe, 20 July 1820, in Gilbert de Lafayette, *Mémoires, correspondance et manuscrits du général La Fayette, publiés par sa famille* (Paris, 1837–38), 6:93: "Cette nouvelle gé-

that same *jeunesse* were seen through rather different spectacles from the other end of the political spectrum. Lamennais, a bitter critic of the secular University, read the future as threatening precisely because it would be inherited by a generation pressing close on his own:

> This youth, which had its baptism of fire against the throne, this youth suckled on revolutionary doctrines and passions, will soon comprise the nation. While certain scoundrels devastate the present, the University corrupts the future; it is preparing an ungovernable future for us.[6]

Even Chateaubriand, sometime idol of the young, resented the inexorable pressure of cohorts who would attain their maturity in his old age:

> A generation is rising up behind us resentful of all discipline, hostile to every king, dreaming of the republic but constitutionally incapable of republican virtues. It advances, presses on us, elbows us aside. Soon it will take our place.

Bonaparte knew how to handle these types, Chateaubriand recalled, by tempting them with glory and decimating them in battle, but for "us" there remained only the appeal of the legitimate monarchy, committed to representative government and supported by a vigorous aristocracy.[7]

It is possible to interpret Chateaubriand's lament as a correct prediction, although I will argue that the contemporary identity of the generation was not completely defined by its opposition to the restored monarchy. It was, however, perceived as forging that identity in the furnace of the struggle against the established elites and received ideas of the Restoration era. This is the way it was characterized by Charles-Augustin Sainte-Beuve (1804), a fascinated participant-observer just on the younger margin of the cohort:

> There is a generation composed of those born at the end of the last century, still children or too young under the Empire, which lib-

---

nération est éclairée et généreuse, supérieure aux impressions du jacobinisme et du bonapartisme. Elle soutiendra, j'en suis sûr, le droit d'une liberté pure." See also Gilbert Chinard, ed., *The Letters of Lafayette and Jefferson* (Baltimore, 1929), 399, 406, 410.

[6] *Correspondance inédite entre Lamennais et le Baron Vitrolles* (Paris, 1886), 41.

[7] François de Chateaubriand, *Mémoires sur S.A.R. Mgr Le Duc de Berry*, in *Oeuvres complètes* (Paris, 1869), 9:579, first published in 1820.

erated itself to don manly garb in the midst of the storms of 1814 and 1815. This generation, whose present age is approximately forty and who fought with virtual unanimity under the Restoration against the political and religious *ancien régime*, today occupies the summits of power and science in business, the Chambers and the Academies. The Revolution of 1830, to which this generation had so greatly contributed by its fifteen years of struggle, was made for it to a considerable extent and was the harbinger of its accession.[8]

Writing only three years after the July Revolution, Sainte-Beuve had already assumed a critical distance from his former mentors, but he still shared their nostalgic self-evaluation.[9] In later years of success and disillusion, they would recall that "springtime of the century" with a retrospective warmth and solidarity envied by their successors.[10] A salient characteristic of the cohort would remain a sense of collective self-confidence and mutual regard. Paul-François Dubois (1793), the biographer of his generation in scattered writings and a key figure in its early history, would remember those years of early manhood as the "climacteric of the century."[11]

Without granting such importance to those years or to the self-estimate of that generation, I do accept the assumption that there was a relationship between age and historically significant behavior in the early years of the Restoration and that the locus of this behavior was in the cohort born between 1792 and 1803. The birthdates that fix the identity of the generation are not self-evident benchmarks but more or less arbitrary boundaries suggested by my reading of the past. Yet to establish boundaries is an indispensable step, and not only for the his-

---

[8] Charles-Augustin Sainte-Beuve, *Portraits littéraires* (Paris, 1862), 1:296.

[9] Sainte-Beuve had been a student of Dubois at the collège Charlemagne and a contributor to Dubois' journal, the *Globe*, at the age of twenty.

[10] Thureau-Dangin, *Le Parti libéral*, 197–98: "Aussi a-t-on pu la proclamer justement une 'génération heureuse.' Même refroidis par l'âge, tous ceux qui avaient vécu de cette vie n'en ont rappelé les souvenirs qu'avec une émotion toujours jeune et un accent ignoré des sceptiques et des matérialistes de l'heure actuelle. Ils redevenaient enthousiastes pour raconter des espoirs qui cependant avaient été depuis lors plus d'une fois déçus; et nous écoutions avec étonnement, mais non sans envie, ces échos du printemps d'un siècle que nous étions condamnés à connaître dans son automne désenchanté et stérile."

[11] Paul-François Dubois, *Cousin, Jouffroy, Damiron* (Paris, 1902), 39.

tory of generations. For, in the words of Fernand Braudel, "The question of boundaries is the first to be encountered; from it all others flow.
To draw a boundary around anything is to define, analyze and reconstruct it; in this case select, indeed adopt, a philosophy of history."[12]
Eminent historians have criticized the very attempt to mark off segments along the seamless continuum of daily births,[13] but the problem
of establishing generational boundaries should inhibit us no more than
does the problem of marking off the categories in any continuum—
such as class, ideology, or political movement—where there is a shad-
ing or ambiguity at the boundaries.[14] The authority for the particular
delimitation is established by argument with reference to the collective
behavior and personal relationships that significantly divided groups
according to age rather than some other variable. In this case I will argue that historically important age relationships can be established by
setting off the cohort born during the last decade of the eighteenth century and emerging into maturity under the Restoration from those too
old to have participated in the imperial educational system or too
young to have reached early maturity by the death of Louis XVIII in
1824.

Here I part from such distinguished authorities as Albert Thibaudet, whose history of French literary generations places Lamartine,
born in 1790, and Théophile Gautier, born in 1811, in the same romantic generation.[15] This is not to argue the question of whether there were
one or more distinct or overlapping "romantic" generations,[16] or

[12] Fernand Braudel, *The Mediterranean and the Mediterranean World in the Age of
Philip II*, trans. S. Reynolds (New York, 1972), 1:18.

[13] See especially Johan Huizinga, *Men and Ideas* (New York, 1965), 73–74; Lucien
Febvre, "Générations," in Bulletin du centre international de synthèse. Section de
synthèse historique, no. 7, published in *Revue de synthèse historique*, 47 (1929): 41–42.

[14] I have discussed this issue in my essay "The Historical Problem of Generations,"
American Historical Review, 78 (December 1973): 1358.

[15] Thibaudet, "La Génération de 1820," 105–292. Brown, "The Generation of 1820,"
22, presents an excellent critique of the broad and inconsistent boundaries of Charléty's
"nouvelle génération" in his volume in the Lavisse series. However, I do not subscribe
to Brown's inclusion of Charles Comte (1782) and Charles Dunoyer (1786), that is, men
of Stendhal's generation, in the crucial cohort of the Restoration *jeunesse*.

[16] For example, James S. Allen, *Popular French Romanticism: Authors, Readers, and
Books in the 19th Century* (Syracuse, 1981), 87–88, argues the question rather inconclu-
sively, identifying a "French romantic generation of 1830" but remarking that too
many romantic authors were born on the wrong date to allow of the concept of a "theoretical romantic generation." In another work, Allen's conclusion, "une génération

whether the term romantic should be confined to art and literature.[17] A plausible case might be made for a romantic literary generation born in the years between 1790 and 1820, or for that matter in the eighty years between the birth of Chateaubriand in 1768 and his death in 1848.[18] The usefulness of such demarcations depends upon the breadth of perspective adopted by the viewer. From a sufficient distance, there is some sense in locating everyone born after 1790 in a "postrevolutionary generation," just as there is in identifying economic developments between 1750 and 1850 as an industrial revolution; but in the narrow and sharpened perspective of the lens I focus on the first decade of the Restoration, salient attributes of those who came of age between 1814 and 1825 distinguish them from their younger brothers, who flamboyantly expressed their alienation in the early 1830s, and their elders, who had already embarked on the careers afforded by Napoleon's military imperium.

Thus I subscribe to Sainte-Beuve's distinction between the generation of Vigny and Hugo, who made their literary debuts around 1820, and that of Auguste Barbier, born in 1805 and only appearing on the literary scene after the Revolution of July 1830.[19] Sainte-Beuve's shadowy boundary between the literary giants born before 1803 and the minor *littérateur* born in 1805 does indicate significant differences in experience and behavior. Not only did Barbier make his literary debut

---

romantique de 1830 semble donc bien exister en France," is followed by, "Donc, l'hypothèse d'une génération romantique ne correspond pas à ce que nous savons de l'histoire littéraire réelle." Allen, "Y-a-t-il en France une génération romantique de 1830?" *Romantisme*, 28–29 (1980): 102–18. Cf. Pierre Barbéris, "Structures et dynamiques du romantisme," in Pierre Abraham and Roland Desné, eds., *Manuel d'histoire littéraire de la France* (Paris, 1972), 4 (Part 1): 484.

[17] As Lucien Febvre remarked, there is no guarantee that a "literary generation" will be chronologically congruent, or otherwise identical, with a "political" or other generation appearing in roughly the same time span. Febvre, "Générations," 42.

[18] See, for example, René Jasinski, *Histoire de la littérature française* (Paris, 1966), 2:244–311.

[19] For an identification of two distinct generations, see Max Milner, *Le Romantisme*, vol. 1, *1820–1843* (Paris, 1973), 43–48; C. A. Sainte-Beuve, *Causeries du lundi* (Paris, 1883), 12:7; see also Emile Deschamps (1791), *Oeuvres complètes* (Paris, 1873), 4:302–3: "A cette époque 1823–24, Alfred de Musset, Théophile Gautier, A. Cosnard, Antoine de Latour et beaucoup d'autres poètes appartenant aux mêmes générations, n'avaient pas encore fait leurs preuves." Pierre Barbéris, *Lectures du réel* (Paris, 1973), 87: "*Enfant du siècle* en 1818–1820 était sacre et signe de promesse. En 1830, *enfant du siècle* est signe de damnation."

after 1830, he was just too young to have rioted in June 1820 or to have conspired with the Carbonari in 1821. The notorious *jeunesse* that flaunted its red waistcoat at the première of Hugo's *Hernani* is not quite coeval with the young Hugo, and the students who, in legend at least, mounted the barricades of July are of a different breed than the veterans of the secret societies—such as Godefroy Cavaignac (1801), Jules Bastide (1800), and J. A. Guinard (1799)—who played a leading part in the July Revolution.

Men like Armand Carrel (1800), the liberal journalist, or Saint-Amand Bazard (1791), the conspirator and Saint-Simonian, or Charles Rémusat (1797), the brilliant second-generation Doctrinaire, passed with the end of the Restoration into the fourth or fifth decade of their lives. They can be distinguished ideologically and temperamentally from such successors as Théophile Gautier and Petrus Borel (1809). This is to refer not merely to their date of birth but to their characteristic behavior: the generation of 1820 was distinguished in its own eyes and in those of its contemporaries by its "gravity," by the high moral tone it struck on issues of cosmic or personal significance. There was little trace among them of Bohemianism, dandyism, or the inclination to shock the bourgeoisie. Their brand of the *mal du siècle*—the emotional tone of stylish melancholy or genuine despair attributed to cohorts of cultivated youth throughout the first half of the century—was laced with a bracing sense of personal and collective superiority.[20]

The boundary that separates the generation of 1820 from its immediate predecessors is also vague and also needs to be established with reference to historical context and collective behavior. The youth of the early Restoration has been plausibly identified as the first postrevolutionary generation,[21] but a sharper focus on its actual historical location will identify it as the first generation formed in the *lycées* and faculties of the new imperial University. The chronological boundary at roughly 1791 or 1792 separates the generation of the *auditeurs* of the Conseil d'Etat, future cadres for the imperial state machine, from a fledgling elite that would center its ambitions on the *grandes écoles* of the late Empire and the early Restoration.[22] The moral and intellectual

[20] This subject is pursued with indefatigable gusto by Pierre Barbéris in *Balzac Et Le Mal du siècle*. It will be discussed at length below in chapter 7.

[21] Isambert, *De la Charbonnerie au saint-simonisme*, 67.

[22] Nicholas Richardson, *The French Prefectoral Corps, 1814–1830* (Cambridge, Eng.,

temperament of a Stendhal (1783), formed out of the ideas of the eighteenth century and hardened in the crucible of the imperial wars, was essentially antithetical to the spirit of the young intellectuals with whom he collaborated and quarreled in the 1820s.

I believe that I can make a plausible case for the relative coherence and distinctiveness of the cohort born between 1792 and 1803, but I scarcely pretend to perfect clarity at its boundaries. The cohort remains on a continuum. Lamartine, born in 1790, or Sainte-Beuve, in 1804, exemplify the blurring at the edges of any such attempt at sociohistorical definition: the former, whose poetry spoke so powerfully to and for his young admirers, had been socialized under different circumstances and would never quite fulfill the role they wished to assign him;[23] the latter would manage to maintain an ambiguous position at the very edge of the cohort that enabled him to assume the role of collaborator or critic according to his convenience.

The distinctions I have drawn proceed from my conviction that what distinguishes the generation of 1820 is precisely its historical location, beginning with its socialization to the sound of martial music and the sight of ceremonies of national self-congratulation but in an atmosphere of institutional stasis and subterranean crisis. Its collective trauma was not the Revolution but the collapse of the Empire. This was the trauma of that "pale, ardent, and neurotic generation" described in the oft-quoted passage from the unforgettable second chapter of Alfred de Musset's forgettable novel, *Confession of a Child of the Century*. An "anxious youth" conceived between battles had awakened from its dreams of the snows of Moscow and the sun of the pyramids to the sound of church bells, its horizon illuminated not by the brilliant sun of Austerlitz but by the pale reflection of the lilies:

> Three elements entered into the life which offered itself to these children: behind them a past destroyed forever, still quivering on its ruins with all the fossils of centuries of absolutism; before them the aurora of an immense horizon, the first gleam of the future, and between these two worlds . . . something similar to the ocean

---

1966), 132: "The auditors came for the most part from the generation born between 1780 and 1790."

[23] Milner, *Le Romantisme*, 249, on Lamartine's *formation* in the spirit of the eighteenth century: "les éléments essentiels d'une enfance et d'une adolescence que tout paraît rattacher au passé."

that separates the old continent from the young America, something vague and floating, a rough sea filled with wreckage, trav-
ersed from time to time by a white sail or by some ship trailing
thick clouds of smoke; the present century, in a word, which separates past from future, which is neither the one nor the other,
and which resembles both, where one cannot know whether at
each step he treads on a seedbed or a heap of refuse.[24]

De Musset himself, born in 1810, was just too young to have experienced the trauma, but he provided a poignant representation of the
self-image of a generation convinced it had been betrayed by the past,
facing with anxiety and confidence its magnificent destiny to shape the
inscrutable future. Its perception of the lessons of the past and the
promise of the future had been permanently colored by the fact that its
emergence into maturity coincided with the death of the Empire and
the rebirth of the monarchy.

All of this remains to be established. Most of the evidence for the argument depends on the traces deposited by an articulate minority of
the cohort. However, the anonymous majority of the "turbulent"
youth of the schools, or the rioters of June 1820, or the audience for the
lectures of Victor Cousin (1792), or the members of masonic lodges and
secret societies have also left tangible evidence of the generational coherence of their collective behavior. To document the influence of the
leaders and spokesmen whose names we have recovered is to imply the
existence of these wider circles to and for whom they spoke. Nevertheless, the major insights of this work depend on the reconstruction of
the ideas and behavior of individuals whose identity has not been lost
to history.

What generalizations about the collective mentality of that vast sea
of anonymous coevals dare one derive from an examination of the
members of the cohort sufficiently educated or sufficiently literate to
enjoy or aspire to social mobility through the manipulation of words
and the application of professional training? This is the question facing
anyone who proposes to characterize a generation, as the characterization invariably depends upon a small minority of those born between
the relevant dates. Most historians of generations have resolutely faced

[24] Alfred de Musset, *La Confession d'un enfant du siècle: Oeuvres complètes en prose*
(Paris, 1951), 85.

away from the question while listing five or twelve or twenty noteworthy individuals presumed to incarnate the spirit of their coevals. Actually, the problem of drawing generalizations about large populations from evidence provided by small minorities is endemic in the social sciences. I have argued that we need not claim that a certain minority is representative while asserting that significant distinctions between populations and significant changes in a population can be attributed to a relevant minority.[25]

Whether the evidence here is in some sense representative of that minority is another question. The list of those cited and discussed is necessarily a partial and arbitrary selection from a much larger population; therefore, it seems appropriate to lay my cards on the table, present the list of those through whom the history of the generation has been derived, and outline the criteria for the construction of the list.[26]

My first criterion responded to historical reputation. Even though I have attempted to fix the history of the generation at an early stage of its existence, it seemed precious to exclude those individuals who attained great distinction only after they passed out of the era of their youth in the Restoration. Perhaps the young Balzac had made a sufficient impression by 1825 to earn him a place on the list even if he had not become the paragon of the novelist; it seemed unthinkable to exclude him. The great economist and philosopher Antoine-Augustin Cournot was still some years away from making any significant impression on his contemporaries, too young to rival those slightly older coevals whose ephemeral reputations his would someday eclipse. Yet Cournot should certainly be entered on the roster of his generation, especially because he left us reminiscences of his youth.[27] All direct testimony from the subjects of the study has been gratefully received and guarantees that the witness will be listed.

Those who seemed outstanding at the time, irrespective of the distinction of their subsequent careers, comprise the core of the list. Salience in contemporary eyes also brings into view those who played

---

[25] Spitzer, "The Historical Problem of Generations," 1359–60. Annie Kriegel remarks, "But the legitimacy of paradigmatic representation has no quantitative basis. It stems purely from the ability to achieve recognition by providing the maximum differentiating identity." Kriegel, "Generational Difference: The History of an Idea," *Daedalus*, 107 (Fall 1978): 29.

[26] See appendix A.

[27] Antoine-Augustin Cournot, *Souvenirs* (Paris, 1913).

something less than stellar roles but whose active participation and widespread association in various organizations, associations, or circles that contributed to the establishment of an age-related collective identity performed an integrative function. Many of those individuals were identified by their multiple membership in organizations, associations, or circles that contributed to the establishment of an age-related collective identity. Membership in one such group by an otherwise unnoted individual has not usually been dignified with an entry. Individuals who came to my attention only as students at the Ecole normale or as recruits for the Carbonari, but who had not distinguished themselves as members of that group and had left no other traces, have rarely been listed. And there are innumerable others—identified in the correspondence of contemporaries, in the records of the authorities, or in the reminiscences of acquaintances—who have not been recorded here. Another way to describe this process would be to admit that wherever an individual of the appropriate age has been cited in this text he (or, rarely, she) has become an operational member of the generation.

Having observed my cards, the reader may wonder whether they are stacked. Anyone can think of names to add to the list. In principle, there may have been as many young intellectuals who extolled the older generation, embraced radical empiricism, and cheered the Restoration purges of the University as there were those who said and did the things that constitute the profile I have drawn, but if this is the case only a handful managed to deposit an entry in the historical record. This is not to assert a perfect homogeneity. The subjects of this study enthusiastically agreed to differ, but in the very formulation of their differences they set themselves apart from their contemporaries in other cohorts.

Some of these issues have been anticipated by distinctions drawn by Karl Mannheim. For Mannheim, a generation, or a "social-generation," is not necessarily identical with an entire age cohort, and a generation itself is composed of distinct generation units. According to Mannheim, "Youth experiencing the same concrete historical problems may be said to be part of the same actual generation; while those groups within the same actual generation which work up the material of their common experiences in different specific ways, constitute separate generation units." Mannheim further refines this two-tiered conception with reference to "concrete groups" within generational units that have developed especially influential "integrative attitudes." With all those who share a common historical location and the conception of a common destiny, they constitute a "generation in actuality."[28]

These distinctions do seem useful, even indispensable, but they do not completely dispose of recalcitrant questions. How can we know that certain attitudes are "integrative"? Apparently when they are so influential that "individuals outside the narrow groups but nevertheless similarly located find in them the satisfying expression of their location in the prevailing *historical configuration*."[29] In that case, to separate out generation units of whatever size does not spare us the task of demonstrating that they do express the attitudes of some larger population, and this entails some characterization of the larger population.

Perhaps we can uncover the relevant evidence in the "prevailing historical configuration." The concrete historical issues that engage our attention—wars, depressions, industrialization, changes of regime, intellectual movements—affect thousands or millions of lives. The more pervasive the historical experience, the larger the number of coevals whose shared experience constitutes a collective identity.[30] The self-defined generation of the Restoration *jeunesse* was comprised of coevals whose identity had been shaped by events on an immense scale, by the distant consequences of the Revolution as well as the immediate consequences of the fall of the Empire.

To emphasize the decisive imprint of the historical situation at a cer-

---

[28] Mannheim, "The Problem of Generations," 304. Mannheim cites as an example, "Those who were young about 1810 in Germany constituted one actual generation whether they adhered to the then current version of liberal or conservative ideas. But insofar as they are conservative or liberal, they belonged to different units of that actual generation" (p. 307, see also 297n).

[29] Ibid., 306–7.

[30] See Wohl, *The Generation of 1914*, 80: "Mannheim's distinction between generation as location and generation as actuality helped further to illuminate the relationship between the masses and the intellectual and political elites who sought to lead them. The more collective the nature of historical events, the greater the number of people they would affect, and hence the larger potential size of the actual generation." See also Hans Jaeger, "Generations in History: Reflections on a Controversial Concept," *History and Theory*, 24 (1985): 291: "Pronounced generational breaks which may affect an entire society apparently occur only after decisive historical events, such as wars, revolutions, and economic crises of great proportions." Also, Robert Tyler, "Of Generations, Generation Gaps, and History," *Connecticut Review*, 5 (October 1971): 9. Raoul Girardet, "De La Conception de génération à la notion de contemporanéité," *Revue d'histoire moderne et contemporaine*, 30 (April–June 1983): 265–66, emphasizes the infrequency of such conjunctures.

tain stage of socialization is to present a generational rather than a life-cycle interpretation of the collective behavior of cohorts. This is to relinquish the assumption that generational coherence is confined to the life stage of youth or to some chronic cultural-biological gap that separates the young from everyone else. A great deal of the literature on the history of generations conceives of such characteristics as rebelliousness, alienation, hubris, idealism, and frustrated mobility as recurrent attributes of an early stage in the life cycle, but as Karl Mannheim has observed, factors presumed to be present in every situation cannot explain "the particular features of a given process of modification."[31] The presumption that the young are always rebellious or underemployed contributes little to the discrimination of variations of youthful behavior in varying circumstances. My intention is definitely not to argue from characteristics assumed to be present at all times and places but to reconstruct a specific context for the behavior of youth in the first decade of the Restoration.

This does not entail a doctrinaire contextualism that would ignore the historical implications of the universal attributes of human growth. How the life stage of youth is defined, how long it lasts, and what social roles it entails all vary according to time and place, but even societies that do not insert a stage of youth between childhood and maturity must deal with the development of the child into the adult.[32] No one is experienced at birth. The young have no one to learn from but their elders. Important social roles may or may not be assigned to youth, but the young must be socialized. They may or may not rebel against their training, but they must be trained. If they are socialized or trained in schools, they will usually experience age segregation. If the schools are concentrated in a city or a *quartier*, they will inhabit an age-related subculture.

[31] Mannheim, "The Problem of Generations," 312.

[32] For a discussion of the historical and social definitions of youth, see Philippe Ariès, *Centuries of Childhood* (New York, 1962); John R. Gillis, *Youth and History* (New York, 1974); S. N. Eisenstadt, "Archetypal Patterns of Youth," in Peter K. Manning and Marcello Truzzi, eds., *Youth and Sociology* (Englewood Cliffs, N.J., 1972), 12–29; and Kenneth Keniston, "Youth: A 'New' Stage of Life," *American Scholar*, 39 (Autumn 1970): 631–54. On the general issue of "the biological principles of aging and cohort flow," see Matilda White Riley, "Aging, Social Change, and the Power of Ideas," *Daedalus*, 107 (Fall 1978): 44–45; and C. John Sommerville, *The Rise and Fall of Childhood* (Beverly Hills, 1982).

The actual consequence for a given youth will depend upon the roles assigned to particular age grades by the society and by the circumstances of the historical moment. The more stable the society, the more likely that age distinctions will be experienced solely as the recurrent differences between regular stages in the life cycle. The sharper and more profound the change in the historical circumstances, the more likely that age groups will differ as a result of their particular experiences. Especially where there has been a radical change in the socialization of cohorts that are contemporary but not coeval, age-related differences may be perceived across a deep generational gap.

The traumatic changes of such importance in forging the unique collective identity of the Restoration *jeunesse* were experienced within the framework of institutions, expectations, and patterns of behavior characteristic of the young. They lived segregated lives in schools and the student milieu, formed voluntary associations with their coevals, and communicated with a dense network of friends and acquaintances of their own generation.

Any description of the public role of the youth of the Restoration will inevitably emphasize the "youth of the schools"—that small minority occupying, or recently promoted out of, the newly established *lycées*, faculties, and *grandes écoles* of the national university system. The virtually universal pattern of the organization of higher education in the modern world—socialization and training of an elite in age-segregated institutions—had already assumed its characteristic French form. The fortunate few (exclusively male) were recruited from privileged social strata. They were segregated under the rigorous discipline of the youth barracks—the *école caserne*—and then resegregated under the rigorous indiscipline of the Parisian student milieu or one of its provincial imitations. They were educated and stratified through a highly formalized examination system. The most successful constituted an elite corps of *lauréats de concours*, prize winners of the ubiquitous academic competitions. The very cream of that cream competed for places at the *grandes écoles*, notably the Ecole normale and the Ecole polytechnique, where they established personal connections through which they would exert an influence far out of proportion to their number.

This is the educational system in which the school assumes its role as a "cohort creator," where long association in the lock step of an "age-hierarchized school system gives the cohort ample opportunity to identify itself as a historical entity."[33] For the majority of students, and ex-students, the unifying effects of secondary and advanced schooling were reinforced by the severing of local and family roots entailed by the migration to Paris, where, "fraternally united solely by their common age, young people from the most varied backgrounds and social origins became aware of their power and their solidarity before falling back, toward their thirtieth year, behind the ramparts of their [social] group."[34] This passage from Louis Mazoyer's still-unrivalled article on the "jeunes générations françaises de 1830" was preceded by the warning that it would be imprudent to attribute to an entire generation the spirit manifested by a segment of the Parisian *jeunesse*. It would be even less prudent to identify the entire generation born between 1792 and 1803 with the most articulate and militant elements of the Latin Quarter. And not even the minority of that minority that has left its imprint on the pages of history can be confined to the personnel of the youth of the schools.

The students and graduates of the Ecole normale, the Ecole polytechnique, and the faculties of law and medicine did enjoy a disproportionate visibility and influence, but they were members of a wider milieu that included cultured young aristocrats, junior officials in the national and municipal administrations, younger members of the professions, clerks apprenticed to the world of commerce, and those with sufficient education to aspire to live by their verbal skills in the French version of Grub Street.

In addition to direct or indirect association with the schools—as students, alumni, or members of the audience of popular academic lectures—they fashioned a generational solidarity in voluntary associations. In the early years of the Restoration, the common tendency of the young to cluster with their coevals was carried to unusual lengths in discussion circles, masonic lodges, and political cabals and conspiracies, and on the editorial boards of influential journals. They were impatient of apprenticeship, preferring to organize and dominate their own associations. As François Mentré and Karl Mannheim have observed, membership in voluntary groups allows the new generation to express

---

[33] Norman R. Ryder, "The Cohort as a Concept in the Study of Social Change," *American Sociological Review*, 30 (December 1965): 854.

[34] Louis Mazoyer, "Catégories d'âge et groupes sociaux: Les Jeunes Générations françaises de 1830," *Annales*, 10 (September 1938): 392.

its originality free of the constraints of such traditional institutions as the schools.[35]

The significance for generational identity of membership in formal institutions or in voluntary associations suggests why discussions of the generation of 1820 refer almost exclusively to males. Women were excluded from most of the groups through which young men expressed their solidarity, realized their career aspirations, and forced themselves on the attention of contemporaries. There were no women in the institutions of secondary or higher education, none to my knowledge in the secret societies, none on the editorial boards of the influential journals. Where French society traditionally allowed a small opening for feminine self-expression, that is, through literature (including the opportunity to compete in literary *concours*), we do find a few names, notably among the contributors to the *Muse française*. Other roles through which French women put their stamp on high culture in salons and social circles were only occasionally available to girls in their twenties. The young poetess Delphine Gay (1804)—called the "French muse" and renowned as much for her beauty as her verse—was perceived by contemporaries as a striking exception. In effect, the experience of the women whose literary talents allowed them to escape from invisibility set them apart not because of their age but because of their sex.

Another aspect of the generational homogeneity so obvious at first glance and so complex upon investigation, was the nexus of personal relationships that constituted what social scientists now call a "social network." Ryder's definition of the peer group as a "subset of one's cohort" is particularly applicable to the young, whose personal associations are most narrowly bounded by age before entrance into mature family life and settled occupations.[36] Even before I came upon the term in the technical literature, I had begun to enter the term "network" in my notes, because the web of those personal relationships seemed to have something to do with the coherence of the cohort and the way in which it experienced its particular historical situation.[37]

[35] Mannheim, "The Problem of Generations," 319; François Mentré, *Les Générations sociales* (Paris, 1920).

[36] Ryder, "The Cohort as a Concept in the Study of Social Change," 854.

[37] For a sampling of recent contributions to what has become a substantial literature, see J. Boissevain and J. C. Mitchell, eds., *Network Analysis: Studies in Human Interaction* (The Hague, 1973); Samuel Leinhardt, ed., *Social Networks: A Developing Paradigm* (New York, 1977); P. W. Holland and S. Leinhardt, eds., *Perspectives on Social Network*

To a considerable extent, the network of personal relationships is an attribute of the complicated overlap of membership in organizations and voluntary associations, but not completely, because individuals were connected by links of personal friendship and social acquaintance outside the boundaries of formal organization. The social network both developed out of and contributed to the connections established in the various groups. Lifelong friendships developed out of the coincidence of attendance at a *lycée* or the Ecole normale; friends formed discussion groups or founded journals through which they made new associations. This is to say, in the current jargon of the craft, that the personal connections were dense and multiplex, that a great many members of the network were connected by more than one association with a great many other members. Indeed, the web of personal relationships is so extensive that the subjects of this study might be conceived of as comprising a single social network. Unfortunately, that conception does reintroduce the problem of the representativeness of my list of subjects. The boundaries of the network are arbitrary. The addition of a number of names to the list might affect any systematic characterization of the total set.[38] Therefore it seems appropriate to settle for an examination of the partial networks whose intersections constitute the larger nexus. These networks have been represented as computer-drawn sociograms in Appendix B.

As suggested above, lasting patterns of personal relationships are often established in the schools. I have identified 71 of the 183 subjects of this study as students at the four great Paris *lycées*, or *collèges royaux* as they were titled under the Restoration.[39] In effect, a considerable

Research (New York, 1979); D. Knoke and J. H. Kuklinski, *Network Analysis* (Beverly Hills, 1982); P. V. Marsden and N. Lin, *Social Structure and Network Analysis* (Beverly Hills, 1982); Ronald S. Burt, *Toward a Structural Theory of Action: Network Models of Social Structure, Perception and Action* (New York, 1982); and Ronald S. Burt, Michael J. Minor, et al., *Applied Network Analysis: A Methodological Introduction* (Beverly Hills, 1983). For further references, consult the extensive bibliographies of the above works and the journal *Social Networks*.

[38] For a statement of this problem, see John A. Barnes, "Network Analysis: Orienting Notion, Rigorous Technique or Substantive Field of Study?" in Holland and Leinhardt, *Perspectives in Social Network Research*, 408–11; and Edward O. Laumann, Peter V. Marsden, and David Perenky, "The Boundary Specification Problem in Network Analysis," in Burt and Minor, *Applied Network Analysis*, 18–34.

[39] The four *lycées* established under the Empire were Imperial, Napoléon, Charlemagne, and Bonaparte, respectively titled under the Restoration: Louis-le-Grand,

proportion of those who attracted contemporary attention as outstanding representatives of their cohort during the 1820s had matriculated at the Paris schools at the end of the Empire or in the early years of the Restoration. Some forged associations that would last a lifetime. For example, a small cadre of the committed republicans who "lost" the Revolution of 1830—Godefroy and Eugène Cavaignac (1802), Joseph Guinard, and Charles Thomas—were together at a distinguished private school, the *collège* of Sainte-Barbe, where a future fellow-conspirator, F. V. Raspail (1794) was *maître d'études*. As they almost certainly attended advanced courses at the *collège royal*, Louis-le-Grand, they would probably have met Victor and Eugène Hugo (1800), Charles Tanneguy Duchâtel (1802), Eugène Lerminier (1803), Emile Littré (1801), and Charles-Joseph Paravey (1801), whose paths into early maturity would sharply diverge from theirs.[40] (See fig. 2 in Appendix B.)

The graduates of the Paris schools formed more or less coherent networks that would intersect with those informal groups identified as circles, or as *cénacles*, clusters, or cliques, depending upon one's taste in the literature. For our purposes, these are roughly equivalent to Mannheim's "concrete groups" that best express "the particular location of a generation as a whole."

During the first decade of the Restoration, the most influential of such groups was the circle of brilliant *normaliens* around Victor Cousin, who presented his first course of public lectures in philosophy at the Sorbonne in 1815 at the age of twenty-three. Actually, Cousin's influence radiated outward through more or less concentric circles. The inner core was comprised of the first generation of his classmates and pupils at the Ecole normale, each of whom was linked to all of the others and some of whom would establish themselves as independent centers of other circles.

On the outer edge of the Cousinian inner circle were a remarkably large number of young intellectuals, many of whom had never studied with Cousin but looked to him as the articulator of their aspirations

---

Henri IV, Charlemagne, and Bourbon. As I was unable to obtain class lists for the four *collèges royaux*, I assembled fragmentary information from many sources, notably from lists of *palmarès*, the winners of various academic competitions.

[40] Sainte-Barbe was technically a private *institution* or *pension* (regulated by the state, of course) whose students were required to take advanced courses at one of the public *lycées* (*collèges royaux*). Jules Quicherat, *Histoire de Sainte-Barbe* (Paris, 1864), 3:191, 218; Doris Weiner, *Raspail: Scientist and Reformer* (New York, 1968), 57.

and the inspiration for their political commitments. There were others who did not acknowledge Cousin as master but responded to his prestige and occasionally submitted to his influence, particularly on philosophic issues. (See fig. 3 in Appendix B.)[41]

The nature of, and reasons for, Cousin's remarkable influence are key questions for the cultural history not only of the Restoration but of nineteenth-century France. Among Cousin's pupils, Paul-François Dubois came to play the most significant autonomous role as cofounder and chief editor of the influential journal the *Globe* and as the center for the group of old schoolmates from his province, the Breton connection, who came to Paris to play a notable role in the agitation in the professional schools, in masonic lodges dedicated to social reform, and in the secret societies of the capital.[42]

There were, of course, other circles remote from or hostile to the influence of the Cousinians. The figure who appears most often at the center of such groups was Saint-Amand Bazard, leader of political activists between 1815 and 1822, founding member of the Carbonari,

---

[41] These categories blur at the edges. Among the *normaliens* close to Cousin or remembered as his admirers were Théodore Jouffroy, Phillipe Damiron (1794), Paul-François Dubois, Charles Loyson (1791), Louis Bautain (1796), Jean-George Farcy (1800), Augustin Thierry, L. P. Delcasso (1797), Nicolas Bouillet (1798), J. J. Darmaing (1794), J. L. Larauza (1793), and Epagomène Viguier (1793). The acolytes outside the school included J. J. Ampère, Eugène Burnouf (1801), Auguste Sautelet (1800), Charles Paravey, Antoine Cerclet, P. F. Franck-Carré (1800), Edouard Alletz (1798), and Marcelin Desloges (1799). Cousin exerted some influence on or maintained personal connections with Gilbert Carriol (or Cariol, 1798), Adolphe Thiers, Godefroy Cavaignac, Armand Carrel, Charles Rémusat, Ary Scheffer (1795), François Mignet (1796), Edgar Quinet (1803), and Jules Michelet. For a further discussion of Cousin's connections, see chapter 3.

[42] The scattered reminiscences of Dubois constitute a key source for the history and the self-image of his generation. Some of them have been collected and published by Adolphe Lair: Dubois, *Cousin, Jouffroy, Damiron*; Adolphe Lair, "Les Souvenirs de M. Dubois," *Quinzaine*, 43 (1 November 1901): 74–87; (1 December 1901): 305–18; 16 December 1901): 462–77; and Dubois, "Souvenirs inédits," in fourteen issues of *Revue Bleue* between 21 September 1907 and 26 December 1908. See the biography by Paul Gerbod, *Paul-François Dubois: Universitaire, journaliste et homme politique, 1793–1874* (Paris, 1967), which cites various unpublished sources, the most important of which were deposited by Gerbod in the Archives nationales. Archives privées, Papiers de Paul-François Dubois, 319 AP[1-3] (cited henceforth as Papiers Dubois, AN 319 AP[1-3]). Unpublished sources are also cited in Jean-Jacques Goblot, " 'Le Globe' en 1827: Lettres inédites de Damiron et de Dubois," *Revue d'histoire littéraire de la France* 72 (May–June 1972): 482–506.

early associate of the young *polytechniciens* and entrepreneurs who launched the first Saint-Simonian journal, the *Producteur*.[43]

There were other groups too, smaller and less homogeneous with regard to age, that would also reflect the influence of some central figure, such as Emile Deschamps (1791), who brought together young romantics and royalists to found the *Muse française*, or J. J. Ampère (1800), center of a group who had gone to school with him at the collège Henri IV, or Etienne Delécluze (1781), whose salon became the center for the interaction of various groups and individuals who might otherwise have had little contact.

It is not surprising to note that most of the leaders of the generational circles are to be found at the older edge of the cohort, sufficiently experienced to command authority but young enough to share the experience of their coevals. Etienne Delécluze does not fall into this group. He belongs to an earlier cohort and was neither the center nor the leader of the youth of the 1820s. Rather, he played the role of a social or cultural broker, bringing into temporary conjunction the liberal *Globe* intelligentsia, the Ampère circle, and other individuals in and out of the cohort, such as Prosper Mérimée (1803), Stendhal, Paul-Louis Courier, or even a representative of the Saint-Simonian coterie, Antoine Cerclet.[44]

The presence of Cerclet at the Delécluze salon suggests a somewhat different role, not so much that of a star or a broker as that of a connector. To cite a small example of the breadth of Cerclet's personal web, we place him at the wedding of Auguste Comte as one of four

[43] For Bazard, see chapters 2 and 6.

[44] Among the *globistes* who attended the Delécluze salon were Rémusat, Thiers, Dubois, Jouffroy, Ludovic Vitet (1802), Charles Tanneguy-Duchâtel, Guy Patin (1793), Prosper Duvergier de Hauranne (1798), Adolphe Dittmer (1795), H. A. Cavé (1794), Charles Coquerel (1797), Nicolas Artaud (1794), and Charles Magnin (1793). Some of the friends of J. J. Ampère appeared: Albert Stapfer (1802), Charles Stapfer (1799), Adrien Jussieu (1797), and Prosper Mérimée. The Saint-Simonians were represented by Cerclet, and by Sautelet and Artaud, who were connected with the Saint-Simonian journal, the *Producteur*. According to Barbéris, *Balzac Et Le Mal du siècle*, 1:329, Balzac also frequented the salon. Detailed information on these relationships chez Delécluze or elsewhere are provided in: Etienne Delécluze, *Journal de Delécluze, 1824–1828* (Paris, 1948); and Etienne-Jean Delécluze, *Souvenirs de soixante années* (Paris, 1862). See also Robert Baschet, *E.-J. Delécluze: Témoin de son temps, 1781–1863* (Paris, 1942), 90–103. For a description of the salon, see Sainte-Beuve, *Nouveaux lundis* (Paris, 1892), 3:107–9.

witnesses, three of whom are known to us. Comte himself was more or less a maverick, reluctantly connected with the self-selected heirs of Saint-Simon. One of the Saint-Simonians, Olinde Rodrigues (1795), was a witness at the wedding and had probably known Comte when Rodrigues had been an instructor at the Ecole polytechnique. Comte had been educated in the provinces, but Rodrigues had been both a student and an instructor at the lycée Napoléon, which became the collège Henri IV. Another laureate from Henri IV, J. M. Duhamel (1797), stood up at the wedding for Auguste Comte, his classmate at the Ecole polytechnique. Duhamel had also studied law at Rennes, where he had become a member of Paul Dubois' Breton circle. Dubois identifies him as a member of the Carbonari, as was Cerclet, a witness for the bride (whom he had passed on from his bed to Comte's). Cerclet had been numbered among the acolytes of Victor Cousin, but he went on from the Carbonari to become the first editor of the Saint-Simonian *Producteur*. (See fig. 4 in Appendix B.)[45]

An even more ubiquitous individual whose brief existence can be traced out along the ramifications of the generational network was Auguste Sautelet (1800), a suicide at the age of thirty but preserved forever in the amber of Balzac and Stendhal scholarship. Sautelet had come up from the provinces, where he had been a condisciple of Balzac at the *collège* of Vendôme, studied at the collège Charlemagne with Balzac and Michelet, then took his degree in law and plunged into the militant world of the youth of the schools.[46] A student and devotee of Victor Cousin's course in philosophy, he was, according to several witnesses, inducted by Cousin into the world of conspiracy in the secret societies. He was probably a member of the subversive masonic lodge, the *Amis de la vérité*, and was certainly a member of a Carbonarist cell, where he

[45] For the wedding of Auguste Comte, see Henri Gouhier, *La Vie d'Auguste Comte* (Paris, 1965), 118–19.

[46] See for example, Barbéris, *Balzac Et Le Mal du siècle*, 1:329; Henri Martineau, comp., *Petit Dictionnaire stendhalien* (Paris, 1948), 434–39. For contemporary descriptions of Sautelet and the testimony on his personal connections, see especially the obituary by Armand Carrel, "Un Mort volontaire," *Revue de Paris* (June 1830), 205–16; "Obsèques de M. Sautelet," *National*, 16 May 1830; Dubois, *Revue bleue* 10 (8 August 1908): 161; Sainte-Beuve, *Portraits contemporains* (Paris, 1891), 1:178–83; Pierre Leroux, *Réfutation de l'éclectisme* (Paris, 1839), 79; Charles de Rémusat, *Mémoires de ma vie*, ed. Charles H. Pouthas (Paris, 1959), 2:282–83; Delécluze, *Souvenirs*, 274–75; and *Journal*, 342. L. J. Arrigon, *Les Débuts littéraires d'Honoré de Balzac* (Paris, 1924), 65; Moïse Le Yaouanc, "Balzac au lycée Charlemagne," *L'Année balzacienne* (1962): 81.

was a close associate of the protorepublican group around Godefroy Cavaignac, Charles Thomas, Joseph Guinard, and J. B. Paulin (1796). He frequented the Delécluze salon and was an intimate of the Ampère circle. (See fig. 5 in Appendix B.)

Like so many of his companions in the secret societies, he deserted political conspiracy for the world of letters, founding a publishing firm with J. B. Paulin. At the age of twenty-five he assumed a key role in the dissemination of the most distinctive works of the new generation. He was a shareholder and *dépositaire* of the *Globe*, published Stendhal's snide critique of the Saint-Simonians, *D'Un Nouveau Complot contre les industriels*, and was also a shareholder and publisher of the *Producteur*, the target of Stendhal's attacks. In introducing such pioneering works as Mérimée's *Théâtre de Clara Gazul*, Sautelet functioned as what Lewis Coser has called "a gatekeeper of ideas," a middleman and broker of concepts through personal relations as well as business associations.[47] After he brought his promising career and life to an end in 1830 he was remembered as one of the best known, most popular, and most attractive young men in Paris, with a flair for bringing his friends together and an uncanny gift for drawing people out.

Sautelet seemed to incarnate the salient attributes of what might be called his generation's *mentalité*. His life had been shadowed, and was eventually destroyed, by the *mal du siècle*, that sense of cosmic despair he shared with so many of his associates.[48] He oscillated between an intolerable metaphysical doubt and the conviction that "man is placed on earth for action," actively expressed in his dynamic pursuit of a precocious career.[49] In this dichotomy, too, he was like his coevals.

The ubiquitous presence of a Sautelet exemplifies the striking attribute of the social network of Restoration youth, its "density"—technically, the proportion of all of the connections in the network to all of

[47] Lewis Coser, "Publishers as Gatekeepers of Ideas," *Annals of the American Academy of Political and Social Science*, 421 (September 1975): 14–22; Charles Kadushin, "Networks and Circles in the Production of Culture," *American Behavioral Scientist*, 19 (July–August 1976): 780–81. Another publisher who played a key role in the dissemination of the ideas of his cohort was Alexandre Lachevardière, who was printer of the *Mémorial catholique*, publisher of the *Globe*, and investor and printer for the *Producteur*. See chapter 6.

[48] For a discussion of the generational *mentalité* and the issue of the *mal du siècle*, see chapter 7.

[49] From a letter of Sautelet quoted in Sainte-Beuve, *Portraits contemporains*, 1:182.

the possible connections, such that in a perfectly dense network, each subject is connected to every other.[50] Not only the outstanding and influential but the obscure and forgotten members of one social circle or organization appear and reappear in the meetings of other groups, in social gatherings, in large-scale manifestations of generational solidarity such as political demonstrations and conspiracies, and, of course, in a wide variety of personal relationships.

In this discussion of intersecting circles and ramified personal relationships, I have referred only to direct links. Social network research is often concerned with indirect links—A does not know C but is indirectly linked through their mutual relations with B—but I could not begin to trace the indirect ramifications. The evidence for the direct connections is so thick on the ground as to suggest that the addition of indirect links would have evoked a perfect, and impenetrable, density.

The density of the network of young Parisian intellectuals scarcely distinguishes the Restoration from other eras. I will argue, however, that the specific historical context for the formation of the network shaped and strengthened the generational identity of the cohort of the 1820s. Especially relevant were royalist policies that temporarily ruptured the intergenerational patron-client nexus and freed the most dynamic elements of a future elite to depend on each other for the fulfillment of occupational and intellectual ambitions. The purge of the University that coincided with the political accession of the ultraroyalists and culminated in the suspension of the Ecole normale in 1822 was an especially striking confirmation of the conviction of the most effective spokesmen for the Restoration youth that they had to depend on their own resources. This is not to say that the paranoid policies of the regime were the sole cause of the alienation of a nascent elite. Well before the period of the purges, activist circles within and outside of the schools had begun to assert their solidarity and autonomy through forms of behavior traditionally, or not traditionally, associated with the young.[51]

This behavior began in the schools, where periodic rebellions against a monastic discipline were multiplied by the shock of the transition

---

[50] Knoke and Kulkinski, *Network Analysis*, 45.

[51] For the story of the student movement and of the formation of secret societies and conspiracies, see chapter 2, where I draw on material from my book *Old Hatreds and Young Hopes: The French Carbonari Against the Bourbon Restoration* (Cambridge, Mass., 1971).

from the empire in which they had been raised to the monarchy into which they were forced to graduate. Yet the fractious activities of the "youth of the schools," amounting on occasion to insurrection, were not exclusively the product of a nostalgia for the imperial glories or a reaction against the clericalization of the educational system, but reflected the conviction that history had bestowed obligations on the new generation that only they were equipped to fulfill.

In the schools and in the city, discussion groups and small *cénacles* were formed to explore new paths to the future. Out of such groups emerged the intention to bring together the educated youth of Paris into some sort of a general movement. The freemasons unwittingly provided a convenient vehicle, as a handful of young radicals founded a lodge as a cover for political meetings and for the recruitment of students and young commercial clerks in the capital. They organized the *Amis de la vérité*, recruited a membership almost exclusively under the age of thirty, and replaced the "superannuated practices"[52] of masonry with instruction in civic rights and duties. The most militant members eventually proceeded from subversive talk to revolutionary action.

With other political activists, the alumni of "turbulence" and sedition in the schools, they would provide the nucleus for the political riots of June 1820, which is very much to the point, because those particular demonstrations, unlike the crowds of the great revolutionary days from 1789 to 1871, were actually led by the young. From the reminiscences of participants and from official sources, we know that when the bitter debates in the Chamber of Deputies over the law of the double vote spilled out into the streets in the first week of June 1820, students and "young people from the shops" were the dominant components of the crowds.

The riots of the June Days petered out in a fiasco that impelled many young malcontents "to cross the space that separated protests from revolt" and to commit themselves to the conspiracies of 19 August 1820, and the French Carbonari.[53] Thousands of students, clerks, halfpay officers, and other Napoleonic veterans, soldiers still in Bourbon uniform, leaders of the antiroyalist opposition in various provincial cen-

---

[52] This phrase was applied to masonic rites in the reminiscences of both B. Pance, "Les Etudiants sous la Restauration," in *Paris révolutionnaire* (Paris, 1833–34), 1:265; and J. T. Flotard, "Une Nuit d'étudiant sous la Restauration," *Paris revolutionnaire*, 2:453.

[53] Pance, "Les Etudiants," 266.

ters, ex-Bonapartists and future republicans, and admirers of Lafayette and enemies of the Jesuits constructed an immense, ramshackle organization whose preferred tactic was the infiltration and subversion of military units on the invalid assumption that the dynasty could be toppled by its own troops.

The young participants in the conspiracy, notably the former leaders of agitation in the schools and founders of masonic fronts, believed then and remembered later that they had controlled the entire movement. They recalled that national figures such as Lafayette and Manuel had been recruited as figureheads and had permitted themselves to be manipulated by obscure activists in their twenties. This recollection of conspiratorial reality seems to me something of a collective delusion, but for our present purposes we need merely note that the Carbonari formed a generational as well as a political coalition in which youth operated as a semiautonomous element. They certainly differed among themselves, but they functioned, especially in Paris and Brittany, as a group, cooperating with, but distinct from, the opposition notables, the lawyers and journalists, and the resentful veterans and disaffected soldiers who joined them in the secret cells—the *ventes* of the Carbonari.

The fantasy of constructing an infiltration-proof nationwide conspiracy was lent a certain plausibility by the prior existence of the various personal networks. The principle of organizing isolated cells connected by a single representative to the next layer of the conspiratorial pyramid depended upon mutual recognition and mutual trust. In Paris at least, recruits could reasonably surmise the membership of other *ventes* and assume a solidarity that inhibited betrayal. In fact, the cells of the young Paris militants were proof against the police; the plot was betrayed by soldiers recklessly solicited by agents in the infected regiments. Perhaps the most remarkable aspect of this ephemeral "mania for conspiracy" was the temporary intersection of networks of individuals of roughly the same age but diverse political temperaments who would proceed along sharply divergent paths when the conspiracy collapsed. (See fig. 6 in Appendix B.)[54]

Even as they diverged, however, the younger cohorts retained a sort of generational identity. In 1824 the ex-conspirators Pierre Leroux and Paul Dubois conceived of a journal dedicated to the enlightenment of "those generations brought up since the Restoration and tormented

[54] For the list of Carbonari, see chapter 2, n. 81.

with a desire for self-instruction."[55] Drawing in alumni of the Carbonari and the Ecole normale in addition to the young luminaries of the
literary salons, they launched the *Globe* into its brilliant and influential
orbit. The striking success of that journal was all the more impressive
in light of the age of its major contributors. Their guiding spirit, Paul
Dubois, was virtually the doyen at the age of thirty-one. The mean age
of the rest was roughly twenty-seven. (See fig. 7 in Appendix B.)

An even greater generational homogeneity characterized the first
board of editors of the Saint-Simonian journal the *Producteur*. The
Saint-Simonian nucleus around Prosper Enfantin (1796), Olinde Rodrigues (1795), and P. M. Laurent (1793) joined with notorious ex-Car-
bonarists such as Bazard and Philippe Buchez to form a tight cluster of
birthdates, if not of political temperaments. Their ages ranged from
that of Saint-Amand Bazard, who was thirty-four in 1825, to Léon
Halévy (1802), who was twenty-three. Six of the ten founders and editors had been born between 1794 and 1797.

With the end of the brief history of the *Producteur* (which was published from October 1825 to October 1826) we come close to the end of
our cohort's "youth." The oldest among them were well into their
fourth decade, and their militant phase was succeeded by a period of
limited goals and political realism. The majority of their generation,
whose members were beginning to move in the separate directions that
would define their sharp differences after 1830, did retain a certain
unity in continued opposition to the regime of Charles X.

Indeed one might suppose, as the royal authorities did, that the only
focus for those ideologically fragmented, quarrelsome coevals, aside
from their age, was their opposition to the Restoration status quo, that
the implacable hostility manifested in the unruly behavior of the youth
of the schools, in mass demonstrations, riots, and conspiracies, and finally in theoretical critiques of the entire social order, was simply the
expression of the junior branch of the permanent opposition to crown
and church. Certain leaders of the militant *jeunesse* were in fact the
sons of revolutionary fathers or the disciples of venerable relics of the
revolution, the most notable of whom was Lafayette.[56] In many French

---

[55] *Globe*, 15 September 1824. The crucial role of the major journals—the *Globe*, the
Producteur, and the *Muse française*—is discussed in chapters 4–6.

[56] One would not expect children of regicides such as Godefroy and Eugène Cavaignac or Hippolyte Carnot (1801) and N. L. Sadi-Carnot (1796) to find a welcome un-

schools, disaffected students had only to follow their teachers. What Keniston calls "the red diaper baby" thesis may fit the children of Jacobins and Bonapartists better than would the theory that rebellious sons had repudiated their "de-authorized" fathers.[57]

There is, however, persuasive evidence that the collective self-definition of the generation of 1820 was not merely the young echo of established antiroyalism. Sébastien Charléty's chapter "L'Avènement d'une génération nouvelle" in his history of the Restoration correctly emphasized the refusal of the Restoration youth, irrespective of its political or artistic tendencies, to be patronized by its elders.[58] The neoliberal editors of the *Globe* were at great pains to distance themselves from the threadbare dogma of their self-appointed mentors at the *Constitutionnel* or the *Minerve française*. The romanticism of the young royalists of the *Muse française*, like the romanticism of the young liberals at the *Globe*, was conceived in opposition to the neoclassic fossils in all political camps.

To illustrate his discussion of generation units, Karl Mannheim selected "romantic conservative" and "liberal rationalist" youth as manifesting "two polar forms of the intellectual and social response to an historical stimulus experienced by all in common."[59] This distinction, which seems obviously applicable to the youth of the Restoration, leads into a tangle of complex and overlapping loyalties in which certain shared assumptions with regard to the historical situation of the cohort can nevertheless be discerned. The constituents of this more or less implicit consensus comprise what S. N. Eisenstadt has called a "youth ideology," in which youth is celebrated as a distinct human type, bearing the indispensable new values of the community, and in which older generations are considered inadequate to new realities by the very fact of their seniority.[60]

The sense in which this familiar form of self-assertion should be dignified as "ideology" will be discussed in chapter 7. It was expressed with almost universal certitude by the most articulate spokesmen for

der the Bourbons. Georges Weill, *Histoire du parti républicain en France (1814–1870)* (Paris, 1928), 7–8.

[57] Kenneth Keniston, *Youth and Dissent* (New York, 1971), 273–74.

[58] Charléty, "L'Avènement d'une génération nouvelle," 197–98.

[59] Mannheim, "The Problem of Generations," 304.

[60] S. N. Eisenstadt, *From Generation to Generation: Age Groups and Social Structure* (Glencoe, Ill., 1956), 102, 311.

the Restoration *jeunesse*. They believed, with Frank Manuel's Saint-Simonians, that "history was bifurcated by their generation,"[61] and that they had been cued onto the European stage in what Léon Halévy called "one of those epochs of sharp transition where the emerging generations are separated from their predecessors to such a degree that in the same country, in the same century, we exist as citizens of two nations and contemporaries of two eras."[62] The assumption of an uncrossable historical divide, of a radical discontinuity,[63] was the condition for what Pierre Barbéris has called "l'extrême valorisation du jeune homme à l'époque romantique," the conviction that the mature cohorts were to be regarded as obstacles rather than as guides to the future and that youth is to be conceived, not as a life stage, but as *valeur*, as the repository of an intrinsic worth.[64]

Two elements comprise the conviction of a separate, superior, age-specific identity. The first is the collective self-perception of a distinct identity as a new generation.[65] The second, the perceived existence of some contemporary "other" against which the coeval self is defined. The obsolete generation of the predecessors was not merely an abstrac-

---

[61] Frank E. Manuel, *The Prophets of Paris* (Cambridge, Mass., 1962), 168.

[62] Léon Halévy, *Producteur*, 1 (1825): 275. This was a common theme conveyed in various metaphors. Feuillet de Conches (1798) characterized the era as divided between two worlds, "dont l'un continue l'autre, et qui, cependant, sont si dissemblables, et l'un à l'autre, si fort inconnus et témoins fatalement de deux sociétés où les enfants sont séparés des pères par cette immense distance des usages, des préjugés, des institutions, qui équivaut à la distance des siècles." F. S. Feuillet de Conches, *Souvenirs de première jeunesse d'un curieux septuagénaire: Fin du premier Empire et commencement de la Restauration* (Vichy, 1877), 258.

[63] See Wohl, *The Generation of 1914*, 39: "The generational idea feeds on a sense of discontinuity and disconnection from the past."

[64] Barbéris, *Balzac Et Le Mal du siècle*, 1:331.

[65] It is sometimes argued that the term "generation" should be applied only to age groups that express a self-conscious identity. See Wohl, *The Generation of 1914*, 209: "The 'generation of 1914' was therefore first of all a self-image produced by a clearly defined group within the educated classes at a particular moment in the evolution of European society," or, categorically, in Brown, "The Generation of 1820," 38: "It is proposed here that the term 'generation' be restricted to those groups of individuals that actually thought of themselves as a generation." I will skirt the issue of whether a generation can exist in the absence of consciousness-for-itself because my group certainly did assert such a consciousness. See also Wilbur Scott and Harold Grasmick, "Generations and Group Consciousness: A Quantification of Mannheim's Analogy," *Youth and Society*, 11 (December 1979): 191.

tion or an historical figment in the first decade of the Restoration, it was a physical reality, dominating the commanding heights of the economic, political, and cultural establishment. Its loyalties defined the dominant conceptions of politics, art, and religion. Its internal divisions adumbrated the crucial cleavages of the political and social order. The frustrations, disappointments, and threatening portents of an unsettled present were presumed to be the fruit of its failures. Its past mistakes constituted the legitimation of its successors' world-historical future.

The prediction of a brilliant future for any particular *jeunesse* depends on the presumption of precocity, to my knowledge scarcely explored as a social or historical phenomenon.[66] Precocity denotes qualities more mature than those considered appropriate to the youthful stage of the life cycle in the light of current social conventions. A penchant for panty raids is not precocious; the drafting of the Port Huron Manifesto for the SDS was the expression of remarkable political maturity or a characteristic assertion of youthful hubris, depending on one's point of view. During the Restoration the critique of obsolescence was itself advanced as evidence of early ripening.

The sclerosis of the cohort in place was contrasted with the splendid promise of a Victor Cousin, at twenty-three arguably the most influential philosopher in France; or an Ary Scheffer, born in 1795, an artistic child prodigy, accepted for the salon of 1819 and a star of the salon of 1824, whose genre paintings enjoyed "one of the great successes of the Restoration, along with the songs of Béranger and the *Messéniennes* of Casimir Delavigne."[67] The remarkable career of Delavigne (1793) was built on poems mourning the national catastrophe at Waterloo, which were published to immense acclaim in 1815, when he was twenty-two, and opened the road to the cultural summit of the Academy, which he attained at the green age of thirty-two.

Beyond the circle of the precocious superstars, there were many who shared a collective self-regard shaped by the experience of competitive success. Their future had been authenticated in the arena of the *concours*, in the innumerable exams and competitions that characterized French culture in and out of school. The small universe of the *lauréats de concours* was also a constituent of the personal network, as schoolboy champions first met and measured each other in classroom competi-

[66] The subject is treated in Ariès, *Centuries of Childhood*, 194–95, 227–28.
[67] Joseph François Michaud, comp., *Biographie universelle* (Paris, 1854), 38:264–65.

tions or in the great *concours généraux* of the Paris *lycées*.[68] The circumstances under which they experienced the successes of a stage of elite apprenticeship led them to confuse it with a decisive generational conjuncture that would transform culture.

It has been argued that the discrepancy between the exaggerated expectations of the Restoration youth and the restricted possibilities of the contemporary job market was the source of the politico-cultural alienation of a fledgling elite. This poignant sense of the contrast between expectations and opportunities gave the generation its transient unity as an excess of educated men. The classic theory of frustrated mobility, applied to virtually every "overeducated" generation since the age of Richelieu, emphasizes the predictable alienation of the surplus products of an educational system that trained more professionals and functionaries than the market would absorb. There is certainly a great deal of evidence on the career frustrations of the Restoration youth and their resentment of the dead weight of a post-Napoleonic gerontocracy, but these attitudes need to be examined in the light of demographic and occupational realities. The career possibilities for any age cohort are most directly affected by its relation to the numbers and situations of its immediate predecessors on the lower rungs of the occupational ladder. The age cohort just preceding the generation of 1820 had been decimated by the last years of the Napoleonic wars, and there is evidence that it did not preempt all of the career possibilities produced by the dismantling of the First Empire. This is to argue that the classic discontents of a Julien Sorel or of De Musset's *enfant du siècle* do not do justice to the opening out of careers in the previously frozen or severely restricted professions of teaching, law, medicine, journalism, and letters in general.

This question, which will be explored in detail in chapter 9, also relates to the issue of generational identity as a function of social class. This is posed with reference to the Restoration era in Georg Lukács' and Pierre Barbéris' Marxian interpretations of the world of Balzac,[69]

---

[68] George Simmel, *The Web of Group Affiliations* (New York, 1955), 155: "A typical example of multiple group affiliations within a single group is the competition among persons who show their solidarity in other respects."

[69] Georg Lukács, *Studies in European Realism*, trans. Edith Bone (London, 1950), 47–64; Pierre Barbéris, "Mal du siècle, ou d'un romantisme de droite à un romantisme de gauche," in *Romantisme et politique, 1815–1851*. Colloque de l'Ecole normale supérieure de Saint-Cloud, 1966, (Paris, 1969), 171, 174–75, 193–94, and various passages

and in a more general sense, in Hans Jaeger's recent critique of Karl Mannheim. The issue is not exhausted with reference to the obvious need to distinguish social groups in the same age cohort. When we speak of a generational identity articulated by Parisian intellectuals, we probably are not speaking to the identity of young peasants in the *massif central*. The more difficult question bears on the historically specific interrelationships of age groups and social classes.

When Karl Mannheim considers both generation and class under the rubric of "social location," he is, in Hans Jaeger's metaphor, attempting to unravel simultaneously the untidy warp and woof of the distinct threads of generational and social development.[70] Or, to put it another way, the axes of age and class are presumed to intersect but on different systems of coordinates. From one perspective, membership in an age cohort is permanent and inescapable, whereas one can change classes; from another, the context for the transition through life stages may be fixed by the permanent boundaries of social class.

The relevance of these considerations to particular experiences of our cohort can be discerned in Barbéris' distinction between successive cohorts of the disaffected Restoration youth, first in the aristocratic nostalgia of the children of victims of the bourgeois revolution, then in the alienation of the sons of the bourgeoisie facing a constricted market for their extravagant ambitions. This is an extended version of Lukács' brilliant evocation of the "Lost Illusions" of a generation that believed it was still called on to fulfill the tasks of the heroic age of the bourgeoisie, when in actuality it would have to merchandise ideals in the cash nexus of a capitalist culture.

I too believe that we cannot understand the history of Balzac's generation without relating it to the general history of the bourgeoisie, but with the proviso that one must examine the actual circumstances under which those particular children of the bourgeoisie confronted the challenge of the new century. A sharpened focus on the transition from the restrictions of the authoritarian Empire to the ambiguous potentialities of the Restoration suggests that the alienation of the young intelligentsia was not so much the expression of frustrated mobility as of a revolution of rising expectations.

---

cited below in his *Balzac Et Le Mal du siècle*. See also Mazoyer, "Catégories d'âge et groupes sociaux," 419. Helmut Stenzel and Heinz Thoma, "Poésie et société dans la critique littéraire du *Globe*," *Romantisme*, 39 (1983): 25–59.

[70] Jaeger, "Generations in History," 285.

However, to rest the issue at this point is to present too mechanical an interpretation of what was a functional relationship. The generational identity of the Restoration youth should not be considered as a variable independent from, though interacting with, class categories, but as a historically specific phenomenon of social class. There is a certain amount of evidence that peasants and artisans continued to experience youth as a recurrent life stage; only the educated children of the upper classes conceived of youth as constituting a unique cohort with a distinctive destiny. They were wrong. In retrospect their world-historical identity diminished into an apprenticeship for satisfying careers. It was not their destiny to transform culture but to pass it on. That is why the balance sheet of so many brilliant individual careers was to be summed up as a collective failure.

As an historical phenomenon the generation eventually dissolved into the larger society, but in its brief experience of significant coherence one can read the complexities of the transition to a new century.

CHAPTER 2

Youth as the
Age of Dissent

"Revolts were in fashion in the *collèges*."
Comte de Castellane, *Journal du maréchal
de Castellane, 1804–1862*

"For a new era, a new generation."
Ulysse Trélat, *Paris révolutionnaire*

On 10 July 1819, a delegation of
students from the Paris Faculty of Law presented a petition to the
Chamber of Deputies protesting the dismissal of a popular lecturer and the suspension of his course. The government's measures were defended before the Chamber by Royer-Collard as
president of the Commission of Public Instruction. In 1819,
Royer-Collard's Doctrinaire constitutionalism still indicated
defense of, and service in, the monarchy according to the moderate royalist version of the Charte. In this case he would justify
the prescription of strong medicine for fairly mild disorders by
placing them in appropriately sinister perspective:

> You all know that disturbances broke out about six months
> ago, first at the *collège royal* Louis-le-Grand, and then at the
> *collège royal* of Nantes. But what you do not know, Gentle-
> men, is that similar disturbances had been simultaneously,
> though unsuccessfully, attempted in many *collèges*—which
> were widely dispersed and had no communication with one
> another. I cite especially the *collèges* of Rennes, of Bordeaux,
> of Périgueux, of Caen, of Lyon, of Tournon, of Vannes.
> And these disturbances were attempted, so to speak, in tran-
> quil times, under the regular discipline and the unremitting
> surveillance of experienced and highly respected authorities
> whose firmness anticipated and stifled them. You are even
> less aware, Gentlemen, of the incontrovertible fact that the
> agitation in some of these institutions came from the out-

side, inspired and stimulated by senseless manifestos distributed in the name of the *collège* Louis-le-Grand. These unfortunate children, egged on to acts of criminal violence, were unable to say what it was they wanted, to formulate a complaint, or to articulate a grievance. A few of them did admit to the desire to destroy the *collège* and go home.

Collège riots have undoubtedly occurred before, but there has been no such an offensive simultaneously launched against many points and made possible only by the odious corrupting of youth and even children. This is a new crime—heretofore absent from the history of political factions.

The agitation has not been confined to the *collèges*. Subsequently we have seen the students of a medical faculty pushing opposition to authority to the point of deserting the school for several months.

These are the events that have preceded, if not prepared, the troubles in the Paris law school.[1]

Actually, the president of the Commission of Public Instruction exaggerated a trifle, at least with regard to the law school. The crisis there arose when persistent applause for the lectures of a popular liberal professor was countered by royalist hisses, which precipitated a general tumult. The official response was to suspend the course, answer the predictable demonstration by arresting the handiest demonstrators, close the school, and indict Professor Bavoux for incitement to sedition. The political police could produce no evidence that the disturbances in the law school, or elsewhere, had been organized or coordinated from a single center. Indeed there was evidence, quietly interred in the police archives, that ultraroyalist nonstudents may have provoked the initial disorders.[2] The government's case against Professor Bavoux and the student demonstrators was lost in the courts. However, Royer-Collard's exaggerations did contain a certain vague truth, or at least the anticipation of truth, for there was an unruly student and youth move-

---

[1] *Archives parlementaires*, 2nd ser., 25:651–52. The *collèges royaux* to which Royer-Collard refers were the *lycées* of the First Empire, renamed under the Restoration.

[2] The document suggesting that the ultraroyalists had organized a provocation is entitled *Quelques conjectures qui font présumer que la scène tumultueuse de l'Ecole de Droit aurait été provoquée*. It is in the *fonds* of the *police générale* in the Archives nationales, Carton F⁷ 6693. (Such sources will hereafter be cited as AN F⁷ 6693.)

ment, it would soon have political or even subversive content, and it was unprecedented in France. What he did not anticipate was that his own protégés were to be numbered among the subversives.

In 1819, Royer-Collard and the other partisans of the centralized, secular University still preferred to believe that student misbehavior was the product of an ill-intentioned minority. For many royalists, however, especially those who believed that the destiny of the dynasty was inseparable from the strength of the Catholic faith, student dissidence was the inevitable product of an inherently vicious system founded to inculcate a hatred of the true faith and the worship of the usurper. The Napoleonic University was both the most characteristic product of "le Génie de la Révolution" and the "legitimate daughter of Bonaparte," a hybrid of revolutionary arrogance and despotic centralism.[3] This conviction was nourished by a dialectic of continuous mutual suspicion between state and student body in which the most trivial incidents, as well as major explosions of "turbulence," were met with harsh reprisals and anticipated by a rigid and niggling discipline, and in which the reprisals and the discipline confirmed new *promotions* in their alienation from the regime.

The roots of the problematic relationship between the Restoration government and the students in secondary and higher education lay in the transition from empire to monarchy. The restored regime contemplated the University from the perspective of its decree of 8 April 1814, which deplored an exclusively statist and militaristic educational system and promised to return children to the authority of their fathers, mothers, tutors, or families.[4]

That system, which was certainly permeated by an *esprit militaire*, had by no means won the hearts of its intended narrow clientele. The Empire had had considerable trouble in finding a sufficient number of

---

[3] "Le Génie de la Révolution" appears in the title of an influential critique of the University by Jean-Baptiste-Germain Fabry, *Le Génie de la Révolution considéré dans l'éducation; ou, Mémoires pour servir à l'histoire de l'instruction publique, depuis 1789, jusqu'à nos jours*, 3 vols. (Paris, 1817–18). *La Fille légitime de Bonaparte* was the title of an anonymous pamphlet that criticized the University. For a thorough treatment, see Jean Poirier, "L'Université provisoire (1814–1821)," *Revue d'histoire moderne*, 1 (1926): 241–79; and "L'Opinion publique et l'Université pendant la première Restauration," *La Révolution française*, 56 (March 1909): 234–70, 330–42.

[4] "Arrêté concernant les formes et la direction de l'éducation des enfants," in Jean B. Duvergier, ed., *Collection complète des lois, décrets, ordonnances, règlements et avis du conseil d'état* (Paris, 1834–38), 19:9.

bourgeois families willing to offer up their children to the *lycées* even though these were designated as the avenues to the professional faculties and to place and preferment in the state.[5] Some of the *lycéens* were delighted to be enrolled in training centers for the conquest of a continent, and they marched happily off to class to the beat of the drum. Other spirits were blighted in the stifling atmosphere *de la caserne et du couvent,* of a barracks crossed with a monastery.[6]

Nevertheless, the official correspondence of the first Restoration government coincides with the reminiscences of former *lycéens* in the portrayal of the stupefaction, rage, and contempt with which the pupils of the imperial *lycées* greeted the collapse of the Empire and the first educational "reforms" of the restored regime.[7] Nourished on victory bulletins almost to the last, totally unprepared for the shock of Napoleon's fall, the disoriented and anxious students of 1814 had conceived of no alternative to the system in which they had been raised. The Bourbon dynasty meant no more to them than the Carolingian.[8] Even at the Breton *collège* of Vannes, where the students had been imbued with the mystique of the *chouannerie,* they had such a vague idea of the dynasty "so completely foreign to our generation," A. F. Rio recalled, "that we had to ask ourselves if Louis XVIII was actually a Bourbon."[9]

[5] Georges Weill, *Histoire de l'enseignement secondaire en France (1802–1920)* (Paris, 1921), 44–48.

[6] The phrase is Adolphe Blanqui's. In fact, he was perfectly at home in "le système d'éducation des lycées de l'Empire, qui a dû exercer une grande influence sur les hommes de notre génération." Adolphe Blanqui, "Souvenirs d'un lycéen de 1814," *Revue de Paris,* 133 (15 April 1916): 861. See also Gerbod, *Paul-François Dubois,* 17; Alphonse Mahul, "Souvenirs d'un collégien du temps de l'Empire," *Revue des langues romanes,* 37 (1894): 517–18; Rémusat, *Mémoires,* 1:70–79; Feuillet de Conches, *Souvenirs de première jeunesse,* 1–2, 89–91; and Jules Simon, *Mémoires des autres* (Paris, 1890), 64–76.

[7] Jean Poirier, "Lycéens d'il y a cent ans," *Revue internationale de l'enseignement,* 67 (1914): 174–88, and "Lycéens impériaux (1814–1815)," *Revue de Paris,* 164 (15 May 1921): 380–401; Adrien Garnier, *Frayssinous: Son Rôle dans l'université sous la Restauration (1822–1828)* (Paris, 1925), 46–48.

[8] Adolphe Blanqui, "Souvenirs d'un lycéen de 1814," *Revue de Paris,* 134 (1 May 1916): 103. "Car alors," remembered Alphonse Mahul (1795), "qui pensait en France aux Bourbons?" Mahul, "Souvenirs d'un collégien du temps de l'Empire," *Revue des langues romanes,* 38 (1895): 87. Dubois quoted in Gerbod, *Paul-François Dubois,* 17: "confiant ... dans l'étoile de l'Empire et la durée de l'Empire que nous regardions comme éternelles."

[9] A. F. Rio (1797), *La Petite Chouannerie; ou, Histoire d'un collège breton sous l'Empire* (Paris, 1842), 52.

Most of the academic officials who were precariously in place struggled desperately to disarm royalist hostility to the University, hastily substituting the white cockade for the tricolor and the tolling of the bells for the roll of the drums and presiding over religious ceremonies celebrating the return of the beloved dynasty. The response to all this is captured in the reminiscences of Adolphe Blanqui (1798), son of a Napoleonic official and member of the revolutionary Convention who had found his heart's desire in the order, sobriety, manly discipline, and opportunity for competitive distinction offered by the imperial *lycée* at Nice. The news of the Bourbons' triumphant reentry was celebrated before the assembled school by officials who days before had zealously shepherded their charges through the rituals of emperor worship. The students could not adapt so quickly. When the school officials announced the defeat and abdication of the emperor to the assembled school, it was stupefied to see its administration decked out in white cockades, which were then distributed by the basketful to an instantly recalcitrant student body. "One would have had to witness this scene," Blanqui recalled, "to have any conception of the attitude of contemporary youth toward these excellent princes whose name we heard pronounced for the first time." The royal cockades were trampled, thrown into the sewer, consigned to the school cesspool, while the precious tricolor was transformed into a sacred relic.[10]

Similar demonstrations disturbed the discipline of schools throughout the kingdom. Such occasions were not always political, although protests that ostensibly reflected local grievances and occasionally amounted to riots that lasted for several days were correctly interpreted as expressions of a broader dissidence and political resentment. The message of student behavior, like the graffiti they chalked on the walls of their *lycées*, confirmed the enemies of the University in their animus. The entire period between March and November 1814 was characterized by a *guerre des brochures* against the secular educational system. When the system was removed from its official provisional status—that is, formally reconstituted by the decree of 17 February 1815—the introduction of clerical influence at virtually every level of the University did nothing to disarm those for whom the only solution was destruction, root and branch: "A curse on the daughter and the mother, the old and the new University," intoned Lamennais. "A curse on the spawners of this infernal brood, a curse on those who gave birth to it

[10] Blanqui, "Souvenirs d'un lycéen," 134 (1 May 1916): 115.

and helped to raise it. A curse on the chiefs, a curse on the lieutenants, a curse on all that infamous *canaille*."[11]

The almost frantic efforts of the university administration to make it a truly "monarchistic and religious" institution by submitting the students to a discipline even more rigorous and far more religious than that applied in the imperial *lycée* seemed to bear fruit in the return of sobriety and order in the spring of 1815. However, the worst expectations of the *bien pensants* were fulfilled when the students of France were confronted with the incredible adventure and the immense temptations of the Hundred Days. Perhaps no one outside the army was less proof against the siren song of the emperor than the *lycéens*, who rushed back into their uniforms and volunteered themselves as cannon fodder in that last, hopeless fight and definitive destruction of any minimal consensus in France. Some of the *lycées*—at Aix, Angers, and Avignon, for example—were Bonapartist islands in a royalist sea.[12] Lazare Carnot, Napoleon's last minister of the interior, had ample reason to praise the students before the Chamber of Deputies.[13] Not many months later they would be assessed in that same tribune from a different perspective. In a speech whose main point was the proposal that a drastically reformed and purged educational system be placed in the hands of the church, the ultraroyalist deputy Murard de Saint-Romain reminded the deputies that Bonaparte's "last usurpation" had found its most devoted partisans in the nation's *collèges* and *lycées*, where "delicate students were transformed overnight into fierce gunners."[14]

Jean Poirier, historian of the University in transition from Empire to Restoration, observed that whatever else the imperial educational system had accomplished, it had attained its primary goal, the inculcation of loyalty in the only segment of the *génération nouvelle* destined to play a public role—those future functionaries who were the children

---

[11] Letter of Lamennais to the Abbé Jean, 6 March 1815, in Félicité de Lamennais, *Oeuvres inédites* (Paris, 1866), 1:202.

[12] Garnier, *Frayssinous*, 49; Poirier, "Lycéens d'il y a cent ans," 186–88, and "L'Université provisoire," 256.

[13] "L'enthousiasme que les élèves font éclater dans les lycées est admirable: les sentiments qui les animent ont été comprimés, il est vrai, mais ils n'en ont acquis que plus d'ardeur." *Archives parlementaires*, 2nd series, 14:417.

[14] Ibid., 16:59. For the suggestion that Murard de Saint-Romain had been briefed by more sophisticated enemies of the University, see Poirier, "L'Université provisoire," 260.

of the bourgeoisie—and that this was precisely where the Restoration would fail. The chronic hostility to the regime within the world of the schools would continue to renew the ranks of its opposition in all the years from 1814 to the Revolution of July 1830.[15] That is certainly the way things looked to contemporary royalists. In fact, however, the currents that flowed from the poisoned imperial spring did not run so clear. As Poirier himself implies, militarism or Bonapartism was not the universal characteristic of the Restoration youth. Even in 1814 the simple combative zeal for the Empire manifested in the provincial schools was considerably diluted among Rémusat's skeptical companions in the great Paris *lycées*.[16] Throughout the following decade, the older students in the professional faculties and *grandes écoles* would remain divided and ambivalent, critical of both the Empire and its successor. These nuances are constituents of the collective mentality of the young elite in the early years of the Restoration. However, there is no doubt that the "youth of the schools" hammered out an identity characterized by a militant hostility toward the authorities that was indistinguishable in its consequences from hostility to the political regime.

The relation of state to student was built, as it had been under the Empire, on the assumption that the nature of the beast required sleepless surveillance, minute regulation, and condign punishment for petty infractions. "PRINCIPE GÉNÉRAL—The students ought never be left to themselves," writes the Inspector of the Academy of Paris.[17] The discipline presumed appropriate to a community of healthy young males was roughly analogous to what would be applied in a training depot of the Foreign Legion. To these standard assumptions the Restoration added an insistent, meticulous religious regimen for the salvation of those corruptible small souls. Oddly enough, these salutary measures did not guarantee that "tranquility" so devoutly desired by the French administrative soul.

In fact, the paranoid surveillance of the student corps helped to create what it was intended to forestall. However, it is not always easy to distinguish perennial rebelliousness, the inevitable periodic explosions of the surplus energy of young males, from genuine dissidence. As

[15] Poirier, "Lycéens impériaux," 401.

[16] Rémusat, *Mémoires*, 1:123–24. See also Quicherat, *Histoire de Sainte-Barbe*, 3:131.

[17] Louis Gabriel Taillefer (ex-proviseur des collèges royaux de Versailles et de Louis-le-Grand. Inspecteur de l'Académie de Paris), *De Quelques Améliorations à introduire dans l'instruction publique* (Paris, 1824), 67.

Adrien Garnier remarked in his thorough study of the University in the era of Bishop Frayssinous, it was easier for school administrators to accuse ill-behaved students of antiroyalism than to inculcate "l'esprit d'ordre et de discipline."[18] Garnier goes on to cite a long list of more or less serious incidents in the *collèges royaux* and the higher faculties between 1815 and 1823–24 in which one can identify some sort of political animus. The *collèges*, which would remain the linchpin of the entire educational system (especially as the Restoration would make the baccalaureate a requirement for entry into the professional faculties), continued to provide occasion for voluminous official correspondence. Between 1815 and 1822 there were major incidents of indiscipline in something like sixteen of thirty-eight *collèges royaux*.

The turbulence and reprisals that wracked the educational system after the Hundred Days would pass, and the secondary schools would settle back into the uneasy calm of the first years of the Second Restoration. But by 1819 the conviction of all of those who thought that the safety of France was threatened by a secularized educational system was fortified by that epidemic of disorders described in Royer-Collard's speech to the Chamber. The revolt at the prestigious *collège* Louis-le-Grand, which was the centerpiece of Royer-Collard's speech, was sufficiently impressive to require the presence of fifty gendarmes. A few weeks after discipline had been restored, the students reexploded in a demonstration of solidarity with their expelled leaders, and this apparently set off sympathetic detonations at other schools at Nantes, Pontivy, Poitiers, Amiens, and Toulouse. Again, it is not always easy to separate out the seditious elements in these activities, although something sufficiently deplorable was usually produced in the course of the crisis. During the affair at Louis-le-Grand, for example, students forced their way into the school's chapel and leaped upon the altar crying, "Pas de Dieu! Vive Royer-Collard!"—not precisely the accolade sought by the president of the Commission of Public Instruction.[19] Such incidents reinforced the conviction that the infected *collèges* were serving as the nurseries of insurrection, and that what had begun as *mutineries d'enfants* in the *collèges* would mature into *révoltes véritables* in the faculties.[20]

[18] Garnier, *Frayssinous*, 50.

[19] Gustave Dupont-Ferrier, *Du Collège de Clermont au lycée Louis-le-Grand* (Paris, 1922), 2:491–93.

[20] Garnier, *Frayssinous*, 60; Liard, *L'Enseignement supérieur*, 2:141.

As early as November 1815 the ceremonial opening of the medical school had to be suspended because of the misbehavior of many of the students. Six months later sterner measures were applied to the Ecole polytechnique, where a breach of discipline led to the provisional dismissal of all the students and the temporary closure and reorganization of the school. Between 1816 and 1818 a rash of dismissals or disciplinary actions followed demonstrations at the law schools of Dijon, Rennes, and Aix. This chapter was introduced with the affair of the Paris law school in 1819, which was preceded and accompanied by disturbances with a political or anticlerical point at institutions of secondary education all across the country. In that year the law faculty at Toulouse was also shut down, and so was the medical *collège* at Montpellier after students boycotted the courses. In June 1820 the Paris riots over the changes in the electoral laws were followed by sympathetic demonstrations in many provincial faculties. In 1821 a long history of agitation that developed into something like an aborted insurrection led to the liquidation of the law school at Grenoble. The year 1822 was a banner year. The scandalous incident at the Paris faculty of medicine precipitated a suspension of classes and a purge and reconstitution of the entire faculty. The meticulous surveillance and the successive purges of the arrogant elite at the Ecole normale were not sufficient to save it, and it went out of existence in 1822.[21]

The reasons for the repressive measures might seem trivial to our hard-bitten or permissive age. Not only genuine riots but the least indication of disrespect for the authorities, or even an excessive public enthusiasm for Louis XVIII's constitution, the Charte, might provide the excuse for the suspension or permanent suppression of entire faculties. There is little doubt that student unrest was the pretext for the convenient reorganizations and purges that contributed to the clericalization

[21] There is a great deal of official material on unrest in the *collèges* and the University faculties in the series AN F⁷ and F¹⁷. These documents provided the basis for Garnier's thorough survey; Garnier, *Frayssinous*, 46–83, 153–65, 198–200. See also Achille de Vaulabelle, *Histoire des deux Restaurations*, 4th ed. (Paris, 1858), 5:54–57; Liard, *L'Enseignement supérieur*, 2:141–44, 160–65; Isambert, *De la Charbonnerie au saint-simonisme*, 59–62; Thureau-Dangin, *Le Parti libéral*, 232–33; Charles d'Haussez, *Mémoires du Baron Haussez* (Paris, 1896), 354–63; G. Vaulthier, "Les Etudiants en droit en 1823," *Revue internationale de l'enseignement*, 63 (1912): 264–68; *Le Centenaire de l'Ecole normale* (Paris, 1895), 220–22; A. Corlieu, *Centenaire de la faculté de médecine de Paris (1794–1894)* (Paris, 1896), 222–23.

of the educational system, especially after the appointment of Frayssinous as grand master of the University. Nor is there any doubt that this process strengthened the identity of the students as *frondeurs* and their solidarity with their teachers in opposition to the régime.[22] A closer look at some of the major incidents will help us to understand how this identity was forged.

The crisis at the Ecole polytechnique in the spring of 1816 has been subjected to close and controversial scrutiny because Auguste Comte happened to be one of the students expelled in that affair. There is rough consensus on the occasion of the crisis, which was the ragging of an unpopular instructor and the student body's truculent solidarity with the student leaders selected for punishment. The draconian response, amounting to a reorganization of the school and a purge of the faculty and student body, was far out of proportion to the precipitating incident.[23] The real point of the policy was served up with relish in an anonymous brochure, *Quelques Réflexions sur l'Ecole polytechnique*, now attributed to Lamennais:

> Now, the Ecole polytechnique, born in the troubled years of the Revolution, has long been suspected of assiduously preserving revolutionary ideals and of passing them on to students who have carried on an all-too-faithful tradition of republicanism and impiety. Undoubtedly their expulsion should be attributed to that rather than to a minor incident of insubordination. Indeed, we can only praise the prudence of a measure which has recognized the gravity of the malady in applying the only efficacious cure.[24]

This remedy left a bitter residue. Auguste Comte despaired of his chances in the civil service exams hypocritically made accessible to *po-*

[22] Paul Gerbod, "La Vie universitaire à Paris de 1820 à 1830," *Revue d'histoire moderne et contemporaine*, 13 (January–March 1966): 35–48, 2; Liard, *L'Enseignement supérieur*, 2:161–68; Garnier, *Frayssinous*, 67–69, 153–65.

[23] Henri Gouhier, *La Jeunesse d'Auguste Comte* (Paris, 1933), 1:116–22. The contemporary official version appeared in A. Fourcy, *Histoire de l'Ecole polytechnique* (Paris, 1828), 333–36. A tendentious positivist version with relevant documents from the police archives is in V. E. Pépin, "Matériaux pour servir à la biographie d'Auguste Comte: Licenciement de l'Ecole polytechnique en avril 1816," *Revue positiviste internationale*, 7 (15 November 1909): 413–34.

[24] [Félicité de Lamennais?], *Quelques réflexions sur l'Ecole polytechnique*, quoted in Christian Maréchal, "Auguste Comte, Andrieux, La Mennais et l'Ecole polytechnique," *Correspondant*, 282 (25 February 1921): 640.

lytechniciens whose dismissal from the school guaranteed their competitive disability.[25]

The Ecole polytechnique was a special case, among other reasons because of the unfortunate distinction its pupils had earned during the Hundred Days, because of its central role in military education, and because of its significance in the formation of a scientific and technical elite. But similar policies were applied wherever the least suspicion of dissidence justified the excision of corrupt tissue from the body of the institution. In 1817, for example, the moderate royalist government exploited the most trivial incident to close the law school at Rennes, dismiss all the students and faculty, and readmit only those who would document a commitment to *bons principes*. The Comte de Corbière, a Breton lawyer and a leader of the ultras in the Chamber of Deputies, was named professor and *doyen* of the faculty at Rennes. A few of the bolder spirits attempted to submit a petition protesting the decree to the Chamber of Deputies, which refused to receive it. The petitioners were, of course, expelled from the school.[26] Two of them, J. M. Duhamel and Alexandre Bertrand, would resurface in that circle of Breton activists who made a disproportionate contribution to the turbulence of the student quarters in the capital. As the government put it in its disciplinary decree on the school at Rennes, law students were of particular concern because the nature of their studies destined them to be interpreters of the law, magistrates, and officials. Therefore it was indispensable that they be submitted to a discipline that guaranteed "orderly conduct and a growing devotion to church and state."[27]

Naturally the various incidents of indiscipline at provincial faculties such as Rennes, Dijon, Aix, Poitiers, Grenoble, and Toulouse caused nothing like the concern produced by the students in the Paris Ecole de droit, who had the tendency to assume rather prematurely their role as the pacesetters for the national bar. In 1819 the crisis at the law school that was the occasion for Royer-Collard's lurid speech to the Chamber became something of a national cause célèbre. The Bavoux affair not only stimulated the usual polemics between the government

[25] Auguste Comte to Xavier Valat, 13 October 1816, in Auguste Comte, *Correspondance générale*, vol. 1, *1814–1840*, ed. Paul E. de Berridô Carneiro and Pierre Arnaud (Paris, 1973), 12.

[26] There is a detailed description of the affair from the viewpoint of the liberal opposition in the *Censeur européen*, 2 (1817): 324–28. See Garnier, *Frayssinous*, 61.

[27] Quoted in *Censeur européen*, 2 (1819): 328.

and its critics, it aroused a sense of combative solidarity in student circles outside the faculty of law.[28] Professor Bavoux's course on criminal
law had attracted a large, enthusiastic audience for his critical gloss on
the harsh and vindictive penal code, a legacy of the imperial approach
to social order. The exploitation of imperial despotism as a stick with
which to beat the monarchy was particularly infuriating to royalists,
who were obliged to defend their precarious order with the instruments that lay to hand. The students, on the other hand, were perfectly
willing to applaud more or less Aesopian attacks on the Empire. Indeed, their spokesmen expressed few regrets for Napoleon's domestic
arrangements even while they mourned the eclipse of national glory.
Their vision of the future did not entail a regime that assigned to the
young the role of service and obedience.

The course of events, described at the beginning of this chapter, that
led to the suspension of classes and the arrest, trial, and acquittal of
Bavoux and two students, provided the occasion for the medical students to express their solidarity with their comrades in the law. Representatives from the two faculties formed their own commission of in-
quiry, which published its findings, thus putting in the shade, as one
nostalgic reminiscence has it, "the committees of all the so-called representative governments."[29] The author of the findings was G. J. Cariol
(1798), a law student whose name will crop up again among the admirers of Victor Cousin, who helped to found the masonic front, the
Amis de la vérité, and to organize the conspiracy of the Carbonari.[30]

The Bavoux affair was interpreted in the press and the Chamber of
Deputies according to factional alignments. Benjamin Constant took
the occasion to praise the *génération naissante* as the hope and future
glory of the nation, while a conservative chorus deplored the arrogance

[28] The Bavoux affair is described in Vaulabelle, *Histoire des deux restaurations*, 5:55–
56; André-Marie Jean Jacques Dupin, *Mémoires de M. Dupin* (Paris, 1861), 1:179–84;
Prosper Duvergier de Hauranne, *Histoire du gouvernement parlementaire en France*
(Paris, 1862), 5:169–73. The Bavoux trials were reported in the *Moniteur universel*, 1-6
August 1819.

[29] Benjamin Pance, "Les Etudiants sous la Restauration," *Paris révolutionnaire* (Paris,
1833), 1:261. Pance (1800) recalled that the *contingents* were furnished only by the faculties of law and medicine, as the other schools were still under the thumb of the authorities.

[30] [J. Gilbert-Antoine-Jules] Cariol, *L'Ecole de droit de Paris au 2 juillet 1819, par plusieurs élèves de cette école. Signé: J. Cariol, président de la commission des élèves* (Paris,
1819).

of a *jeunesse* that presumed to petition the Chamber on matters better left to its masters.[31] This characteristic patronizing dismissal of youthful self-assertion was to cost the regime dearly in the end.[32]

Despite his defense of the sleazy administrative tactics applied in the Bavoux affair,[33] Royer-Collard was regarded, and is remembered, as the paladin of the embattled University.[34] In the fall of 1819, not long after the Bavoux fiasco, he resigned his post as president of the Commission of Public Instruction, and the administration of the educational system proceeded along the path that led to the appointment in 1822 of a grand master of the University. This was Monsignor Frayssinous, the bishop of Hermopolis, first *aumônier* to His Majesty, and an eminent defender of Christian dogma in the light of modern science.

The new administration's intentions were made sufficiently clear in the circular that the bishop addressed to his principal subordinates shortly after his appointment. In appointing a man of the cloth to head the educational system "His Majesty" had indicated his desire that the youth of his kingdom be inculcated with religious and monarchist values. Therefore, "He who had the misfortune to live an unreligious life and who was not devoted to the royal family should understand that he lacked what was required in a worthy teacher of the young," and so forth.[35]

The attempt to resacralize the educational system is an example of the monarchy's ambivalent reception of the imperial legacy. It could neither live with, nor live without, the secular University. On the one hand, the period after 1819 was marked by a series of decrees that brought the system out of the administrative limbo in which it had floundered since the fall of the Empire and reestablished it as an arm of the state, not a dominion of the church. On the other, it was to be

[31] *Archives parlementaires*, 2nd ser., 25:652–53.

[32] The conservative luminaries Fiévée, Chateaubriand, and De Serre contributed commentaries on this subject; see chapter 11.

[33] In 1819 Royer-Collard's concern with the students' political chastity was probably sincere. At dinner with the Doctrinaire circle he is reported to have said, "Ces jacobins d'aujourd'hui tentent sur la jeunesse, à présent, ce que leurs prédécesseurs ont tenté sur le peuple; et cela prouve à quel point il eût fallu s'occuper de l'Instruction publique, et s'attacher à gagner ces jeunes têtes qu'on peut égarer facilement." Charles de Rémusat, *Correspondance de M. de Rémusat* (Paris, 1866), 6:41.

[34] See, for example, Paul-François Dubois, *Fragments littéraires* (Paris, 1879), 2:74–75; Liard, *L'Enseignement supérieur*, 2:146–47.

[35] Quoted in *L'Ami de la religion et du roi*, 32 (1822): 207–8.

administered and staffed by those with impeccable religious and political—not necessarily equivalent to first-class academic—credentials.
The *conseil royal d'instruction publique* was packed with such erstwhile
enemies of the University as Abbés Nicolle and Elicaragay, the curriculum was sanitized, and the teachers were tested for the appropriate
shade of white.[36]

Thus the piecemeal consolidation of the University was accompanied by an increasing supervision of the content of instruction and
by an unsystematic purge and replacement of cadres. There was a practical and symbolic coincidence in the promulgation of the decree of 1
November 1820, which laid out the "definitive organisation," of the
University, and the roughly contemporaneous suspension of Victor
Cousin's enormously popular course of public lectures in philosophy at
the Sorbonne.[37] The termination of the lectures was interpreted by
Cousin's large following as a triumph for obscurantism and a harbinger of a wider purge. This had been predicted by his devoted student,
Théodore Jouffroy, as early as April 1820: "If you are dismissed, my
resignation, and that of your other pupils who teach philosophy, will
follow."[38] Jouffroy was right. He and Cousin would hang on at the
Ecole normale until its liquidation in 1822, but by that time many
promising *normaliens*—former students of Cousin and others—had
been dismissed from their teaching posts.

The suppression of the Ecole normale struck iron into the souls of a
small but crucial student elite, already influential far out of proportion
to its numbers. The bitterness is recaptured in the reminiscences of the
school's old boys well past the middle of the century, and it persists in
the republican historiography of education in the Restoration era. The
volume of Liard's monumental history of higher education published
in 1888, or for that matter Paul Gerbod's article published in 1966, read
as if the Restoration obscurantists had been beaten back only the other
day.[39]

[36] Liard, *L'Enseignement supérieur*, 2:151; Poirier, "L'Université provisoire," 2
(1927): 261–306; Gerbod, "La Vie universitaire à Paris," 34–37.

[37] The issue of the suspension is described in detail in Jules Barthélemy-Saint-Hilaire, *M. Victor Cousin: Sa Vie et sa correspondance* (Paris, 1895), 1:95–126, and is discussed below in chapter 3.

[38] Jouffroy to Cousin, 30 April 1820, ibid., 98.

[39] For fresh references to the atrocity of 1822 well into the 1870s, see *Mémorial de
l'association des anciens élèves de l'Ecole normale, 1846–1876* (Versailles, 1877), 444. See

The "reforms" in the other faculties, which often amounted to the replacement of outstanding scholars by lesser men with better political credentials, undoubtedly contributed to the alienation of successive *promotions* of the most promising elements in the student population.[40] A little verse tossed off by clever young Charles de Rémusat begins, "When the young annoy us, we change their professors."[41] As I will argue in detail below, the aspirations of the Restoration *jeunesse* did not preclude an accommodation with some versions of the constitutional monarchy, but with the ultraroyalist version, no accommodation was possible.

The policy of ideological purification was accompanied by a tightening of discipline in and outside of the faculties. The infiltration of nonstudents, always identified as the true source of student turbulence, was to be checked by the rigorous surveillance of identity papers. Students who fomented trouble when school was out or who publicly displayed disrespect for constituted authority, the king, or the legislature were to be suspended or expelled whether or not they were technically subject to criminal justice.[42] There is a paranoid tone to the prolifera-

---

also *Le Centenaire de l'Ecole normale*, 222; Liard, *L'Enseignement supérieur*, 2:160; and Gerbod, "La Vie universitaire à Paris," 34–37.

[40] For the relation of such policies to the general "alienation" of the Restoration youth, see chapter 9.

[41] The entire verse, published in André Armengaud, "Charles Rémusat, poète méconnu," in *La France au XIXe siècle: Etudes historiques. Mélanges offerts à Charles Hippolyte Pouthas* (Paris, 1973), 87, reads as follows:

PROCLAMATION MINISTÉRIELLE AU MOIS DE DÉCEMBRE 1820
Air: *La Treille de sincérité*
Les jeunes gens nous embarrassent,
Nous changerons leurs professeurs;
Si les brochures nous tracassent,
Nous quadruplerons leurs censeurs.
Il faut, si les moeurs sont frondeuses
Multiplier les espions;
Si les lumières nous inondent,
Laissons faire les missions.
Renais, ô France, à l'espérance,
Tu dois à nos soins diligents
La Charte et les honnêtes gens (bis).

[42] See, for example, a circular to the rectors of the Académies from the Commission de l'instruction publique, Paris, 15 April 1820, AN F⁷ 6693, one of many communications on student turbulence in the dossier.

tion of draconian decrees after 1819, but this is not to say that there was no objective correlative for official *angst* or that refractory students were merely responding to reactionary stimuli. The first decade of the Restoration was characterized by the determination of the rising generation to liberate itself from the authority of age whether imposed as discipline or extorted in the form of deference.

The commitment to an autonomous search for solutions to the problems of the era was expressed in a conscious effort to give breadth and focus to an age-linked community developing out of friendships, attendance at the same school, residence in the same *quartier*, and participation in the same process of socialization. Especially, but not exclusively, in Paris, informal or somewhat formal organizations—*petits cénacles*, discussion circles, and masonic lodges—enjoyed a brief existence as centers for the discussion of current and cosmic issues free from the supervision of anyone over the age of thirty.

What emerged from these inchoate efforts was something like a youth movement with an ill-defined but increasingly influential leadership. Our understanding of the motives and tactics of this activist general staff depends on the reminiscences of its most militant alumni, particularly those who published their reminiscences under the July Monarchy in the collective work *Paris révolutionnaire*. Their recollections coincide in tracing the modest and obscure antecedents of the movement in the resolution of four clerks of the Paris municipal administration to provide a unifying focus for the "jeunesse studieuse de Paris."[43]   The four *commis*, all in their twenties, were Philippe Buchez, Saint-Amand Bazard, Nicholas Joubert, and J. T. Flotard. The first two were taking their first steps in lifetime careers as political agitators and social theorists. Saint-Amand Bazard's passage through the conspiracies of the 1820s and on into the Saint-Simonian movement would terminate with his untimely death in 1832. Philippe Buchez would follow a similar path through the Saint-Simonian movement and into his own version of Christian socialism. He was to have a fairly distinguished career as a historian and a leader of moderate working-class elements, and he would play a salient if equivocal role in the po-

[43] This is the phrase of J. T. Flotard in "Une Nuit d'étudiant sous la Restauration (Du 19 au 20 août 1820)," *Paris révolutionnaire* (Paris, 1834), 2:451. The other key accounts of the radical youth movement in this publication are Ulysse Trélat (1795), "La charbonnerie," ibid., 277–341; and B. Pance, "Les Etudiants sous la Restauration," ibid., 1:253–80.

litical history of the Second Republic. The others made the greatest impression on their contemporaries in the years before 1830, especially in the subterranean role of the conspirator. Portrayed in a characteristically acute and patronizing sketch by his former schoolmate Charles Rémusat as a man of courage and intelligence and one of the leaders of the militant youth, Nicolas Joubert played a significant role in the conspiracies of the early twenties, in the electoral politics of the late Restoration, and in the July Revolution. He eventually settled into the office of Director of the Paris Octroi under Louis Philippe. Flotard's career was composed of similar materials. He built an impressive clandestine reputation among his young coevals in the various secret societies of the Restoration and emerged into an unremarkable career on the fringe of belles-lettres after 1830.[44]

It is rather difficult to explain the rapid success of these four anonymous young men in persuading their fellows to engage in demanding and dangerous enterprises. Hindsight does reveal the personal attractions of Buchez and Bazard. The latter was especially remembered by various contemporaries as a man of unusual personal authority.[45] At the elder edge of the generation, he had made a reputation in the defense of Paris in 1814. The other three had also volunteered for the fight against the invaders in 1814 and 1815. By 1818 they were no longer schoolboys and were gainfully employed outside the educational system. They were, however, closely tied to the schools, not only through social connections, but through the enrollment in the faculties; both Buchez and Bazard had begun to study medicine.

It may well be that the recollections of the influence of those four

[44] On Buchez, see A. Ott, "Une notice sur la vie et les travaux de l'auteur," in Philippe-J. B. Buchez, *Traité de politique et de science morale* (Paris, 1866); François-André Isambert, *Politique, religion et science de l'homme chez Philippe Buchez (1786–1865)* (Paris, 1967); Isambert, *De la Charbonnerie au saint-simonisme*; and Henri Godlewski, "L'Etudiant en médecine Philippe Buchez, fondateur du carbonarisme français," *Bulletin de la société française d'histoire de la médecine*, 31 (February 1937): 43–48. On Joubert, see Rémusat, *Mémoires*, 2:52–53. On Flotard, see the 1848 election poster, *Les Murailles révolutionnaires de 1848*, 16th ed. (Paris, 1868), 351–52; and J. T. Flotard, Secrétaire général de la Mairie de Paris, *Aux Electeurs du département de la Seine, 24 mai 1849* (Paris, 1849).

[45] The article on Bazard in the *Encyclopédie nouvelle* (Paris, 1836), 2:519–24, published by Pierre Leroux and J. Reynaud devoted more space to Bazard than to the celebrated chemist Berthollet or to Gracchus Babeuf. For further citations on Bazard see chapter 6.

municipal clerks are exaggerations. However, they are a useful correc-
tive to the emphasis on the unique role of the minuscule elite from the
first few *promotions* of the Ecole normale. Victor Cousin and his protégés—Paul Dubois, Théodore Jouffroy, Augustin Thierry, and the
rest—did have a remarkable effect in shaping and articulating the
identity of their generation, particularly in the realm of ideas. But their
retrospective evaluation of their own importance obscures the extent to
which other leaders, especially the young veterans of the last battles before the walls of Paris, could command a following.

In the early years of the Restoration these individuals and groups
proceeded from widely disparate backgrounds to a sense of an amor-
phous collective identity, an identity that would pit a youthful, dynamic, and disinterested "we" against a historically compromised, obsolescent, aging "they." This identity is evident but elusive and will
require considerable elucidation. In a sense it is the subject of this book.
The binding element, the temperamental cement, of the emerging
leaders of a youth movement in Paris between 1817 and 1822 was the
conviction that the regeneration of the nation depended upon the autonomous enterprise of the young. This was the conviction behind the
various discussion circles organized during the first few years after the
fall of the Empire as agencies for the liberation of the imagination from
the received ideas of the older generation. The notables of the house of
intellect had pontificated together in a *Société philosophique*, their jun-
iors would sally into the realm of ideas in a *Société diablement philosophique*.[46]

This society, among whose founders was Buchez and other future
activists, was one of the early tentative efforts to forge some sort of intellectual identity for the student elite of Paris. This was the goal of the
four *commis*, clerks who initiated, with incredible self-confidence, an
ambitious program to transform the isolation of the "patriotic youth."
Their strategy was to rally to the students from the faculties of law and
medicine the other *jeunes gens* engaged in special studies at the Ecole

[46] On the Société diablement philosophique, see François de Corcelle, *Documens
pour servir à l'histoire des conspirations des parties et des sectes* (Paris, 1831), 18; Ott's preface in Buchez, *Traité de politique*, 1:xvi; Duvergier de Hauranne, *Histoire du gouvernement parlementaire*, 6:18; Isambert, *De la Charbonnerie au saint-simonisme*, 70–71. On
Balzac's fictional re-creation of such a cenacle in *Illusions perdues*, see Bruce Tolley,
"The Cenacle of Balzac's *Illusions perdues*," *French Studies*, 15 (October 1961): 324–37.

polytechnique and at the schools of pharmacy, mines, and *beaux-arts*.[47] Quite an undertaking, but not sufficient for Bazard, who proposed to add to the educated cream of the generation the much larger mass of young men who came to Paris from all over France to be trained in commercial occupations—*se former aux habitudes commerciales*. This conception was so striking as to be reproduced verbatim in reminiscences long after the event. According to these accounts, Bazard had observed that

> the apprentices to commerce live in even greater isolation than do the students; the very nature of their occupations tends to weaken the patriotic instincts of the young. To put them in touch with students would give birth to the wish to cultivate their intelligence and liberate them from the selfish commercialism assiduously preached and exemplified by the employers.[48]

The instrument chosen to assemble, and to serve as a "patriotic seminar" for, the students and commercial clerks of Paris was an ostensibly orthodox lodge of the freemasons, the *Amis de la vérité*. According to Flotard, his quartet joined the parent organization, the Grand Orient, and recruited thirty sympathizers—ten law students, ten medical students, and ten sales clerks—"admittedly in a scarcely orthodox manner."[49] After sufficient drilling in the detailed observances of the Scottish Rite, they successfully petitioned for authorization to form a new lodge. The precise chronology of the establishment of the *Amis de la vérité* (and the *Amis de l'Armorique*, its sister lodge, recruited from the Breton circle), the exact number and identity of its members, and the details of its actual relation to extramasonic activities have remained as problematic for historians as they were to the contemporary police and the masonic officials in the Grand Orient.[50]

We do know that the lodge became a forum for the boldest exploration of current political and philosophic issues and eventually a front for revolutionary conspiracy. Although surviving documents in the

---

[47] Flotard, *Paris révolutionnaire*, 2:451.

[48] Ibid., 452.

[49] Ibid.

[50] This question is discussed in Spitzer, *Old Hatreds and Young Hopes*, 220–21. The fragmentary source materials on the lodges, the *Amis de la vérité* and the *Amis de l'Armorique*, are in the Bibliothèque nationale, Fonds Franc-maçonnerie, FM² 39 and FM² 35 respectively. Henceforth cited as BN FM² 39.

masonic archives do not match contemporary testimony as to the vast numbers of recruits or the identity of notorious individual members of the lodge, we can be certain that it did recruit a large number of individuals of varied antecedents who shared the attribute of age. It was probably in the *Amis de la vérité* that veterans of the defense of Paris— Bazard and the rest—came to know the *normalien* coterie, the admirers of Victor Cousin, and the circle of Breton liberals around Paul Dubois. We can identify with reasonable certainty such familiar names as Auguste Sautelet; Gilbert Cariol, spokesman for the law students in the Bavoux affair; J. M. Duhamel, condisciple of Dubois at Rennes and Comte at the Ecole polytechnique; Arnold Scheffer, journalist, friend of Victor Cousin, and member of the circle that had begun to gather round the Count de Saint-Simon; and some two dozen others whose names would appear and reappear in the archives of the political police first as student agitators and then as conspirators.[51] The turn to freemasonry was, in effect, a phase in the process of knitting together personal networks into a web of dissidence that would eventually encompass a political conspiracy on a national scale.

The attraction of the two lodges lay in the fact that they were conceived and controlled by the young. The generational tone of the organization is conveyed in the reminiscences of Flotard and Benjamin Pance, which describe the superannuated practices of traditional freemasonry.[52] Their recollections are partially confirmed from the other side of the generation gap in the fragments of masonic correspondence preserved in the Bibliothèque nationale. The Grand Orient was distressed by the free and easy manner in which the *Amis de la vérité* submitted its membership lists and financial records and by the lack of

---

[51] For a discussion of the discrepancy between the number of names on the surviving membership lists of the *Amis de la vérité* and the *Amis de l'Armorique* (forty-five members on the longest list) and reminiscences of a much larger membership, and for an attempt to identify members whose names do not appear on the lists, see Spitzer, *Old Hatreds and Young Hopes*, 219–24. The following members of the lodges figure in our history of the *génération*: J. M. Baradère (1793), Saint-Amand Bazard, Charles Beslay, Philippe Buchez, Louis-Joseph Antoine Cahaigne (1796), Gilbert Cariol, François de Corcelle, Frédéric Degeorge, Marcelin Desloges, Pierre Dugied, J. M. Duhamel, Fernand Flocon (1800), J. T. Flotard, Joseph Guinard, Nicolas Joubert, Joseph-Antoine Limpérani (1798), André Marchais, Benjamin Pance, P. I. Rouen, Frédéric Salveton, Auguste Sautelet, Arnold Scheffer, Ary Scheffer, and Claude Sigaux. See Brown, "The Generation of 1820," 305–10.

[52] Flotard, *Paris révolutionnaire*, 2:452; Pance, *Paris révolutionnaire*, 1:265.

mature prudence in a promising lodge whose oldest member was twenty-eight.[53]

The *Amis de la vérité*, which would function as a conduit into the conspiracy of the Carbonari, foreshadowed that secret society in the assumption of the young freemasons that they were obliged to lead their elders willy-nilly into the new era. There was a foreshadowing also in the question of who was actually leading whom. Joseph Rey, a Grenoble lawyer deeply engaged in the clandestine resistance to the Bourbons between 1816 and 1820, believed that he and Victor Cousin had maneuvered behind the scenes to establish the lodge, a fact of which its founders were themselves unaware.[54] Through the mist of honest, self-serving, and deluded reminiscences, we can discern the outlines of a contest for control of the militant opposition to the regime, or at least of an inchoate attempt to construct a generational coalition in opposition to resurgent ultraroyalism.

The ambiguous possibilities of this tendency (policy is too strong a term) were revealed during the riots of June 1820 over the so-called law of the double vote. During the first two weeks of June, Parisian youths did for the first time what has been wrongly assumed they often did. They provided the leadership for mass demonstrations over a national political issue. The issue was the electoral reform that gave the richest one-quarter of the small Restoration electorate double representation. This apparently minor adjustment in the minuscule electorate can be seen as the hinge of the political history of the Restoration. It closed the door to the realization of the liberal, or moderate parliamentarian, version of the monarchy according to the Charte, and split the royalist center, propelling the Right Center into the arms of ultraroyalism and the moderate royalists into eventual coalition with the opponents of the entire regime. It was debated in the Chamber of Deputies with a polemical animus that carried the debate outside the boundaries of the Constitution—and from the parliamentary terrain into the Paris streets. These debates were followed with passionate interest by citizens throughout the country and by the intensely partisan crowds assembled in front of the Palais Bourbon.[55]

---

[53] BN FM² 39.

[54] *Patriote des Alpes*, 9 November 1847.

[55] There are detailed accounts of the June Days in Vaulabelle, *Histoire des deux restaurations*, 5:146–69; Duvergier de Hauranne, *Histoire du gouvernement parlementaire*, 5:528–60; Louis de Viel-Castel, *Histoire de la restauration* (Paris, 1865), 8:558–613; and

According to contemporary accounts, these crowds were characterized by the presence of young people, who formed a boisterous escort
to and from the Chamber for the current hero of the liberals, the Marquis de Chauvelin, and clashed with groups of men engaged in an apparently disciplined harassment of the opposition deputies.[56] On the
evening of June 2 a violent confrontation occurred when several students were singled out for beatings by what seemed to be royalist officers out of uniform supported by the belligerent neutrality of the police
and the *gendarmerie*. The next day, larger and more pugnacious crowds
encountered soldiers, this time very much in uniform. As the troops
moved into disperse knots of truculent youths, a soldier fired off a shot
that killed a law student, Nicholas Lallemand, and contributed the first
student martyr to French radical hagiography.

On Sunday the fourth, when the Chamber was not in session, there
was an ominous calm, but on the fifth when the Chamber convened to
reenact in the verbal clash at the rostrum the murderous conflict in the
streets, placards were up on the walls of the Ecole de droit and five or
six thousand people flowed out of the student quarter and into a great
demonstration outside the Chamber. Inside, the accusations of police
brutality were answered by warnings against revolutionary appeals
from the parliamentary arena to the arena of the streets. The wealthy
and influential opposition deputy Jacques Laffitte read a letter from
Lallemand's father denying allegations that his son had provoked a
shot in the back. "This young man had cried 'Vive la Charte!'" Laffitte remarked, "and these words were the signal for murder under the
very walls of the royal palace."[57] The minister of justice assured the
deputies that their inviolability would be preserved; let them repudiate
in their turn those shameful attempts to stir up the peaceable mass of
the population on the part of a handful of malcontents, "or of a mis-

---

in Etienne Denis Pasquier, *Mémoires du Chancelier Pasquier* (Paris, 1896), 4:412–17.
The bulk of the official correspondence on the June Days is in the AN F⁷ series. Var-
ious documents were published in [P. F. Hercule de Serre], *Correspondance du comte de
Serre (1796–1824)* (Paris, 1877), 6:222–36.

[56] The royalist leader Villèle identified, "Des étudiants en médecine, de jeunes lit-
térateurs montés par Benjamin Constant, des commis poussés par Lafitte, voilà je crois,
le fonds des premiers rassemblements qui ont eu lieu et qui chaque jour s'accroissent."
Villèle to Mme. de Villèle, 4 June 1820, in Joseph de Villèle, *Mémoires et correspondance
du Comte de Villèle*, 2:382. For the version of sympathetic bystanders, see Rémusat, *Correspondance*, 6:486–89; see also Charles Beslay, *Mes Souvenirs* (Paris, 1873), 69.

[57] *Archives parlementaires*, 2nd ser., 28:275.

guided youth whom they manipulate." But the turbulence outside the Palais Bourbon continued as mounted troops charged and dispersed the angry crowds. A number were arrested, and the authorities were happy to report that "no inhabitant of the *faubourg* had joined the rebels."[58] The inhabitants of the old revolutionary *faubourgs* continued to be the object of anxious or optimistic expectations. There is the story of one of the spectators of the demonstration, an aged veteran of the revolutionary era, impatiently consulting his watch. "Three o'clock," he cried, "and the *faubourgs* still haven't arrived."[59] The *faubourgs* never did show up. On the morning of the sixth, a huge funeral procession accompanied Lallemand's coffin to Père Lachaise, and late that afternoon cheering columns led by students swept eastward to cries of "Aux faubourgs!" and "Vive la Charte!" in the most determined effort to tap the great insurrectionary tradition of the Faubourg Saint-Antoine. This time the troops were reinforced by a heavy rain, and the "insurrection" petered out in the shelter of cafés, doorways, and colonnades. During the next few days similar efforts around the Portes Saint-Denis and Saint-Martin raised large crowds, which were effectively and bloodily dispersed by the cavalry.

During the entire affair, the government characterized the crowds as *jeunes gens, jeunes gens égarés*, and *jeunes gens, la plupart étrangers à la capitale*—undoubtedly a factious minority of the predominantly loyal and peaceable student body. The official correspondence noted that the "seditious youth" from the schools were joined by some young types from the boutiques and by a certain number of discharged or halfpay officers and a few men "of a mature age."[60] The police made a point of arresting the more visible "mature" men, especially if they had attained high rank in the Napoleonic armies, but in general the authorities attributed the June Days to youthful agitators egged on by malevolent elders from behind the scenes.

In the records of the police we can pick out threads of the web woven by militants from the schools, the *cénacles*, and the masonic front organizations. Among those expelled from the law school for participation in the "unlawful assemblies" of June 1820 was Frédéric Degeorge, who had come down from Lille to study law in the capital

58 Ibid., 279; [de Serre], *Correspondance*, 6:226.
59 This tale is spun in Vaulabelle, *Histoire des deux restaurations*, 5:152.
60 [de Serre], *Correspondance*, 6:222–36.

where he plunged into the subculture of political sedition as a member of the *Amis de la vérité* and participated in the conspiracies of August 1820 and the Carbonari. Recruited into the desperate band that tried to turn back the French troops as they crossed the border in the Spanish campaign of 1823, Degeorge was fortunate to escape with his skin to London, where he joined the émigré community and became a foreign correspondent for the *Globe*—founded by his fellow conspirators.[61] A report of the king's attorney—the *procureur du roi*—on the shooting of Lallemand identifies in the crowd one Isidore Rouen, lawyer, whom we recognize as P. I. Rouen (1796), member of the *Amis de l'Armorique*, Carbonarist, and cofounder of the Saint-Simonian journal, the *Producteur*. According to family tradition, Augustin Thierry was among the demonstrators forced into a ditch by the horses of the dragoons. A brilliant young lawyer, Félix Barthe (1795), spoke at Lallemand's grave.[62]

The identification of the June Days of 1820 as a quasi-insurrection of the young is congruent with the reminiscences of participants. At the time, of course, spokesmen for the militant youth simultaneously affirmed their protest against political repression while denying that their actions had any subversive intent. Speaking, as he said, in the name of French youth, Senemaud, a law student, published a pamphlet signed and approved by a commission, the members of which were selected from "commercial establishments and the schools of law and medicine."[63] Senemaud described the unwarranted persecution of the militants of the June Days as one more example of "Gothic oligarchs." Yet, he wrote, in the face of persecution,

> How might thoughtful young men describe a *jeunesse* whose hands are unstained by blood, whose lives have not been tarnished, whose heart is not black and guilty but candid, sensitive,

[61] André Fortin, *Frédéric Degeorge* (Lille, 1964), 16–25; Frédéric Degeorge, "Les Proscrits de la Restauration," *Paris révolutionnaire*, 4:103–27.

[62] [de Serre], *Correspondance*, 6:229; A. Augustin Thierry, *Augustin Thierry (1795–1856) d'après sa correspondance et ses papiers de famille* (Paris, 1922), 63.

[63] [Edmond Senemaud], *Détails historiques sur les évènements de la première quinzaine de juin MDCCCXX, par M. Senemaud, élève de la Faculté de Droit à Paris* (Paris, 1820), 24. The members of the commission named are Senemaud, Limpérani, Degeorge, and Baudet. The first three would be active in the conspiracies that followed the June Days.

generous, and always responsive to the sacred names of Fatherland and Honor?[64]

This conviction of the peculiar virtues of Senemaud's coevals was not
universally shared at the time but would color their retrospective accounts. Pance's version in *Paris révolutionnaire* does grant the clandestine influence of mature politicians. The schools had massed before the
Chamber of Deputies at the summons of the opposition notables who
did not know what to do with them once they had appeared. Here is
planted the seed of the conviction that the consequence of submitting
to the prudent guidance of the old was the surrender of the dynamic of
youth. However, Pance was not willing to admit that this first courageous affirmation of his cohort was a complete fiasco. In the June Days
of 1820, he claimed, they took their first steps in the direction of July
1830. Even at the time, the affair bore fruit, as "solidarity was sealed by
a student's blood and none of his brothers forgot it."[65]

Poor Lallemand certainly did contribute to the solidarity of his surviving brothers. The funeral procession and graveside ceremony were
organized as generational rites. The contribution of Armand Marrast
(1801) to *Paris révolutionnaire* features a florid description of that "revolutionary funeral" dominated by a *génération* confident of its destiny
and bold enough to use a language that passed the bounds of *la prudence parlementaire*:

> It didn't require a terribly clairvoyant observer to foretell what
> France was to become in the hands of that youth, which would
> henceforth assume the vanguard of progress for all nations. . . .
> The challenge of the new generation was first heard ten years be-
> fore [the Revolution of 1830] at the funeral of a comrade and
> friend that the generation of the past was to answer with a *coup
> d'état* only to draw down on itself a *coup de foudre*.[66]

Even if the martyrdom of Lallemand did not have the long-term and
profound effects attributed to it by Pance or Marrast, it certainly contributed to the solidarity that is often produced by the experience of
repression. The bystander may preserve a prudent neutrality until the

[64] Ibid., 65.

[65] *Paris révolutionnaire*, 1:264.

[66] Armand Marrast, "Les Funérailles révolutionnaires," *Paris révolutionnaire*, 3:235–
36.

moment when the policeman clubs someone like himself. That is the moment, as we say nowadays, when he becomes politicized.

How this may have been the case in 1820 is suggested in the solitary musings of the twenty-one-year-old scholar Jules Michelet. In his journal for June 5–7 he writes, "It would require a stable temperament to remain tranquil and self-absorbed in the midst of these political convulsions." He quotes Benjamin Constant's speech in the Chamber of Deputies eulogizing his generation, is stirred by the courage with which they faced the sabers of the *gendarmerie*, and indulges in the speculation, "What glory for the *jeunesse française* if it alone were to make that sublime revolution!" To his friend Poinsot he writes, "My dear friend, I feel a strong need to learn how to handle a gun."[67] Even the sober, ambitious *collégien* Jules Baroche (1802) was tempted to join the action. "Fortunately," he recalls, "it rained." He went home wet, disconsolate, and preserved from the sort of behavior he would implacably repress as Louis Napoleon's minister of justice.[68]

The effects of the June Days and the martyrdom of Lallemand rippled out far beyond the confines of the Latin Quarter. The obvious idea of a subscription in memory of Lallemand spread from Paris to various schools in the provinces and continued to provide a focus for agitation after the initial crisis had subsided. There were "attroupements et désordres" fomented by the law students at Poitiers; at Brest "des jeunes inconsidérés" initiated scandalous scenes; at Rennes "attroupements tumultueux" were joined by students from the faculties of law, medicine, and the *collège royal*; at Toulouse crowds of law students gathered on the "pretext" of raising a subscription for a mausoleum for Lallemand.[69]

The turbulence in Paris and the provinces subsided by mid-June. The faculties were purged of notorious agitators, and as early as June 10 the minister of justice would reassure the *procureurs généraux* of the

---

[67] Jules Michelet, *Ecrits de jeunesse* (Paris, 1959), 83–84, 262.

[68] Bibliothèque Thiers, Papiers Baroche, T Mss 967, 37.

[69] Various repercussions of the June Days are reported in AN F¹⁷ 2105, BB³⁰ 192, F⁷ 6667, BB³⁰ 280. See also [de Serre], *Correspondance*, 6:235–36; Duvergier de Hauranne, *Histoire du gouvernement parlementaire*, 5:550–65. Prefect of Police Baron Anglès to Director General of Police Claude Mounier, 9 June 1820, in Bibliothèque historique de la Ville de Paris, MS 810. Anglès thought a law student, De George, arrested on June 8, was a courier from Paris to the provinces. This almost certainly was the ubiquitous Frédéric Degeorge.

insignificance of the handful of troublemakers who disturbed the public order.[70] The *Moniteur universel* of June 9 reproduced the remarks delivered by the historian Lacretelle "*le jeune*" to a large and appreciative audience at the Faculty of Letters. After the decree of the Commission of Public Instruction stipulating the expulsion of any student convicted of participation in the recent disorders, Professor Lacretelle delivered a "frank and affectionate" sermon. The young must shun the spurious attractions of the revolutionary temperament, keep their anxious parents ever in mind, and above all:

> Beware of those who flatter you. Beware of those who praise your precious gifts, the brilliant but sometimes deceptive portion of a fortunate few, and never the common lot. Reject the ridiculous notion of constituting yourselves, in all your inexperience, as an autonomous power within the state, bizarre and tyrannical judges of all the rest.

These and other candid observations were received, the *Moniteur* tells us, with "the unanimous and prolonged applause of the young and numerous audience."[71]

But somehow the message did not reach all of the studious *jeunesse*. It was at this point, Pance recalled, that the schools had crossed the gap that separates protest from revolt. The students were about to exchange the "canes and umbrellas of June" for more serious weapons. And this time they were to act on their own, except perhaps "to unite, under certain circumstances, with eminent men, who would lead the way."[72] Pance's recollection of the chronology of the application of these resolutions is not precisely congruent with other reminiscences or with the record of events. The commitment to direct insurrectionary action that followed hard on the June Days, that is, the conspiracy of August 1820, was again a sort of coalition in which the young Paris militants were only one of several groups that came together to overthrow the dynasty. As in the case of other conspiratorial coalitions, the precise composition and relative influence of the various elements in the secret organization are obscure, but on the basis of what the police knew then and what the participants later remembered, we can recon-

[70] [De Serre], *Correspondance*, 6:231.

[71] *Moniteur universel*, 9 June 1820.

[72] *Paris révolutionnaire*, 1:264–66.

struct the rough outlines of the amalgam of officers in uniform and on half pay, national leaders of the parliamentary opposition, and the leading lights of the militant *jeunesse*, who contrived the attempt to topple the Bourbons through a military pronunciamento that was to be the signal for a general insurrection.

The attempt was aborted when soldiers in the royal legions reported the insubordination to their superiors. The police net hauled in a miscellany of disaffected officers, as well as some notorious Bonapartist agents and other civilians long suspected of clandestine agitation. The authorities also strongly suspected but were unable to indict such national dignitaries as Lafayette and the wealthy ultraliberal deputy Voyer d'Argenson. They were unable to identify and bring to book those student leaders and indefatigable agitators we have followed through the organization of the *Amis de la vérité*, the piecemeal agitation in the schools, and the mass demonstrations of June.[73]

Nevertheless, a certain amount of information about their implication in the August conspiracy, unavailable to the police, is available to us. It seems probable that Nicholas Joubert, one of the original four *commis*, and Charles Beslay, from the *Amis de l'Armorique*, established connections with some of the older conspirators through Lafayette. They also established other contacts through François de Corcelle, son of the liberal deputy, and through such intermediaries as Joseph Rey, a Grenoble lawyer whose unpublished and published recollections provide the fullest account of the August conspiracy from the inside and a great deal about the background of all the clandestine operations against the regime between 1815 and 1822.[74] Rey provides the best account of the relations between his organization in southeastern France, L'Union, and the key groups of veterans and half-pay officers at Paris and in the vulnerable units of the royal army. He also describes the role of Victor Cousin, which is especially relevant to our general concerns because of Cousin's immense public and personal influence over the apprentice intelligentsia of the Restoration and because so many per-

---

[73] There is a detailed account of the conspiracy in Spitzer, *Old Hatreds and Young Hopes*, 39–49, 212–16.

[74] Rey's revelations appeared in the *Patriote des Alpes*, 1 October 1841 and in various issues between 26 October and 16 December 1847. There is a great deal of relevant material in his manuscript memoirs at the Bibliothèque historique de la Ville de Grenoble, fonds T3938, T3939, T3940. See Spitzer, *Old Hatreds and Young Hopes*, 213.

sonal threads crossed at the intersection of Cousin and his coterie.[75] Despite the denials of Cousin and his biographers, there is persuasive mutually supporting testimony to implicate Cousin in the organization of the conspiracies of 1820 and the Carbonari, although not in the risks of direct action. Rey recalls that Cousin and his followers Auguste Sautelet and J. Cariol were engaged in the formation and drilling of an armed band of students recruited in anticipation of a "great popular movement to force the king to follow the Charte."[76] In the event, Cousin happened to be traveling outside France when the great movement sputtered and collapsed.

Whatever Cousin's actual role in organizing an armed company of devoted *jeunes gens*, there was certainly some sort of an armed company attached to the conspiracy. It is identified in Flotard's memoir as the "compagnie franche des écoles." It went into action on the night that the rising of army units at Vincennes was to signal the outbreak of the insurrection. Several hundred students fell out with alacrity at the summons of the leading members of the *Amis de la vérité* and the *Amis de l'Armorique*. They answered the call without question and without the remotest idea of the real goal of, or the actual means available to, the conspiracy. In those days, says Flotard, the members of the lodge could rely on one another. If later on members of that sacred battalion would fall short of their civic duties, "the fault lay in the times, which corrupted the young by making them 'wiser,' that is to say, less prompt to act; more prudent, that is to say, more timid; more moderate, that is to say, more egotistical." At that moment on the night of 19–20 August 1820, excessive prudence was not the problem, at least not for the students. They drew up in their improvised squads, received the arms and the passwords, and were assigned commanders under the supreme leadership of the eldest among them, Saint-Amand Bazard, "little dreaming then," says Flotard, "of his future as a Saint-Simonian pope." In a narrow alley across from the Panthéon, they waited coolly for the order from the grand quartier-général to join the military insurrection at Vincennes.[77] The moment never arrived. At 11:30 Bazard appeared at the quartier-général, exhausted but icily calm, to reveal that the signal from above was not forthcoming and that there was to

[75] On the evidence for Cousin's involvement in the conspiracies, see Spitzer, *Old Hatreds and Young Hopes*, 221, 226, 227, 240, 268. Also see below chapter 3.

[76] Joseph Rey in Bib. Grenoble, T3938, 43.

[77] *Paris révolutionnaire*, 2:459.

be no attempt that night. The youthful rank and file were convinced that this last-minute cancellation was caused by the cowardice of the older leaders of the plot. The promise to admit their representatives to the inner council of the conspiracy had not been honored. The self-protective caution of the older generation had prevailed. "That was our first Waterloo," Pance recalls, "and the second for France."[78] But not the final defeat, for, unlike their elders, the youth of the schools preserved the resolution to prevail, but this time with a different instrument—the secret insurrectionary network of the Carbonari. This network was to have unintentional ramifications when it intersected with a group of young lawyers who would found careers on the defense of their less prudent coevals.[79]

There are two aspects of the obscure, complex, tragicomic history of the Carbonari that are of particular relevance to the self-definition of the generation of 1820: the widespread recruitment through a dense network of interpersonal connections that brought so many individuals of disparate circles and backgrounds into an age-based political movement, and the extent to which this movement was the political expression of, and was dominated by, an autonomous *jeunesse*.[80]

There seems no doubt that the Carbonari was founded by a handful of veterans of the leadership of the *Amis de la vérité* and the August conspiracy. Two of them, so the story goes, left France for a brief stint as freedom fighters in the Neapolitan revolution, in which they absorbed the organizational forms and conspiratorial techniques of the Italian Carbonari. Sometime in the spring of 1821, Nicholas Joubert, one of the four original *commis*, and Pierre Dugied, a young wine merchant who had been a member of the *Amis de la vérité*, returned from Italy with ideas that seemed applicable to the French milieu. Some ten to fifteen students, ex-students, young lawyers, doctors, and clerks proceeded from the implausible assumption that they could spin out of their own heads a national network of secret cells, *ventes*, into which

---

[78] Ibid., 1:269.

[79] Among the lawyers who played a part in the conspiracy trials were Barthe, Chaix D'Est Ange (1800), H. G. Boulay de la Meurthe (1797), Arthur-Auguste Beugnot (1797), Charles Renouard (1794), F. A. Isambert (1792), E. E. Boinvilliers, and Désiré Dalloz (1795).

[80] The following account of the Carbonari is drawn from my book *Old Hatreds and Young Hopes*.

they could recruit a sufficient number of conspirators to contemplate bringing down the state. The assumption was correct.

In his anything-but-neutral participant's account, Trélat celebrates the universal enthusiasm that greeted the proposed conspiracy, which rapidly spread from the faculties of law and medicine and "a considerable number of young people in trade" in Paris to people throughout the country.[81] The proposal to conspire seemed to give many of them precisely what they had been dreaming of and thirsting after. This is probably a not-too-rosy version of the remarkable response that greeted most reckless and ill-defined proposals. Somehow at that moment "the need to conspire" was so intense as to impel a great many individuals from various backgrounds to accept the evident risks and implausible opportunities of membership in the secet *ventes* of the Carbonari. They had entered the organization from many directions and at its demise would fan out again on diverging paths. In transitory union with those veterans of agitation and conspiracy led by the notorious four *commis*, we find the sober, complacent young savants from the Ecole normale and the circle of Victor Cousin—notably Paul Dubois, Théodore Jouffroy, and Augustin Thierry. Admirers of the fiery orator and prudent conspirator Jacques Manuel mingled with acolytes of Lafayette, future republicans and Saint-Simonians with the embryo cadre of the *juste milieu*.[82]

It is not easy to recapture the common element that cemented these diverse individuals into such a dangerous and far-fetched enterprise. Years later one of them, Armand Carrel, wondered, "how could we ever have had the mad hope of overthrowing a government supported on the laws and on the inertia of thirty million men by plots led by law

[81] *Paris révolutionnaire*, 2:282–83.

[82] The members of the Carbonari who are subjects of this work are: Etienne Arago (1802), J. M. Baradère, Félix Barthe, Jules Bastide, Jean-Jacques Baude (1792), Saint-Amand Bazard, Louis Belmontet, Charles Beslay, E. E. Boinvilliers (1799), Philippe Buchez, Gilbert Cariol, Armand Carrel, Eugène Cavaignac, Godefroy Cavaignac, Antoine Cerclet, François de Corcelle, Victor Cousin, Marcelin Desloges, J. J. Dubochet (1798), Paul Dubois, Pierre Dugied, J. M. Duhamel, James Fazy (1794), J. F. Flotard, Camille Henri Guillier de la Touche (1800), Joseph-Auguste Guinard, Nicholas Joubert, Théodore Jouffroy, Pierre Leroux, Joseph-Antoine Limpérani, André Marchais, Marthe-Camille Montalivet (1801), J. B. Paulin, François-Vincent Raspail (1794), Pierre-Isidore Rouen, Frédéric Salveton, Auguste Sautelet, Arnold Scheffer, Ary Scheffer, Henry Scheffer, Senemaud, Claude Sigaud, Augustin Thierry, Charles Thomas, Ulysse Trélat.

students and second lieutenants?"[83] It is just such a question that is *not*
elucidated with reference to the recklessness and idealism of the young.
Why at that time and in that place? Why that particular alignment of
such different attitudes and temperaments? Why as a resolutely autonomous element in a generational coalition?

Perhaps political ideology was the cement. In Ulysse Trélat's detailed and authoritative account of the Carbonari, the association's
goals are remembered as republican.[84] Trélat, who would remain on
the virtuous side of the barricades during the July Monarchy,[85] nostal-
gically portrayed a generation outraged by the national humiliation
that had returned the *royauté-cosaque* to the throne but inoculated by
its love of liberty against the popular cult of the Empire. "Proud of the
glory of France," Trélat wrote, "it was innocent of the despotism that
had oppressed it."[86] The ideal of the student revolutionary was liberty,
a republican ideal. There is other testimony to the same effect.

There was, no doubt, a universal enthusiasm for "liberty" however
conceived, but a universal commitment to a republican constitution is
not to be found even among the most militant of the young revolutionaries. François de Corcelle recalled that a majority of the enthusiasts in
the discussion societies and the *Amis de la vérité* settled for something
like a federative republic (more or less the model for the organization
of the Carbonari), while others upheld the ideal of a constitutional
monarchy or of a centralized republic with a strong central administration.[87] In fact, the conspiratorial coalition could not have survived if
there had been any clarity or serious debate as to its political goals.
Something like the right of the French people to establish its own form
of government seemed to have provided a convenient provisional
catchall.

In a sense, the ideological diversity of the young members of the
Carbonari reflected that of the general political opposition to the Bourbon regime, an opposition that, particularly after Napoleon's death, enjoyed the opportunity to coalesce against the common enemy without
having to specify precise, divisive goals. Pance speaks of the desire to

[83] *National*, 22 September 1830.

[84] *Paris révolutionnaire*, 2:257.

[85] He would eventually cross to the other side as the Minister of Public Works in
1848.

[86] *Paris révolutionnaire*, 2:277.

[87] Corcelle, *Documens pour servir à l'histoire des conspirations*, 18–19.

"reintegrate the French student into the great revolutionary family."[88] Indeed, as we have seen, many contemporaries believed that young radicals had merely signed on to the party of the disloyal opposition, for whom the settlement of 1814 was but a lost battle in a long war.

Certainly the commitment to conspiracy was no monopoly of the young. Carbonarism itself was a coalition of generations as well as political tendencies. The period between 1815 and 1823 was characterized by an "epidemic of conspiracy," and not only in France. The choice of the Italian model of conspiracy at the moment of its debacle can be partly understood in light of the accumulated precedents of freemasonry and of the secret societies organized by republicans and royalists against moderate royalism, as well as by Bonapartists and republicans against the Bourbon line.[89] Yet there was a difference. What distinguished Carbonarism from the other conspiracies was the resolution of its young founders to retain control of the revolutionary coalition in the hands of their own generation. This was the lesson drawn from the earlier debacles, and this was the conviction at the very core of their *politique*. "To a new era, a new generation," said Trélat. "The older cohorts had been used up, worn out or drained of all initiative."[90]

This conviction was deeply felt by many of Trélat's coevals who did not share his taste for conspiracy. The premise of the obsolescence of the older generation and the world-historical mission of the new informed the dominant ideas and actions of the entire generation. In response to contemporary circumstances—the harassment of the schools, the outrageous law of the double vote, the apparent threats of clericalism and censorship—the generational mission was briefly identified with the politics of insurrection.

The sense of generational mission imposed the resolution to dominate the revolutionary coalition, specifically to retain control of the secret organization despite the tactical necessity of recruiting certain notables with national reputations. In my book on the Carbonari, I tried to work through the problematic relationship of the young founders of the secret society with the dignitaries of the national opposition. There I argued that it was not plausible to suppose that such distinguished conspirators as Lafayette or Jacques Manuel or the Marquis Voyer

[88] *Paris révolutionnaire*, 2:257.

[89] See the insightful remarks of Isambert, *De la Charbonnerie au saint-simonisme*, 89–91.

[90] *Paris révolutionnaire*, 2:277.

d'Argenson accepted their role as figureheads for obscure young scholars and clerks. It seemed to me that various groups shared the incompatible belief that they and no other were at the decisive center of the
society.[91] The point for the present study, however, is that the young
organizers sincerely believed that the direction of the conspiracy belonged to them, that the notables had been admitted to the association
without depriving it of its "force and character," as Trélat put it. Of
course, a few of the impressionable young recruits permitted themselves "a certain amount of flattery and occasional symptoms of servil-
ity," but in general the notables came to know their place. Saint-
Amand Bazard, the thirty-year-old president of the *vente suprême*, did
not hesitate to issue the great Lafayette "a sharp rebuke" for missing a
meeting.[92] (A few years after this, Bazard would be remembered as a
spokesman for the young Saint-Simonians, effectively refuting the patronizing remarks of Benjamin Constant.)[93] Paul Dubois recalled how
his relationship with the famous orator Manuel had been established
"by the mandate of my political associates and the Charbonnerie bretonne; sometimes his equal in authority, sometimes his superior, as
well as that of old general Lafayette."[94] Armand Carrel would defend
the older leaders against the accusation that they had used and then deserted their young followers under fire: "Never did the leaders of the
ancienne opposition ... never did Manuel, Lafayette, or a single one of
their political associates, make a practice of subverting sergeants, junior
officers, or students only to abandon them to the guillotine of the Restoration. ... It is they (the younger generation) who attempted to subvert the members of the chamber."[95]

There were, on the other hand, those who believed that the failure
of the Carbonari, as of the August 1820 plot, could be assigned to the
irresolution or even the cowardice of the senior conspirators. They reconciled the contradictory convictions that the Carbonari had been led

[91] Spitzer, *Old Hatreds and Young Hopes*, 238–41.

[92] Trélat, *Paris révolutionnaire*, 2:287. For similar versions of relations between
young and old conspirators, see Corcelle, *Documens pour servir à l'histoire des conspirations*, 10–11; Duvergier de Hauranne, *Histoire du gouvernement parlementaire*, 6:395;
Guizot, *Mémoires*, 1:239.

[93] [Saint-Simon], *Oeuvres de Saint-Simon et d'Enfantin*, (Paris, 1865), 1:181.

[94] Papiers Dubois, AN 319 AP³; see also Dubois, "Souvenirs inédits," *Revue bleue*, 8
(5 October 1907): 422.

[95] Armand Carrel, *Oeuvres politiques et littéraires* (Paris, 1857), 3:169–70.

by the young but betrayed by the old by maintaining that somehow the notables had gradually infiltrated the leadership of the organization. Even Trélat managed to square that circle: "It was evident that the young no longer controlled the Charbonnerie as they had when it was organized; they had been outmaneuvered."[96]

Thus the failure of the Carbonari was ascribed to what its founders had been especially concerned to avoid: the growing influence and the faltering of the older generation. In fact, the difference in revolutionary temperament was not exclusively a division between rash youth and prudent middle age. Old notables and young enthusiasts were unified in opposing camps defined by differences in ideology and political temperament. Lafayette, the hope of the young republicans and the most desperate activists, was opposed by the coterie around the cool, pragmatic Manuel, who would be posthumously accused of proto-Orleanism. Paul Dubois would remember that he himself had had the wisdom to preserve the Charbonnerie bretonne "against all illusions and to prevent any premature rising there." To the militant Doctor Trélat, this wisdom reflected "a doctrinaire spirit continuously committed to combating all clear and precise ideas, all direct propositions."[97]

What finally tore the generational fabric of the Carbonari was not so much its incipient divisions as its failures. The collapse of the conspiracy was felt both as a moral and a practical fiasco. The unresisted execution of ten comrades, and especially the calvary of the "four sergeants of La Rochelle," were ineradicable stains on the honor of those whose ritualized solidarity had failed their most vulnerable brothers. The organization disintegrated in an atmosphere of mutual recrimination. The transient identity of disparate individuals temporarily unified through the shared sense of mission was lost.

Yet the generational identity that had informed the clandestine assemblies of the young Carbonarists did not disappear but would be expressed in other ways with greater success. As Augustin Thierry recalled:

This revolutionary effervescence was almost immediately succeeded by outstanding scholarly activity. Starting in the year 1823,

[96] *Paris révolutionnaire*, 2:231; cf. Marcellin Desloges in the *Patriote des Alpes*, 7 December 1847.

[97] Dubois, "Souvenirs inédits," *Revue bleue*, 9 (14 March 1908): 322; *Paris révolutionnaire*, 2:331.

a fresh breeze stimulated the simultaneous revival of all the branches of literature. The dawn of the ambition to grasp the truth in all of its forms, in art as well as science, was to be seen among a large number of young and distinguished intellects. This ambition continued to be fruitful throughout the next seven years and to encourage generous and noble aspirations for the future.[98]

The most impressive manifestation of this *souffle de rénovation* was the appearance of remarkable journals launched and edited by a corps of ex-students and erstwhile conspirators, most of them still in their twenties. The cofounder and guiding spirit of the *Globe*, Paul-François Dubois, would, with poignant nostalgia, turn again and again throughout the rest of his long life to the golden moment when he had been the standard-bearer for the literary and political crusade of an "entire generation."[99] Not long after Dubois and Pierre Leroux had drawn the *normaliens*, ex-Carbonari, and other associates into the exciting editorial work on the *Globe*, Saint-Amand Bazard followed a different path out of the world of conspiracy:

> Scarcely had I sounded the void and sensed the sterility for our era of critical philosophy and revolutionary politics when the works of Saint-Simon captured my attention, and it did not take me long to perceive in the ideas of this bold innovator the germ of the new world for which I had long instinctively searched.[100]

The Saint-Simonians who founded the *Producteur* and the young liberals at the *Globe* would take their stand on opposed terrains, or so it seemed to them. I hope to demonstrate in the following chapters that the premises from which they argued were not in fact as far apart as their polemics seemed to suggest and that they shared with the entire intelligentsia of their generation the views adumbrated by Bazard's remarks on the sterility of critical philosophy and the quest for the germ of a new world.

[98] Augustin Thierry, *Dix Ans d'études historiques*, in *Oeuvres d'Augustin Thierry* (Brussels, 1867), 321; Duvergier de Hauranne, *Histoire du gouvernement parlementaire*, 8:113.

[99] See, e.g., Papiers Dubois AN 319 AP³, dossiers 1 and 3.

[100] Saint-Amand Bazard, from a copy of a letter to Resseguier printed in [Saint-Simon], *Oeuvres de Saint-Simon et d'Enfantin*, 8:54.

CHAPTER 3

Victor Cousin:
The Professor as Guru

"At present he is the only man who can inspire
me because he is the only one in whom I perceive
the glow of genius."
Edgar Quinet to Mme. Quinet, November 1825

"... the most insufferable poseur whom I have
ever met."
Etienne Delécluze, *Journal de Delécluze,*
1824–1828

The repudiation of political for
intellectual adventuring was not a departure from, but a continuation of, tendencies characteristic of the *jeunesse* from the beginning of the Restoration. That first vibrant, confusing decade after
Napoleon's fall was marked by an intense intellectual ferment in
which educated youth in and out of the schools groped toward a
collective destiny defined in opposition to obsolete ideologies and
informed by a sense of millennial potentialities. The thrilling in-
timation of vast intellectual opportunities and obligations had begun to germinate beneath the icy authoritarianism of the late
Empire, at least among the fortunate few who were spared the
decimation of the last military campaigns. This was especially apparent in that sheltered workshop of the Ecole normale where,
by a "fortunate inconsequence," the greatest intellectual liberties
flourished in the midst of the narrow discipline of the waning
Empire.[1] It was at the Ecole normale in the years between 1810
and 1814 that the individual whose personal influence would
place an indelible stamp on his own generation had begun his

[1] Lair, "Les Souvenirs de M. Dubois," (1 November 1901): 87; Dubois,
Cousin, Jouffroy, Damiron, 7; Joseph-Daniel Guigniaut, *Institut impérial de la
France: Notice historique sur la vie et les travaux de M. Augustin Thierry* (Paris,
1863), 5.

career and had created a brilliant and dedicated coterie. This individual was Victor Cousin. Some conception of the nature and extent of his influence is indispensable to any characterization of the spirit of the generation of 1820.

Cousin certainly did not have a monopoly on the admiration of the young intellectuals of the early Restoration. Chateaubriand continued to inspire successive cohorts of young Renés, Lafayette persisted as an ivy-covered revolutionary institution, and, while young intellectuals sedulously avoided service in Napoleon's armies, his demonic presence undoubtedly left its mark on the older brothers of Julien Sorel. But the spirit of the generation is most fully expressed in its interest in the ideas of Saint-Simon and its reverence for the brilliant pedagogues of the Restoration University—Guizot, Villemain, and above all, Victor Cousin. Saint-Simon appealed to a much smaller contemporary circle, but his influence ramified far beyond his era. That of Victor Cousin was diminished by the disrepute into which his philosophy fell.

The attempt to reconstruct the nature of Victor Cousin's appeal to his contemporaries in the early years of the Restoration puts a considerable strain on our historical empathy.[2] There is no question as to the existence of the phenomenon.[3] Cousin's philosophy lectures at the Sorbonne between 1815 and 1820 attracted and enraptured a large audi-

---

[2] This treatment of Cousin's influence is an expanded version of my essay "Victor Cousin and the French Generation of 1820" in Dora B. Weiner and William R. Keylor, eds., *From Parnassus: Essays in Honor of Jacques Barzun* (New York, 1976), 177–94.

[3] The question of Cousin's influence on the youth of the Restoration received considerable attention in such nineteenth-century works as: Hippolyte Taine, *Les Philosophes classiques du XIXe siècle en France*, 7th ed. (Paris, 1895), 79–202, 289–315; Barthélemy–Saint-Hilaire, *Victor Cousin: Sa Vie et sa correspondance*, 1:49–50; Jules Simon, *Victor Cousin* (Paris, 1891), 7–8, 16–19; Paul Janet, *Victor Cousin et son oeuvre* (Paris, 1885), 15–31; Charles Dejob, *L'Instruction publique en France et en Italie au dix-neuvième siècle* (Paris, 1894), 333–36. It has been taken up again in several useful recent studies: W. M. Simon, "The 'Two Cultures' in Nineteenth-Century France: Victor Cousin and Auguste Comte," *Journal of the History of Ideas*, 26 (January–March 1965): 45–58; Doris S. Goldstein, "Official Philosophies in Modern France: The Example of Victor Cousin," *Journal of Social History*, 1 (Spring 1968): 259–79; André Canivez, *Jules Lagneau: Professeur de philosophie* (Paris, 1965), 1:144–77, 203–22; Lucien Sève, *Philosophie française contemporaine* (Paris, 1962), 95–96; Armand Hoog, "Un Intercesseur de romantisme: Victor Cousin vu par Stendhal," *Revue des sciences humaines*, new series, 62–63 (April–September 1951): 184–200; Barbéris, *Balzac Et Le Mal du siècle*, 1:240–43; D. G. Charlton, *Secular Religions in France, 1815–1870* (London, 1963), 97–99. I will discuss the testimony of Cousin's contemporaries below.

ence, distinguished by the presence of the Parisian notables but dominated by aficionados under the age of thirty.[4] In a manner strikingly
similar to the cult of Henri Bergson before the First World War, attendance at the lectures of the young philosopher functioned as the de-
fiant expression of a distinct generational identity. In a sense, the problem lies in reconciling Cousin's contemporary reputation with the
subsequent evaluation of his work. Cousin enjoyed one of those inflated reputations, so devastatingly, so decisively, so wittily deflated (by
Taine above all) that their real merits and the nature of their original
appeal seem lost to the historical imagination.[5]

One might argue that a historian concerned with how ideas were
received when they were articulated should not dwell on subsequent
evaluations. My emphasis on the actual situation of the generation of
1820 is so contextual that this prescription might seem self-evident.
Cousin's philosophy will be considered in the light of its meaning for
his coevals in the 1820s, not its enshrinement in the academic establish-

---

[4] For contemporary testimony on the success of Cousin's first series of lectures, see
Thierry, *Dix Ans d'études historiques*, 461–75, first published in the *Censeur européen*, 4
August and December 1819; Théodore Jouffroy, *Nouveaux mélanges philosophiques*,
3rd ed. (Paris, 1872), 127–30; J. S. Cariol, "Cours de M. Cousin," in *Journal général de
législation et de jurisprudence* (Paris, 1820), 1:491–503; 2:112–15; Dubois, *Cousin, Jouffroy, Damiron*, 35–51; Carné, *Souvenirs de ma jeunesse*, 15; Charles de Rémusat, *Séance
de l'académie française du 23 avril 1868. Discours de réception de Jules Favre. Réponse de
M. De Rémusat* (Paris, 1868), 64–65; H. J. G. Patin, *Discours de M. S. de Sacy . . . prononcé
aux funérailles de M. V. Cousin le 24 janvier 1867, et discours de MM. de Parien et Patin*
(Paris, 1867), 16: *Surveillant politique et littéraire* (1818), 28 (a journal edited by Cousin's
admirer J. J. Darmaing); Philippe Damiron, *Essai sur l'histoire de la philosophie en
France au dix-neuvième siècle* (Paris, 1828), 362. F. Chambon, "L'Ecole normale en
1816–1818," *Revue internationale de l'enseignement*, 54 (1907): 320–25, publishes a poem
by the *normalien* Laurent Delcasso (1797), "Epitre à Victor Cousin: Souvenirs de
l'Ecole normale, 1816–1818," which celebrates the *voix souveraine* of the master in ring-
ing alexandrines.

[5] There is a long list of those who have consigned Cousin to the philosophical scrapheap, starting with such contemporary critics as Auguste Comte. See, for example,
Comte to Valat, 3 November 1824, in Comte, *Correspondance générale*, 1:132; Armand
Marrast, *Examen critique du cours de philosophie de M. Cousin (leçon par leçon)* (Paris,
1828); Eugène Lerminier, *Lettres philosophiques adressées à un Berlinois* (Paris, 1832).
For characteristic negative evaluations of Cousin, see Taine, *Les Philosophes classiques*,
129–78; Félix Ravaisson, *La Philosophie en France au XIXe siècle* (Paris, 1904), 32–34;
George Boas, *French Philosophies of the Romantic Period* (Baltimore, 1925), 197–233;
Emile Brehier, *The History of Philosophy*, volume 6, *The Nineteenth Century: Period of
Systems, 1800–1850*, trans. Joseph Thomas (Chicago, 1968), 6:74–91.

ment of the July Monarchy or its ultimate relegation to the scrapheap of intellectual history.[6] It would be dogmatic, however, to exclude all consideration of the intrinsic merit of the philosophic argument.[7] To emphasize the striking discrepancy between contemporary and subsequent evaluations of Cousin's philosophical system is not to patronize the past but to pose the problem.

In his stimulating article on Stendhal's ambivalent reception of Cousin, Armand Hoog solves the problem almost too well when he concludes that Cousin, like Bergson, was the voice of his epoch, a "sonorous echo" of the movements of his age. There is a certain circularity in this insight, at least to the extent that the presumed identity with the spirit of an age is presented as an explanation for specific influence over a particular audience. Hoog attempts to break out of this circle by specifying the timeliness of Cousin's articulation of a "nascent romantic sensibility."[8] A somewhat similar solution is implied by Taine's mordant suggestion that the eclectics satisfied the contemporary taste for sublime abstraction that made reason the dupe of the heart. Taine also advanced the familiar conception of the alternation of generations: "Raised to believe, the fathers doubted, brought up in doubt, the sons wished to believe."[9]

Another general explanation for the particular influence of Cousin is provided by Marxists such as Lucien Sève, who characterized Cousin as the first of the "great ideological functionaries of the bourgeoisie in power."[10] But even if one accepts Sève's interpretation of Cousinian spiritualism as a cloth cut to the precise political measure of the bourgeoisie, one still has to explain why such a philosophy would be the focus of the enthusiasm of the militant youth of the early Restora-

[6] I subscribe to the assessment of Barbéris, *Balzac Et Le Mal du siècle*, 1:241, "Cousin nous semble aujourd'hui parfaitement démodé; il a contre lui sa longue carrière officielle, ses prises de position gouvernementales sous la monarchie de Juillet, et plus tard. Mais il faut essayer de le juger (comme Guizot), avec l'esprit de ceux qui l'entendirent aux premiers temps de la Restauration, alors qu'il apportait vraiment quelque chose, et qu'il parlait un langage qu'on attendait, dont on avait besoin."

[7] For a discussion of the issue, see John Dunn, "The Identity of the History of Ideas," *Philosophy*, 43 (April 1968): 86.

[8] Hoog, "Un Intercesseur du romantisme," 186, 192.

[9] Taine, *Les Philosophes classiques*, 290–96.

[10] Sève, *Philosophie française contemporaine*, 105, 111. See also O. Cecconi, "La 'Restauration' intellectuelle," in Pierre Abraham and Roland Desné, eds., *Histoire littéraire de la France, 1794–1830* (Paris, 1976), 7:324–32.

tion. Hoog himself has posed the central question: "What privileged quality attracted the public to Cousin rather than to someone else?"[11] Hoog's question requires two answers, one an explanation of what there was in the lectures and early writings of Cousin that specifically appealed to his young public, and the other an explanation of what there was about that public that made it receptive to Cousin's particular arguments. I believe that the second explanation is to be sought in the historical location of the generation of 1820 and in the preoccupations that its historical situation imposed.

It is not difficult to identify specific elements in Cousin's first course of lectures that might appeal to an educated audience in the early years of the First Restoration. Doris Goldstein has provided a clear summary of the salient points:

> To the University youth who applauded him, Cousin's philosophy stood for the ability of reason to arrive at truth unaided by theology and, in politics, for Constitutional monarchy. In short, by 1830 Cousin had attained prominence with a philosophy which was secular and yet not irreligious, liberal and yet not revolutionary.[12]

Yet, in 1820, Cousin's philosophy *was* considered revolutionary by students and other young admirers, and by the authorities. The problem lies in relating the anodyne content of "this nice, relaxing tepid bath into which fathers dip their children as a healthful precaution"[13] to its bracing effects. It seems scarcely revolutionary to send off a student body convinced that rigorous introspection guarantees the existence of the self, the soul, the external world, God, immortality, and universal objective criteria of truth and beauty; that good and evil receive their eternal rewards; that liberty is an inviolable element of human nature and property a sacred component of liberty; that sovereignty is not to be found in the hands of despots or in the whims of the masses but in the absolute idea of justice; and that a constitutional monarchy is the best of all regimes.

The familiar and most obvious explanation of Cousin's remarkable appeal for the Restoration *jeunesse* refers to his age. In 1815, when he

[11] Hoog, "Un Intercesseur du romantisme," 188.
[12] Goldstein, "Official Philosophies in Modern France," 261.
[13] Taine, *Les Philosophes classiques*, 311.

began his course of lectures at the Sorbonne as Royer-Collard's substitute he was twenty-three, an inspiring teacher and comrade of the brilliant young *normaliens* such as Dubois, Damiron, and Jouffroy, who already constituted his coterie. He was not only the teacher, but the spokesman for, and the personal incarnation of, the first generation fed through the imperial University. His legendary ascent from humble origins by way of an unrivaled series of triumphs in scholastic prize competitions made him the first great athlete of the meritocracy, star of the first *promotion* of the Ecole normale in 1810.[14] He represented an answer to Julien Sorel's question, "Napoleon was truly God's gift to French youth. Who will replace him?" an answer that had not occurred to Stendhal.

One cannot separate the effect of Cousin's doctrine from his personal impact on students only a few years younger than their charismatic instructor. Even as a fifteen-year-old schoolboy, his enthusiasm and eloquence fascinated his fellow students. As *élève répétiteur* (tutor), then as *maître de conférences* at the Ecole normale, he inspired and dominated his young charges.[15] No one in the early days of the school, Paul Dubois would recall, approached Cousin without "feeling an electric charge."[16] In those vernal days before he became the supreme pontiff of French philosophy, Cousin treated his student companions more like collaborators than disciples. Philippe Damiron, for whom Cousin's personal conversations were even more inspiring than his public lectures, paints a portrait of his comrade-mentor that bears little resemblance to Jules Simon's depiction of the commander of the philosophic regiment under the July Monarchy. In his Restoration phase Cousin wanted nothing more than students who could think for themselves. Damiron recalled that "There was nothing less regimented than his teaching, which was the essence of freedom and sincerity."[17]

---

[14] See the insightful analysis of Cousin's popularity in Canivez, *Jules Lagneau*, 1:158: "Il est jeune, il est d'origine populaire, il semble être le fils de ses oeuvres, sorti de néant par l'énergique impulsion de son génie."

[15] Dubois, *Cousin, Jouffroy, Damiron*, 30.

[16] Lair, "Les Souvenirs de M. Dubois," (16 December 1901): 476. The same image appears in the *Souvenirs* of the Catholic royalist Count de Carné, who attended the lectures "de recevoir en pleine poitrine la décharge électrique de M. Cousin." Carné, *Souvenirs de ma jeunesse*, 15.

[17] Philippe Damiron, *Souvenirs de vingt ans d'enseignement à la Faculté des Lettres de Paris* (Paris, 1859), xlii. This was also the way Cousin remembered it. "Formés à la méthode philosophique, les élèves s'en servaient avec le professeur comme eux-mêmes;

As he began to forge his brilliant university career under the patronage of Royer-Collard, Cousin in turn became the patron of the careers of his favorite students from the Ecole normale. Until the suspension of his philosophy lectures in 1820, or the termination of the Ecole normale in 1822, he saw to the future and sustained the hopes of that hierarchy of young talents that he had begun to construct beneath him. Théodore Jouffroy, who occupied the next rung below him, held up the model of their mentor to his less successful but equally ambitious comrades:

> When you ask me to encourage you, you have come to the wrong place, for I myself have little energy and I would fail if Cousin did not revive and rekindle my spirit with the warmth of his philosophic zeal. That man communicates a fervor; simply to converse with him is to acquire unexpected force and new vigor.[18]

For several years Cousin remained the inspiring center of that dense personal network of the successive *promotions* of the Ecole normale, but his influence extended well beyond the *normalien* coterie. His lectures at the Sorbonne were attended by a large circle of serious students, somewhat younger and less sophisticated than his students at the Ecole normale but passionately interested in philosophy.[19] From outside the University he attracted such enthusiastic partisans as the young *littérateur* J. J. Ampère, son of the distinguished scientist. Ampère himself was the center of a cluster of talented coevals, including Jules Bastide, Prosper Mérimée, and Auguste Sautelet.[20] To his friends (whose feel-

---

ils doutaient, résistaient, argumentaient avec une entière liberté, et par-là s'excerçaient à cet esprit d'indépendance et de critique qui je l'espère portera ses fruits." Victor Cousin, *Fragments philosophiques*, 3rd ed. (Paris, 1838), 1:370. See also Dubois, *Cousin, Jouffroy, Damiron*, 33–34; Jouffroy, *Nouveaux mélanges philosophiques*, 129–30. One can discern intimations of his tendency to dominate in, for example, a patronizing, avuncular letter to a young admirer in the provinces. Victor Cousin to M. Charlot, 13 August 1825, Bibliothèque Victor Cousin, Cousin Ms. no. 262.

[18] Jouffroy to Damiron, 5 March 1817, in Théodore Jouffroy, *Correspondance de Théodore Jouffroy, publiée avec une Etude sur Jouffroy par Adolphe Lair* (Paris, 1901), 115–16.

[19] Cousin, *Fragments philosophiques*, 1:374.

[20] André-Marie Ampère and Jean-Jacques Ampère, *Correspondance et souvenirs (De 1805 à 1864)* (Paris, 1875), 1:137; Baschet, *E. J. Delécluze*, 95. Other members of the circle were the botanist Adrien Jussieu, his younger brother Alexis (1802); Charles and Albert Stapfer, Franck-Carré, Edmond Morel (1798), and Mérimée's cousin, the future orientalist Fulgence Fresnel (1795).

ings toward Cousin were rather mixed) Ampère confessed that he hated philosophy but loved Cousin.[21] Through Royer-Collard and the Doctrinaire junto, Cousin established close relations with the young aristocrats of the literary salons, notably Charles de Rémusat, who would become a lifelong advocate of his philosophy.[22] Rémusat's memoirs, so rich in detail on his personal relationships, trace out the rather tenuous connections with Thiers and Mignet, scarcely disciples but sharing with Cousin the doctrine of "historical fatalism" (the words are Rémusat's) that justified the excesses of the Revolution. They periodically dined with Cousin and other intimates or casual acquaintances, such as Ary Scheffer, J. J. Ampère, Augustin Thierry, Auguste Sautelet, and Armand Carrel.[23]

By the age of thirty, independent of any formal affiliation or official status, Cousin had assumed the role of unofficial doyen of educated youth in and out of the University. It seemed natural to Jules Michelet to seek an introduction to the philosopher in order to obtain advice on the best way to undertake the systematic study of history; Quinet at twenty-two writes ecstatically of Cousin's kindness; even Delacroix looks forward to attending his lectures.[24]

Cousin was also in touch with the political activists: deeply involved with Sautelet and G. J. Cariol in the paramilitary organizations behind the August 1820 conspiracy; on friendly terms with such young firebrands as Godefroy Cavaignac, Marcelin Desloges, and Antoine Cerclet; and closely associated with the most militant of his ex-students in recruiting for the subversive lodge of the *Amis de la vérité* and the underground *ventes* of the Carbonari. This was denied by Cousin then

[21] Ampère to Jules Bastide, 1 June 1820, Ampère, *Correspondance*, 1:162.

[22] In the Avertissement to his *Essais de philosophie* (Paris, 1842), 1:iv, Rémusat wrote: "Cependant au premier rang de ses amis et de ses maîtres, il en est un qu'il ne peut se défendre de nommer, c'est celui qui depuis vingt-cinq ans inspire tout la philosophie française, M. Cousin."

[23] Rémusat, *Mémoires*, 2:145–46.

[24] Paul Viallaneix, *La Voie royale* (Paris, 1971), 207, 216; Quinet to Mme. Quinet, November 1825, in Edgar Quinet, *Correspondance de Edgar Quinet—Lettres à sa mère* (Paris, 1877), 1:306, 381. Delacroix to J. B. Pierret, 6 November 1818, in Eugène Delacroix, *Correspondance générale* (Paris, 1936), 1:35: "Je serais bien content aussi, car je ne finis pas, si nous pouvions encore cette année assister à l'ouverture du cours de Cousin, qui, j'imagine, n'est pas encore commencé." Patrice Vermeren, "Une Politique de l'institution philosophique, un de la tactique parlementaire en matière de religion et de philosophie: Edgar Quinet et Victor Cousin," *Corpus*, 1 (May 1985): 104–7.

and by his admirers ever since. The question is technically moot, but as I argued in my book on the Carbonari, there is plausible, mutually supporting testimony to his role as recruiter for illegal organizations and dangerous actions in which he did not directly participate.[25] Paul Dubois was probably on target in his reminiscence:

> Cousin, ever the hierophant, not precisely an initiate, or at least affiliated to no *vente*, as he later stated, when imprisoned at Berlin, and I believe him, but knowing all, perhaps hovering over the *haute vente* thanks to the confidences of Manuel, Girod de l'Ain, . . . and . . . de Schonen.[26]

Less charitably, Pierre Leroux took occasion to remind the academic pope of the July Monarchy how much of a revolutionary he once had been. The fact that Cousin had not personally joined a Carbonarist cell had enabled him to "forget" his involvement, but others remembered. Others, such as Sautelet (whom Leroux called "that comrade of your youth, and of mine, who was long your disciple, and who killed himself after having lost all hope and all belief in life"), remembered Cousin as the woman of the Holy Scriptures, "quae comedit, et tergens os suum decit: Non sum operata malum" (who eats, and, wiping her mouth, says, I have not done badly).[27]

Whatever the extent of Cousin's cautious maneuvering on the margin of the conspiracies, it did not dim his luster for his coevals. His major impact was public, delivered from the platform. Here too it had to do with personality and manner of delivery as well as with philosophic content. In a brilliant passage, Taine elucidates the integral relation of content and form. The very essence of Cousinian philosophy, according to Taine, was in its style, that is, in the language of oratory. In an age of orators, Cousin was the supreme master of that polished eloquence not completely appropriate to a rigorous metaphysics but magnificently suited to the presentation of *"vérités moyennes."* Oratorical style and ideational content were perfectly wed in the discussion of those comfortable truisms that, Taine observed, "are more appropriate to conversation than to science, that are in the reach of everyone rather than just a few, that one knows and loves not because he is a superior

[25] Spitzer, *Old Hatreds and Young Hopes*, 221, 227–28, 240, 268.
[26] Dubois, "Augustin Thierry," *Revue bleue*, 5th series, 10 (12 December 1908): 742.
[27] Leroux, *Réfutation de l'éclectisme*, 79. Leroux is quoting Proverbs 30:20.

person but because he is well-bred. . . . They appeal to common sense rather than to rationality; the truths they establish are plausible rather than valid, and they are loved rather than demonstrated. . . . M. Cousin is one of the masters of this genre."[28] One is tempted to give up writing and just go on quoting Taine, whose pungent observations were not so far, for all that, from the enthusiastic consensus of Cousin's contemporary admirers.[29]

As Royer-Collard's substitute, Cousin recapitulated that high seriousness in the exposition of philosophic problems that had captivated the audience for his predecessor's first course in 1811. In contrast to the urbane lectures of an autumnal ideologue such as Laromiguière—"occasional *causeries* full of nostalgic charm"[30]—Cousin's course was perceived as an intense personal statement expressing "the gravity of the moral commitment contracted in public and under the authority of science."[31] The moral intensity of Cousin's delivery, the impression conveyed of an intellectual effort so intense that it threatened to drain him of his very life, were indispensable contributions to the reception of the abstruse arguments.[32]

By Cousin's second series of lectures, in 1828—again a personal triumph—a hostile young critic like Armand Marrast was able to identify the studied oratorical effects and to characterize him as "the most artful actor of the faculty."[33] The response to Cousin's brand of oratorical delivery eventually became a matter of taste and philosophic temperament. But in the beginning his facile eloquence was the perfect medium for the message his audience wanted to hear.

---

[28] Taine, *Les Philosophes classiques*, 84–85, 100–3. See Cousin on the facile eloquence of Laromiguière, where he observes, "Malheureusement le talent d'exposition, qui se prête aussi bien à l'erreur qu'à la vérité, ne prouve rien pour ou contre un système." Cousin, *Fragments philosophiques*, 1:151.

[29] See, for example, Rémusat, *Séance de l'Académie française*, 64–65.

[30] Lair, "Les Souvenirs de M. Dubois," (16 December 1901): 471.

[31] Thierry, *Dix Ans d'études historiques*, 203.

[32] Ibid., 221–22; Dubois, *Cousin, Jouffroy, Damiron*, 38.

[33] Marrast, *Examen critique*, 7; Cousin was characterized as "le comédien le plus désagréablement grimacier que j'aie jamais recontré" by Etienne Delécluze in his *Journal*, 226. In 1828 Victor Jacquemont was taken by Ampère to a Cousin lecture: "J'allais là, sans doute à bien des extravagances et des niaiseries prétentieuses. But it was beyond all my expectations. [In English.] Non, l'on ne peut se faire une idée de la platitude de cette comédie si on ne l'a entendue, si on ne l'a vu jouer." Jacquemont to Achille Chaper, 31 May 1828, in Victor Jacquemont, *Letters to Achille Chaper*, ed. J. F. Marshall (Philadelphia, 1960), 235.

Following Stendhal, Armand Hoog emphasizes the emotional effect of Cousin's virtuoso performance, which conveyed "less a system of thought than a system of fascination," but in a manner perfectly suited to the content of the lectures. According to Hoog, Stendhal was the only contemporary to identify the philosopher's appeal with the fact that he was the aesthetician of a nascent romantic sensibility. Cousin did not articulate a full-fledged romanticism, but he did suggest that many romantic themes derived from the premise of the supremacy of the imagination over reality. It was Stendhal's great merit to see that "the vast majority of well-bred youth had been converted to romanticism by the eloquence of M. Cousin."[34]

Lucien Lévy-Bruhl makes a similar case in his lucid summary of Cousin's philosophy. To the extent that he worked German metaphysics into his lectures, Cousin was a romantic philosopher,

> and this chiefly accounts for the enthusiasm with which the youth of the time received his lessons. Perhaps they did not understand very thoroughly such abstruse metaphysics, but a genuine feeling apprised them that Cousin's brilliant but obscure precepts sprang from the same soil as the poetry of Hugo, Lamartine and de Vigny, or the pictures of Scheffer and Delacroix.[35]

There are many elements in Cousin's lectures that can be subsumed under the various definitions of romanticism. However, we cannot explain the influence of a particular thinker on a particular audience merely by identifying aspects of his thought that happened to coincide with our prior assumptions about the climate of opinion. Any definition of a romanticism to which Cousin *then* appealed would have to include such terms as "severe," "rigorous," "the experimental method," "founded on incontestable facts," and above all "scientific," because they adumbrate the contributions that were most admired by his public.[36] Augustin Thierry, who managed to admire Cousin and

[34] Hoog, "Un Intercesseur du romantisme," 194, quoting, somewhat out of context, Stendhal's *Racine et Shakespeare*, vol. 37 of *Oeuvres complètes* (Paris, 1970), 123.

[35] Lucien Lévy-Bruhl, *History of Modern Philosophy in France* (Chicago, 1899), 341. For the relation of Cousin's aesthetics to romanticism, see Frederic Will, *Flumen Historicum: Victor Cousin's Aesthetic and Its Sources* (Chapel Hill, N.C., 1965).

[36] See, for example, Damiron, *Essai sur l'histoire de la philosophie*, 362; Jouffroy, *Nouveaux mélanges philosophiques*, 122–28; F. A.-A. Mignet, *Institut Impérial de France. Notice historique sur la vie et les travaux de M. Victor Cousin* (Paris, 1869), 9; and Rémusat, *Séance de l'Académie française*, 56; G. J. Cariol in *Journal général de législation et de ju-*

Saint-Simon almost simultaneously, characterized Cousin in exact contradiction to his subsequent reputation: "The same mental rigor that made him reject vaguely liberal theories without practical application also excluded from his lessons everything that he did not perceive as rational and scientific."[37] Some of Cousin's critics even accused him of the defects of these alleged scientific virtues. As late as 1839, Pierre Leroux attacked Cousin for excluding sentiment from philosophy, thereby reducing the discipline to "a science of observation analogous to geometry or physics" that did not speak to human feelings or human needs.[38]

But Cousin convinced his first audience that precisely in the science of observation lay the answers to all the big questions, the questions of how to live and what to believe, that history had forced on a generation coming to maturity during the collapse of one regime and the rebirth of another. This admirable science did not require laboratories, observatories, or field expeditions but could be practiced on the podium. There Cousin would occasionally refer to the physical sciences, not to illustrate the application of the scientific method, but to establish the authority of his own philosophic viewpoint by analogy. Thus he referred to the discipline of physics to make the point that a body of knowledge only attains the status of a science when its particular observations have been subsumed under general laws, for "in philosophic terms, the idea of something absolute is the very idea of science."[39]

---

risprudence, 1:491. For the romantics' positive attitude toward science, see Jacques Barzun, *Classic, Romantic and Modern* (Boston, 1961), 64–66.

[37] Thierry, *Dix Ans d'études historiques*, 213.

[38] Leroux, *Réfutation de l'éclectisme*, 266; Alfred de Vigny characterized eclecticism as "une lumière sans doute, mais une lumière comme celle de la lune, qui éclaire sans réchauffer. On peut distinguer les objets à sa clarté, mais toute sa force ne produirait pas la plus légère étincelle." Alfred de Vigny, *Le Journal d'un poète* (Paris, 1913), 34.

[39] Victor Cousin, *Cours de l'histoire de la philosophie moderne* (Paris, 1846), 2:36. No text of Cousin's first series of lectures (1815–1820) has been preserved. The several published versions are lecture notes put into publishable form by former students but somewhat revised by Cousin in successive editions. Janet, *Victor Cousin*, 13, 60–61, identifies the most authentic edition as that published by Cousin's students—Garnier, Danton, and Vacherot—in five volumes between 1836 and 1841. The catalogue of the Bibliothèque nationale lists one volume, *Cours de philosophie professé à la Faculté des lettres pendant l'année 1818, par M. V. Cousin, du beau et du bien, publié . . . par M. Adolphe Garnier* (Paris: L. Hachette, 1836), and four volumes, *Cours d'histoire de la philosophie morale au dix-huitième siècle, professé à la Faculté des lettres en 1819 et 1820, par V. Cousin* (Paris: Ladgrange, 1839–42), published by Danton and Vacherot. I have

The assertion that "fixed and absolute principles" were the indispensable concomitant of any science indicates how Cousin managed to have his empiricism and transcend it too. Such absolute principles were approached by experiment but could only be established by Reason, which for Cousin is quite distinct from mere *raisonnement* or *raison appliquée*.[40] Thus he rejected the radical empiricist version of Newtonian science and clung to the rationalist tradition that discovers Reason in the structure of the natural order with which the operations of individual minds are more or less congruent.[41] To assert the supremacy of Reason, however, was not to reject the empirical side of any valid science; indeed: "To unite observation and reason, to attain the ideal of science, and to attain it by the route of experience, that is the scientific problem; to the extent that it has not been solved, science does not exist."[42]

Cousin was not concerned with proposing solutions to specific scientific problems but with lending the authority of science to his philosophy through the development of a method that would successfully unite reason with observation. This method was psychological and constituted a science of self-observation. The analysis of thought was thus the point of departure for any philosophic (which is to say scientific) research. For this analysis to be empirical rather than arbitrary, it had to be applied to the self with meticulous objectivity. The scientific communication of a philosopher began with a description of his apperception, and scientific replication depended upon the ability of the audience to repeat the process for themselves.

The paradoxes of a science of self-perception were not perceived by

---

drawn my citations from a "Nouvelle Edition, revue et corrigée," published in 1846 by Cousin, who, says Janet, "en a perfectionné la forme et plus ou moins modifié le fonds." This remains a source for the lectures from 1815 to 1817 not covered in the Garnier, Danton, and Vacherot volumes. Where it is possible to establish a concordance between the earlier and the 1846 editions, I have checked my citations against the more "authentic" versions, including an 1815 edition of Cousin's Introduction. The most useful summary of Cousin's early ideas is in the Preface to the first edition of Victor Cousin, *Fragments philosophiques*, drafted in 1826. I will cite the third edition, published in Paris in 1838.

[40] Cousin, *Cours de l'histoire de la philosophie moderne*, 2:36.

[41] See the distinction drawn by Max Horkheimer, *The Eclipse of Reason* (New York, 1947), 5.

[42] Cousin, *Cours de l'histoire de la philosophie moderne*, 2:37.

Cousin's admirers.[43] The great appeal of this procedure was that it carried the necessary empirical credentials while charting a path out of the swamps of skepticism. It was the method through which the insights of the Scottish philosophers of common sense and Kant's critical idealism could be brought to bear against the sensationalism of the ideologues and the other pernicious variants of Lockean empiricism. Cousin pursued two fundamental lines of argument in disposing of the British and French versions of the Lockean tradition. The first was epistemological and borrowed from the Scottish philosophers of common sense, subsequently embellished with some of the insights of Maine de Biran and German idealism. The second line of argument, of greater moment to his audience I think, was historical.

The entire course of his lectures from 1815 to 1820 was presented and received as a vast effort of moral pedagogy transcending the treatment of the technical problems of philosophy, but his presentation began with the "solution" of certain technical problems. These problems could be approached by way of a course organized as a history of modern philosophy because they were posed by the British empiricists who followed Descartes' first steps on to the highroad of untrammelled speculation. Perhaps it is more accurate to say that for French philosophy the problems had been posed by Condillac and the sensationalism of the Idéologues. In 1813, Cousin's thesis at the Faculty of Letters had been a celebration of Condillac and the analytical method, but he had already begun to free himself from the influence of what he would subsequently label "sensualism" under the influence of Laromiguière, Royer-Collard, and Maine de Biran. The first of these is numbered among the last of the Idéologues, but he had qualified the standard Condillacian approach with the conception of the active role of the mind in transforming sensations.[44] Cousin credited Laromiguière with having inspired him to devote his life to philosophy,[45] but it was Royer-Collard—annointed philosopher-in-chief by Napoleon as a palatable

---

[43] They were certainly perceived by his early critics, Auguste Comte for example; Auguste Comte to Valat, 24 September 1818, in *Correspondance générale*, 1:58–59.

[44] On Laromiguière see François Picavet, *Les Idéologues* (Paris, 1891), 520–48; Prosper Alfaric, *Laromiguière Et Son Ecole* (Paris, 1929); Taine, *Les Philosophes classiques*, 1–20.

[45] Cousin, *Fragments philosophiques*, 1:23, 139–85; "Leçons de philosophie, ou Essai sur les facultés de l'âme par Laromiguière."

alternative to the cranky independence of the Idéologues—who had pointed the way out of the valley of skeptical despair.[46]

As George Boas remarked, the story that Royer-Collard received the inspiration for his philosophy lectures (1811-1814) from a volume by Thomas Reid that he picked up along the quais seems too good to be true, but the discovery of Reid was providential for the antagonists of the Idéologues.[47] We can gather from fragmentary lecture notes that Royer-Collard borrowed his refutation of a philosophy that confined itself to the association of "ideas" from Reid's assertion of the principles of cognition posited in the very nature of the human mind.[48] This was presented by Royer-Collard rather more in the form of a proclamation than an argument,[49] but it provided the foundation on which Cousin was to erect an immense edifice designed to provide a total world view adequate to the unprecedented demands of the new century.[50]

Given the contemporary state of the philosophic art, this effort could only proceed from a disposition of the technical problems posed by a radical empiricism. During the first two years of Cousin's course, this task was accomplished by drawing upon the Scottish school of com-

---

[46] Royer-Collard was appointed to the chair of the history of philosophy when it was vacated by Pastoret in 1811. Although his last lectures were delivered in 1814, he occupied the chair until his death in 1845. For the circumstances of the appointment, see Prosper de Barante, *La Vie politique de M. Royer-Collard* (Paris, 1861), 1:105; Eugène Spuller, *Royer-Collard* (Paris, 1895), 72–73.

[47] Boas, *French Philosophies of the Romantic Period*, 158. The story appears in most accounts of Royer-Collard's philosophic stint, for example: Barante, *La Vie politique de M. Royer-Collard*, 1:108.

[48] The *Fragments philosophiques* of Royer-Collard was published by Théodore Jouffroy in volume 3 of his *Oeuvres complètes de Thomas Reid* (Paris, 1836). These lecture notes plus the texts of his inaugural *discours* in 1811 and 1813 were assembled in André Schimberg, *Les Fragments philosophiques de Royer-Collard* (Paris, 1913). The inaugural *discours* for 1813 is also published in Barante, *La Vie politique de M. Royer-Collard*, 112–34.

[49] See Taine's brief disposition of Royer-Collard, hors d'oeuvre to his evisceration of Cousin, in *Les Philosophes classiques*, 30: "Il [Royer-Collard] fut roi en philosophie, il ne fut pas docteur." For continued veneration of the spiritualist school, see Philippe Damiron, *Discours prononcé à la Faculté des lettres (Cours d'histoire de la philosophie moderne)* (Paris, 1845).

[50] Charlton, *Secular Religions in France*, 98: "We shall never understand the expectant enthusiasm of his young listeners and the influence he exerted on philosophers like Jouffroy, Simon, Janet, Quinet and others, unless we appreciate the ambitious range of what he was attempting."

mon sense and certain Kantian notions for ammunition to demolish Hume, Condillac, and the Lockean tradition. The conceptual core of the early lectures was a summary of the arguments of Thomas Reid purportedly refuting Locke's theory of ideas: the theory constructed on the premise that the sole objects of mental perception were those so-called ideas.[51] From this conception Locke's successors had proceeded step by inexorable step to the intolerable conclusion of David Hume: "It is certain . . . that neither spirit nor matter exist, that only ideas without subject, object or any real interconnections exist as vague shadows, and that the imagination is all there is, suspended as it were, over a universal void."[52] (Such a version of Hume could be presented with little fear of contradiction, since the content of his philosophy was virtually unknown in France.)[53]

The great merit of Reid—and of Kant, who was treated in the second set of lectures—was to have undermined this monstrous creation with the very instruments of its construction—rigorous induction and the experimental method. The application of the experimental method, which was nothing other than that science of self-observation called psychology,[54] helped Reid to the conclusion that human knowledge depended upon first principles—*lois de pensée*, the constituent principles of our very nature that comprise the common sense of humanity.[55]

Neither Cousin nor Reid celebrated the common sense of humanity in order to defer to the unmediated opinions of the man in the street but to appeal to the immutable convictions that prevailed, beyond demonstration, as the very constituents of thought. Cousin ultimately refined the number of these irreducible *lois de pensée* to two: substance and causality. From them he derived his universe.

This effort, he believed, took him beyond Reid and Kant, who stopped short of the recognition that the validity of the premises of human cognition transcend the operations of the individual mind. They were *vérités indépendantes*—independent of the thinking subject as

[51] Cousin, *Cours de l'histoire de la philosophie moderne*, 1:37: "les seuls objets des perceptions de l'esprit ce sont des pensées: toutes nos connaissances roulent sur nos idées."

[52] Ibid., 70.

[53] The target of French philosophers was Condillac. However, see Jouffroy, "Préface du traducteur," in *Oeuvres complètes de Thomas Reid*, 1:ccxiv.

[54] Cousin, *Fragments philosophiques*, 1:48–49, 54.

[55] Cousin, *Cours de l'histoire de la philosophie moderne*, 3:69.

Reason was independent of the reasoner. As *lois de raison* they partook of the universality and necessity of the rational nature of things; they were, in Cousin's words, "les lois de la raison en elle-même."[56]

To his own satisfaction, Cousin had contributed an improved version of Descartes' feat of self-levitation.[57] His lectures, Cousin believed, had partially realized, "the dominant ideal of my life, to reconstitute the eternal verities with contemporary conceptions and thus to attain the universal by way of the experimental method."[58] Cousin proceeded very rapidly along that route once he had disposed of the obstacles left in the way by the radical empiricists. In a passage that is virtually self-caricature, he demonstrates how far and fast one can go once rigorous self-observation has established "the universal and necessary principle of causality":

> Similar procedures lead to the cause of all causes, to the First Cause, to God, and not only to an omnipotent Deity, but to a moral Deity, to a holy Deity; such that this experimental method, which, narrowly applied to a single set of phenomena, was the death of ontology and the higher morality, applied with a resolute integrity to every phenomenon, raises up what it had toppled and supplies ontology with a sound approach and firm foundations. Thus from modest beginnings one can arrive at conclusions whose importance equals their certainty.[59]

The "scientific" demonstration of metaphysical certainties in the form of an oratorical tour de force made an impression on Cousin's contemporaries that would not be felt by subsequent critics of his printed word.[60]

---

[56] Cousin, *Fragments philosophiques*, 1:60–62.

[57] For a characterization of Descartes that reads like a description of Cousin, see Richard Schacht, *Hegel and After* (Pittsburgh, 1975), 21: "Descartes, at the dawn of modern philosophy, had hoped that, starting with a systematic suspension of belief in everything which is in the least dubitable, he would be able to proceed to erect an edifice of knowledge which would be completely certain and would moreover—as luck would have it—accord with the basic ideas of the world, man, God, and morality adhered to by Scholastic philosophers and theologians, and by ordinary men of common sense as well."

[58] Cousin, *Fragments philosophiques*, 1:82.

[59] Ibid., 57.

[60] See, for example, the ironical remarks of Brehier, *The History of Philosophy*, 6:85,

In justice to Cousin it must be remarked that he was presenting to a large Parisian audience the first systematic public exposition of the major issues of modern philosophy. Perhaps this is to say that we have merely situated Cousin in the great international campaign to rescue metaphysics from the specter of David Hume. Seen from this perspective, he was not so much satisfying a particular age group as expressing the philosophic preoccupations of an entire age. Like contemporary audiences for philosophy throughout Europe and America, the French desired a refutation of materialism and skepticism that did not depend on the reiteration of outworn pieties but proceeded from the most rigorous application of the successful principles of scientific investigation. However, in presenting his version of the standard arguments of the Scottish and German critics of empiricism, Cousin also articulated the special preoccupations of the French generation to, and for which, he spoke.

Those preoccupations constituted the context for the historicist cast of Cousin's philosophy. The justification of an emerging dogma with reference to its antecedents confirmed his generation's conviction of the peculiar relevance of its historical location. Maurice Mandelbaum has argued that what shaped "the tendency to view all matters in the light of their histories" into a dominant nineteenth-century idea was not so much a product of the profound transformation associated with the revolutionary era as a response to the strictly philosophic problems posed during the Enlightenment.[61] I believe that, at least for Cousin and his coevals, the preoccupation with the recent history of the revolutionary-imperial era was inseparable from the philosophic debate with the eighteenth century. It would not have occurred to them to separate the question of philosophic validity from the appreciation of historical context.

Just as Cousin appropriated the authority of science without practicing it, he asserted the authority of his philosophy for historical practice without contributing to the contemporary renaissance of historical studies. His fragmentary pronouncements on the writing of history had their influence, however. Michelet, among others, was inspired by an early essay that argued that any true historical science would be a

---

regarding Cousin's progress from "irreproachable inductions to metaphysical assertions which thus assume a character as scientific as physical laws."

[61] Maurice Mandelbaum, *History, Man, and Reason* (Baltimore, 1971), 51.

philosophy of history, which is to say that any valid historical science would be founded on the premises of Cousin's philosophy.[62]

In his discussion of historical method, Cousin proceeds with his usual dexterity from the empirical to the metaphysical. Historical investigation could only begin with the rigorous observation of successive events. The fruit of this indispensable empiricism was the history of reality from which all understanding must proceed, but reality is not truth—*le réel n'est pas le vrai*. The surface events, the "accidents" of human experience that provide the stuff of historical description, are but reflections of ultimate truth. "To grasp the unmediated truth is impossible, since one can only arrive at the truth by way of reality; to understand nothing but reality is insufficient, as reality is nothing but the manifestation of truth." Modern man, buffeted by "the tempests of revolution," needs to understand the underlying meaning and direction of the chaotic welter of events. This is the task that historians have left to the philosophy of history. To discern the ultimate truths, to penetrate beneath the phenomena of the exterior world to the invisible world of ideas, would be to create "la science historique par excellence."[63] In a sense, historical was assimilated to philosophic truth but in a dialectical rather than a subordinate relationship, because philosophic truth was to be established by historical analysis. For Cousin, any study of philosophy was a history of philosophy. His task as he saw it was "to carry out the reform of philosophical studies in France, clarifying the history of philosophy by a system and demonstrating this system by the entire history of philosophy."[64]

Out of this historical justification of his philosophical system, Cousin developed his philosophy of eclecticism. Using a method he supposed to be that of the physical sciences, he proposed to select the correct elements in all past philosophies, uniting all of the truths to be found in the preceding doctrines in a higher synthesis. He believed that he and his coevals were ideally situated to undertake such a task because, un-

---

[62] My citations are from the essay republished in the third edition of *Fragments philosophiques*, 1:233–39. Michelet read it in a supplement to the third volume of J. A. Buchon's translation of Dugald Stewart, *Histoire abrégée des sciences métaphysiques, morales et politiques depuis la Renaissance des lettres* (Paris, 1820–23); Michelet, *Ecrits de jeunesse*, 408. For a further discussion of the generation's historicism, see below, chapter 7.

[63] Cousin, *Fragments philosophiques*, 1:236–38.

[64] Ibid., 83.

like their fathers, they were able to do justice to the past while recognizing that ideas appropriate to one era were inadequate to the next.[65] A reading of recent history revealed the great contributions and the sinister consequences of eighteenth-century sensationalism and materialism; it imposed the recognition both that the experimental method had been "the necessary fruit of time" and that "the analytical spirit" had wreaked considerable destruction.[66]

In *his* version of the transition from a critical to an organic epoch, Cousin granted to the eighteenth century an indispensable role in clearing the ground, or rather littering the ground with the wreckage of old prejudices and obsolete authorities, thus freeing humanity for its irreversible advance across the debris. It had left to its heirs in the nineteenth century the legacy of an "energetic and fertile love of truth," and the task of "filling in the chasm and replacing what had been destroyed."[67]

Again, one might argue that Cousin struck notes already in the air and played on themes whose appeal was scarcely confined to a Parisian youth. His assumption that the contemporary situation was historically necessary but intolerable and transitory was the commonplace conviction of his circle of students, and it was widely shared—by the Saint-Simonians and Auguste Comte, among others.[68] They all believed that society could live neither by the obsolete conceptions of the Old Regime nor by the negative ideas of its opponents, and that the task on the intellectual agenda of the nineteenth century was the formulation of a new unifying doctrine.

Cousin's agenda was an early sketch of what was to become a familiar scenario: a metaphysical system that no longer met fundamental aspirations or answered basic questions must give way to a pervasive skepticism whose inevitable, but merely negative, function was to clear the ground for the new synthesis, which was in the making. It would provide the answer to the question of not only what to believe but how to live. This was the point and promise of lectures that Cousin intended

---

[65] Ibid., 49: "et pourtant si nous sommes plus justes que nos pères envers le passé, nous ne pouvons pas y reposer plus qu'eux; nous amnistions nos pères et le temps, et nous n'avons foi qu'à l'observation et à l'expérience."

[66] Ibid.

[67] Cousin, *Cours de l'histoire de la philosophie moderne*, 2:10–11.

[68] See chapter 7.

to transcend the narrow issues of a technical philosophy and to bring together, as Barbéris puts it, "abstract philosophy and practical morality, speculation and action."[69]

Therefore Cousin's lectures were celebrated as a contribution to the civic education of his contemporaries. The entire performance constituted a manifesto of the moral obligation to be intelligent. What the *jeunes gens* loved in the lectures of Cousin, reported Augustin Thierry, "was the austere alliance of patriotism and science" and the presentation of civic precepts under the aegis of a higher morality.[70] In 1828, Philippe Damiron looked forward to Cousin's return to the lectureship, "which he honored by that philosophic patriotism which is the obligation and should be the commitment of every professor."[71]

What subsequent critics would damn as a polemical subterfuge that affirmed or refuted problematic doctrines in the light of their social consequences was precisely what the generation of Thierry and Damiron was waiting to hear.[72] Disoriented by the annihilation of the cynical certainties of the Empire, the young audience was surprised and enchanted to hear someone say "Take heart!" to insist that philosophic truths transcended the depressing vagaries of war and politics, and to urge them to reaffirm and purify the legacy of the Revolution. "It is difficult today," remarked Charles Rémusat, "to reconstruct what those lectures meant to the generations who heard them. They brought about a spiritual rebirth of hope, confidence, and pride."[73]

In the introduction to his first course of lectures in 1815, Cousin presented the task of ideological reconstruction as the special challenge and responsibility of the new generation:

[69] Barbéris, *Balzac Et Le Mal du siècle*, 1:243. Royer-Collard had already emphasized the social and political implications of philosophic controversy: "C'est donc un fait que la morale publique et privée, que l'ordre des sociétés et le bonheur des individus sont engagés dans le débat de la vraie et de la fausse philosophie sur la réalité de la connaissance"; quoted in Barante, *La Vie politique de M. Royer-Collard*, 1:134.

[70] Thierry, *Dix Ans d'études historiques*, 215.

[71] Damiron, *Essai sur l'histoire de la philosophie*, 363.

[72] See Taine, *Les Philosophes classiques*, 219, for the most trenchant critique of Cousin's moralizing philosophy as reducing science, "à une machine oratoire d'éducation et de gouvernement"; also Boas, for Cousin's "insistence upon the practical effects of a doctrine as a means of refuting it." *French Philosophies of the Romantic Period*, 201.

[73] Rémusat, *Séance de l'Académie française*, 54–55.

It is to those of you whose age is close to mine that I dare to speak at this moment; to you who will form the emerging generation; to you the sole support, the last hope of our dear and unfortunate country. Gentlemen, you passionately love the fatherland; if you wish to save it, espouse our noble doctrines.[74]

Taine quotes the passage in full, emphasizing the irresistible effects of the demagogic appeal to patriotism, which was fused with an appeal to the generational solidarity and *amour-propre* of Cousin's audience.[75] What he presented as a challenge, they would accept as a birthright.

The vast social, moral, and essentially theological pretensions of a pedagogy directed beyond the classrooms were not well received by the hardening conservatism of the Restoration legitimists. The Catholic church never would be persuaded, even by Cousin's convoluted diplomacy under the July Monarchy, that the faith was served by a dialectic that arrived independently and "scientifically" at truths it had long established under its own authority. In the 1820s it was even less satisfied with a philosophy that reeked of pantheism and a patronizing dismissal of obsolete metaphysics.[76]

There was nothing overtly subversive in the manifest political content of Cousin's course of lectures, but the ultraroyalists who dominated the educational establishment after 1819 were not disarmed by his celebration of the monarchy of the Charte as "at once the best of monarchies and the best of republics." In principle, he argued a relativist approach to political systems, asserting that there was no ideal form of government, but that different systems were appropriate to various places, times, and the "genius of diverse nations."[77] In fact, his analysis of political institutions inevitably concluded with a repudiation of the absolutism of both monarchs and masses, and the affirmation of a "balanced" constitution remarkably like the combination of crown and chambers in the Charte of 1814.

---

[74] Cousin, *Cours de l'histoire de la philosophie*, 1:22–23. A few lines have been edited out of this version, according to an 1816 edition of the opening *discours*. Victor Cousin, *Discours prononcé à l'ouverture de cours de l'histoire de la philosophie, le 13 décembre 1815* (Paris, 1816).

[75] Taine, *Les Philosophes classiques*, 301–2.

[76] Writing in the *Catholique*, 15 (1829): 318, the Baron Eckstein made that point: "Il [eclecticism] s'annonce avec la prétention hautement avouée de se substituer à l'Eglise, ou, plutôt, de jouer le rôle de l'Eglise, sous forme philosophique."

[77] Cousin, *Cours de l'histoire de la philosophie moderne*, 3:332, 317.

Not all celebrations of the Charte were gratefully received. Cousin's characterization of the providential Constitution as the incarnation of rights gloriously won in the Revolution seems calculated to stir the enthusiasm of young students and the bile of old royalists. Other references to the Revolution were even more provocative. The Declaration of the Rights of Man, for example, was described as "the finest, the holiest, the most beneficent, document to have appeared on earth since the Gospel."[78]

There were other, less explicit but possibly sinister, political references. At least twice for his impressionable audience Cousin evoked the image of a young man willing to mount the scaffold rather than to betray his ideals.[79] Of course, few contemporaries could know that young men were indeed to go to the scaffold as a consequence of conspiratorial projects directly or indirectly encouraged by the magnetic professor. Perhaps, as Liard observes, the ability to arouse the young with vague and stirring affirmations of liberty was a sufficient threat to an insecure establishment.[80]

There is no evidence of an overt official objection to the political content of Cousin's lectures or publications before 30 November 1820, when the Council of Public Instruction suspended his course of lectures at the Faculty of Letters. Technically, Cousin's status was not affected; he was kept on as *maître de conférences* at the Ecole normale, but the nonrenewal of Cousin's annual performance as the *suppléant* of Royer-Collard was universally interpreted as an official repudiation.

The liquidation of one of the most popular courses in, and outside of, the University is often assimilated to the general purge of the Doctrinaires, prime targets of the ultraroyalist offensive after the assassination of the Duc de Berry, and Cousin's triumphant return to the rostrum in 1828 is seen as a significant consequence of the political defeat of the Villèle ministry. This is true enough, but I do not believe that Victor Cousin was gagged merely because of his association with Guizot and Royer-Collard, or even because the police suspected him of connections with foreign revolutionaries.

The University's repudiation of Cousin's efforts to reconstruct an in-

---

[78] Ibid., 323.

[79] Ibid., 1:313, 2:355.

[80] "Pour le Conseil royal et pour son chef, c'était de la politique et la plus dangereuse de toutes, celle qui agit sur l'esprit public et a le pouvoir de le modifier." Liard, *L'Enseignement supérieur*, 2:158.

dependent metaphysics is illuminated by its continued toleration of the sensationalist philosophy of Laromiguière. Napoleon had sensed that the skeptical spirit of the Idéologues was less appropriate to his bureaucratic imperium than were the Doctrinaire gravities of Royer-Collard, and we know how appropriate Cousin's philosophy would appear to the political and social *juste milieu* after 1830. Yet, the *bien-pensants* who had come to dominate the Restoration University found it possible to live with a more or less diluted version of eighteenth-century materialism and sensationalism, while they were thrown into a state of perpetual anxiety by Cousin's eloquent demonstrations of a just God and a providential constitutional monarchy.

Despite the obvious discrepancies between Ideologue philosophy and Restoration ideology, the regime preferred to retain Laromiguière so that, as Prosper Alfaric concluded, "By a curious irony of fate, the doctrine of this secularized priest, of this Idéologue friend of Garat, Sieyès, Cabanis, and de Tracy was vested by the clerical reaction with something like a university monopoly.[81] This irony was apparent to contemporaries. In 1818, well before the culmination of the clerical offensive in the University, Jouffroy remarked that "those who cling to the old dogmas prefer the skepticism that has replaced faith to the enlightened dogmatism that threatens, in turn, to replace skepticism."[82]

There is indeed a sense in which materialism and skepticism were "directly contrary to the needs of the Restoration," but the official preference for a housebroken empiricism over a presumptuous metaphysics was neither anomalous nor unprecedented.[83] Max Horkheimer notes that religious authorities have characteristically chosen to persecute the metaphysicians, the Brunos and the Spinozas, rather than the empiricists such as Telesio and Locke. A metaphysics that presumes to recapitulate the objective reason inherent in reality aspires "to replace traditional religion with methodical philosophical thought and insight and thus to become a source of tradition all by itself." Cousin persistently denied that he wanted to replace traditional religion, but, to continue Horkheimer's brilliant insight, "the real issue was whether revelation or reason, whether theology or philosophy, should be the agency for determining and expressing ultimate truth."[84]

---

[81] Alfaric, *Laromiguière Et Son Ecole*, 97–98.

[82] Jouffroy to Damiron, 8 August 1818, in Jouffroy, *Correspondance*, 220.

[83] Pierre Orecchioni, "Tentatives de restauration intellectuelle," in *Manuel d'histoire littéraire de la France* (Paris, 1972), 4:590.

[84] Horkheimer, *Eclipse of Reason*, 14–17.

This is not to suggest that the objections to Cousin were narrowly, or even primarily, theological. A self-appointed seer with a large following was even more obnoxious on political than on religious grounds. Cousin was not preaching subversion, but his commitment to a completely unfettered exploration of fundamental questions implied the strong possibility of unacceptable conclusions. This concern was reflected in the anxious, hypocritical, and increasingly acrimonious correspondence over Cousin's failure to submit, and to stick to, a detailed lesson plan for his courses at the Ecole normale and the Faculty of Letters.

The *Moniteur* of 29 November 1820 conveyed the announcement of the termination of the lecture course in what might have been the template for all subsequent academic double-think. M. Cousin had not been suspended, since he had never been a professor of philosophy (that is, he had merely lectured as Royer-Collard's *suppléant*). Rather, since he was "engaged in important studies of ancient Greek philosophy, he will not replace M. Royer-Collard this winter."[85] In response to Cousin's predictable objections, Cuvier, the president of the Royal Council of Public Instruction, expressed regret that he had not followed well-meant advice and submitted a printed, unambiguous outline of his course. In effect, Cousin's ambitions did not go so far as to incline him to submit to a more or less tacit censorship.[86] Not long after the suspension, the faculty of the Collège de France nominated Cousin for a vacancy in the chair of natural law, but the government rejected his candidacy for that of a M. de Portets, who is known to history only because of that fact.[87]

Cousin's young admirers shared the conservative establishment's view of his revolutionary potential. According to Jouffroy, two men had initiated the revival of French philosophy from the slumbers of the Empire: Laromiguière, who reconstructed the philosophy of Condillac, and Royer-Collard, who refuted it. Two camps rallied to their standards:

> The elegant and skeptical minds were for the old doctrines; fiery types, naturally more revolutionary, were for the new. . . . A man

---

[85] Barthélemy-Saint-Hilaire, *M. Victor Cousin*, 1:110.

[86] Ibid., 114. The behind-the-scenes correspondence has left deposits in Cousin's dossier in the archives of educational personnel. Correspondence of Director, Ecole normale with Cuvier, 15, 25 May 1820. AN F^{17} 20492.

[87] Liard, *L'Enseignement supérieur*, 2:158.

[Cousin] still quite young, but never since more eloquent, was found at the head of the latter faction.[88]

The termination of Cousin's course was widely interpreted as a signal victory for obscurantism and a blow aimed directly at the generation to and for whom he spoke.[89] His martyr's crown would be sanctified in 1824 when he was arrested while travelling through Germany and handed over to the Prussian political police.[90] His release in 1825 and even more the reconstitution of his philosophy course after the electoral defeat of the ultraroyalists in 1828 were hailed as milestones on the highroad of the human spirit.

Victor Cousin is rightly remembered as "the first of the *chiens de garde*,"[91] destined to apologize for regimes, not to subvert them, but in the first decade of the Restoration the suspension of Cousin's course, the liquidation of the Ecole normale, and the purge of the University merely confirmed the assumption of the literate youth that they were destined to forge their country's future outside of, and against, its established institutions.

[88] Jouffroy, *Nouveaux mélanges philosophiques*, 117–18.

[89] In April 1820 Jouffroy had predicted the purge that would follow the suspension of the course. In May all the *maîtres de conférences* of the Ecole normale communicated their anxiety regarding Cousin's future to the director of the school. Barthélemy-Saint-Hilaire, *M. Victor Cousin*, 1:97–102.

[90] Cousin was accused of complicity in an international conspiracy and held under questioning in Berlin until February 1825. He denied everything. I have discussed this event in Spitzer, *Old Hatreds and Young Hopes*, 206–9, 268.

[91] Cecconi, "La 'Restauration' intellectuelle," 332.

CHAPTER 4

The *Globe*:
Flagship for a Generation

"Goethe spoke about the *Globe*. 'The contributors,' he said, 'are men of the world—serene, lucid, bold in the highest degree. When they censure they are polite and gallant, while in contrast
the German scholars always feel immediately that
they must hate those who do not think as they do.
I count the *Globe* among the most interesting periodicals and could not do without it."
        J. P. Eckerman, *Conversations with Goethe*

"I read the *Globe*, which bores me, and what
vexes me is that I cannot exactly say why. There
is something rather insipid in these ideas, without
consequence and corresponding to nothing."
Prosper de Barante, *Souvenirs du Baron de Barante*

The educational politics of ultra-
royalism, culminating in the purge of the University, reinforced
the resolution of the Restoration *jeunesse* to cut its own path into
the future. After 1822 that aspiration was most effectively expressed in the founding of the various periodicals controlled and
edited by many of the same individuals who had traced out a
complex network of personal affiliations in the schools, in informal associations, and in the secret societies. The erstwhile conspirators who assembled the staffs of the *Globe* and the *Producteur* were able to bring in talented coevals who had not
necessarily shared their enthusiasm for political subversion. The
young royalists who edited the *Muse française* were less tightly
concentrated according to age than were the *normalien* circle at
the center of the *Globe* or the coterie of Saint-Simonians who
organized the *Producteur*, but they thought of themselves as
carrying out a cultural mission that could only be consummated
by the young. The foreword of the first issue of their journal,

which appeared in 1823, identified obligations imposed on literary criticism by recent events and in which *les pères de la critique* had little interest:

> As the French Revolution has launched society along unfamiliar paths and into unprecedented relationships, literature, which is the expression of society, has been profoundly affected by these violent shocks and strange innovations. Criticism, purposefully or out of habit, seems to lag somewhat behind the general movement. Thus it is not always sufficiently relevant to contemporary literature; for in order to guide it one must march along with it. To consolidate and not to paralyze such youthful, untrammeled progress the *Muse française* will devote its efforts and its solicitude.[1]

The mild suggestion that the "fathers of criticism" suffered from a sort of intellectual sclerosis was the reverse of the coin whose face was stamped with the conviction that only a new generation could provide guidance along the unfamiliar path of the new century.

The preoccupations and potentialities of *la génération actuelle* were also evoked in the first issue of the *Producteur*, introduced by the Saint-Simonian circle in 1825:

> Our efforts will be fruitless, useless, and inglorious to the extent that we attack or defend a past that survives only for a few timid minds and obsolete interests. The struggle is over, there is no point in further combat, liberty has been won, we must profit from it. This particular generation has been summoned to prepare the organization of the new system; our task will be to help it comprehend the valid application of its talents, to persuade it to drop pointless debates in order to undertake the tasks required by the present state of knowledge and civilization.[2]

It was, however, the *Globe* that would become the most influential vehicle of the generational perspective on contemporary culture and the publication most consequentially committed to the edification of the "generations brought up since the Restoration and tormented with

[1] Jules Marsan, ed., *La Muse française* (Paris, 1907), 1:5.
[2] *Producteur*, 1 October 1825.

the desire to educate themselves."[3] I will therefore begin with a consideration of the *Globe* (although it was preceded by the publication of the *Muse française*) and devote the attention to it which its unique role in the expression of a generational *esprit* deserves, without sharing the conviction of some of its editors that the staff and the contributors of the journal monopolized virtually all the available talent of the literate *jeunesse*.

The familiar story of the founding of the *Globe* is the most striking example of the self-confident solidarity of that network of intellectuals under the age of thirty-two and of the career opportunities open to them under a regime that most of them despised. The project of a periodical devoted to the ideas of the new generation had been canvassed by young literati ever since journalism had been liberated from the lockstep of the Empire. There had been such precedents as Darmaing's ephemeral *Surveillant politique et littéraire*; the *Conservateur littéraire*, founded by the brothers Hugo, whose guiding spirit and chief contributor, Victor Hugo, was all of nineteen when the review terminated in 1821; the *Muse française*, whose contributors were drawn predominantly, if not exclusively, from the younger romantics; and the *Memorial catholique*, edited by two twenty-seven-year-old priests.[4]

The most direct inspiration for the publication of the *Globe* was probably the *Tablettes universelles*, which appeared between 1820 and 1824. This weekly was not monopolized by the young,[5] but along with

---

[3] *Globe*, 15 September 1824.

[4] J. J. Darmaing, a *normalien* of the *promotion* of 1812 and an admirer of Victor Cousin, published the *Surveillant politique et littéraire*, dedicated to the exposure of arbitrary acts of the government, for a few months in 1818. He also floated the highly successful *Gazette des tribunaux* in 1825. The *Conservateur littéraire* (1819–1821) was edited by Victor Hugo assisted by his brothers Abel (1798) and Eugène (1800).

[5] It was first published by J. B. Gouriet (1774) but taken over in 1823 by Jacques Coste with the public endorsement of the liberal establishment. Its promising future was aborted when Coste sold out to the royalist combine attempting to buy up the opposition press. The government feared its influence on "la jeunesse." Claude Bellanger et al., *Histoire générale de la presse française* (Paris, 1969), 2:75; see also Duvergier de Hauranne, *Histoire du gouvernement parlementaire*, 7:438–41, 506–7; Rémusat, *Mémoires*, 2:84–88, 100–4, and *Passé et présent*, 2:205; Eugène Hatin, *Histoire politique et littéraire de la presse en France* (Paris, 1861), 8:497–98; Irène [Collins] Fozzard, "The Government and the Press in France, 1822 to 1827," *English Historical Review*, 66 (January 1971): 58–59; Charles-Marc Desgranges, *La Presse littéraire sous la Restauration,*

the literary lights of the established opposition it did recruit youthful talent and thus served as

> the first attempt at a union of the young generation of various origins—the *proscrits* of the University (Jouffroy, Dubois, etc.), the young doctrinaires, flower of the highbrow salons (Rémusat at their head), and the two southerners directly committed to the revolution, Messieurs Mignet and Thiers.[6]

Various personal networks intersected in the office of the editor, Jacques Coste (1798). It was a meeting place for *jeunes gens* committed to liberal ideals and all sorts of new ideas. That was Rémusat's recollection of gatherings at which he first encountered, and established close relations with, the keen young journalists such as Thiers and Mignet and the coterie of the *universitaires* around Dubois, Damiron, and Trognon, and participated in the tentative fusion of the *mouvement romantique* with the *mouvement philosophique*, at a moment of personal and intellectual rapport.[7]

The columns of political commentary, unsigned but drafted by Rémusat and Thiers, struck the standard chords of the liberal opposition, but occasional pieces by Dubois, Damiron, Rémusat, and others sounded the notes of a new generational leitmotif. Dubois defends the University against the clerical offensive, condemns academic appointments influenced by political or religious partisanship instead of competitive distinction, and summons his cohort to the standard he was soon to raise as editor of his own journal:

> we above all, *jeunes gens*, innocent of error, unsullied by crime and treason, let us live as we have promised to live, and let us remember that to sit in judgment one must be wise, honorable, and worthy even of his enemy's esteem.[8]

1815–1830 (Paris, 1907), 149–54; Lucienne de Wieclawik, *Alphonse Rabbe dans la mêlée politique et littéraire de la Restauration* (Paris, 1963), 301–24.

[6] Sainte-Beuve, *Portraits contemporains*, 4:83.

[7] Rémusat, *Mémoires*, 2:101: "C'est alors que les rapports entre les idées formèrent les relations avec les personnes"; cf. Papiers Dubois, AN 319 AP³, Dossier 3, 22. The young writers who contributed to the *Tablettes universelles* were Dubois, Rémusat, Trognon, Damiron, Thiers, Mignet, Coquerel, Alphonse Mahul, Pierre Dumon (1797), Louis Guizard (1797), and Félix Bodin (1795). Most of the contributions are unsigned, some are initialed.

[8] *Tablettes universelles*, 40 (27 August 1823); 43 (September 1823); 49 (8 November 1823). Gerbod, *Paul-François Dubois*, 48–50.

Damiron places the latent superiority of the new generation in appropriate historical perspective:

> It is not because we scorn the heritage passed on to us by our fathers that we have not completely accepted it; but enriched by experience that they did not enjoy, free of their illusory prejudices, we renounce only their errors, while taking infinite pains to preserve the intermingled truths.[9]

François Mignet introduces the themes of second-generation liberalism: the aristocracy opposes the evident truths of modern political economy because its power is founded on the poverty of the masses; resistance to the contemporary counterrevolution does not entail a regression to the "counterrevolution of the 18th Brumaire," but a fulfillment of the principles of the Revolution preserved in the Constitution of 1814.[10]

A remarkable passage in a long review of Walter Scott's *Quentin Durward* (which I quote at length in chapter 7) evokes the sensibility of the *générations actuelles* tormented by "this double sense of strength and weakness," by the antinomy of the unlimited possibilities for individual aspiration and the crushing weight of external circumstance.[11]

Any opportunity afforded to youthful aspirations by the *Tablettes universelles* evaporated when the journal was purchased by royalist agents in the campaign to buy out the opposition press. "La jeune garde est battue," said Thiers, who proceeded to cast about for some other vehicle for himself and his friends.[12] But this was not yet Thiers' hour. The dream of a completely new, autonomous, and iconoclastic journal was to be realized by the unlikely combination of Pierre Leroux and Paul-François Dubois.

This *was* an unlikely combination despite their similar social antecedents and shared experience when they were *boursiers* at the *lycée* at Rennes and when they conspired together in the Carbonari and socialized with their former classmates and other young Bretons come up to the capital.[13] They were marked for different destinies, of course—Du-

---

[9] *Tablettes universelles*, 56 (27 December 1823).

[10] Ibid., 32 (March 1823); 42 (17 September 1823); Yvonne Knibiehler, *Naissance des sciences humaines: Mignet et l'histoire philosophique au XIXe siècle* (Paris, 1973), 68–69.

[11] *Tablettes universelles*, 36 (17 July 1823).

[12] Rémusat, *Mémoires*, 2:104.

[13] Leroux's father was a *limonadier* a beverage dealer, who died in 1808. Leroux received a scholarship from the city of Paris to the *lycée* at Rennes. Dubois' father, who

bois, never to be an Orleanist insider or complete success but essentially a spiritual citizen of the July Monarchy, and Leroux, not the least of the prophets of social democracy in France—but their paths had already diverged toward the end of the First Empire when Dubois had been recruited for the Ecole normale and Leroux had been forced to drop his application to the Ecole polytechnique in order to support his poverty-stricken family and his widowed mother.

Things had been hard enough for Dubois after his brilliant ascent up the first few rungs of the ladder. Driven out of the university system during the purges of the early twenties, he had to survive by hand-to-mouth literary expedients but managed to maintain and extend his connections among the alumni of the elite schools and also in the circles of well-born literati. Leroux had fallen back into the limbo of the almost-proletariat, working his way up to the level of *prote*, foreman in a printing shop, and in what might have been a decisive act of derogation, establishing a permanent liaison with a woman from the working class.

How these misfortunes were perceived by his happier coevals is suggested by Dubois' recollections: "Whether out of an exaggerated independence, *bizarrie d'esprit*, or necessity, in place of striving for a liberal career like law, medicine, or some employment appropriate to his talents, Leroux apprenticed himself and became a printer," and to cap this, took up with a good, pure, unintelligent, lowborn woman—"*née de bas.*"[14] Despite these handicaps Leroux managed to maintain some of the old connections, tried unsuccessfully to float an improved system

descended from a line of respectable artisans, attained the position of *garde-magasin de l'Armée de l'Ouest* during the Revolution, managed the unprecedented feat of not making a fortune out of the job, and returned to the family *atelier* in 1806. Dubois received a *bourse* to attend the *lycée* from the municipal council of Rennes. P. Félix Thomas, *Pierre Leroux: Sa Vie, ses oeuvres, sa doctrine* (Paris, 1904), 1–14; Jack Bakunin, *Pierre Leroux and the Rebirth of Democratic Socialism, 1797–1848* (New York, 1976), 23–27; M. E. Vacherot, "Notice biographique," in Paul-François Dubois, *Fragments littéraires* (Paris, 1879), 1:i–xiv; Gerbod, *Paul-François Dubois*, 13–52; Jean-Pierre Lacassagne, "De la Charbonnerie au socialisme: l'Itinéraire politique de Pierre Leroux," *Revue des travaux de l'Académie des sciences morales et politiques* (1971): 189–206; Jacques Viard, "Leroux, 'Ouvrier typographe,' carbonaro et fondateur du *Globe*," *Romantisme*, 28 (1980): 239–54; Jean-Jacques Goblot, *Aux Origines du socialisme français: Pierre Leroux et ses premiers écrits* (Lyon, 1977), 1–14.

[14] Papiers Dubois, AN 319 AP3, Dossier 1, 84–85. According to Charles Rémusat, Leroux "avait les formes et la vie d'un ouvrier aisé et intelligent, familier et négligé, et de plus ayant, selon l'usage beaucoup d'ouvriers, une femme qu'il n'avait pas épousée et un troupeau d'enfants." Rémusat, *Mémoires*, 2:139.

for setting type, and then had the good fortune to be employed in the printing establishment of a wealthy young childhood friend, Alexandre Lachevardière. There, possibly stimulated by the example of the *Mémorial catholique*, which was printed at the shop, Leroux conceived the idea of founding the periodical that became the *Globe*.

As the years rolled on and the great days of the *Globe* were lit with a nostalgic glow, the founders would differ over the extent of their respective contributions, but their accounts coincide on the development of the original idea. Leroux had first conceived of a publication that would collect and summarize contemporary scientific, literary, and philosophic contributions from "the civilized nations of the world." According to Dubois, he refashioned Leroux's flabby prospectus into the project for "an authentic literary journal, illuminating the general development of philosophy, letters, and art in Europe, free from all political implications except to the extent that they related to science." Leroux grants that the original project required a doctrinal focus—and that this was provided by the "principle of liberty."[15]

Principles do not float papers. The wherewithal was contributed by Leroux's employer, Lachevardière, who had recently purchased the printing house where he worked and was apparently easily persuaded to invest in the chancy venture. Thus the indispensable first step was the product of that generational network in which Paul Dubois was so tightly enmeshed, initially by way of his Breton schoolmates, including Leroux.[16]

[15] For the somewhat conflicting testimony on the founding of the *Globe*; see Pierre Leroux, "D'Une Nouvelle Typographie," *Revue indépendante*, 6 (25 January 1843): 274; and his article on Alexandre Bertrand in *Encyclopédie nouvelle*, 2 (1836); Dubois repeatedly in *Souvenirs* and autobiographical notes in AN 319 AP³, especially "Souvenirs," 29 January 1843, and "Fragments pour servir à une histoire du *Globe*," 26 August 1869. The key citations and quotes are in Gerbod, *Paul-François Dubois*, 51–52; and Goblot, *Aux Origines du socialisme français*, 3, which cites additional materials in the Fond Rémy Buffet that I have not seen. See also Sainte-Beuve, *Portraits littéraires*, 1:314–17; Rémusat, *Mémoires* 2:137–44; Vacherot, "Notice" and [anon.], "M. Dubois au Globe," in *Fragments littéraires*, 1:xiv–xxix; lxxi–cx; Adolphe Lair, "Le Globe": Sa fondation—sa rédaction—son influence: D'après des Documents inédits," *Séance et travaux de l'Académie des sciences morales et politiques*, 161 (May 1904): 570–98; Thureau-Dangin, *Le Parti libéral*, 217–64; Paul Janet, "Le Globe de la Restauration et Paul-François Dubois," *Revue des deux mondes*, 34 (1 August 1879): 481–512. Thomas, *Pierre Leroux*, 15–31; Gustave Michaut, *Saint-Beuve Avant Les Lundis* (Paris, 1903), 51–133.

[16] Leroux and Dubois had known Alexandre Bertrand, Jean Duhamel, and Désiré Roulin (1796) at the Rennes *lycée*. Bertrand, Duhamel, and Roulin also joined the Car-

In 1831, when Leroux, still mellow after his expropriation of the *Globe* for the Saint-Simonians, summed up its history, he graciously acknowledged that its "practical unity" resided in the person of Dubois, who managed to hold together the diverse temperaments of its contributors by a sort of electrical attraction.[17] There is ample confirmation that Dubois was the "soul of the journal," although admiration for his leadership was to be tempered by the recollection of his abrasive personality.[18] His own reminiscence was that "as a journalist I briefly held sway by way of the *Globe*. An entire generation of writers, and I dare say, of statesmen, was formed around me."[19] This rather exaggerates his importance, but he did play a leading role in those early years. Of all those precocious, somewhat disappointing destinies, his was perhaps the most profoundly marked by the poignancy of unfulfilled promise. Paul Janet struck off what became the received opinion of Dubois: "Many writers enjoy a reputation superior to their merits. A few, merit superior to their reputations. Among the latter was Dubois."[20]

Not that there was unanimity about his reputation. Dubois was a difficult person. It was easy to perceive his irascible rectitude as self-righteousness, but his patent sincerity made a profound impression on youthful companions then and on his students ever after. Above all, it was the sincerity that struck the chord for his coevals—the intense moral seriousness, the evangelistic devotion to ill-defined but deeply felt principles of the good life. Dubois seemed to be perched on the edge of that Great Discovery in the light of which they all might live. Like so many of his confrères, he had begun his career as a self-made scholar, after Victor Cousin the archetype of the poor, talented *normalien*. Even more than Cousin, his permanent identity was shaped by

---

bonari, as did Marcelin Desloges, Charles Beslay, and P. I. Rouen, all three members of the masonic lodge, the *Amis de l'Armorique*, BN FM² 35. The Bretons in Paris continued to meet and dine together. Ange Guépin, *Philosophie du socialisme* (Paris, 1850), 580.

[17] Leroux, *Globe* (18 January 1831); this is partially reproduced in Thomas, *Pierre Leroux*, 16.

[18] Sainte-Beuve, *Portraits littéraires* 1:316. For a recent assertion of the relative importance of Leroux's contribution, see Viard, "Leroux"; for a negative assessment of Dubois, see A. G. Lehmann, *Sainte-Beuve* (Oxford, 1962), 21–23.

[19] Papiers Dubois, AN 319 AP³, Dossier 1, "Mes Mémoires," 1.

[20] Janet, "Le Globe de la Restauration," 481; Adolphe Lair, "Un Maître de Sainte-Beuve," *Correspondant*, 199 (1900): 317–26.

the institutional and emotional relationship to the school whose director he would become. Despite his prickly personality, he had the talent
for the sort of friendship that was favored then—completely devoted,
grave, candid relationships that were constructed to last a lifetime.[21]
Charles Rémusat, who managed to temper his admiration for Dubois'
editorial drive and personal rectitude with a characteristically patronizing description of his irritable temperament and "flinty" literary
style, concludes, "Fortunately, he had friends."[22]

Indeed, Dubois' brash assurance that he had something exceptional
to offer depended on the correct assumption that he could tap the nascent talents of his cohort. "Our recruits," he said, "were there all ready
to go. There were, first of all, our old comrades from the Ecole normale, some in disgrace, others still on active service."[23] For Dubois it
would always be the Ecole normale first of all, starting with his dearest
friends at the inner core of the Cousinian coterie, then widening out
from Jouffroy and Damiron through the intersecting circles of ex-nor-
maliens, former Carbonari, and the Parisian branch of the Breton connection. Additional contributors were recruited through the extended
ramifications of these personal networks.

The young professors brought along their most promising pupils
from the succeeding *promotions*. Thus at the age of twenty Sainte-
Beuve had his foot placed on the bottom rung of a fabulous career by
Dubois, who had been his teacher at the lycée Charlemagne; and Jouffroy recruited Vitet and Tanneguy-Duchâtel, young lights of the liberal aristocracy, from the private course he had undertaken after his
dismissal from the University. Other coevals from the liberal salons,
such as Charles Rémusat and Prosper Duvergier de Hauranne, had
met the *normaliens* socially, or in the audience for Cousin's lectures, or
in such earlier ventures as the *Tablettes universelles*.[24]

---

[21] Dubois describes this ideal in characterizing the relation between Jouffroy and
Damiron in *Cousin, Jouffroy, Damiron*, 112–13: "Les lettres échangées entre Damiron
et lui sont un véritable tableau à nu de deux âmes qui se confessent comme à Dieu, ne
se cachant rien, ne déguisant rien; allant, avec la sagacité d'une conscience qui se
cherche de toutes ses forces au fin fond des choses, et disant tout, et peignant tout, la
vie, le bien, le mal, les idées vraies, fausses ou folles, à mesure qu'elles paraissent sur le
fond de l'âme, laquelle se regarde faire, constate et décrit, avec la plus scrupuleuse fi-
délité, on peut même dire quelquefois, sans vouloir ni dessein prémédité."

[22] Rémusat, *Mémoires*, 2:139–40.

[23] Quoted in Lair, " 'Le Globe': Sa Fondation—sa rédaction—son influence," 579.

[24] In addition to Dubois, Jouffroy, and Damiron, the *normalien* coterie included

This was the brilliant "brigade" of the *Globe* that, according to Rémusat, "would have encompassed the entire *jeunesse*, and therefore the future, if it had included Thiers and his friends."[25] However small the articulate elite of the new generation, it was not quite that small. The *Globe* circle did not encompass the promising writers—Hugo, Vigny, the Deschamps—who frequented the Nodier *cénacle* and founded the *Muse française*; nor did it monopolize that formidable company of former Carbonari who turned to the Saint-Simonian movement and the publication of the *Producteur*. To draw these distinctions is not to suggest complete separation. The networks intersected at the journals as they had in the schools, the secret societies, and the salons.[26]

Although Dubois intended to staff the *Globe* with those "as young, as independent, as impatient as I with any patronage of previous generations and of celebrities out of the past," he welcomed contributors from any quarter.[27] Thus the *Globe* would publish a piece by that middle-aged, ambivalent observer of the younger generation, Henri Beyle. Stendhal's *D'Un Nouveau Complot contre les industriels*, one of the earliest attacks on the Saint-Simonians, was answered in the columns of the *Producteur* by Armand Carrel, ex-Carbonaro, secretary of Augustin Thierry, sometime contributor to the *Globe*, and future collaborator of Thiers and Mignet in the editing of the *National*.[28]

Thierry, Guy Patin, Nicolas Géruzez (1799), Charles Renouard (1794), Auguste Trognon (1795), Nicolas Artaud, J. D. Guigniaut, and Georges Farcy. The ex-Carbonari— Dubois, Jouffroy, and Leroux—were joined by Thierry, Bertrand, Carrel, and Desloges. The political exile Frédéric Degeorge was overseas correspondent. Charles Rémusat, Ludovic Vitet, Charles Tanneguy-Duchâtel, and Duvergier de Hauranne represented the aristocratic salons. Other members of the cohort who figure in this history were Eugène Lerminier (1803), Cavé, Dittmer, Ampère, Magnin, Ernest Desclozeaux (1803), Adolphe Blanqui, Roulin, Thiers, Casimir Bonjour (1795), Coquerel, Sainte-Beuve, and Madame Belloc (Louise Swantin) (1796). Sautelet was one of the proprietors. For the best list of *globistes*, see Gerbod, *Paul-François Dubois*, 55. See also, Jean-Jacques Goblot, "Un 'Mistérieux Rédacteur' du 'Globe': Marcelin Desloges," *Revue d'histoire littéraire de la France*, 85 (March–April 1985): 234–47.

[25] Rémusat, *Mémoires*, 2:143. Thiers did contribute articles on the salon of 1824.

[26] Sautelet and Lachevardière were closely associated with the publication of both the *Globe* and the *Producteur*. At various times Carrel, Artaud, Adolphe Blanqui, and Adolphe Garnier wrote for each of the journals. Cerclet, first editor of the *Producteur*, knew the *Globe* circle at Delécluze's salon. For the gradual *rapprochement* of the *globistes* and Victor Hugo, see below, chapter 5.

[27] Quoted in Gerbod, *Paul-François Dubois*, 55n.

[28] For a convenient reproduction and analysis of the exchange, see Stendhal, *D'Un*

There would be a scattering of articles from such teachers and pa-trons as Cousin and Guizot, but their relation to the journal was mar-ginal. Cousin disapproved at first—at least Dubois remembers that the young master deplored an enterprise that tempted his disciples away from the fabrication of folio volumes to the primrose path of "prema-ture and unwholesome publicity." Dubois adds that Cousin changed his tune when it became apparent that the journal was to be a great success.[29] Guizot, who contributed a few short pieces, inflated the sig-nificance of his role in his memoirs, where he characterized the *Globe* as the work of young Doctrinaires associated with other writers.[30] This patronizing reminiscence stimulated an indignant denial from Paul Dubois. The *globistes* were not junior Doctrinaires, he wrote. Indeed, the journal owed its success to the generational autonomy of its board of editors:

> It was young and free of all ties to the past. Among us there was not one old or well-known writer. Come, so to speak, from the four points of the compass—Carbonari, liberals of every type, we constituted, out of our various opinions and temperaments, a brand new army.[31]

Dubois was scarcely a neutral witness. His entire life was to be per-meated with an obsessive recapitulation of the "memories of that great literary and political crusade of which I had been the chief, the stand-ard-bearer, so to speak, in the midst of my friends."[32] In his seventy-

---

Nouveau Complot contre les industriels, Nouvelle Bibliothèque Romantique, no. 3 (Paris, 1972). Also, see below, chapter 7.

[29] Dubois, *Cousin, Jouffroy, Damiron*, 64–66. Additional evidence to this effect is mixed. During the period prior to the founding of the *Globe*, Dubois informed Jouf-froy that "Cousin . . . est enchanté et a promis secours." Dubois to Jouffroy, 4 August 1824, Papiers Dubois, AN 319 AP¹. Later, in a moment of discouragement, Dubois wrote to Jouffroy, "Cousin aurait-il donc raison et nous faudrait-il nous réfugier dans la science?" Dubois to Jouffroy, 17 September 1827, published in Jean-Jacques Goblot, " 'Le Globe' en 1827, Lettres inédites de Damiron et de Dubois," *Revue d'histoire litté-raire de la France*, 72 (May–June 1972): 505.

[30] Guizot, *Mémoires*, 1:198. Guizot's version is accepted by Charles Pouthas, *Guizot pendant la Restauration* (Paris, 1923), 351–52. Evidently the *globistes* were not model Doctrinaires, as Guizot criticized them for theoretical vagueness and the spirit of co-terie. Guizot, *Mémoires*, 1:324–25.

[31] Quoted in Lair, " 'Le Globe': Sa fondation—sa rédaction—son influence," 588.

[32] Papiers Dubois, AN 319 AP³, Dossier 1, 18. This passage is cited from his *Journal* of 1843. For as long as it seemed remotely possible, he canvassed the possibility of

seventh year he was still compiling notes, in a trembling almost illegible hand, for a history of the *Globe*.

However self-serving, Dubois' version is convincingly supported by other accounts. Rémusat remarked that Guizot would have loved to pass for the patron of the enterprise, but "what was called the 'young university' and was soon to be known as Young France—for Dubois is the first to use that expression—was resolved to advance alone and without a master." Sainte-Beuve also denied that the *Globe* had been founded or developed under the aegis of the Doctrinaires; the true founders were talented young refugees from the University.[33]

From the beginning, a primary concern of the founders was not to be confounded with the press of the established liberal and anticlerical opposition. Pierre Leroux would recall that the originality of the *Globe* lay in its repudiation of the narrow and puerile prejudices of a fossilized liberalism.[34] We have contemporary confirmation of the attitude toward the dignitaries of the liberal press in a letter from Jouffroy to Dubois in the summer of 1824 commenting on Dubois' project for the *Globe*. Jouffroy urged that the journal concentrate on literature, eschew political allusions that reek of prison, and dispense with "shopworn peddlers of bad taste," such as Messieurs Jay and Jouy. The patronage of the fading *vedettes* of the liberal journals was scarcely required by those about to assume the "honorable, lucrative, and safe mission of revolutionizing literature." That mission "can only belong to the young, for the entire previous generation has been discredited; too cynical to appreciate the good; through force of circumstance too skeptical and immoral to speak frankly; too corrupted by thirty years of scandal to command confidence or avoid ridicule."[35]

Jouffroy's letter articulated the premises of the *Globe*. It was not at

---

launching a new *Globe*. See, for example, Georges Weill, "Paul Dubois, un Intellectuel Député," *Revue de synthèse historique*, 46 (December 1928): 96.

[33] Rémusat, *Mémoires*, 2:140–47; Sainte-Beuve, *Portraits littéraires*, 1:316; Thureau-Dangin, *Le Parti libéral*, 221: "c'était donc l'un des caractères du *Globe*, d'être l'oeuvre exclusive d'une jeunesse livrée à ses seules forces, et même en réalité à ses propres inspirations."

[34] *Globe* 18 January 1831. The policies of the *Globe*, Leroux wrote, were not informed "par haine et par colère, comme les autres feuilles libérales, mais par une sympathie généreuse pour une ère d'avenir qu'il entrevoyait confusément et dont il voulait hâter la venue. Destructeur et pacifique tout ensemble, il combattait le catholicisme avec la liberté et réclamait la liberté pour les jésuites."

[35] Jouffroy to Dubois, 16 August 1824, in Jouffroy, *Correspondance*, 374.

first to be political—or not ostensibly political; politics were latent in almost everything treated in the contemporary press. In addition to the desire to avoid the payment of caution money and the censorship imposed on political journals, there was the overriding intention to transcend narrow partisanship and to survey contemporary literature—in the largest sense—with a fresh and unprejudiced eye. Above all, it was to be autonomous. Jouffroy also predicted, more or less accurately, what came to pass. It would be honorable, relatively safe, and lucrative—at least in the light of current career prospects—to edit the *Globe*.

Once the story of the *Globe* had been cast into the bronze of the historical record, its success was remembered as historically appropriate or even inevitable. In an insightful passage, Adolphe Lair related the international repute of the journal to *l'avènement d'une génération nouvelle* whose generous illusions and boundless aspirations were best expressed in Lamartine's poetry and in the columns of the *Globe*.[36] Lair puts his finger on the crucial point; and yet there would have been few to forecast that the twenty-seven-year-old foreman of a small printing house and an unemployed teacher aged thirty-one could conceive, launch, and edit an uncompromisingly highbrow, remorselessly didactic publication that after a few issues would conquer the interest and respect of cultivated circles in France and abroad.[37]

The success of the *Globe* is to be understood in the context of contemporary journalism and in contrast to what was offered by the competition. There was nothing like a modern newspaper then. Politics

[36] Lair, " 'Le Globe": Sa fondation—sa rédaction—son influence," 590: "C'est à ce moment où les hommes de la Révolution et de l'Empire commençaient à disparaître ou à vieillir, que la jeunesse née dans les dernières années du XVIIIe siècle, et les premières années du XIXe arrivait à l'âge viril. Eprise de liberté, avide de gloire, jeune par-dessus tout, ayant de la jeunesse la foi naive, l'illusion généreuse, l'espérance sans bornes, elle se flattait d'éviter les écueils où avaient échoué ses pères, d'assurer ce qu'elle appelait les conquêtes de la Révolution en en répudiant les crimes; et pour emprunter au *Globe* et à M. Dubois lui-même une image aussi vive que fidèle, elle croyait entrevoir comme "l'aurore d'un monde nouveau." De même que les *Méditations* de Lamartine étaient l'expression des ardeurs poétiques de cette génération, le *Globe* devint l'interprète de ses aspirations philosophiques, littéraires et bientôt de ses idées politiques."

[37] It is virtually *de rigueur* to cite Goethe's respect for the journal; for example: Lair, "Le Globe," 592. Describing J. J. Ampère's visit to Goethe in 1827, Sainte-Beuve engages in an extended fantasy on how each of the major contributors to the *Globe* might have represented the *jeunesse* of France to the German monument and concludes that Ampère was, in fact, the most appropriate representative. Sainte-Beuve, *Nouveaux lundis*, 13:207–16.

was the obsession of the most widely circulated journals, such as the
Constitutionnel, but political reporting was uniformly tendentious, and
often Aesopian because of the censorship, and the opposition press was
characterized by a snide pseudo-Voltairian polemical tone. Political
bias also pervaded literary commentary. A great deal of space in all of
the journals of opinion was devoted to literary criticism, to reviews of
books, poems, and plays treated as significant current events and usually evaluated in the light of obvious *parti pris*. Of course, the *Minerve*
or the *Courrier français* or the *Journal des débats* could boast of distinguished contributions from such luminaries as Constant or Chateaubriand, but the regular fare was not terribly substantial.

Substantial fare was what the *Globe* set out to provide. Leroux's
original project was reflected in the first few issues with short notices
on foreign and provincial cultural and social developments, but the
journal soon hit its stride with serious analyses of a wide range of subjects of interest to a cultured clientele. The *Globe* had advertised its
mission as the regeneration of literary criticism and would devote considerable space to that permanent French preoccupation with literature
as the essential touchstone of the national culture, but it would extend
the range of subject matter well beyond the literary boundaries as it
responded to a growing public for a broadly based coverage of subjects
inadequately presented in the educational system or anywhere else.

The *Globe*'s coverage not only included up-to-date surveys of issues
of current interest, such as the Greek revolution, or secondary education in France, or the role of women in Latin America, but also provided the subscriber with serialized essays on such subjects as the main
currents of recent economic thought, major themes in the development
of modern philosophy, an extended survey of contemporary musical
drama, and an unprecedented series of reports on the meetings of the
Académie des sciences.

Even more important than the substance was the spirit. The *Globe*
intended to replace the shallow, frivolous, and tendentious tone of contemporary journalism with a fair, objective, and, above all, morally serious treatment of the subjects that preoccupied the generations come
to maturity since the Restoration. This was the pledge of the *Globe*'s
"Profession of Faith" drafted for its first issue by Paul-François Dubois. In this brief prospectus, whose manifest subject was literary criticism, Dubois managed to articulate the cultural assumptions of his

generation in language that conveyed its characteristic moral tone.[38]
Dubois justified the new journal's existence in the light of the intellectual poverty of its predecessors. While literature had flourished during
the past decade, literary criticism had degenerated into personal anecdote and the gossip of the Paris salon. No wonder the young turned to
political agitation, deprived as they were of any "subject worth serious
consideration." Much of what passed for criticism was either narrowly
partisan, in political periodicals masquerading as literary journals, or
crassly commercial, promoted for the profit of publishing houses. With
reputations the gift of the political coterie or the literary entrepreneur
(Dubois strikes the familiar chord of occupational resentment), what
chance has a modest and unknown youth to escape hopeless obscurity
except by pandering to some patron? To transcend this fate was the
Globe's raison d'être. The editors could not cite great names or powerful authorities in their support; "L'utilité, la vérité, le temps," these
would constitute the elements of their success. *Le temps*: thus Dubois
appeals to the spirit of the age to authenticate the credentials of those
born into it.

The editors of the *Globe* promised to substitute justice and independence for commercial and political motives and to confine criticism
to works worth contemplating, but to extend it beyond the horizon of
the Paris salon to survey (here the remnants of Leroux's original project) the progress of the arts and industry in the provinces and abroad.
Their literary doctrines could be summed up in the phrase, "liberty
and respect for national good taste." The latter repudiated the admiration for German and English models when carried to the point of
threatening the language of Racine and Voltaire; the former defied the
academism that stifled creativity by venerating the past. The intensity
of their convictions might impel the young journalists to dogmatism
but never to intolerance. They welcomed opposing opinions and called
on "the cooperation of all men who loved their country, *des bonnes
études et des beaux-arts*." Summoning up the men who love their country, Dubois' manifesto, like the philosophy lectures of Victor Cousin,
preempts the patriotic terrain for his version of right thinking and
good taste. The pervasive qualities of this brief, clear statement are can-

[38] This was published in the 14 September 1824 issue of the *Globe* and reproduced
in Pierre Trahard, "Le Romantisme défini par 'le Globe,'" in Henri Girard, ed., *Etudes
romantiques* (Paris, 1925), 2–8. Dubois, *Fragments littéraires*, 1:1–8.

dor and gravity—staple elements in the self-image of Dubois and his companions. The commitment is to "sound research, the integrity of good intentions, fair mindedness with independence, this serious interest in what is useful." Thus the humble but intrepid band of youthful truth-tellers launches its fragile bark.

The journal would rather faithfully conform to its initial commitments, most consistently in Dubois' own articles. It was certainly never guilty of frivolity but was inexorably earnest and didactic, a *"journal raisonneur* that sometimes bored its own friends."[39] While it was not above partisan polemics and slanted arguments, it was relatively fair and open-minded, at least in light of the contemporary state of the journalistic art. Occasionally it criticized the works of its own contributors, a virtually unprecedented violation of the *esprit de corps* of the literary coterie.

The *Globe* is probably most often praised for the defense of the liberties of its adversaries.[40] Its repudiation of the dogmatic anticlericalism of the *Constitutionnel* and other champions of the campaign to expel the Jesuits, close church schools, and forbid the publication of religious propaganda constituted an exemplary defense of the right of obnoxious groups to spread pernicious ideas. The question of the civil liberties of the Jesuit order was the conclusive test of contemporary liberal ideas. There could have been no more authentic commitment to principle against the grain of one's profoundest instincts and the prejudices of one's closest allies than the assertion of the right of Jesuits to preach, teach, and even to exist, in France. Dubois struck to the heart of the issue. "The Jesuits," he wrote, "are men and citizens like ourselves. . . . Liberty, even for the Jesuits, but liberty for all."[41] In a running debate with anticlerics such as the mossbacked aristocrat Montlosier and the liberal publicist Kératry, who wanted the state to intervene against the "criminal" machinations of an aggressive clericalism, Dubois followed the classic libertarian arguments to their ultimate conse-

---

[39] Pierre Moreau, *Le Classicisme des romantiques* (Paris, 1932), 197: Prosper de Barante, *Souvenirs du Baron de Barante* (Paris, 1893), 3:326: Barante to Rémusat, 20 June 1826: "Je lis le *Globe* qui m'ennuie et ce qui me fâche c'est que je ne saurais trop dire pourquoi. C'est quelque chose un peu d'insipide que ces idées sans résultats, et qui ne correspondent à rien."

[40] Rémusat, *Mémoires,* 2:149–50; Janet, "Le Globe de la Restauration," 503–12; Gerbod, *Paul-François Dubois,* 64–70.

[41] *Globe,* 4 March 1826; also in *Fragments littéraires,* 1:151.

quence: "The science of the absurd is the condition of the science of the true; he who wishes to prohibit the former, kills the latter."[42]

Beneath all of this lay the unifying conviction: The other side is obsolete. No one would wish to return to the clerical censorship of the Old Regime, and no one should wish to return to the total control over religious, and all other, ideas exercised by Napoleon's despotic state. The running tide was with the libertarians. When Kératry accused the *Globe* of being out of step with informed opinion, the indignant response struck a familiar chord: "Our opinions are those of the rising generations; their support sustains us. With them we proceed peaceably and calmly to the conquest of the religious freedoms promised us by the Constitution, without restriction or reference to laws of the past."[43] The reference to rising generations as the court of last resort was an appeal to the very principle of the *Globe*'s existence. This was a theme repeated with great effect, notably in several long essays by Théodore Jouffroy, Paul Dubois' dearest friend and, in his generous estimation, the brightest star in the Pleiades of contributors to the journal.[44]

The issue of 24 May 1825 had a special supplement featuring Jouffroy's essay "Comment les dogmes finissent" his most widely praised

[42] *Globe*, 21 November 1826; also in *Fragments littéraires*, 1:264; a letter to the editor of the *Globe*, 2 August 1826, argued, "Pour être conséquent, il faudrait cependant se décider entre le respect absolu de la pensée et son entier esclavage."

[43] *Globe*, 5 August 1826; also in *Fragments littéraires*, 1:204. This "Réponse à l'article de M. Kératry" was followed in the 8 August 1826 issue by "Sur la Dénonciation de M. de Montlosier," in which Dubois celebrated the principles that "passionent pour la cause de la liberté toute cette jeunesse appelée à la conquérir un jour"; also in *Fragments littéraires*, 1:206. The *Globe*'s position was supported in a pamphlet written by two young lawyers, J. F. Dupont de Bussac (1803) and Victor Guichard, to refute a brief by Dupin that cited laws of Ancient Rome and the Old Regime to justify repression of the Jesuits: "Il faut donc regarder comme indignes d'une attention et d'une réfutation sérieuses toute argumentation qui repose sur les doctrines et les institutions des générations qui ne sont plus, puisque leur état social est en contradiction avec le nôtre. C'est d'après les besoins de la société actuelle et les lois que ces besoins ont déterminées qu'il faut raisonner en matière de législation." J. F. Dupont [de Bussac] and Victor Guichard, *Consultation ni jésuitique, ni gallicane, ni féodale, en réponse à la consultation rédigée par M. Dupin* (Paris, 1826), 12.

[44] "Jouffroy . . . incomparablement le premier entre nous." Papiers Dubois, AN 319 AP³, Dossier 3, "Mes collaborateurs au Globe." Rémusat, "Théodore Jouffroy," *Passé et présent*, 2:206: "M. Jouffroy primait parmi nous." Sainte-Beuve, *Portraits littéraires*, 1:318.

and best remembered work.[45] The essay was cast in the form of a universal history of the circulation of dogmas but unmistakably spoke to the immediate French past. It contained the familiar representations of a degenerate Old Regime destined to be swept away and of the revolutionary generation whose task it was to wield the iron broom but whose destructive accomplishments rendered it incapable of reconstruction. Although incapable of reaping the fruits of their own labors, those first soldiers of reform had not fought in vain. They had broken the spell, and on their young and enlightened successors this spell can never be cast again. The revolutionary fathers, burned out in the cosmic struggle, have necessarily to be outstripped by their fresh and unscarred heirs, who have already gone beyond their fathers and perceived the emptiness of their doctrines:

> A new faith appears before them, they advance toward this enchanting prospect with enthusiasm, conviction, and resolution, the hope of the new era rests in them, they are its predestined apostle, and in their hands rests the salvation of the world.

Their contemplation of a glorious future, however, does not veil their perception of the misfortunes of the present. The desolation they see around them "rooted a bitter contempt for society and a profound indignation against its masters and its corrupters in young souls informed by a love of truth and virtue."[46] In their alienation from their epoch, they rediscover the sense of their mission.

We can understand the contemporary acclaim for this mediocre tract in the light of its articulation of the fundamental assumptions of Jouffroy's coevals.[47] It was, said Sainte-Beuve, "the most effective manifesto of the aspirations of the *jeune élite persécutée*." It was twice republished in the 1840s by Pierre Leroux as a comment on the *trahison* of the Restoration *clercs* and as a reproach to Jouffroy's mature career:

[45] This is reproduced in Théodore Jouffroy, *Mélanges philosophiques* (Paris, 1833) and in *Le Cahier vert* (Paris, 1924).

[46] Jouffroy, "Comment les dogmes finissent," in *Le Cahier vert*, 73–74.

[47] I agree with Henri Peyre, *Les Générations littéraires*, 59, that Jouffroy's essay was "peut-être trop loué." It is still admired. André Thirion describes how as a young radical writer he was prescribed "Comment les dogmes finissent" by Louis Aragon and how much benefit he drew from the text. At one time he planned "to use Jouffroy's approach to explain the origins of opportunistic or leftist deviations and the development and issue of socialist heresies." André Thirion, *Revolutionaries without Revolution* (New York, 1975), 214.

"He was put on earth to publish those few pages without ever improving on them, and they alone guarantee his place in the history of French thought."[48] At the time of its publication in 1825, the response to Jouffroy's piece was immense, recalled Dubois, who thought that his superb evocation of the condition of their generation put the definitive stamp on the character of the *Globe*.[49]

Jouffroy's contribution to the journal's character was couched in a style somewhat different from that of Dubois. In contrast to the latter's earnest disquisitions lit by flickers of mild sarcasm, Jouffroy is almost grandiloquent, but he also manages to establish an ironic distance from which the young critic might take the measure of his seniors. The tone of ironic and faintly patronizing raillery is even more apparent in an influential essay that Jouffroy remembered as the declaration of principles for the *Globe*.[50]

The substance of "De la Sorbonne et des philosophes" is a critique of the contemporary descendants of the doctors of the church and the philosophers of the eighteenth century in the light of Cousinian eclecticism. The basic argument, a virtual axiom for intellectuals in Jouffroy's age group, was historicist: Each of the old schools had contributed conceptions appropriate to its era, but the imperatives of the present century eluded them. They had been refuted not so much by argument as by "the force of things."[51]

In subsequent publications Jouffroy would provide the technical refutation of dogmatic "spiritualism and materialism," but in this piece the argument is carried by the polemical tone. One feels obliged to inform "the belligerent parties," Jouffroy writes, "that the generation which succeeds them . . . is not as interested in their wrangles as they imagine." Whatever direction it may take, it has no intention of trudging along in their old ruts or consuming itself in their old passions. The

---

[48] Sainte-Beuve, *Portraits littéraires*, 1:297, 313–14. Pierre Leroux, *De La Mutilation d'un écrit posthume de Théodore Jouffroy avec une lettre à l'Académie des sciences morales et un appendice pour faire suite à la réfutation de l'éclectisme* (Paris, 1843), 23; also, see below, chapter 11.

[49] Papiers Dubois, AN 319 AP³, Dossier 1, 6 March 1844.

[50] Jouffroy, *Mélanges philosophiques*, 20n. This essay appeared in the *Globe*, 15 January 1825, and was republished in *Mélanges philosophiques*. Rémusat confirms Jouffroy's reminiscence: "Deux articles, l'un: *La Sorbonne et les philosophes*, l'autre: *Comment les dogmes finissent*, furent comme la déclaration de principes du *Globe*, et cette déclaration de principes fut bien accueillie." Rémusat, *Mémoires*, 2:152.

[51] For a further discussion of the generation's historicism, see chapter 7.

reverend Jesuit fathers and the esteemed friends of the philosophes can continue to have it out; their young auditors will simply enjoy the spectacle and digest the arguments with a dose of agnostic salt: "We read Monsieur Bonald and Monsieur Benjamin Constant with the same sang-froid; we peruse the *Mémorial catholique* and the *Mercure* with equal admiration; and the excellent sermons preached at us from one direction or the other do not touch our hearts." Given the antecedents and published opinions of Jouffroy and his associates, it was not really necessary to say that they did not completely subscribe to the dogmas of Bonald and the *Mémorial catholique*; the important point was to distance themselves from the publicists of the opposition establishment. Jouffroy entered the lists, after such young paladins as Charles Loyson and Saint-Amand Bazard, to have his turn at the old liberal giant, Benjamin Constant.

The same challenge was accepted by Philippe Damiron, the third member of the *normalien* triumvirate at the *Globe*. His long review of Constant's ambitious project, "De la Religion considérée dans sa source, ses formes et ses développements," managed to mix praise and criticism in just the right proportions to appropriate Constant's liberal credentials while establishing his obsolescence.[52] Adopting a tone of tranquil authority (to borrow the expression), the young philosopher complimented Constant on the brilliance and facility with which he presented invariably felicitous, and often correct, interpretations of vital issues.[53] Constant's demonstration, for example, of the inherent religiosity of human nature was sound and well argued, but it was vitiated by his failure to distinguish between "religious sentiment" as an emotion and as an intellectual conviction. In effect, Constant had not rooted his argument in a systematic, a "scientific," conception of the human psyche. That, of course, lay to hand in the science of self-observation practiced so effectively by the Cousinian philosophic circle. Damiron does not say *that* in so many words, but the message is clear enough. Constant had effectively demolished the errors of eighteenth-century philosophy but had not replaced them with clear and positive truths. One would have preferred a bit less brilliance and somewhat more profundity.

[52] *Globe*, 4, 6, 8 October 1824.

[53] The expression is borrowed from Charles Seignobos' characterization of the French school of unscientific history, quoted in William Keylor, *Academy and Community: The Founding of the French Historical Profession* (Cambridge, Mass., 1975), 81.

Altogether a fair-minded, balanced, and objective review that left the reader in no doubt as to who vibrated to the intellectual rhythms of the new era and who did not.

One expects ambitious young intellectuals to measure themselves against peaks on the contemporary horizon—against Constant, Bonald, or Destutt de Tracy. Those peaks did not, however, stand out from the surrounding range with the clarity afforded to our hindsight. The intellectual (and occupational) horizon of the Restoration *jeunesse* was more immediately confined by those who had clawed their way to the cultural heights and maintained and exploited their *situations acquises* by a ubiquitous presence on the literary, philosophic, theatrical, and political scene.

Many of those reputations, now so diminished in historical memory as to be beneath disrepute, were then perceived as the necessary, virtually providential, "other," against which youth could define its unique identity. Two such figures come to mind, not merely as illustrations but because they presented themselves as targets of choice to the publicists of the *Globe*. Louis Simon Auger, born into the revolutionary era in 1772, steered a characteristic course of parallel careers through the new bureaucracy and the world of letters, ultimately fusing them into the office of literary functionary.[54] He published prolifically, notably in the *Journal de l'Empire*, and eventually obtained the position of inspector of the University, as the *Dictionnaire des girouettes* (a biographical dictionary of turncoats) put it, "under the reign of him whom he has since described as the poltroon of Fontainebleau."[55]

After 1814 Auger earned his *girouettes* as royal censor, and the enmity of the liberal intelligentsia for his election to the Académie française just at the moment when it had undergone a political purge. With the support of a coterie of writers of similar tastes, he established himself as the cultural *grand commis par excellence*, attaining the eminence of Perpetual Secretary of the Academy and the role of its mouthpiece on issues of high policy. In this role he delivered the philippic against romanticism that guaranteed his literary immortality as the target of Stendhal's sarcasm.[56]

[54] *Dictionnaire de biographie française*, 4:517–19.

[55] [César de Proisy D'Eppe], *Dictionnaire des girouettes: ou, Nos Contemporains Peints d'après eux-mêmes* (Paris, 1815), 20.

[56] [Louis Simon Auger], *Discours sur le romantisme prononcé dans la séance annuelle des quatre académies du 24 avril 1824, par M. Auger de l'Académie française* (Paris, 1824).

The second volume of *Racine et Shakespeare*, published in 1824 as an answer to Auger, was reviewed with relish in the *Globe*.[57] The journal's gratified response to Stendhal's mischievous handling of that verbose grandee was predictable. Auger's peroration—a tour de force of its kind—was addressed to talented "young writers," urging them to abjure the affectations of excessive melancholy and misanthropic Satanism, the indiscriminate mingling of the sacred and the sensual, and to control their genius with the bridle of wholesome rules. In another *discours* Auger reminded the "masters of the lyre" that under the benevolent rule of their beloved monarch *la patrie* demanded no more of them than "hymns of joy, love, and gratitude."[58]

Not only was Auger obnoxious, he was ubiquitous, especially in his repeated appearances at the public sessions of the Academy to deliver its official response to the *discours* of its new members. As Paul Dubois dryly remarked, the wit and fecundity of Voltaire himself would scarcely have been adequate to so many challenges.[59] With the complacent eloquence of a midget Bossuet, Auger spouted out his flowing periods, delivering the customary effusions on the qualities of the departed member and his brilliant successor, scoring facile debating points against immature literati who had traded the great national classic tradition for foreign pottage, winning the applause of a complaisant audience with appeals to its cultural chauvinism and corporate self-regard. From time to time the *Globe* would pick up a particularly egregious example, as in Auger's welcoming speech to the poet Alexandre Soumet, which congratulated him for refusing to make common cause with those *amateurs de la belle nature* who would trade *Phèdre* and *Iphigénie* for *Faust* and *Goetz von Berlichingen*. This morsel was delivered

---

Stendhal's young friend Victor Jacquemont (1801) suggested that he include in his piece some quotations from the "manifeste d'Auger; et que je trouve supérieures à ce que l'homme le plus spirituel peut inventer. C'est exactement le réquisitoire de Bellart contre les Carbonari." Jacquemont to Stendhal, 22 June 1824, H. Martineau, ed. *Cent soixante-quatorze lettres à Stendhal (1810–1842)* (Paris, 1947), 1:71.

[57] *Globe*, 7 April 1825.

[58] This was in response to Casimir Delavigne's acceptance speech at the Académie française. Casimir Delavigne, *Discours prononcés dans la séance publique tenue par l'Académie française pour la réception de M. Casimir Delavigne, le 7 juillet 1825* (Paris, 1825), 24. After praising the Academy for its politically disinterested appointment of Delavigne, Auger concludes (with obvious reference to Delavigne's *Messéniennes*) that the poets of France had no further reason to write about its conflicts and divisions.

[59] *Globe*, July 1825; also in *Fragments littéraires*, 1:86.

in a "barbarous burlesque accent" that apparently tickled Auger's audience, reported the editor of the *Globe*, who could only pity someone capable of praising Racine by sneering at Goethe.[60]

It is easy enough to see why both the style and content of Auger's effusions had little to commend them to young literary and political *frondeurs*. But one cannot simply place old royalists on one side of the political and literary barricade and young romantics on the other. The fatuous attack on romantics that stimulated Stendhal was, after all, praised in the liberal opposition's more or less official organ, the *Constitutionnel*, as a long overdue critique, "wise and calm."[61] The distance between young liberals and conservative academicians was plain to see; to establish their autonomy, they had to repudiate the condescending fellowship of such "liberal" journals as the *Constitutionnel* and such independent literary dignitaries as Etienne Jouy.

Born in 1764, Joseph-Victor Etienne Jouy managed to tack his way from career to career across the stormy seas of the revolutionary era before sailing into a snug berth as a successful man of letters. Junior officer in the prerevolutionary armies, soldier of the Revolution, briefly imprisoned as an accused counterrevolutionary in 1795, Napoleonic functionary, journalist, dramatist, librettist, essayist—the first half of Jouy's biography is scarcely consonant, in the words of a modern critic, with the subsequent image of a *vieille perruque*, a "powdered wig," petrified in his nostalgia for the cultural artifacts of the Old Regime.[62]

Toward the end of the Empire, Jouy's success as a playwright and librettist was surpassed by the popularity of the serialized observations of *l'Hermite de la Chaussée d'Antin* on "Parisian manners and morals at the beginning of the nineteenth century," a rather bland mixture of anecdote, local color, and reflections on the current scene, a contribution to a minor genre that is still gratefully exploited by historians. These popular sketches of the daily lives and times of the Parisians were followed by sequels that took the "hermit" to the provinces, to Guyane, and even to prison.

Jouy welcomed the return of the Bourbons in 1814 by composing an

---

[60] *Globe*, 30 November 1825; also in *Fragments littéraires*, 1:39–40.

[61] *Constitutionnel*, 26 April 1824.

[62] Claude Pichois, "Pour Une Biographie d'Etienne Jouy," *Revue des sciences humaines*, 118 (April–June 1965): 227–52; Ephraim Harpaz, *L'Ecole libérale sous la Restauration: Le "Mercure" et la "Minerve," 1817–1820* (Geneva, 1968), 11–12; Philarète Chasles, *Mémoires*, 2nd ed. (Paris, 1876), 1:224–37.

opera "in the midst of the first transports of joy caused by the most fortunate and memorable event," a passage appropriately quoted in the *Dictionnaire des girouettes*. Thus, as the Dictionnaire put it, he obtained the king's assent to his nomination to the Institut. During the Hundred Days, he earned additional *girouettes* with an "objective" analysis of the failure of the Bourbons to frustrate the flight of the eagle from Elba to Paris, and an appointment as commissioner of the Théâtre Feydeau.[63]

His royalist credentials rather frayed at the second coming of the king, Jouy joined the ranks of the liberals under the Second Restoration and effectively played up to the widespread tendency to assimilate a nostalgia for the Empire to an affirmation of public liberties. He was the hero of battles with royal censors over his historical dramas, *Bélisaire* and *Sylla*, onto which the most obtuse audience could project the memory of a recently departed hero, especially when the great actor Talma was got up to look just like Napoleon. With characteristic ineptitude, the regime even managed to ornament Jouy with a small martyr's halo. He and his journalistic confrere, Jay, were given a month's prison sentence for placing articles in a biographical dictionary that referred to the hasty trial and execution of Bonapartist officers after the Hundred Days. Jouy's cell became a salon thronged with admirers of the "martyrs of liberalism," and he and Jay subsequently capitalized on their calvary with the publication of a plural version of the hermit—*Les Hermites en prison*.

None of this disarmed Jouy's young critics. In part they reacted to that familiar patronizing of the young by the old. As early as 1811 l'Hermite was deploring the tendency of *les jeunes gens* to lay down the law on any subject—with characteristic snide comments on their bad manners.[64] Although Jouy insisted that he was not an enemy of fruitful

---

[63] [Proisy D'Eppe], *Dictionnaire des girouettes*, 243–49.

[64] Etienne Jouy, *L'Hermite de la Chaussée d'Antin: ou, Observations sur les moeurs et les usages au commencement du XIXe siècle*, 2nd ed. (Paris, 1813), 139. This selection from the "Observations détachées" of 24 October 1811 conveys Jouy's tone: "Ce qui distingue plus particulièrement le ton de la société actuelle, c'est la confiance que les jeunes gens y apportent, et l'influence qu'ils y exercent; point de question qui ne soit à leur portée; ils disputeront avec Humbold sur les voyages; avec Delille et Méhul sur la poésie et la musique. Il n'est pas rare, dans un salon où vingt personnes sont assises autour de feu, de voir un jeune homme debout devant la cheminée (tantôt jouant d'une manière assez indécente avec les basques de son habit, tantôt en face de la glace qu'il consulte avec complaisance), s'emparer de la conversation et débiter aussi sérieusement,

innovation and directed his facsimile of Voltairian wit against doctrinaire *classiques* as well as vaporous *romantiques*, he could not resist
crude little ad hominem quips about types whose romantic exultation
paved the road to the madhouse.[65]

Jouy was not obnoxious to young intellectuals merely because he
criticized them. To the editors of the *Globe*, Jouy was the exemplar of
that shallowness and frivolity that had come to characterize Parisian
letters. The prospectus of the *Globe* had dismissed *croquis de moeurs*,
those sketches of the local scene for which Jouy was best known, as the
sort of literary contribution that left the younger generations famished
for serious fare. An even deeper objection, I think, stemmed from the
Globe's distaste for the least attractive legacy of the eighteenth-century
philosophes—the tradition of the literary coterie publicly dedicated to
liberty and perfectly willing to call on the state to punish the enemies,
and advance the fortunes, of its members. With a notable lack of enthusiasm, the *Globe* observed the *lettrés de l'Empire* as they dined,
schemed, and arrived at the cultural summit together. Like Auger,
Jouy was known as a member of a group of cronies who plotted their
collective advance at the dinner table. Services rendered were repaid in
the coin of public compliments. "There is a new etiquette among the
lettrés de l'Empire," remarks Dubois, "when Boileau spoke of his friend
Racine, he said simply, Monsieur Racine. Messieurs Arnault and Jouy
say my illustrious friend; that is a little more than the *noble et honorable*,
exchanged by peers and deputies."[66] Jouy's ingenuity in self-advertise-
ment, his parading of a cult of Voltaire, his ostentatious name-drop-
ping, his palpable exploitation of sentimental Bonapartism in his historical dramas, all suggested to Dubois that the essential message of the
versatile publicist was "buy my books."

---

aussi péniblement qu'on l'écoute, une vieille anecdote rapportée dans tous les *Anas*, et
qu'il gâte en la déguisant sous des noms modernes."

[65] Pichois, "Pour Une Biographie d'Etienne Jouy," 245, points out that Jouy, like
most of the parties to the *bataille romantique*, rejected the categories of classic and romantic, but Pichois does cite the following lines: "L'exaltation *romantique* vous conduit
à l'extase mélancolique, d'où vous n'avez plus qu'un pas à faire pour arriver aux *Petites-
Maisons*." See also Pichois, *Philarète Chasles Et La Vie littéraire au temps du romantisme*
(Paris, 1965), 1:136. Jouy's refusal to identify with either romanticism or classicism is
in the *Pandore*, 29 March 1824, but that periodical, of which Jouy was one of the senior
editors, is filled with snide gibes at the romantics—for example, "Nécrologie, mort
d'un romantique." *Pandore*, 1 October 1824.

[66] *Globe*, 24 November 1824; also in *Fragments littéraires*, 1:30.

The ambitious young coterie of the *Globe* was itself, as contemporary critics would begin to note, perfectly willing to engage in back-
scratching and mutual puffery. Generously citing an article in another
journal by one of its own key contributors, the *Globe* praises Théodore
Jouffroy and identifies him as "one of those young professors" of the
Ecole normale, an institution whose termination was regretted by the
entire nation. This reveals a certain flair but is amateurish compared,
let us say, to the *Pandore*, one of several ephemeral periodicals floated
by Jouy and his companions, which was inspired by an edition of Jouy's
works to confess: "We have often praised even more than his wit and
his talent, the usefulness, the profundity, and the superior organization
of his ideas," and so forth.[67]

The *Globe* sardonically noted fulsome reference to the master in the
preface of a novel by Philarète Chasles (1798), a versatile young writer
who was constructing a career by describing Jouy on appropriate occasions as the contemporary equivalent of Pascal, Bossuet, Voltaire,
and Rousseau.[68] To the reviewer it seemed odd that someone fortunate
enough to be young and not an *académicien* should be so taken with a
prophet who preferred the past to the future. In this case, Jouy was the
antediluvian boulder in the path of progress, but he was only one of the
more visible members of the coterie, temporarily excluded from political power, which attempted to dominate culture, and careers in culture, especially through the control of influential journals. The *Globe*
urged young poets not to tremble before "that other Academy" of the
Constitutionnel and the *Mercure*, "which totters along like M. Auger
and is only sustained by the weekly eulogies that its members exchange
with habitual sand-froid and the regularity of men of affairs."[69]

It was the *Globe*'s defiance of "that other Academy" that enrolled it
on the side of the innovators in the *bataille romantique*. This is not the
place to refight this battle, but the issue of the relation of the generation
of 1820 to romanticism is inescapable. While I believe that the question
of whether there was a single romantic generation is misplaced, I
would apply Max Milner's comment, "Romanticism is perhaps above

[67] *Globe*, 20 October 1824; *Pandore*, 30 October 1824.

[68] Pichois, *Philarète Chasles*, 1:141. For Chasles' retrospective contempt for his mentor Jouy, see his thoroughly unreliable *Mémoires*, 1:229–327, and an even more negative
version in an expurgated passage published by Claude Pichois, "Les Vrais Mémoires
de Philarète Chasles," *Revue des sciences humaines*, 81 (January–March 1956): 78–79.

[69] *Globe*, 15 February, 31 March 1825.

all a revenge of the young,"[70] to the romanticism of the 1820s. Youth was the common denominator of what Milner identifies as "the generation of 1820," but, Milner adds, not necessarily in the biological sense—*pas forcément celle des artères.*[71] This qualifier responds to the fact that the definition of romanticism according to age distinctions is no more watertight than any of the other definitions. Charles Nodier, and Stendhal in his ambivalent way, belong on the youthful side of that barricade, while young liberals such as Thiessé (1793) and unreconstructed ultramontanes such as the abbé Gerbet (1798) took their stand in the classicist camp.[72] For our purposes, we need merely remark that whether or not romanticism was a generational phenomenon, that was certainly what the critics at the *Globe* intended it to be.

On what reasonable grounds, asked Ludovic Vitet, do *jeunes gens* who are friends of liberty refuse to accept romanticism? For liberals, he wrote, to do so was to accept a sort of moral servitude; for the young, it was to embrace old age.[73] Youth and liberty belonged on one side of the literary barricade, and all of the partisans of repression of whatever sort and from whatever camp belonged on the other. Thus, to Paul Dubois, the fundamental anomaly of contemporary culture was that "free thinkers in politics and religion are absolutists in literature and the protestants against the Academy almost all belong to the political party that is the enemy of change."[74] The history of the romanticism of

[70] Milner, *Le Romantisme*, 17.

[71] Ibid., 44. Milner notes here that "La notion de génération nous offrirait, pour jalonner notre période, des repères plus solides. Le romantisme français, cela ne fait pas de doute, est autant l'affaire d'une génération (ou plus exactement de deux) que d'une doctrine littéraire. . . . Car c'est bien la jeunesse—pas forcément celle des artères—qui constitue le dénominateur commun le plus évident de cette première génération romantique."

[72] See the citation in Chapter 1, note 16, and Paul Bénichou, *Le Sacre de l'écrivain, 1750–1830* (Paris, 1973), 302: "Mais si dans l'ensemble les idées nouvelles en littérature sont plutôt le fait de la génération suivante, le romantisme et l'anti-romantisme, pas plus chez les critiques libéraux que chez les ultras, ne sont essentiellement une question d'âge." Bénichou does entitle his section on Vigny, Hugo, and Sainte-Beuve, "Les Débuts de la grande génération." In *Le Romantisme*, Pierre Moreau identifies a romantic "Génération de 1815," and in *Le Classicisme des romantiques* distinguishes "la Génération du 'Génie du Christianisme' " from "la Génération d'Hernani." For a different approach, see Barbéris, "Mal du siècle," 1:164–82. For a recent attempt to make sense of the various ages of romanticism, see Allen, "Y-a-t-il en France une 'génération romantique de 1830'?" 103–18.

[73] *Globe*, 2 April 1825; also in Trahard, "Le Romantisme," 25–26.

[74] *Globe*, 12 October 1824; also in *Fragments littéraires*, 1:9.

the younger generation was to be the dissolution of that anomaly in the rapprochement of the partisans of political change and artistic innovation.[75]

The assimilation of literary criticism to liberal ideology allowed the *Globe* to engage in militant polemics in favor of a rather conservative aesthetic. It is often correctly remarked that the journal's liberalism aligned it against the counterrevolutionary, pietistic, and sentimental romanticism of the political right, and texts can be cited to characterize the *Globe* as more a critic than a defender of literary innovation.[76]

No doubt the journal's watchword was not, in literature or anything else, "revolution, that is to say, novelty at any price, but liberty, that is to say, reason."[77] However, the standards of truth and reason that were applied with a complacent severity to the self-indulgent melancholy of Lamartine or to the emotive "excesses" of Hugo or Vigny were leveled with real ferocity at the petrified classicism of the liberal literary establishment. The balance is struck in Dubois' review—more prescient than he dreamed—of the third volume of Hugo's *Odes et Ballades*:

> In rereading these verses, one dreams and is moved in the reading, while those cold versifiers, proud of their vulgar elegance, cannot even elicit a momentary pause before their pallid *tableaux*. Monsieur Victor Hugo is in poetry what Monsieur Delacroix is in painting; there is always a great idea, a profound sentiment, beneath their harsh infelicities; and I must admit, I like this youthful, abrasive vigor.[78]

[75] See Michaut, *Sainte-Beuve Avant Les "Lundis"*, 108–9: Stenzel and Thoma, in "Poésie et société dans la critique littéraire du *Globe*," 33–35, situate this development in the *Globe*'s effort to formulate an aesthetic appropriate to the ideological requirements of a capitalist society.

[76] The section of Gerbod's biography of Dubois devoted to this question is entitled "Mises en garde contre le romantisme"; *Paul-François Dubois*, 70–74; cf. Moreau, *Le Classicisme des romantiques*, 195–230; Michaut, *Sainte-Beuve Avant Les "Lundis,"* 97–110. For the opposing view—or, rather, a different emphasis—see René Bray, *Chronologie du romantisme (1804–1830)* (Paris, 1932), 130: "On s'est demandé si *Le Globe* était vraiment romantique. Cela ne semble pas discutable, à la condition qu'on veuille bien ne pas réduire le romantisme au credo de *La Muse française*."

[77] *Globe*, 6 November 1824.

[78] *Globe*, 4 November 1826; also in *Fragments littéraires*, 1:258. Christian A. E. Jensen, *L'Evolution du romantisme: L'Année 1826* (Geneva, 1959), 94, attributes this sympathetic evaluation to Hugo's poem in praise of Napoleon, but I believe that Dubois was responding to the virtues he described in the quoted passage.

Little wonder that Stendhal's version of a defense of romanticism was to the *Globe*'s taste, especially in his evocation of the shopworn rhetoricians. These were the types, observed the reviewer of *Racine et Shakespeare*, whose careers depended on persuading the "young people of the schools of law and medicine" that the introduction of a new genre constituted an attack on good taste and the crime of *lèse-nation*. Given a few more pamphlets by Monsieur Stendhal to help the *jeunesse* apprehend the vested interests of the literary pundits, and all will be lost for the editors of the *Mercure*, the *Constitutionnel*, and the *Pandore*.[79]

This treatment of the question scarcely amounts to the formulation of a new aesthetic theory, much less a contribution to innovative literary practice. At one point, the journal characterized the beliefs and theories of romanticism as entirely negative; not in the sense of a reluctance to grant praise, but as a repudiation of the routine official and authoritarian approach to culture.[80] Its critics were more comfortable with theoretical assertions favoring freedom from convention than with poetic practices violating their conventional expectations, and most at home in defending romanticism by attacking the neoclassical theater.

Their emphasis on the reform of the drama was also most consonant with the quest for artistic forms appropriate to the new era. The critical acumen of their reviews of the dreary succession of "successful" neoclassical dramas and historical tragedies and their clever and sensible polemics against the academized defenses of classical unities and dramatic proprieties helped to corrode the crumbling bastions of a moribund neoclassicism but could not constitute alternative texts for a living theater. The young partisans of a regenerated drama searched the horizon in vain for someone to bell their critical cat.

The disappointing results are suggested by the fact that literary histories still refer to plays read in various sympathetic salons by Charles Rémusat that were never published or performed. We know that one of these, *L'Insurrection de Saint-Domingue*, was read at the home of Paul Dubois to an audience that included most of the major contributors to the *Globe* and such familiar members of the intellectual network as Ary Scheffer, Thiers, Mignet, Cerclet, and Auguste Sautelet.

[79] *Globe*, 7 April 1825; also in Trahard, "Le Romantisme," 31–40.
[80] *Globe*, 29 October 1825.

Etienne Delécluze, old friend and friendly opponent of the young romantics, recalled that this and other readings had greatly stimulated
the interest and anticipation of the young intelligentsia.[81] Their expectations were gratified in the form of several short plays read before a
similar audience *chez* Delécluze by the twenty-two-year-old Prosper
Mérimée. The *Théâtre de Clara Gazul* was not to be staged but was almost immediately published by Sautelet. This was the providential text
for which the explications had already been provided, cut to the measure of the market for literary innovation.

Mérimée's collection of six short plays has often been characterized
as a hoax or a mystification because it was introduced as the work of a
Spanish actress, Clara Gazul, whose "portrait" on the cover was actually Ary Scheffer's lithograph of a sketch by Delécluze of Mérimée
draped in a mantilla.[82] This transparent disguise deceived almost no
one except the obtuse reviewer for the *Journal des débats*, who took the
bohémienne Clara Gazul and her French translator, M. L'Estrange, at
face value.[83] The androgynous portrait does express the ambiguity that
pervades the entire work. Critics still differ over the extent to which
the plays should be read as parody, or a pastiche of Spanish drama, or
as a serious attempt to break away from conventional representations,
or as a hastily written *jeu d'esprit*.

I defer to the distinguished scholars who continue to find in Mérimée's "sober and compact" theatrical art a psychologist of surprising
precocity, an early incarnation of the aesthetic doctrine of Stendhal, or
the first successful expression of romantic realism, even though the
"penetrating insights into the human passions" are formulated in mel-
odramatic clichés.[84] The plots of the plays are salted with sundry mur-

[81] Delécluze, *Souvenirs*, 268–72, and *Journal*, 136–43; Rémusat, *Mémoires*, 2:148–49.
There is a manuscript copy of Rémusat's play, titled, *L'Habitation de Saint Domingue;
ou, l'Insurrection*, in the Archives municipales of Toulouse that has been edited and
published under the direction of J. R. Derré: Charles de Rémusat, *L'Habitation de Saint
Domingue; ou, l'Insurrection* (Paris, 1977).

[82] This "portrait" is reproduced in *Théâtre de Clara Gazul*, with an introduction and
ancillary documents in Pierre Trahard and Edouard Champion, eds., *Oeuvres complètes de Prosper Mérimée* vol. 3 (Paris, 1927). I have cited this edition throughout. In
later editions Mérimée added three plays that I have not discussed here.

[83] From the 4 July 1825 issue, reproduced in a collection of reviews of *Clara Gazul* in
Mérimée, *Oeuvres*, 3:518–25.

[84] See Jules Marsan, *La Bataille romantique* (Paris, 1912), 135–38; Pierre Trahard, *La
Jeunesse de Prosper Mérimée* (Paris, 1925), 1:223; W. D. Howarth, *Sublime and Gro-*

ders, betrayals, adulteries, self-mutilations, suicides, and the transgressions of men of the cloth. Mérimée's sympathetic but bemused older friend Delécluze concluded that the dramas made fascinating reading but were scarcely appropriate to an audience of women and children.[85] Yet, however they appear to posterity's taste, they did enjoy a modest but unquestionable contemporary success. Stendhal, another close friend and mentor, thought that one would have to go back to Beaumarchais to find a work of equal merit. They were praised not only by Mérimée's friends but by such implacable opponents of romantic excess as the *Pandore*, the *Mercure*, and even the conservative *Journal des débats*.[86]

The *Globe* welcomed *Clara Gazul* as the answer to its critical prayers. Duvergier de Hauranne triumphantly proclaimed that the last weapon of the *classiques*, the challenge to the innovators to produce something worthwhile, had been struck from their hands. But even in the most enthusiastic reception of the work, even in the review of Mérimé's intimate friend J. J. Ampère, one senses a certain lack of conviction. Hailing the work as a brilliantly successful response to the demand for "a new literature appropriate to our times," Ampère enthusiastically praised it for its natural, unaffected, and "naive" manner and mildly criticized its somewhat brusque and hasty dramatic style. The gentle qualifications of the encomium stimulated a letter to the editor (probably written in the editorial office) chastising the reviewer for the discrepancy between the "extreme merit" of the work and the measured praise of the review. Ampère's answer was to thank the correspondent for an improved version of his own thoughts and for providing the opportunity to reaffirm his admiration of *Clara Gazul*.[87]

Somehow, all these effusions seemed to conceal a canker of doubt. Mérimée's contribution simply was not strong enough to carry the last

---

tesque: A Study of French Romantic Drama (London, 1975), 113–14; Robert Baschet, *Du Romantisme au Second Empire: Mérimée (1803–1870)* (Paris, 1958), 28–34; A. W. Raitt, *Prosper Mérimée* (New York, 1970), 45–62. For a useful survey of the recent literature, see Barbara T. Cooper, "Mérimée's Romantic Theater: The Present State of Scholarship," *Nineteenth-Century French Studies*, 6 (Fall–Winter 1977–78): 72–81.

[85] Delécluze, *Journal*, 156.

[86] Stendhal's references to the plays are collected in Baschet, *E.-J. Delécluze*, 170. A selection of the reviews is reprinted in Mérimée, *Oeuvres*, 3:503–37.

[87] Duvergier de Hauranne in the *Globe*, 11 June 1825; Ampère in the *Globe*, 4 June and 9 July 1825; letter to the editor on Ampère's review, *Globe*, 18 June 1825; all are reprinted in Mérimée, *Oeuvres*, 3:503–14.

CHAPTER 5

The *Muse Francaise*, the Literary Orbit of Victor Hugo, and the Generational Fission of the Romantics

> "Our fathers, who had not suffered, only asked of
> the arts that they divert the mind; we wish them
> to fortify the soul."
> Victor Hugo, *Le Reveil*, 25 September 1822

The history of the *Muse française*
was over before that of the *Globe* began. Its editors claimed to
speak for youth, although they were not as tightly clustered as the
cohort of the *Globe* and the *Producteur*. The journal's brief career
comprises a chapter in a story of generational conflict that began
several years before its founding in the articulation of a royalist
romanticism and culminated after its demise when Victor Hugo,
the most brilliant and precocious paladin of the new aesthetic,
passed with all his literary baggage into the camp of the opposition to the conservative cultural establishment.

The relation of the literary *jeunesse* to a conservative romanticism was complex and unstable. It was first manifested through
the minority of young writers who expressly repudiated the rationalist, anticlerical, revolutionary heritage of the eighteenth
century and who fought the *bataille romantique* in a coalition of
conservative advocates of artistic innovation. The coalition was to
split under the pressures of the campaign and fracture to some
extent along generational lines. One cannot confine the cohort of
young royalist writers to the person of Victor Hugo, who left
some of his closest friends and coevals under the old white banner
when he crossed the political barricades, but Hugo's incredible
precocity incarnated the attempt to assimilate youth with nostalgia and to identify the rejection of the revolutionary legacy with
the poetic affirmation of the spirit of the new century.[1]

[1] Reference to Victor Hugo can now proceed from the new chronological edi-

Hugo made his debut at the age of fifteen with the award of an honorable mention at the *concours poétique* of the Académie française and took his first step toward public recognition as a mature talent in yet another *concours*—the poetic Jeux floraux of Toulouse. This institution, which could trace partly authentic, partly legendary antecedents back to the Middle Ages, boasted its own forty-member academy, which honored worthy authors as masters and mistresses of the Jeux floraux and awarded jeweled flowers to contestants in various poetic categories each year in May.[2] In the early years of the Restoration, this was the special preserve of poets whose political sentiments were royalist and whose literary efforts seemed to place them somewhere in the movement to liberate literature from the heavy hand of the great Paris Academy.

In 1819, the seventeen-year-old Hugo submitted two conventional poems on irreproachable topics. "The Virgins of Verdun" was awarded the golden amaranth, "réservée" (a sort of second prize), and his "Ode to the Restoration of the Statue of Henry IV" carried off the special prize of the golden lily.[3] They elicited a flattering letter from Alexandre Soumet, Master of the Jeux floraux, rising star of the poetic and theatrical horizon, and soon to become a central figure in the founding of the *Muse française*.

That milestone of the romantic movement was anticipated in 1819 by the publication of the *Conservateur littéraire* by Victor Hugo and his brothers, Abel and Eugène.[4] The senior member of the editorial board

---

tion of his complete works, which includes extensive commentary, notes, and a bibliography. Victor Hugo *Oeuvres complètes*, ed. Jean Massin (Paris, 1967–70), henceforth cited as Hugo, *Oeuvres*. Volumes 1 and 2 cover the period to 1827. See also Edmund Biré, *Victor Hugo Avant 1830*, 2nd ed. (Paris, 1883); Abbé Pierre Dubois, *Bio-Bibliographie de Victor Hugo de 1802 à 1825* (Paris, 1913); Géraud Venzac, *Les Origines religieuses de Victor Hugo* (Paris, 1955), and *Les Premiers Maîtres de Victor Hugo* (Paris, 1955); Jean-Bertrand Barrère, *Victor Hugo: L'Homme et l'oeuvre* (Paris, 1952).

[2] Frédéric Ségu, *L'Académie des jeux floraux et le romantisme de 1818 à 1824* (Paris, 1935). Also, see below, chapter 8.

[3] The *Vierges de Verdun* were martyrs of the revolutionary tribunal, in royalist legend the objects of Fouquier-Tinville's lust. The ode on the *Rétablissement de la statue de Henri IV* was the subject of a special competition.

[4] The *Conservateur littéraire* survived from December 1819 to March 1821. Two of its three volumes have been reissued with an introduction by Jules Marsan. See Marsan, *Le Conservateur littéraire, 1819–1821*, 4 vols. (Paris, 1922-26, 1935–38). Victor Hugo's contributions to the journal are reproduced in *Oeuvres*, 1:467–771.

was Abel, who was twenty-one. This example of the remarkable opportunities available to very young writers with sufficient nerve and
ambition was not precisely launched into a void. The brothers had all
fashioned reputations, and their journal, which was named in deference to Chateaubriand's political paper, the *Conservateur*, received
that journal's benediction.[5] The militant ultraroyalist François Agier
commended it as a touching example of filial piety, recompense for the
devotion of the editors' saintly—that is, implacably royalist—mother,
and as a healthy fruit of good principles and a sound education. It was
reassuring, he wrote, to observe "this throng of *jeunes gens* who love
literature for itself" and to forecast a brilliant future for the *grands talents* in their midst.[6]

The *grand talent* already manifest was that of Victor. The *Conservateur littéraire* was the product of his precocity—remarkable even in
a world of twenty-three-year-old professors of philosophy and brilliant
barristers under the age of twenty-five—and of his immense creative
energy.[7] Until the paper folded, he provided most of the contributions—reviews, essays, poems—revealing a grasp of classical literature
and a general erudition that allowed him to pose, not too implausibly,
as a world-weary old (anonymous) critic, deploring the decline in literary education, admonishing the young poets not to confuse the *genre
érotique* with the *genre purement élégiaque*, and warning *jeunes gens* not
to be too hasty in trying their wings—better to conserve their energies:
"You will need them on the day of battle; lesser birds cast themselves
aloft; eagles gain momentum before mounting on their wings."[8] But,
of course, everyone knew where a young eagle was testing his wings.

Without pretending to contribute to the immense literature on the
precise nature of Victor Hugo's early ambivalences, one can observe

[5] Abel, the eldest, had co-authored a *Traité du mélodrame* in 1817. Eugène's ode on
the death of the Duc D'Enghien had been "crowned" by the Academy of the poetic
Jeux floraux at Toulouse in 1818. Victor had managed the phenomenal feat of winning
an honorable mention in the poetry competition of the Académie française at the age
of fifteen. See chapter 7.

[6] *Conservateur*, 6 (1820): 470.

[7] In 1827 Sainte-Beuve wrote that Hugo owed his "étonnante précocité et à la
trempe de son âme et aux circonstances de ses plus tendres années." *Globe*, 2 January
1827, reprinted in Hugo, *Oeuvres*, 2:1588.

[8] "Réflexions morales et politiques sur les avantages de la monarchie, par MMe C.
de M### (Premier article)," *Conservateur littéraire*, no. 4, January 1820; "Revue poétique," no. 14, July 1820; "Marie Stuart," no. 9, April 1820.

that, in the midst of all the royalist pieties, religious effusions, and reactionary sentiments affected by the *Conservateur littéraire*, he and his
fellow contributors struck familiar chords in the new generational leitmotif.

The hope of the future lay with the *jeunesse lettrée*, a predictable prediction in light of Hugo's restriction of the poetic spirit to those who
had never "calculated the price of wrongdoing or the wages of deceit."
His satirical poem, "L'Enrôleur politique" which introduced the first
issue of the journal, opposed the model of the principled young poet to
the familiar figure of the cynical *girouette*.[9] Of course the turncoats tar-
geted in the *Conservateur littéraire* were all stationed in the liberal or
ministerial camp, but, the poet muses, how few mature men of letters
had not tuned their lyres to the prevailing political winds. This last is
an observation inserted in his review of Lamartine's *Méditations poétiques*, which concludes with the passage often cited as an anticipation
of the reviewer's own Promethean future:

> Courage, young man, you are one of those whom Plato wished to
> cover with honors and banish from his Republic. You too can ex-
> pect to be banished from our land of anarchy and ignorance, and
> your exile will even lack the recognition of palms, parades, and
> flowered crowns that Plato granted the poets.[10]

Yet there is little in all of this to identify idealistic youth with literary
innovation. When Hugo contrasted Lamartine, "classic among the romantics," with Chenier, "romantic among the classics," referring to
"more or less insignificant distinctions," or when he remarked that
"the works of Shakespeare and Schiller only differ from the works of
Corneille and Racine to the extent that they are more faulty," or when
he praised the *directeur* of the Académie française for his sage discourse
on the danger of literary innovation, he revealed how far he had yet to
travel on the road to an artistic revolution.[11] Paul Bénichou is, however,
surely correct to remark that the intensity with which Hugo lived the
"adventure of the *poésie royaliste*" led by an integral logic to rebellion

---

9 "Préface (au tome troisième)," *Conservateur littéraire*, no. 21, September 1820;
"Méditations poétiques," no. 10, April 1820; "L'Enrôleur politique," no. 1, December
1819. Hugo also wrote (but did not publish) a poem, "Dialogue entre le drapeau et la
girouette." *Oeuvres*, 1:417–18.

10 "Méditations poétiques," *Conservateur littéraire*, no. 10, April 1820.

11 "Marie Stuart," *Conservateur littéraire*, no. 9, April 1820; "Séance publique annuelle des quatre académies," no. 12, May 1820.

against the classic forms. That rebellion would ultimately entail the repudiation of a *poésie royaliste*, but the first steps along that path revealed no discrepancy between a creative reconstruction of the arts and the conservative *politique*. In 1822 the first preface to Hugo's collected odes asserted that "human history only presents poetry judged from the height of monarchical ideas and religious beliefs."[12]

Monarchical ideas and religious beliefs were to cement a literary coalition committed to a crusade against the frozen authority of the classic forms, a coalition that was anticipated in a notice in the August 1820 issue of the *Conservateur littéraire* announcing the arrival at Paris of Alexandre Soumet, "who enjoys such a distinguished place among our young poets." This was the Toulouse connection. Soumet (1786) and his friends from the Midi, Alexandre Guiraud (1788) and Jules de Rességuier (1788), brought the prestige of the Jeux floraux to a Parisian circle that included Hugo and his young friends Adolphe de Saint-Valry (1796), Alfred de Vigny, and Gaspard de Pons (1798), to form a *cénacle* whose spiritual and chronological center was Emile Deschamps.

Thanks to the magnetism of charm and enthusiasm, rather than distinguished publication, Deschamps assembled at his father's home a group rather heterogeneous in age, talent, and literary taste but possessing in common a transient sentimental affinity for monarchy, religion, and the resolution to rejuvenate poetry in France.[13] They are fixed forever in that cold, unflattering, retrospective light that Sainte-Beuve cast on so many of his contemporaries:

> ... young men distinguished by their education or their refined sensibilities, loving art, poetry, flattering portraits, and tasteful recreations, royalists born, Christians out of decorum and vague sentiment, [who] had come to believe that the time was ripe to fashion a small, sheltered world apart.[14]

However sheltered and sentimental, this group did not lack the energy and talent to carry their convictions into the public arena and to organize and edit an influential literary journal, the *Muse française*. Under

[12] Bénichou, *Le Sacre de l'écrivain*, 386; Hugo, *Oeuvres*, 2:5.

[13] The fullest description of the group is in Henri Girard, *Un Bourgeois dilettante à l'époque romantique: Emile Deschamps, 1791–1871* (Paris, 1921), 90–104. For Deschamp's characterization of this *cénacle*, see Emile Deschamps, *Oeuvres complètes* (Paris, 1873), 4:301–2.

[14] Sainte-Beuve, *Portraits contemporains*, 1:409.

the leadership of Emile Deschamps, several young writers, including Hugo and Vigny, joined those luminaries from the south, Guiraud and Soumet, to launch the *Muse* into that brief career that has guaranteed it a permanent niche in the histories of French romanticism.[15]

The lasting interest in the periodical owes a great deal to the towering presence of Victor Hugo, and also to Vigny, but at the time it was the collaboration of Soumet that added luster to the enterprise. Soumet's contemporary reputation, especially the enthusiasm he aroused in the young, puts the sort of strain on the historical imagination that we have associated with the remarkable prestige of Victor Cousin.[16] Master of the Jeux floraux, brilliantly successful poet, Soumet now gloriously fulfilled his promise with two openings on the Paris stage within a week. The plays, *Clytemnestre* and *Saul*, provoked considerable indignation among the guardians of the classical proprieties and fulsome praise from such youthful partisans of literary innovation as Hugo, who defended Soumet in an open letter to the *Moniteur* against a literary faction, "that is antipoetic because it is irreligious and antisocial."[17] To our hindsight, Soumet's dramas seem rather conventional efforts at historical tragedy, and, in the event, his commitment to the camp of the literary rebels was not to be proof against the lure of the cultural establishment.[18]

In the beginning, under the aegis of Soumet and Guiraud, the *Muse française* enjoyed the shelter of established reputations and the support of such royalist strongholds as the Société des bonnes lettres.[19] The

[15] The *Muse française* was republished in a two-volume edition with a useful introduction by Jules Marsan. See Marsan, ed., *La Muse française* (Paris, 1907). It is mentioned in virtually every work on French romanticism. See Léon Séché, *Le Cénacle de la "Muse française," 1823–1827* (Paris, 1909); Girard, *Emile Deschamps*, 104–18; Bray, *Chronologie du romantisme*, 78–117; Marsan, *La Bataille romantique* (Paris, 1912), 55–105.

[16] Séché, *Le Cénacle de la "Muse française"*, 1–53, 114–17; A. Beffort, *Alexandre Soumet: Sa Vie et ses oeuvres* (Luxembourg, 1908); Milner, *Le Romantisme*, 359–60. See, for example, Alfred de Vigny, *Correspondance d' Alfred de Vigny, 1816–1863* (Paris, 1905), 5, where Vigny compares Soumet favorably to Lamartine.

[17] *Moniteur universel*, 26 November 1822.

[18] Howarth, *Sublime and Grotesque*, 102.

[19] The Société des bonnes lettres was founded in 1821 as the royalist answer to the liberal association, the Athénée. Such leading conservative writers and politicians as Chateaubriand, Vitrolles, and Polignac provided a platform for young defenders of throne and altar, such as the brothers Hugo, Emile Deschamps, and Vigny. Bray,

journal certainly did live up to its royalist credentials, but it welcomed among its contributors such mavericks as Jules Lefèvre (1797) and the Bonapartist poet and sometime conspirator Louis Belmontet.[20] It also welcomed the poetic contributions of a group of women who were praised for their tenderness and sensibility (for being "romantic" in the hackneyed sense of the term) but who were still accepted on less patronizing terms than customary even in the liberal reviews.[21]

Although the contributors to the journal were drawn from various age groups,[22] it presented itself as the voice of youth, determined, as its prospectus promised, to take up where the obsolescent "fathers of criticism" left off, speaking in the name of Hugo's "sweet and serious generation," and complaining of a "vast system of persecution organized at all points of the republic of letters against the new romantic generation."[23] For a brief period, as Bénichou acutely remarks, counterrevolutionary royalism had managed to place the stamp of youth on the prestige of the past.[24]

Chronologie du romantisme, 58–61; Margaret H. Peoples, "La Société des bonnes lettres (1821–1830)," in *Smith College Studies in Modern Languages*, 5 (October 1923): 1–50.

[20] Jules Lefèvre (subsequently Lefèvre-Deumier, to honor a relative who left him an inheritance), thought to be a liberal or even a republican, published an ode in honor of the opposition orator General Foy in 1825. He was the incarnation of his generation's *mal du siècle*. P. L. Jacob, "Notice biographique," in Jules Lefèvre-Deumier, *Sir Lionel D'Arquenay* (Paris, 1884), 1:i–lvi; Georges Brunet, Introduction to Jules Lefèvre-Deumier, *Les Vespres de l'Abbaye du Val* (Paris, 1924), ix–cxi; Sainte-Beuve, *Portraits contemporains*, 2:249–61. Louis Belmontet, probably a member of the Carbonari in the 1820s, was a lifelong Bonapartist. Germain Sarrut and B. Saint-Edme, *Biographie des hommes du jour* (Paris, 1836), 1 (Part 2): 14; Rémusat, *Mémoires*, 2:536; Adolphe Robert and Gaston Cougny, comps. *Dictionnaire des parlementaires français* (Paris, 1889), 1:248–49.

[21] The women published in the *Muse française* were Delphine Gay, Adelaide Dufrenoy, Marceline Desbordes-Valmore, Amable Tastu, and Hortense Céré-Barbé.

[22] The founders and major contributors to the *Muse française* cluster into two cohorts (with the few exceptions noted below). One was the generation of 1820: Victor Hugo (1802), Alfred de Vigny (1797), Adolphe de Saint-Valry (1796), Gaspard de Pons (1798), and Jules Lefèvre (1797). The other was the older generation: Alexandre Soumet (1786), Alexandre Guiraud (1788), Jules de Rességuier (1788), and Ulric Guittinger (1785). Emile Deschamps (1791) was, chronologically and practically, the link between the two groups. Other contributors range along the age spectrum from Jacques Ancelot (1794) to Baour Lormain (1754).

[23] Citations to the *Muse française* refer to volumes 1 and 2 of the Marsan edition. "Avant-Propos," July 1823, 1:4; "Essai sur l'indifférence," August 1823, 1:75; "La guerre en temps de paix," May 1824, 2:272.

[24] Bénichou, *Le Sacre de l'écrivain*, 297.

The *Muse française* conceived its raison d'être as renewal of poetic theory and practice, opening "an immense field yet to be harvested by the new generation." This commitment proceeded from the assumption that the new era required new modes of literary expression and from the virtually universal metaphor of an era of ruins. "The young and observant man who enters the world immediately after a revolution seems to have come upon the theater of a vast conflagration" where, amidst the tragic wreckage of the old civilization, he can discern the outlines of a new art: "We march across the ruins," sobered by memories that limit our muse to songs that are sad and severe.[25]

According to Alexandre Guiraud, the solution to the problem of reconciling a literature appropriate to a "new world regenerated by the baptism of blood" with the veneration of the old idols destroyed by the Revolution would be the repudiation of those products of eighteenth-century culture subversive of the monarchic and religious old order. Irreligion, above all, was in essence antipoetic, and the frivolous and shallow language of the eighteenth-century literati had nothing to say to those born into the new century. "It is not in the century of Bonaparte that one can continue Voltaire," says Hugo.[26] The royalist romantics attempted to maintain their connection with the cultural Great Tradition of the monarchy by reaching across the eighteenth century to the seventeenth. "Don't our recent glories," asked Alexandre Guiraud, presenting a rather eclectic list of contemporary literary stars, "attest to the literary fellowship of our young century with the *Grand siècle?*"[27]

This solution did not resolve all of the tensions and contradictions of the attempt to define the relationship between a literature appropriate to the new era and the literary monuments of the French past. This is to say that the contributors to the *Muse française* can be subsumed under the rubric of the "classicism of the romantics" as appropriately as the editors of the *Globe* and that they expressed their ambivalence in much the same language.[28] Emile Deschamps advises young poets to remember "that beside the imagination that creates should always be found the good taste that preserves, and that the music of the modern

[25] *Muse française*, 1:243, 2:328, 86, 21, 301.

[26] Ibid., 2:21, 301.

[27] Guiraud lists Soumet, Lamartine, Ancelot, Casimir Delavigne, Victor Hugo, Charles Nodier, Pichald, and Alfred de Vigny. Ibid., 86.

[28] Moreau, *Le Classicisme des romantiques*, 164–95.

muse needs to be played on the magnificent instrument of the Racines and the Boileaus."[29]

The tension involved in advocating a new aesthetic while continuing to venerate the old characterized the entire course of French romanticism, but the tensions in the circle of the *Muse française* were peculiarly sharpened because of the context in which they had to operate, a context that was inescapably political. The editors of the *Muse* did not conceal their loyalties, but they had promised that their critical judgments would transcend their political preferences. In his reaffirmation of "our doctrines" at the beginning of the second volume, Guiraud remarked that the struggle over literary values was not exclusively between "two political parties" but between those who felt with their hearts as well as their heads and those who trusted only to reason and memory to guide them through well-worn routes in the realm of the imagination.[30]

Despite sincere affirmations of the priority of the poetic imagination, it would be impossible for the *Muse* to transcend the pressure of political commitment. From the first it was the object of ferocious attacks from the left, especially in the columns of the *Mercure*, where the mutual admiration of the editors of the *Muse* was presented as the self-promotion of a literary clique.[31] The critics of the *Muse* did indeed burn incense at each other's altars as thick as anything sent up by Jouy and Company, but in the face of such aspersions they stoutly defended their obligation to give credit where credit was due.[32] They were less resolute in facing down criticism from another quarter. The sharp attacks from the liberal direction did not bestow credentials sufficient to placate the increasingly vocal defenders of all the orthodoxies. The *Société des bonnes lettres*, which had welcomed young recruits to the royalist platform, and even the Academy of the Jeux floraux, turned against those whose repudiation of the grand tradition of French letters was seen as one more expression of the spirit of the revolution.

Auger's famous fulmination at the Academy was the centerpiece of this campaign, but other distinguished spokesmen for the established

---

[29] *Muse française*, 1:244.

[30] Ibid., 1:5–6; 2:23.

[31] Bray, *Chronologie du romantisme*, 98–119.

[32] As Victor Hugo put it in his review of Vigny's *Eloa* in the *Muse française*, 2:257: "Je ne sais par quelle bizarre manie on prétend refuser aujourd'hui au génie le droit d'admirer hautement le génie."

order, including Bishop Frayssinous, conveyed the unmistakable warning that the aggressive denigration of literary conventions might prove to be a grave practical mistake. The royal government's attitude toward artistic innovation remained ambivalent—Lamartine and Hugo were granted various perquisites by the ministry—but the powers of the Academy and the critics in the royalist journals spoke with sufficient clarity to encourage some of the contributors to the *Muse française* to change camps or at least to take a prudent distance from the literary rebels.[33]

The sad result was that just as victory had begun to crown the cohorts of the *bataille romantique*, the combatants at the *Muse française* fell back in a retreat that ended with the liquidation of the journal. Not that the retreat was a sudden rout. Some positions were bitterly defended almost to the last, and divisions in the staff were reflected in the variety of critical perspectives. As late as the issue of April 1824, Charles Nodier sallied out of his secure fortress at the Arsenal to contribute "De Quelques Logomachies classiques," the only essay he wrote for the *Muse*. Among other pungent observations, he noted that the politics of antiromanticism made strange bedfellows:

> It has become good form to attack the romantic genre without knowing precisely what it is. Politics itself has momentarily suspended its exclusive pretensions, forgetting notorious incompatibilities to adjust itself to literary alignments. The *Quotidienne* has offered a holocaust of the romantics to the *Courrier*, and there has been a temporary truce in order to consummate the immolation between friends.[34]

Nine days after Nodier's clever polemic, Auger delivered the establishment's anathema on the "new literary schism." As we have already covered that ground, it is sufficient to note that the *Muse française* believed itself to be directly in the line of fire. This was "war in time of peace," as Deschamps entitled his response to Auger in the May issue of the *Muse*. The ambivalent and self-contradictory nature of this piece foreshadows the journal's demise. The essay falls into two disparate parts; the first and longest is a witty pastiche of the various antiromantic clichés. Deschamps concludes that the *classiques* have identified as

---

[33] Bray, *Chronologie du romantisme*, 98–119.
[34] *Muse française*, 2:196.

romantic that which is poetic and that therefore the conflict "between classics and romantics is nothing but the eternal war between prosaic spirits and poetic souls." Then, just at the point where he caricatures Auger as the *procureur général* of the literary supreme court, there is an abrupt change of tone. Deschamps' evident disagreement with Auger is diluted with expressions of respect for the severe but objective critique of this "wise academician." After entering a few additional tentative, respectful objections to some of Auger's remarks, Deschamps promises to continue the discussion in a subsequent issue. That issue never appeared. The discussion had been temporarily suspended, wrote Deschamps in the following number, because Byron had died, and the issue of June 1824, the last to appear, was devoted to his memory.[35]

The story of the self-destruction of the *Muse française* exemplifies the extent to which artistic production and aesthetic ideals were enmeshed in a nexus of personal, political, and institutional relationships. The immediate source of the journal's demise was not so much intimidation as temptation. The Academy let it be known that Alexandre Soumet, the oldest and, with the possible exception of Victor Hugo, the most successful of the original *Muse* circle, might be a viable candidate for one of the immortal seats, but only if he freed himself from any association with those literary adventurers dedicated to the corruption of the French language and the worship of foreign idols. This *démarche* of cultural diplomacy is the background of Emile Deschamps' ambivalent response to Auger's anathema. Deschamps was about to contribute to his friend's ascension to Olympus by liquidating the last obstacle to the ascent.

Various authorities have questioned Soumet's candidacy as the cause of the termination, citing the split among the editors over a critical review of Lamartine and the dismissal of their hero Chateaubriand from the government. But S. Irving Stone has plausibly argued, with reference to letters bearing on the crisis, that the candidacy was indeed the immediate cause.[36]

[35] Ibid., 2:263–79.

[36] Séché, *Le Cénacle de la Muse française*, 96–110; Girard, *Emile Deschamps*, 115–18. For the view that Soumet's candidacy was indeed the cause, see S. Irving Stone, "La Fin de la 'Muse française,'" *Revue d'histoire littéraire de la France*, 36 (1929): 270–77; and Bray, *Chronologie du romantisme*, 112–15. The most recent variant of this interpretation is Jean Massin, "La Fin de la 'Muse française' et la mort de l'enfant sublime," in

The conflict over the decision to liquidate the *Muse* was conducted roughly, if not completely, along generational lines. As the date for the elections to the vacant chair at the Academy approached, Soumet retired from the staff. Then Deschamps insisted that the July issue carry the statement disassociating himself, Soumet, Guiraud, and de Rességuier from the journal, and then, in the teeth of Hugo's resolution to carry on, and objections mailed in from the provinces by Vigny, it was decided that the July issue must never appear.[37] Vigny consoled himself with the thought that Soumet would be their Trojan horse within the walls of the Academy. "We have given up the *Muse* in exchange for his seat,"[38] he wrote with misplaced optimism, for Soumet's acceptance speech celebrating the French monopoly of the rules of literary taste revealed that he had passed over, bands playing and banners flying, into the enemy lines.[39]

There is something in all of this of young idealists let down by somewhat older literary operators, or, as Jean Massin puts it, the "adventurers" (Hugo and Vigny) were outmaneuvered by the "intriguers" (Soumet and Deschamps). Massin concludes that the real issue was whether romanticism was a party whose interests demanded the tactics of compromise or a movement that had to obey its own dynamics.[40] These positions represented contradictory conclusions drawn from the ultimate irreconcilability of literary innovation with the ideology of the Restoration.[41] The very justification for the founding of the *Muse française*, the conviction that the French Revolution had created a new era requiring new forms of literary expression, could not be assimilated by a regime that had defined 1814 as the nineteenth year of the reign of Louis XVIII.

Shortly after the demise of the *Muse française*, Bishop Frayssinous,

---

Hugo, *Oeuvres*, 2:1446. This is also the interpretation of Adèle Hugo, *Victor Hugo raconté par un témoin de sa vie*, which, however, confuses the *Revue française* with the *Muse française*. Hugo, *Oeuvres*, 2:1022.

[37] Guiraud subsequently said that his name had been added without his permission.

[38] Vigny to Edouard Delprat, 1 September 1824, in Vigny, *Correspondance*, 81.

[39] This should have come as no surprise. In his laudatory review of Hugo's *Nouvelles Odes* in the *Muse française*, 2:143–54, Soumet observes that, like Hugo, he does not know what "romantique" means but that such "bizarres compositions" as *Faust* and *Goetz von Berlichingen* had only been admired in France out of ignorance.

[40] Massin in Hugo, *Oeuvres*, 2:1447.

[41] Bénichou, *Le Sacre de l'écrivain*, 297: "Ainsi l'idée d'une rénovation, littéraire et sociale, finit par l'emporter, dans un milieu tout royaliste, sur celle de la restauration."

Grand Master of the University and champion orator of the *bien-pensants*, nailed on the lid in his discourse at the ceremony for the distribution of the prizes for the yearly *concours* of the great Paris *collèges*. In the light of his solemn duty to warn his young charges against "the invasions of bad taste," he was obliged to deliver a rebuke to those who presumed themselves superior to Fénelon, Racine, Bossuet, and the other giants of "our *grand siècle littéraire*," and who affected

> a secret aversion for whatever is simple, clear, natural, and beautiful; they seem to prefer anything affected, false, bizarre, and nebulous; a new style had entailed new theories, and literature as well as philosophy has its Sophists. Let us never forget that common sense should be the touchstone and that the uncontrolled imagination is close to madness.[42]

Frayssinous' malediction, like the admonitions of Auger, ran counter to the aspirations of a generation that, in the words of Max Milner, "had thought it possible to consummate the alliance of the aristocracy of the intellect with the aristocracy of birth." Faced with implacable opposition of the fogeys in the royalist camp, those who staked themselves on the future were impelled to seek an ideology that would liberate them from the shackles forged by the partisans of the past.[43]

This is not to imply that the political regime did not do everything possible to bind young talent to the system. Lamartine and Hugo were granted the glorious assignment of composing Charles X's coronation odes. Hugo wrote the odes and savored the celebrity but by 1825 was well on his way to assuming the leadership of that "sacred band" in his crusade for a new cultural order. Even before the birth of the *Muse française*, he had taken his stand with the "genius of this century" against that "moribund literature of the last century" and those critics who persecuted the reborn spirit of Racine in the name of his corpse.[44] As late as the preface to the 1824 edition of his *Nouvelles Odes*, however, Hugo still affected the familiar stance of not grasping the distinction between classic and romantic. "In literature," he said, in virtually the

[42] *Moniteur universel*, 17 August 1824.

[43] Milner, *Le Romantisme*, 60.

[44] Review of "Le Parricide" by Jules Lefèvre, in the *Réveil*, 19 February 1823, in Hugo, *Oeuvres*, 2:49–52.

words of Jouy, "as in everything else, there is only the good and the bad, the beautiful and the deformed, the true and the false."[45]

In his contributions to the *Muse française*, Hugo had continued to exercise a certain restraint, but he made it clear enough that he had no intention of deserting the field. As the pressure mounted, he hardened his position. In the eleventh issue of the *Muse*, which contained Deschamp's equivocating answer to Auger, Hugo enthusiastically praised Vigny's mystical poem *Eloa* with sarcastic reference to "the classical defenders of healthy literary doctrines."[46]

The last issue, dedicated to the memory of Byron, contained Hugo's heroic effort to square the ideological-aesthetic circle. There was simply no way to evaluate Byron's demonic spirit from the perspective of "monarchic ideals and religious beliefs," but he could be justified as an authentic voice of the new era in contrast to "that Muse that had celebrated Cardinal Dubois, flattered *La Pompadour*, and outraged our Joan of Arc." It was a mistake to identify the satanic defiance of the English poet with the laughter of Voltaire. "Voltaire had not suffered."[47] Thus Hugo made one more attempt to assimilate the defenders of classicism, many of whom were enthusiastic supporters of restored crown and church, to the atheistic, cynical, subversive literature of the eighteenth century.

The time for such subtle distinctions was almost past. Within a month of the demise of the *Muse française*, Hugo answered an attack on romanticism in the *Journal des débats* with a vigorous and combative defense of the new school.[48] He was yet to draw out the political consequences of his literary rebellion. His coronation ode pealed out the praise of a crown "weighed down with the glory of sixty kings," but the ninth day after the coronation found him writing to his friend Saint-Valry, "I understand that they are saying that I have abjured my 'literary heresies,' as has our great poet Soumet. Vigorously deny that assertion wherever possible. You will be doing me a favor."[49]

The preface to the 1826 edition of Hugo's *Odes* proceeded from the familiar prudent assertion that "the only genuine distinction in the works of the mind is that of good and bad," but he no longer referred

[45] Hugo, *Oeuvres*, 2:470.
[46] *Muse française*, 2:248.
[47] Ibid., 297–309.
[48] Ibid., 553.
[49] Hugo to Saint-Valry, 7 May 1825, in Hugo, *Oeuvres*, 2:1468.

to the religious essence of the poetic spirit. Nature and truth were now identified as the sole models for the poet. The preface pointedly rejected, in words very like those of the gladiators of the *Globe*, the self-proclaimed *classiques* who confounded imitation, pedantry, and routine with art.[50]

In March 1826 the *Globe* reviewed *Bug-Jargal*, the second version of Hugo's novel on the slave insurrection in Saint-Domingue. The generally favorable review discerned Hugo's embarrassment as a royalist in portraying rebellion with sympathy but credited him with an eloquent repudiation of slavery.[51] With all deliberate speed and appropriate reservations, the *Globe* was moving toward recognition of Hugo as one of its own.

Dubois' review of the 1826 edition of the *Odes et Ballades* was matched with a personal rapprochement. On receiving a copy of the book, Dubois made a visit to the young poet and came away with the resolution to do justice to Hugo's work. The pressure of time forced him to assign this task to his protégé Sainte-Beuve,[52] whose two-part review in the *Globe* in January 1826 was, with certain reservations, a laudatory retrospective survey of the *oeuvre* of a major poet. Hugo came round to see the young critic and forged that friendship and intellectual partnership that might serve as the convenient termination of our discussion. At this point, Sainte-Beuve, who stood just at the junior edge of our cohort, rallied to the banner that was to be borne by Victor Hugo as the standard of a new generation—the generation of *Hernani* and the Revolution of 1830.

I have not intended to present the transformation of Victor Hugo, who was *sui generis*, as the incarnation of the history of his coevals, or even of those who passed from the romanticism of the royalists to the romantic liberalism of 1830. His personal path was marked out by the logic of his artistic maturing as well as by the efforts to come to terms with his relation to his father. Hugo was, however, the most dynamic, precocious, and culturally significant representative of those whose search for liberation and fulfillment through literature brought them into an alliance with the young writers such as the *globistes*, who arrived at literary innovation as a deduction from liberal premises. This

---

[50] Ibid., 709–13.

[51] *Globe*, 2 March 1826.

[52] Lair, "Un Maître de Sainte-Beuve," 326; Sainte-Beuve's reminiscence in Hugo, *Oeuvres*, 2:1047–49.

is the point at which the unity of romanticism had been consummated,[53] more perhaps on negative than positive grounds, for literature as conceived by the editors of the *Constitutionnel* or by Bishop Frayssinous could not conceivably meet the youthful demand for a means of expression appropriate to the postrevolutionary era.

[53] Bray, "Vers l'Unité du romantisme," *Chronologie du romantisme*, 140–59.

CHAPTER 6

The *Producteur* and the Search for a "New General Doctrine"

"There are good reasons for believing that the most recent doctrine is the best."
                                        Enfantin, *Producteur*, 1826

The process that brought romantic poets into the cultural coalition with liberal critics reflected the power of shared assumptions to imprint a generational unity on the surface conflicts of militantly independent intellectuals. Perhaps the greatest tension between the assertion of a completely autonomous ideology and the internalizing of common conceptions was manifested in the brief history of the *Producteur*, the first periodical publication of the self-designated heirs of Saint-Simon.

The personal and intellectual background of the Saint-Simonian coterie was much closer to that of the founders of the *Globe* than to the political inclinations or the personal ramifications of the *cénacle* that directed the *Muse française*. Key figures in the founding of the *Globe* and the *Producteur* had been close associates before 1825, especially in the conspiracy of the Carbonari. To some extent, the personal network and intellectual solidarity provided the *Globe* by graduates of the Ecole normale would be supplied to the *Producteur* by the self-assured technocratic elite from the Ecole polytechnique.[1]

Instead of Victor Cousin as role model and all-purpose guru there was that incredible figure from another era, the Count Henri de Saint-Simon. The nature and intensity of Saint-Simon's influence on a chosen fragment of the Restoration cohort was as remarkable in its way as was the vast temporary prestige of

[1] This connection was rather tenuous at first. Of the contributors to the *Producteur*, only Enfantin, Comte, and Adolphe Gondinet had been students at the school. Olinde Rodrigues had been a mathematics tutor there.

Victor Cousin, and more significant in the long run. This influence has sometimes been treated as a simple matter of historical fact, but just as we wish to explain why a talented, bumptious cohort of ambitious, bright young men should want to plunge into Victor Cousin's tepid philosophic bath, we might pause to wonder what a succession of promising trained minds from elite schools and scientific disciplines—in succession, Thierry, Comte, Olinde Rodrigues, and the rest—saw in the farrago of crankish ramblings, fabricated facts, vainglorious prognostications, and autobiographical confidences published by that venerable relic of failed careers just at the moment of transition from Bonaparte to Bourbon.

To a considerable extent, they were drawn to Saint-Simon by his powerful personality. So different from Victor Cousin in age, background, and personal style, the aging count had something that captured youthful imaginations at just that historical moment. The point is succinctly put in Frank Manuel's definitive biography: "To a whole group of young *bourgeois* who had been drawn from the province to Paris for their studies, Saint-Simon in his middle fifties was a grand figure of the *ancien régime*—an impression he did nothing to discourage."[2] He combined the polished courtesy of the *grand seigneur* with an artless enthusiasm and a conceptual recklessness extremely appealing to young imaginations starved for some generous vision of their problematic future. At his best in small groups or tête-à-tête, he, like Cousin, was most effective with the spoken word, another star of the age of oratory. For Léon Halévy, one of the last to have received the living word, "His conversation, occasionally halting and obscure, often exhibited charm and force. But whether his discourse was more or less rich or felicitous, his ideas were always fresh, bold, and paradoxical."[3]

Saint-Simon did not have Cousin's platform eloquence, but in his

[2] Frank E. Manuel, *The New World of Henri Saint-Simon* (Cambridge, Mass., 1956), 191.

[3] Léon Halévy, "Souvenirs de Saint-Simon," *France littéraire*, 1 (March 1832): 537–38. This passage is reproduced in a truncated version of Halévy's reminiscence in the *Revue d'histoire économique et sociale*, 13 (1925): 173. See also the "Notice sur Saint-Simon et sa doctrine et sur quelques autres ouvrages qui en seraient le développement," by an anonymous secretary of Saint-Simon, in Alfred Pereire, *Autour de Saint-Simon* (Paris, 1912), 180; Hippolyte Auger, *Mémoires d'Auger (1810–1859)* (Paris, 1891), 127. Hippolyte Carnot, "Sur le Saint-Simonisme," *Académie des sciences morales et politiques, compte rendu*, 128 (1887): 127–31.

way he did convey a similar impression of a life devoted to the service of truth—a great gentleman who had abjured old *habitudes féodales* and sacrificed his social prerogatives in his dedication to the ideal. In an age of shattered illusions and successful *arrivistes*, the vagaries of his strange career were perceived as milestones in an exemplary voyage of the mind. According to Rodrigues, Saint-Simon had never been swept away by the revolutionary flood but had spent those turbulent years reflecting on "the reorganization of the system of ideas." Comte (in the first flush of discipleship) thought that this grand comrade in arms of Lafayette and Washington had never stained his political escutcheon, had never flattered Bonaparte, and sought no favors from the Restoration court: "Everyone has acknowledged that his conduct from the beginning of the Revolution through the stern trials of thirty years has been stainlessly pure."[4] A portrait, as Comte's biographer observes, that reveals a certain ignorance of the count's picaresque past.[5]

However accurate, the perception of a life of selfless dedication contributed greatly to Saint-Simon's influence on an impressionable *jeunesse*, but, of course, if there had been no attraction in the substance of the ideas, there would have been no following for the ideologist. The major works on Saint-Simon and his school have persuasively identified the major sources of the influence. Manuel, for example, concludes that:

> The appeal for a new synthesis, for the inauguration of the new age, were the central aspects of Saint-Simon's thought which attracted young men of talent in his last years. They were all longing for an organismic culture, an end to the contemporary period of transition.[6]

In Saint-Simon's conception of the legacy of the immediate past, we find, once again, the metaphor of "ruins." In 1817 he and Thierry published their pamphlet, *L'Industrie*, taxing the philosophes with having overfulfilled their historical task in totally demolishing the obsolete ideological structure of the Old Regime before they had conceived of

[4] Olinde Rodrigues, "De Henri Saint-Simon," *Producteur*, 3 (1826): 89; Comte to Valat, 15 May 1818, in Comte, *Correspondance générale*, 1:35-36; Hippolyte Carnot, "Résumé général de la doctrine saint-simonienne fait en 1831," *Revue socialiste*, 17 (March 1893): 316-17.

[5] Gouhier, *La Jeunesse d'Auguste Comte*, 3:171.

[6] Manuel, *The New World of Henri Saint-Simon*, 235.

anything to replace it. This categorical and unrelieved negativism bore the primary responsibility for the excesses of the Revolution and for the militaristic despotism that had succeeded it. Having providentially survived these catastrophes, the French nation should not hope to construct a new order out of the debris of the old. Once-dominant conceptions will never reassume their old authority. "A new foundation is needed for social thought, just as a new institution had been required by society."[7]

Therefore it was pointless to attempt to revive a system of ideas whose destruction had been "complete, radical, and irrevocable." What was needed was a "new general doctrine," appropriate to the present stage of civilization and the development of knowledge.[8] Saint-Simon intended not merely to call for the new doctrine but to provide it. There were many who would reject his particular solution to the problem while echoing his formulation of it.

In 1822, Auguste Comte, who by this time had broken with Saint-Simon, also discovered "in the nature of things" that the necessary crisis of the feudal and theological old order had been succeeded by the preponderance of "the critical doctrine." The unrestrained exploitation of this tendency, the essential cause of the terrible convulsions of the crisis of the Old Regime, had left society in a state of terrifying spiritual and secular disorganizaton, and it remained the greatest obstacle to the progress of civilization.[9]

This is Comte's version of that familiar thirst for synthesis that made the *jeunesse* so open to systematic constructs and more responsive to "simplicity than to the infinite complexity of things."[10] Charléty's comment on the attractions of Saint-Simonism is not terribly different from Taine's picture of the popularity of Victor Cousin,[11] and, as I will argue below, what Saint-Simon's young admirers discovered in his

[7] Augustin Thierry, *L'Industrie* in *Oeuvres de Claude Henri de Saint-Simon* (Paris, 1966), 1:207. This was originally published in May 1817 under the name of "A. Thierry, Fils adoptif de Henri de Saint-Simon," *L'Industrie* (Paris, 1817).

[8] Saint-Simon, *Du Système industriel*, in Saint-Simon, *Oeuvres*, 3:50–51.

[9] Auguste Comte, "Plan des travaux scientifiques nécessaires pour réorganiser la société," in *Ecrits de jeunesse 1816–1828*, (Paris, 1970), 241–52.

[10] Sébastien Charléty, *Histoire du saint-simonisme (1825–1864)* (Paris, 1931), 46.

[11] "S'ils [les gens de 1820] avaient perdu les habitudes d'analyse, ils avaient gardé la passion de la métaphysique; ils étaient à la fois sentimentaux et systématiques et demandaient des théories à leur coeur." Taine, *Les Philosophes classiques*, 297–98.

"science" was not so far from what Cousin's audience wanted to find in the philosophy of eclecticism.[12] This is not to insist that Saint-Simon and Cousin advanced identical ideas, but that they provided answers to similar questions.

The intersection of ideas produced by common concerns and shared assumptions was also a phenomenon of personal relationships. Cousin and Saint-Simon had themselves established a relationship of sorts. Shortly before the latter's death, he would appeal to the younger man for assistance in the dissemination of his *Catéchisme des industriels*.[13] Their young disciples would mingle and part as they passed from Saint-Simon's chamber to the lecture hall where Victor Cousin held forth, contributed to the *Globe*, joined the staff of the *Producteur*, and fractured old friendships and formed new ones along the ideological fault line.

The story of Saint-Simon's acquisition of young secretaries and collaborators, and finally of that conventicle of disciples who gathered at his grave, has been thoroughly explored.[14] It begins in the last years of the Empire, when Saint-Simon renewed his long search for the ideal collaborator among the fledgling geniuses of the Ecole normale. Probably in 1813, possibly through his friendship with the *normalien* Eugène Péclet (1793), he was put in touch with the nineteen-year-old Augustin Thierry and sufficiently impressed to offer him the position of secretary or editor-secretary.[15] After the fall of the Empire had dis-

---

[12] See chapter 7.

[13] A note from Saint-Simon to Cousin, Bibliothèque Victor Cousin, Victor Cousin Manuscripts, Ms. 247, reads as follows:

> Permettez-moi, mon cher Cousin, de vous rappeler que vous m'avez promis d'obtenir pour moi la bienveillance de votre ami Guinan [sic] relativement à mes travaux, je vous envoye un exemplaire complet du catéchisme je vous prie de le lui remettre le plus tôt possible.
>
> J'ai mille choses à vous dire, donnez moi un rendez-vous à Paris ou à la campagne à votre choix.
>
> Tout à vous,
Saint-Simon
Rue de Richelieu No 34

[14] Notably in Manuel, *The New World of Henri Saint-Simon*; Charléty, *Histoire du saint-simonisme*; and Gouhier, *La Jeunesse d'Auguste Comte*.

[15] *Eugène Péclet, normalien* of the *promotion* of 1812, professor of science and physics at Marseilles in 1816, writes an admiring letter to Saint-Simon that mentions Thierry.

posed of Thierry's initial reluctance to compromise his teaching career by associating with such an unorthodox individual, they established a relationship that rapidly transformed the young man from secretary to collaborator, to coauthor of a series of publications, and to publicly acknowledged adoptive son. With some of Saint-Simon's older acquaintances, Thierry and his friends the Scheffer brothers and Hyacinthe Didot (1794) joined a loose circle around Saint-Simon but did not yet constitute that chapel of the true disciples.[16]

Thierry shucked off the filial relationship almost as soon as it had been assumed, breaking with Saint-Simon more or less amicably sometime in mid-1817. His place was immediately filled by a sometime student from that other *corps d'élite*, the Ecole polytechnique. The nineteen-year-old ex-*polytechnicien* Auguste Comte assumed Thierry's role as secretary-editor and surrogate son. This was a far more intense relationship that ended in the explosion whose reverberations are still heard round the scholarly world.[17]

For Thierry, whose intellectual career developed in directions quite remote from the governing conceptions of Saint-Simon, there never was that clash over priority of discovery produced by the jealous messianisms of Comte and Saint-Simon, yet Comte and Thierry did share the inability of arrogant young intellectuals to accept permanent subordination to an older mentor. Despite Saint-Simon's financial generosity (when he had the cash) and his willingness to publicize the contributions of collaborators who were, after all, only just out of their teens, the essence of the relationship was to be that of high priest to acolyte, which was essentially incompatible with the self-image of a Comte or a Thierry.[18] It is my unverifiable conviction that the disciples

---

Péclet to Saint-Simon, undated, Bibliothèque nationale, Nouvelles acquisitions françaises, 24605: Correspondance et manuscrits du Comte Henri de Saint-Simon.

[16] Thierry's relations with Saint-Simon are detailed in A. Augustin-Thierry, *Augustin Thierry*, 22, 33, 36–44; Gouhier, *La Jeunesse d'Auguste Comte*, 3:71–79; Manuel, *The New World of Henri Saint-Simon*, 172, 194–97; Roulon Nephi Smithson, *Augustin Thierry: Social and Political Consciousness in the Evolution of a Historical Method* (Geneva, 1973), 31–49.

[17] For thorough, but not identical, treatments of the Comte–Saint-Simon controversy, see Gouhier, *La Jeunesse d'Auguste Comte*, 3:336–407; and Manuel, *The New World of Henri Saint-Simon*, 332–43, 419n, and *The Prophets of Paris*, 251–96. For the most recent Comtean salvo, see the Preface to Comte, *Ecrits de jeunesse*, 29–30.

[18] Even before the definitive break, Comte grew restive over Saint-Simon's paternalism: "M. de Saint-Simon a eu, comme les pères vis-à-vis des enfants, les métropoles

who gathered around Saint-Simon in his last years were saved from similar apostasies by the death of the prophet. There was not time enough for Rodrigues or Halévy, or even the formidable egos of Bazard and Enfantin, to resent the subordinate's role.

The last gathering to receive the living word was formed in May 1823 with the meeting of Saint-Simon and Olinde Rodrigues, a twenty-eight-year-old mathematics tutor at the Ecole polytechnique, broker at the Bourse, and student of the banking system.[19] Rodrigues introduced Saint-Simon to his cousins Emile (1800) and Isaac (1806) Pereire and to Léon Halévy (1802), all Jews and scions of banking families who were leaders of the Jewish religious community. They, with the later recruit, Gustave d'Eichtal (1804), formed the Jewish connection often emphasized in histories of the movement.[20]

With Olinde Rodrigues as his alter ego and young Halévy as his last secretary-collaborator, Saint-Simon embarked on one further attempt to present his doctrine in a coherent form. With the additional assistance of the jurist J. B. Duvergier (1792) and Dr. Etienne Bailly (1796), they undertook the publication of a series of essays on Saint-Simonian themes, the *Opinions littéraires, philosophiques et industrielles*, and planned the publication of a periodical devoted to the development of the central doctrines.[21] Before the journal could appear, Saint-Simon was gone, but he left a devoted nucleus determined to proceed to the fulfillment of his project.

à l'égard des colonies, le petit inconvénient, que la physiologie montre comme presque inévitable, de croire qu'ayant été son élève, je devais continuer à l'être indéfiniment, même après que la barbe m'aurait poussé." Comte to Tabarié, 5 August 1824, in Comte, *Correspondance générale*, 1:76.

[19] There is some question as to whether Rodrigues was born in 1794 or 1795; see Isambert, *De la Charbonnerie au saint-simonisme*, 142.

[20] Georges Weill, "Les Juifs et les saint-simoniens," *Revue des études juives*, 31 (1895): 261–80; Zosa Szajkowski, "The Jewish Saint-Simonians and Socialist Antisemites in France," *Jewish Social Studies*, 9 (January 1947): 33–60; Manuel, *The New World of Henri Saint-Simon*, 340–46; Robert B. Carlisle, "The Birth of Technocracy: Science, Society and Saint-Simonians," *Journal of the History of Ideas*, 35 (July–September 1974): 453; and "Saint-Simonian Radicalism: A Definition and a Direction," *French Historical Studies*, 5 (Fall 1968): 436; Barrie M. Ratcliffe, "Saint-Simonianism and Messianism: The Case of Gustave d'Eichtal," *French Historical Studies*, 9 (Spring 1976): 486, and "Some Jewish Problems in the Early Careers of Emile and Isaac Pereire," *Jewish Social Studies*, 34 (July 1972): 202.

[21] The essays were collected in one volume: Saint-Simon, *Opinions littéraires, philosophiques et industrielles* (Paris, 1825).

The intellectual legacy as received by the young disciples was out-lined in Dr. Bailly's discourse at Saint-Simon's grave. Those fortunate enough to have heard Saint-Simon's discussion of the major questions of philosophy, Bailly said, had witnessed that incredible ability to as-similate widely disparate methodologies into a unified conceptual sys-tem. His powers of synthesis had enabled him to lay the foundations of a new science, "the physiology of the human species."[22] Most precious of all to the generation of Saint-Simon's successors was the legacy of hope:

> We who have been instilled with the prejudices of our society have often regretted being born in this old continent of Europe which has appeared to us as a mass of ruins incapable of stimulat-ing our imagination. Consumed by the need for action, which made a torment of an existence whose futility wearied us, we ar-raigned nature for having endowed us with sentiments that set us in conflict with our situation.
>
> But today, gentlemen, formed in the school of this great man, you have embarked on a career for which he showed the way. To-day, your sense of living has been heightened by the impulse with which he awakened your faculties, by the delights born of an imagination passionate for the general good. Today, finally, when the conviction of belonging to a society full of energy and vitality has replaced the inertia to which you believed yourselves con-demned, you are indebted to him for a new moral existence whose worth you alone can appreciate.
>
> ... The melancholy illness of which he cured you is the same one of which you must in turn cure society. As a result of your efforts the changes which have been wrought in your morale will be effected in the human species. Worthy successors of a man to whom you owe such keen joys, the finest testimony of your grat-itude will be the continuation of his work in developing the intel-ligence of man.[23]

The first step into the new existence was taken on 1 June 1825, twelve days after the funeral, when a *société en commandite* was formed

[22] Etienne-Marin Bailly, *Discours prononcé sur la tombe de M. Henri Saint-Simon par le Docteur E. M. Bailly de Blois* (Blois, 1825).

[23] I have borrowed Frank Manuel's translation of this passage; *The New World of Henri Saint-Simon*, 366.

to publish the *Producteur*. That project had been conceived by Saint-Simon and his devoted followers, but the magnetism of the ideas drew in a group of posthumous disciples who joined Rodrigues, Bailly, J. B. Duvergier, and Léon Halévy in financing and editing the new journal.[24] Among the shareholders were some of those businessmen who had contributed to Saint-Simon's projected series of publications celebrating the civic merits of *les industriels*.[25] Jacques Laffitte headed the list with ten shares. He and other wealthy shareholders, such as the banker A. Ardouin and the industrialist Guillaume-Louis Ternaux, were not expected to contribute anything but their cash. The journal was to be directed and edited by the original circle—Olinde Rodrigues, Dr. Etienne Bailly, J. B. Duvergier, and Léon Halévy—enlarged by promising recruits from the pool of Parisian talent. Among individuals of widely diverse social antecedents and educational background, the common attribute of the editorial coalition was age. The oldest of nine founders and "principal editors" of the *Producteur* was Saint-Amand Bazard at thirty-four; the youngest, the twenty-three-year-old Léon Halévy. Their mean age in 1825 was thirty; six of them had been born between 1793 and 1796. With one exception, the additional *rédacteurs ordinaires*, including Antoine Cerclet, the first editor-in-chief, had been born between 1794 and 1803.[26]

The first of the new associates in the order of his appearance and in the light of his subsequent significance, was Prosper Enfantin, who joined Rodrigues in signing the share certificates as *fondateur-gérant*. Enfantin was a former *polytechnicien*, class of 1813, and veteran of combat before Vincennes in 1814. Like Auguste Comte, he had never graduated from the school, and like Comte he would continue to sign him-

---

[24] Henri-René d'Allemagne, *Les Saint-Simoniens* (Paris, 1930), 30–56.

[25] The names and *actions*, or shares, of the shareholders are listed in Saint-Simon, *Oeuvres de Saint-Simon et d'Enfantin* (Paris, 1865), 1:150. Jacques Laffitte held ten, Ardouin five, Rodrigues and Enfantin three each, Sautelet and Cie two each, and the following people held one each: Ternaux, Basterrèche, Vorms de Romilly, Odier, Achille Bégé, Comynet, Blanc Collin, Ve Vannard and son, Loignon, Mesnier, Holstein, Cerclet, Lachevardière, Duvergier, Rouen, Léon Halévy, and Dr. Bailly.

[26] The founders were: E. M. Bailly, J. B. Duvergier, O. Rodrigues (1795), L. Halévy, and P. Enfantin (1796). The *rédacteurs principaux*: Rodrigues, Enfantin, S. A. Bazard, Buchez, P. I. Rouen, and P. M. Laurent de l'Ardèche (1793). The *rédacteurs ordinaires*: Cerclet, J. Allier (1794), N. Artaud (1794), Adolphe Blanqui, A. Carrel, Comte, F. Bodin (1795), Decaen, J. J. Dubochet, A. Garnier (1801), A. Gondinet, L. Halévy, J. Huot (1790), and A. Senty (1803).

self "ex-*polytechnicien.*" He maintained his connections, corresponding with classmates, organizing a student campaign to raise money for the Greek rebellion, and when his pursuit of a business career briefly landed him in St. Petersburg, participating in a discussion group of *polytechniciens* stranded in the Russian capital.[27]

There are few traces of Enfantin's prior connections with the Saint-Simonians. He had subscribed to the *Catéchisme des industriels* and had been granted a brief audience with the master himself. Rodrigues, his tutor at the lycée Napoléon, had introduced him to Saint-Simon and seems to have brought him into the movement, where, in the summer of 1825, he assumed a leading, if not yet dominant, role. The letters that he wrote during the period of the gestation of the *Producteur* laid out the elements of the doctrine that impelled him to stake his talent, energies, and slender resources on its dissemination.

There was, above all, that cosmic optimism enshrined in the epigraph they had chosen for the masthead of the journal, enthusiastically quoted in a letter to his cousin Thérèse Nugues: "L'âge d'or qu'une aveugle tradition a placé jusqu'ici dans le passé est devant nous." This was the premise that would enable Saint-Simon's successors to refute the reactionary philosophies of the ultras and the cyclical theories of the liberals through the demonstration of the inevitable secular ascent of civilization to a better future.[28] Enfantin repeats this formulation in another letter, adding that these conceptions had been anticipated by Condorcet and Mme. de Staël. But only Saint-Simon, so far ahead of his century that he had been dismissed as a dreamer, had proposed as a theorem the vast problem of the optimum organization of the productive apparatus—a Kepler who left to his successors the mission to produce "the Newton of social physics."[29] It was Saint-Simon who had pointed the way past the "outworn and destructive metaphysics of the last century" and the liberal metaphysics of the Rights of Man, to a new positive science of society.

Enfantin's scientism brings to mind the familiar association of Saint-Simonism with the technocrats of the Ecole polytechnique, but at the

[27] For Enfantin's biography, see *Oeuvres de Saint-Simon et d'Enfantin*, 1:135–224; 2:1–224; Henry-René d'Allemagne, *Prosper Enfantin et Les Grandes Entreprises du XIXe siècle* (Paris, 1935); J. P. Alem, *Enfantin: Le Prophète aux sept visages* (Paris, 1964).

[28] Enfantin to Thérèse Nugues, 18 August 1825, in Saint-Simon, *Oeuvres de Saint-Simon et d'Enfantin*, 24:46.

[29] Enfantin to Pichard, 23 August 1825, ibid., 56.

beginning, aside from Rodrigues, who had been a math tutor there, Enfantin was the sole member of the editorial staff associated with the school. The other recruits had been shaped in a rather different milieu. The first editor-in-chief, Antoine Cerclet, three of the six *rédacteurs principaux*—Saint-Amand Bazard, Philippe Buchez, and P. I. Rouen—and the publisher and subscriber Auguste Sautelet, came out of the Carbonari. There is more to this than the coincidence of having conspired. What was represented, especially through Bazard and Buchez, was the network of Paris activists, in and out of the schools, who had crossed paths in clubs, masonic lodges, secret societies, and salons.

Among them Bazard was preeminent: old enough to have been decorated for bravery at Vincennes in 1814; with Buchez one of the fabulous "four *commis*" who had set out to radicalize the students, the apprentices to the professions, and the commercial clerks of the capital; *vénérable* of the lodge *Amis de la vérité*; contributor to liberal journals; chieftain of the student legions in the "conspiracy of August" in 1820; cofounder of the Carbonari and key representative of the younger element in its *haute vente*; and mouthpiece for that generational effrontery that gave Lafayette his marching orders and told Benjamin Constant where to go.[30]

Bazard is chiefly remembered for his subsequent partnership and disastrous conflict with Enfantin in the high-priesthood of the Saint-Simonian church, but he came to the movement in 1825 with an established reputation among the young, one that owed nothing to preeminence in the scholarly *concours* or the *promotions* of the *grandes écoles*. He represented, I think, the tip of that submerged Parisian *jeunesse* who provided the rank and file for the mass demonstrations of 1820 and the crowd that attended the funeral of Lallemand and the lectures of Victor Cousin.

The precise ramifications of the network of personal relationships that connected Bazard, Buchez, and the other activists to the Saint-Simonian circle immediately after the master's death have not been identified. Perhaps Enfantin had met his fellow volunteers in the defense

[30] *Encyclopédie nouvelle*, 2:519–24; Willy Spühler, *Der Saint-Simonismus: Lehre und Leben von Saint-Amand Bazard* (Zurich, 1926); Johann Ruppert, *Das Soziale System Bazards* (Würzburg, 1890); *La Grande Encyclopédie*, 5:970–71; Karl Schmidtlein, "Saint-Amand Bazard: Ein Beitrag zur Entstehungsgeschichte des Sozialismus," *Schmollers Jahrbuch*, 46 (1922): 65–107.

of Paris, or there may have been Saint-Simonians in the masonic lodge, the *Amis de la vérité*, or in one of the other Parisian *cénacles*.[31] It is clear enough that Bazard's conviction of the sterility of critical philosophy and revolutionary politics was widely shared and that the general search for synthesis would temporarily unite disparate intellects around the Saint-Simonian standard.

The coalition of mixed antecedents and incompatible temperaments that proceeded to publish the journal was agreed, at first, on general policy. This policy was to withhold the more unconventional, and especially the religious, elements of the doctrine until the public had been educated through the presentation of more assimilable materials. "These are the subterfuges," confides Enfantin, "that we propose to employ to arrive at an approach to the truth, almost always in the form of a literary, scientific, or industrial critique."[32] The general idea was to examine institutions in the light of their concrete contributions to human welfare, to advance practical proposals for the harnessing of productive capacity, and to arouse general interest through an appeal to specific interests. We cannot know whether this ideological restraint reassured the *Producteur*'s readers, but it did allow the journal to recruit young writers who would have been put off by messianic pretensions and a religious tone.

There was nothing in Cerclet's introduction to the first issue to turn away apprentice political economists like Adolphe Blanqui, although it did present a temperate survey of major Saint-Simonian themes. The immense ambitions of the movement—to construct a new philosophy on the foundations of a new conception of human nature—were not concealed but introduced in sober, measured, reassuring language. Proceeding from the premise of the cumulative amelioration of the human condition, the new philosophy was to identify the developments and institutions that had contributed to material and scientific progress in the past and that would guarantee it in the future. The Saint-Simonian trinity of *savants, artistes,* and *industriels,* who deserved the credit for all the significant contributions to human progress, were to be educated to an awareness that the direction of organized society belonged to them. The task of the *génération actuelle*—Cerclet is speaking

[31] Isambert, *De la Charbonnerie au saint-simonisme*, 80, 142–43.
[32] Enfantin to Thérèse Nugues, 18 August 1825, in Saint-Simon, *Oeuvres de Saint-Simon et d'Enfantin*, 24:44; Louis Reybaud, *Etudes sur les réformateurs contemporains ou socialistes modernes* (Paris, 1864), 1:87.

to his articulate coevals, with no reference yet to a "priesthood"—was to bring them that message, to teach them to transcend the obsolete preoccupations of the political arena in order to assume their rightful place at the summit of society. Signposts were suggested. The job of the *savants* was to destroy the empire of "vague and mystical concepts." The *industriels* were to value themselves at their true worth and to indoctrinate the entire class of producers with "the profound sense of the public weal." The *artistes* were urged to eschew the wilder flights of imagination in order to serve humanity through the propagation of correct and useful ideas.[33]

The early issues of the journal pursued these subjects, not precisely with circumspection, but with an emphasis on specific developments and practical proposals. Enfantin and Rouen described and extolled the actual and potential functions of joint-stock companies. In "Considérations sur l'industrie," Olindes Rodrigues sketched out something like a primer of industrial capitalism. Léon Halévy wrote on literary questions, to which subject the *Producteur* devoted considerable space, for like the other journals it freighted cultural issues with great moral and political significance. There were pieces on industrial innovations; on public works, such as canals; and on significant developments in foreign countries—notably, lengthy contributions by Adolphe Blanqui on Latin America and Armand Carrel on Greece.

In style and content the *Producteur* was at least as "serious" as the *Globe*, the absence of the flippant Voltairian tone signifying that its grave young editors were members of the postrevolutionary generation. Enfantin once remarked that Saint-Simon's more or less incomprehensible language inhibited the reception of his message and that the new journal intended to present the ideas in a palatable form, "à la Voltaire."[34] No danger of that, however; instead of whimsical *croquis des moeurs* or facetious *pensées diverses* there were descriptions of canals and the topography of Sardinia.

Then, in the seventh number, a more profound and ambitious chord was struck in Auguste Comte's "Considérations philosophiques sur les sciences et sur les savans."[35] Comte was on reasonably friendly terms with several of the editors, including Cerclet, whose former mistress

---

[33] *Producteur*, 1 (1825): 1–11.

[34] Enfantin to Pichard, 2 February 1826, in Saint-Simon, *Oeuvres de Saint-Simon et d'Enfantin*, 24:86.

[35] This is now accessible in Comte, *Ecrits de jeunesse*, 323–59.

became Comte's wife, but he was contemptuous of Saint-Simon's epigoni and had no intention of enlisting under someone else's banner. He needed the money, however, and was reassured by the reflection that even if the journal turned out to be characteristically vacuous or mediocre, it would scarcely be compromised by any revolutionary content.[36]

For the first time the readers of the journal were presented with the law of the three stages. Who had first conceived of the precise Comtean or Saint-Simonian terminology for what was a fairly widespread contemporary conception is no more our concern than it was that of the *Producteur*'s public in 1825. Comte's reading of the past as the history of systems of thought, proceeding from the theological through the metaphysical to the positive stage of human intellectual development, was a sharply defined formulation of the widespread conviction that the correct application of the scientific method enabled one to "see in the profound study of the past the authentic explanation of the present and the general manifestation of the future." This historical science was presumed to validate two somewhat contradictory assumptions: the fact of the integral relationship between conceptual and social systems and the belief that the postrevolutionary social order still awaited the ideological system appropriate to its unprecedented historical situation. Comte's historicism affirmed not only the historical inevitability of a new and higher positive synthesis, but its social necessity; the only cure for the present state of social anarchy was the reimposition of a universally accepted ideology.

Despite his distance from the Saint-Simonian inner circle, Comte's essays contributed major statements to what became the journal's leitmotif, "the need for a new general doctrine," Saint-Simon's phrase, which was reproduced as the title of one of Bazard's essays on this theme. Bazard took up the subject in an article soon after the appearance of Comte's first piece. Indeed, he followed Comte so closely as to reproduce with almost literal fidelity his remarks on "liberty of conscience" in the 1822 essay that was an early formulation of his "système de politique positive." There, Comte has argued that the spiritual reorganization of the social order was inhibited by a doctrinaire adher-

---

[36] Comte to Eichtal, 24 November 1825, in Comte, *Correspondance générale*, 1:172. Comte was reassured by the appointment of Cerclet as the journal's director. He called Cerclet, "un homme de mérite étrange à cette coterie."

ence to the principle of the "unlimited liberty of conscience." The triumph of this principle had been the historically necessary product of the decadence of theology, but it now threatened to inhibit the establishment of any general system of ideas whatsoever. The absurdity of the unlimited application of freedom of conscience is exposed by the unassailable authority of the physical sciences. A system of political principles remains to be established, but Comte asserted, "to convert this transitory fact into a fundamental and eternal dogma is surely to proclaim that society should remain forever without general doctrines."[37]

Bazard advanced identical arguments in the *Producteur* in 1825. His article "Des Partisans du passé et de ceux de la liberté de conscience," identified the two camps whose irreconcilable differences had to be transcended before society (in the midst of ruins) could find the coherence to march forward out of postrevolutionary doubt and spiritual anarchy.[38] The bankruptcy of a conservative nostalgia was indubitable, but the present generation had burdened itself with prejudices in favor of an unlimited freedom of conscience whose historical function could never be anything but destructive. Like Comte, Bazard looked forward to the time when the unquestioned authority of the physical sciences would be extended to demonstrated principles of social organization and the sterile struggles between partisans of the past and advocates of intellectual anarchy would be forsaken for the great work of reconstruction.

The denigration of an unlimited freedom of conscience immediately made the Saint-Simonians the target of those critics, from Benjamin Constant to George Iggers, who identify their dreams of a unifying doctrine with authoritarian fantasies.[39] In a brief polemic with the *Producteur*, Constant disposed of a doctrine that granted liberty of conscience as long as error endured but not after truth had been discovered, "as if each person did not perceive his own opinion as the truth and would not authorize himself in the light of this new doctrine to stifle the liberty of his adversaries, accusing them of error." To this classic liberal critique, editor-in-chief Cerclet gave the classic reply:

[37] Comte, "Plan des travaux scientifiques nécessaires pour réorganiser la société," *Ecrits de jeunesse*, 246–47.

[38] *Producteur*, 1 (1825): 399–412.

[39] George G. Iggers, *The Cult of Authority: The Political Philosophy of the Saint-Simonians, A Chapter in the Intellectual History of Totalitarianism* (The Hague, 1958).

They were not proposing to call out the gendarmes against bad ideas but were asserting that when the moral and political sciences attained the certainty of the physical sciences, "it would be necessary, willy-nilly, to accept the scientific truths in morals and politics as today one believes in the scientific truths of astronomy and physics."[40] In the light of recent efforts to obtain equal classroom time for the science of creationism, we can see that the Saint-Simonians were optimistic about the authority the hard sciences would obtain, let alone the social sciences, but during the early period at least, they did not advocate the political enforcement of social theory.[41]

The point, however, was to discover and affirm the larger truth, and this entailed rejection of the critical, negativist, skeptical spirit that had fulfilled its necessary role in the eighteenth century but had inhibited the affirmation of the historically necessary positive synthesis. The editors of the *Producteur* not only recoiled from the intellectual anarchy of every-man-his-own-scientist but also from the skeptical and tentative state of mind that refused to attempt to make general sense of phenomena. This is the point at which they separated themselves from the liberal economists of the previous cohort, whose views they by and large supported.

In a series of articles devoted to a generally laudatory review of Charles Dunoyer's *La Morale et l'industrie, dans leurs rapports avec la liberté*, P. I. Rouen deplored the distinguished journalist's "excessive timidity" in dealing with the fundamental causes of human progress. Dunoyer was willing merely to "hazard an explanation" for the causes of revolution and the collapse of civilization. Rouen concluded that "whoever undertakes to establish a political system will fail if he does not proceed from a profound confidence in his own authority. He should possess the unshakeable conviction that the truth he seeks is accessible to his thought."[42] The unshakeable conviction of Truth's ac-

---

[40] *Producteur*, 1 (1825): 537–38.

[41] There *were*, in fact, certain inconsistencies. In his presentation of Saint-Simonian doctrine, Olinde Rodrigues posits an ideal European state that "tout en proclamant une liberté de conscience illimitée" would repress all religions, "dont les principes seraient contraires au grand code de moral qu'il aurait établi." *Producteur*, 3 (1826): 87.

[42] Ibid., 2 (1826): 454. See also Enfantin's critique, *Producteur*, 3 (1826): 420–25, of Charles Comte's *Traité de législation; ou, L'Exposition des lois générales* (Paris, 1835), where Comte had defended the analytic method against "des hommes qui ont l'esprit

cessibility, expressed with a special fervor by the Saint-Simonians, was axiomatic for virtually all of their coevals, who were engaged in the quest for new truths in the ruins of the old order. One did not set out on a search for the grail burdened with an excess of skeptical scruples.

Sharing these attitudes, the editors began to chafe under their self-imposed restraints. Now, more than a year after the death of Saint-Simon, the time seemed ripe to introduce the esoteric core of the doctrine and the individual whose seminal thoughts had spawned it. In the April 1826 issue, Olinde Rodrigues published the first of four articles on Henri Saint-Simon.[43] The first two volumes of the journal had at least introduced readers to a new philosophic terrain; now, Rodrigues promised, it would satisfy the demand for a greater precision and detail with regard to the origin and history of the "school" of industrial science to which the *Producteur* belonged.

The Saint-Simon introduced by Rodrigues had providentially appeared just at the historical moment when there was an overriding necessity for a "general doctrine consonant with the progress of knowledge." Recognizing that the revolutionary crisis marked an *époque climatérique*, Saint-Simon had transcended the particularistic obsessions of his contemporaries, and the vision of his great predecessors, Kant and Condorcet, to formulate a philosophy of history that incarnated the principles of a science of society. As Keith Baker has remarked, this was to transform Condorcet's carefully circumscribed relation of a philosophy of history to a projected social science into a historicist legitimation of a predicted social order.[44]

This reciprocal legitimation of a social science and a philosophy of history—we would say, of Saint-Simon's scientism and his historicism—was precisely what appealed to Olinde Rodrigues. He could now reveal that Saint-Simon's theory of the three stages was the pure germ of the doctrine of the *Producteur*. The history of thought culminating in the scientific or positive stage was also the history of the emergence of a new social system out of the ruins of the old. The organic relationship of the scientific ideology and the industrial order was demonstrated in Saint-Simon's reading of the past. An intellectual system

rempli de systèmes imaginaires" (p. 74). Bazard criticizes Guizot and Constant for their reluctance to synthesize. *Producteur*, 4 (1826): 112–22, 136–38.

[43] *Producteur*, 3 (1826): 86–109, 281–304, 426–43; 4 (1826): 86–112.

[44] Keith Michael Baker, *Condorcet: From Natural Philosophy to Social Mathematics* (Chicago, 1975), 377.

appropriate to the new order was necessarily a total synthesis of knowledge, thus the immense promise of Saint-Simon's project for a universal encyclopedia, the virtual equivalent of a religion that would serve as "the intermediary between the *savans* and the people and as the basis of a moral education."[45]

The journal's new turn entailed a reorganization of staff as well as a modification of content. The fellow travelers dropped away. Léon Halévy left too. In retrospect, he would give the rather unconvincing reason that the journal fell short of a "religious respect" for the ideas of Saint-Simon.[46] Adolphe Blanqui contributed a few minor reviews before fading out of the picture. In the last few months of the *Producteur*'s existence, virtually all of the articles were written by Enfantin, Bazard, Buchez, and Laurent. In their assumption of the role of masters of the school, we begin to see their future as pillars of the church.

Enfantin's announcement of the new monthly format in April 1826 restated the fundamental themes. Their goal was to unite the *savants, artistes*, and *industriels* through a philosophic doctrine in harmony with the actual state of civilization. The sciences would be considered in the light of their relation to social progress, political economy as it reflected on the unity and amelioration of the productive classes, and the *beaux-arts* with regard to their contributions to the reconstruction of the social order. The *Producteur* intended to recall artists to their "noble mission," to demonstrate the uselessness of the attempts to "make vibrate in the human heart chords that time had broken," to remind them that "an active generation," weary of an obsolete past, required not regret but hope.[47]

Enfantin's summons to artists sounded a theme repeated throughout the life of the journal.[48] The *Producteur* fused a direct and literal rendering of Bonald's conception of art as the expression of society with a characteristic confusion of the "is" and the "ought." The conviction that "chaque temps a son beau"—that literary beauty was nothing but "the poetic expression of the mass of dominant ideas at each epoch"— was combined with the exhortation to create new forms appropriate to

[45] *Producteur*, 3 (1826): 296.

[46] Halévy, "Souvenirs de Saint-Simon," 541.

[47] *Producteur*, 2 (1826): 628–29.

[48] There is brief, perceptive discussion of the aesthetics of the *Producteur* in Marguerite Thibert, *Le Rôle social de l'art d'après les saint-simoniens* (Paris, 1925), 21–26.

an emerging era.[49] Poets and painters were urged to eschew those obsolete paeans to military glory, those yearnings after medieval fantasies, those imitations of antique models, for a celebration of the new ideas and the *mouvement industriel*.

The logical tension implicit in these prescriptions is highlighted by Adolphe Garnier's categorical assertions, "Let's not forget that literature and the arts are entirely passive, that they cannot represent a moral system before it is established, nor anticipate a social structure of which they are in any case only its reflection or expression."[50] But the editors of the *Producteur* could not have sustained their conception of an art oriented to the future in the face of such a rigorous determination of the cultural superstructure. The positivist and utilitarian orientation of the early issues gave way to that aesthetic sentimentalism that conformed to the journal's messianic intentions.[51] The changing emphasis is exemplified in Enfantin's introduction to the 1826 volume, which informed the artists of their noble mission to reveal the brilliant future to their generation, and in Buchez's "reflections" on literature and the *beaux-arts*, which denied that the function of art was merely to express the sentiments of its time: "The genius of the *beaux-arts* is not a vulgar genius, it is not a slave destined to follow in the footsteps of society; it ought to strike out in front, and serve as a guide; it should take the lead, and society should follow."[52]

What all of this came to in the evaluation of specific works was the requirement of an edifying content. The medium was to send the appropriate message. Soumet, that improbable object of youthful enthusiasm, was hailed for his progressive, forward-looking ode to the Languedoc canal. Victor Chauvet's "Haiti, chant lyrique," celebrating the Villèle government's recognition of that republic, was a promising augury of the poetry of "new ideas"—that is, of sentiments appropriate to the progress of humanity.[53]

The utilitarian standard that reduced art to the expression of appropriate sentiments is what one would have expected of the Saint-Simonians, but their assertion of this standard, if somewhat more consequential, was in principle no different from that of their coevals. The *Globe*

[49] *Producteur*, 1 (1825): 279.
[50] Ibid., 524.
[51] Thibert, *Le Rôle social de l'art d'après les saint-simoniens*, 23.
[52] *Producteur*, 4 (1826): 204.
[53] Ibid., 1 (1825): 179, 579, 276–78.

also praised Chauvet's poem as the work of a poet able to find *belles inspirations* in contemporary events and to contribute to a poetics that had at last begun to align itself on contemporary mores and to find the language appropriate to its new destiny.[54]

The critics of the *Producteur* and of the *Globe* not only posited a didactic art in which beauty was inseparable from right thinking but wrestled in similar ways with the question of an appropriate form for a progressive content. The themes we have followed out in the columns of the *Globe* are repeated in those of the *Producteur*: the same ambivalence in the contest of classic and romantic; the same contempt for the servile imitations of antique models on the one hand and scorn for affectations of medievalism and self-indulgent Byronism on the other; the same repudiation of a narrow chauvinism in the arts and the affirmation of receptivity to creative forces from abroad, especially from Germany and England, qualified by an unfailing commitment to the ultimate superiority of the great French tradition; the same rejection of the neoclassical conventions of the contemporary theatre; and the same search for the undiscovered dramatists who would create a theatre appropriate to the new era; and—here we are on familiar ground—the same assessment of the chances of an obscure poet to find an audience if he had not been puffed in the organs of the cultural establishment— the *Journal des débats* or the *Constitutionnel*.[55]

Joseph Allier articulated what the *Producteur* conceived as its difference from the aesthetics of the *Globe* in a piece that praised the latter journal as the most balanced and acute of all the literary journals but criticized it for the elitism that eschewed the commitment to move the masses through art.[56] Allier's piece was a rather tangential expression of the ambivalence with which the editors of the *Producteur* viewed the journal edited by their erstwhile friends and associates. Their feelings, while not precisely reciprocated by the editors of the *Globe*, were informed with something like the spirit of sibling rivalry.

An examination of the odd, truncated dialogue between the *Globe* and the *Producteur* not only illuminates the similarities and differences between those groups but also sheds light on fundamental, often unar-

[54] *Globe*, 7 January 1826. The *Muse française* published Victor Chauvet's ode to the Greek revolution.
[55] *Producteur*, 1 (1825): 184-85.
[56] Ibid., 3 (1826): 39-40.

ticulated, assumptions that provided the ideological cement for the generation. This examination is intended to introduce a broader discussion of those general assumptions in the following chapter.

The dialogue appropriately proceeded from philosophic foundations laid down in Laurent's review of Cousin's "Fragments Philosophiques" published in the *Producteur* in the issues of May and July 1826.[57] This was cast more or less in the form of a defense of "industrialism," which Laurent saw as having been misunderstood and misrepresented by Cousin and his school. As Cousin's book had scarcely considered the school of industrialism except to dismiss it for its unscientific spirit, Laurent's commentary concentrated on a review of Cousin's work in the *Globe*, which devoted considerable space to a critique of the ideas of the Saint-Simonians.[58] Damiron's piece sought to distance Cousin's philosophy from the opposing poles of "la théocratie et l'industrialisme." The former, which was exclusively concerned with spiritual and theological solutions, inevitably subordinated the truths of science to those of dogma and revelation; the latter was concerned with nothing but science, rejecting not only theology but all moral and psychological conceptions. Theocracy and industrialism did, however, have something in common—they both desired the institution or reinstitution of a common ideology. The disciples of Saint-Simon had not successfully disguised their intention to replace the intellectual anarchy of contemporary society with a unified doctrine provided by a sovereign body of self-elected *savants*. At this point I do not wish to dwell on the obvious liberal critique of the Saint-Simonians' supposed authoritarianism but on the more or less philosophic issue that seemed both to divide and to unite the young neoliberals and the Saint-Simonians.

Laurent's answer to Damiron's review, while mildly contemptuous of Cousin's sycophants, showed respect and admiration for the young master. It was unfortunate that such an upright, eloquent, and judicious professor should so misrepresent the school of thought precisely dedicated to science in the larger sense and to moral conceptions that manifestly transcended any narrow materialism. Indeed, there was significant agreement in certain fundamental propositions. "This distinguished professor," wrote Laurent, "approaches *l'industrialisme*

[57] Ibid., 3 (1826): 325–38; 4 (1826): 19–37.
[58] *Globe*, 6 May 1826.

through his affirmation of the law of individual and collective perfect-ibility as he does through his appreciation of the general phenomena revealed in the history of the gradual education of the human species."[59]

Cousin's grasp of the history of the education of humanity enabled him to grant to each era the respect due its characteristic contribution to human progress. Thus he rightly praised the great eighteenth-cen-tury triumphs of "the spirit of analysis and observation" without, how-ever, granting any merit to its posthumous children, whose sterile in-sistence on total intellectual autonomy could only lead to emotional and intellectual anarchy and the erosion of social unity. Cousin shared with the prophets of industrialism that conviction of the absolute moral and social necessity of a unifying doctrine; unfortunately, his method led to a doctrine even more obsolete than those of the critical spirit. His attempt "to create experimentally a psychological doctrine that could carry him from induction to ontology" led him through a labyrinth of speculation to the dead end of metaphysical abstraction. Cousin's psy-chologism began with "positive" observations of the facts of sensation but ascended from conjecture to conjecture into the realm of empty ab-straction as it abstracted the individual from the social context, which is the sole domain of human reality.

Laurent seemed to be saying in vaguer terms what Comte had al-ready expressed with deadly precision in 1819. The positivistic predis-positions of Comte and the Saint-Simonians enabled them to identify the contradiction in the attempt to found a human science on intro-spective psychology. To assume the role of observer simultaneously with what is being observed was, Comte wrote, as if one could "divide his mind, that is to say, his brain, into two parts, one of which acts while the other observes."[60]

Victor Cousin, his immediate circle, and his distant heirs, never did seem to take that point, but the polemicists at the *Globe* managed to locate with some accuracy the mote in the Saint-Simonian eye. The generally sympathetic obituary for Saint-Simon in the 4 June 1825 issue of the *Globe* picked out a decisive flaw in his tendency to appeal to the future to vindicate prescriptions for the present social order—"to wish to improvise and organize, on the basis of no authority but his desires,

---

[59] *Producteur*, 3 (1826): 332; Laurent's *Résumé de l'histoire et de la philosophie* (Paris, 1826), 425–28, treated Cousin with great respect.
[60] Comte to Valat, 24 September 1819, in Comte, *Correspondance générale*, 1:58.

a social system of which time alone conceals the secrets in its bosom."[61] Somehow the critical spirit lingered on, a deplorable legacy of the eighteenth century, except when applied to someone else.

The critical dialogue on a relatively lofty and fair-minded philosophic plane eventually deteriorated into an ill-tempered exchange, the best-remembered example of which is the polemic between Stendhal and Armand Carrel over the former's pamphlet, *D'Un Nouveau Complot contre les industriels*, which was reprinted in the *Globe*.[62] In what is scarcely one of his most distinguished works, Stendhal reduces the Saint-Simonian philosophy to the unqualified glorification of businessmen, which straw man he then demolishes with anecdotes of commercial amorality, appeals to the contributions of other professions, comparisons with military and literary heroes, and ad hominem references to the motives of journalists who burn incense at the altars of Mammon.

The *Producteur*'s editor, Cerclet, who knew Stendhal in the Delécluze salon, fired off a letter composed in equal parts of heavy sarcasm and moral indignation. Stendhal's piece was characteristically witty and well written, but superficial cleverness—"You are indeed witty"— was no substitute for some understanding of the subject. Writers "such as you who approach things superficially and reduce everything to wisecracks," he wrote, are ill-advised to navigate into deep water where they only look foolish. And how deplorable to impugn the motives of individuals whom one does not even know. Stendhal returned the compliment in an urbane response that expressed the hope that "while you scarcely appreciate my pleasantries and I your pretentious obscurities, we can continue to live on a friendly footing," and promised to leave personalities out of a subsequent edition (the version that appeared in the *Globe*).[63] This small exchange of unpleasantries exposes

---

[61] *Globe*, 4 June 1825.

[62] A recent critical edition containing the documents, relevant correspondence, and a structural analysis of Stendhal's pamphlet is in the series Nouvelles Bibliothèque Romantique, No. 3, Stendhal, *D'un Nouveau Complot contre les industriels* (Paris, 1972). See Fernand Rudé, *Stendhal Et La Pensée sociale de son temps* (Paris, 1967), 101–80. For a positive evaluation of Stendhal's pamphlet, see J. Birnberg, " 'D'Un Nouveau Complot' contre les industriels: Pamphlet possible ou impossible?" in O. Schellekens, ed., *Stendhal, Le Saint-Simonisme et les industriels: Stendhal et la Belgique* (Brussels, 1979), 103–11.

[63] A. Cerclet to Stendhal, 30 November 1825; H. Beyle to Cerclet, 30 November 1825, both reprinted in Stendhal, *D'Un Nouveau Complot*, 33–37.

the chasm dividing the literary-moral sensibility of the forty-two-year-old charter member of the Happy Few from that of the young prophet of the new industrial order—a difference far deeper than their differences over the amount of esteem deserved by contemporary captains of industry.[64]

Cerclet concluded that the *Producteur* would not care to dignify Stendhal's work with public notice, but a few weeks later the journal did publish Armand Carrel's review of the pamphlet. Although only briefly a fellow traveler of *industrialisme* (Carrel and Stendhal were both out of place in the columns of the respective journals), Carrel struck the authentic note in a restrained exposition of standard Saint-Simonian themes without deigning, as he said, to engage in pointless polemics, "above all if tilting with a would-be adversary requires a descent into triviality," the chosen terrain for the launching of *pasquinades*.[65]

The *Globe* ambiguously praised, and published, Stendhal's piece, but scarcely as a characteristic expression of its own views on political economy, which were in fact quite similar to those outlined in the *Producteur*.[66] Tanneguy-Duchâtel's series of articles on economic theory contained little that would have been rejected by the Saint-Simonians.[67]

The editors of the *Producteur* did make a conscious effort to distance themselves from other progressive publicists, especially in a not completely successful attempt to transcend the aesthetic-moral obsessions of the "merely literary" journals. But even the literary journals were prepared to celebrate the construction of a new industrial order. The theme that did distinguish the Saint-Simonians from the young liberals as early as the mid-1820s referred to what came to be called the *question sociale*. Everyone respected the contributions of the English political economists and assumed a universal thirst for new facts about the progress of industry; the *Globe* would publish respectful reviews of Villermé's survey of working-class living conditions and would deplore

[64] For a further discussion of the temperamental generation gap, see chapter 7.

[65] *Producteur*, 1 (1825): 437–41.

[66] *Globe*, 17 December 1825.

[67] *Globe*, 20 November, 4, 7, 25 December 1824; 5 February, 19 March, 23 April, 21 May, 11 June, 30 July, 13 August 1825. For a similar, and perhaps more sophisticated, example of contemporary economic thought, see A. de Carrion-Nisas (1794), *Principes d'économie politique* (Paris, 1825).

their brutalizing effects, but only the *Producteur* characterized the circumstances of the class of "the most numerous and the most poor" as a fundamental social issue.[68]

The intermittent dialogue between the *Globe* and the *Producteur* continued to deteriorate. The *Globe* grouped the Saint-Simonians with the devotees of a secular papacy characterized by "a hatred of individualism and a mania for reorganization," and Enfantin dismissed the editors of the *Globe* as facile literati, hopelessly mired in the "ontology" of a dedication to govern the world by abstractions.[69] In the midst of this unedifying exchange, the two journals dealt passing blows to the mainstream liberal publication, the *Courrier français*, which had directed a patronizing lecture to the "young friends of the country" who had abandoned the grand old doctrines in pursuit of utopias, and to "certain inexperienced thinkers who cling to the skirts of Voltaire and Rousseau." Curious language, remarked the *Producteur*, "in the mouth of men who themselves had abandoned their fathers' doctrines in 1789." Voltaire's robe was indeed sewn with stars, but nowadays the young were looking for a new mode, which was unlikely to be provided by those who continued to think in 1826 precisely as they had in 1789. Dubois, writing in the *Globe*, deplored the *Courrier*'s shopworn device of ritual appeals to the sacred heritage of the Revolution—appeals turned against the very generation that had dedicated itself to the rehabilitation of the Revolution through unprejudiced research and had produced the two finest works in its honor. "Like the entire generation to which we have the honor to belong," continued Dubois, "we have come of age, and our self-appointed tutors should at least get things right." The editorial board of the *Producteur* was not only in agreement with, but was virtually the collective representation of, these sentiments.[70]

Although they struck the generational chord less often than did the publicists of the *Globe*, the Saint-Simonians certainly shared their coevals' convictions that they "bifurcated history." Their older generation consisted of Saint-Simon, the great exception to the inability of the human imagination to transcend its own era, providentially summoned

---

[68] For an example, see *Producteur*, 5 (1825): 199.

[69] *Globe*, 9 September 1826; *Producteur*, 4 (1826): 499–508.

[70] The offending article appeared in the *Courrier français* of 17 September 1826. It was answered by Enfantin in the *Producteur*, 4 (1826): 442–53, and by Dubois in the *Globe*, 19 September 1826.

up by "the progress of the human spirit" to proclaim a new doctrine. Save for this magnificent exception, "it was not to be the old who will have the most influence on the future of humanity."[71] The conviction that the human future was incarnate in the cohort coeval with the new era situated the young Saint-Simonians among the spokesmen for their generation and distinguished them from their older contemporaries.

[71] *Producteur*, 4 (1826): 46.

CHAPTER 7

Shared Assumptions and a Common Temper of Mind

"In general, up to the age of thirty, one produces
ideas; after thirty, one has fixed ideas."
André F. Carrion-Nisas, *De la jeunesse française*

My emphasis on the common
assumptions that underlay the differences between the *Globe* and
the *Producteur* might be construed as a preamble to W. M.
Simon's suggestive essay "The 'Two Cultures' in Nineteenth-
Century France: Victor Cousin and Auguste Comte." After describing the century-long opposition of the intellectual traditions
that more or less derived from Cousin and Comte, Simon concludes, "Between them it was a 'dialogue de sourds'; but later it
turned into a general conversation because in fact there were not
'two cultures,' but one with many streams."[1] My concern is not
with the ultimate convergence of the streams but with their common source in the premises of a generational ideology shared by
the Cousinian circle, the Saint-Simonian coterie, and most of
their articulate coevals.

The application of "ideology" may seem to impose a spurious
coherence on the welter of ideas expressed by members of a particular age group in the Restoration era, but I believe that a modified version of Karl Mannheim's distinction between a "particular" and a "total" conception of ideologies allows us to identify
the conceptual amalgam that distinguished the cohort from its
contemporaries. In Mannheim's usage, *"particular"* refers to a
reading of ideology as an expression or rationalization of interest
specific to a group and *"total"* refers to the interpretation of the
"total structure" of a group's mind as a "Function of its social
existence."[2] I therefore distinguish the particular expression of

[1] Simon, "The 'Two Cultures' in Nineteenth-Century France," 58.
[2] Karl Mannheim, *Ideology and Utopia* (New York, 1955), 55–59. Mannheim
relates these "conceptions" of ideology to the identification of distortions in an

the distinct identity, destiny, and superiority of the cohort in S. N. Eisenstadt's sense of a "youth ideology" from the *Weltanschauung*, the articulated principles and the unstated premises that shaped the consciousness of its spokesmen. These are conceptually separable,
although of course they intermingle in any discourse.

Reference to ideology, or to ideologies, in this sense does not completely serve to identify what distinguishes the characteristic behavior
of the generation from that of its contemporaries. The very language
in which it casts its ideas, its rhetorical tone, proceeds from something
like a common sensibility or temperament, or what French scholars
might identify as a collective *mentalité* in contrast to a collective *prise de
conscience*.[3] This is scarcely a recent preoccupation. More than forty
years ago Lucien Febvre proposed an investigation of "the nuances of
sensibility that separate epochs, or more precisely, generations, from
each other."[4] I have found it impossible to characterize the ideas that
separated the cohort of 1820 from its predecessors and successors without reference to nuances of sensibility, to what Robert Mandrou calls,
"the affective domain of sentiments and passions."[5]

"opponent's" view. I introduce the terms particular and total without reference to the
truth or falsity of the ideologies.

[3] These are often viewed not as separate but as functionally interrelated attributes.
Michel Vovelle refers to two systems of thought, "aux uns que les mentalités s'inscri-
vent tout naturellement dans le champs de l'idéologique, aux autres que l'idéologie au
sens restrictif du terme pourrait n'être qu'un aspect ou un niveau du champ des mentalités: disons celui de la prise de conscience, de la formalisation ou de la pensée claire."
Michel Vovelle, *Idéologie et mentalités* (Paris, 1982), 11.

[4] Lucien Febvre, "Comment Reconstituer La Vie affective d'autrefois? La Sensibilité et l'histoire," in *Combats pour l'histoire* (Paris, 1953), 234, first published in the *Annales d'histoire sociale*, 3 (1941). For the somewhat similar conception of "styles of
thought," see Karl Mannheim, *Essays on Sociology and Social Psychology* (London,
1969), 74–77.

[5] Robert Mandrou, "L'Histoire des mentalités," under the entry *"Histoire"* in the
Encyclopaedia Universalis (Paris, 1968), 8:436. Mandrou's definition seems applicable to
the relatively privileged and educated subjects of this study. For a conception of *mentalité* that emphasizes "the attitudes of ordinary people toward everyday life or the culture of the common man," see Patrick H. Hutton, "The History of Mentalités: The
New Map of Cultural History," *History and Theory*, 20 (1981): 237–59. For a sampling
of the proliferating literature, see Louis Trénard, "L'Histoire des mentalités collectives: Les Livres—Bilan et perspectives," *Revue d'histoire moderne et contemporaine*, 15
(October–December 1968): 691–703; Jacques Le Goff, "Les Mentalités," in Jacques Le
Goff and Pierre Nora, eds., *Faire De L'Histoire* (Paris, 1974), 3:76–94; G. Bouthol, *Les
Mentalités* (Paris, 1971); Georges Duby, "L'Histoire des mentalités," in *Encyclopédie de*

To venture into the domain of collective psychology is to navigate in deep waters. I will not attempt to identify some common psychological state produced by widely shared experiences, such as patterns of child rearing or the transition from the loving family to the oppressive school.[6] I believe there is no way to reconstruct a generational psyche equal to the sum of the individual personalities the evidence for which could only be found in each case history. This does not preclude the possibility of identifying certain shared attitudes or modes of response that reflect the experience of common historical circumstances at a certain life stage. This is challenge enough. In addition to the chronic problem of establishing the extent to which the assertion of widely accepted ideas might be age related, there is the task of showing how a certain style of discourse or pattern of behavior—or, even more vaguely, a temperamental tone—can be considered distinctive. Such characteristics as the deep, tender, and romantic friendships between young males do not seem to me to distinguish our cohort from other age groups, at least until past the middle of the century.[7] It is difficult to discern some distinctive pattern of explicit sexual attitudes, not to mention repressed desires and sublimated drives. The mixture of sentimental effusion and coarse appetite in the sexual awakenings of the young Comte or Delacroix, or the affected cynicism of Mérimée or Duvergier de Hauranne, do not especially differentiate their sexual sensibilities from familiar attributes of the youthful phase of the life cycle.

---

la pléiade. L'Histoire et ses méthodes (Paris, 1961), 937–66. For the application of the concept to the history of generations, see Anthony Esler, Generations in History (Author's copyright, 1982), 85–107; Brown, "The Generation of 1820," 35–39.

[6] For example, I find little to distinguish the socialization of successive cohorts in Anthony Esler's hypothesis that the "generational rebellion of the 1830's" owed something to the childhood experience of parental overindulgence followed by extreme repression at school. Anthony Esler, "Youth in Revolt: The French Generation of 1830," in Robert Bezucha, ed., Modern European Social History (Lexington, Ky., 1972), 308. For a view similar to mine, see Mazoyer, "Catégories d'âge et groupes sociaux," 387. See Fred Weinstein and Gerald M. Platt, "The Coming Crisis in Psychohistory," Journal of Modern History, 47 (June 1975): 212. "Historians cannot treat all the conceptual and environmental variables suggested by the need to fulfill ego requirements as subsidiary to the residual factors of childhood experiences."

[7] There are many examples of a rhetoric of friendship that in our day would be confined to lovers. Commenting on her father's schoolboy diary and correspondence, the daughter of Emile Bary (1799) characterized, "Ces expressions d'amitié que la fin du dix-neuvième siècle ne comprendrait plus." [Emile Bary], Les Cahiers d'un rhétoricien de 1815 (Paris, 1890), 170.

There were, however, salient attributes of the generation of 1820 that scarcely fit the traditional descriptions of the youthful stage. They were, in their own eyes at least, a sober generation—*grave* was their word for it—"sweet and serious," as Hugo had it, parading their dedication to *méditation sérieuse* and *saines études* (even Delacroix indulges in a certain amount of that) in self-conscious contrast to the meretricious cleverness of the Old Guard. They responded to familiar representations of feckless youth with quiet distaste. The *Globe* reviewed a Scribe play featuring the comic expedients of a young debtor with the remark, "we are tired of these good fellows, gamblers, and débauchés who are always attractive to women and who reform in the last act. . . . Fortunately our *jeunesse* is more serious and has better things than debts to create."[8] Not all of them are humorless—Balzac is in the cohort too, Rémusat writes humorous verse, the columns of the *Globe* supply a certain ration of polemical wit—but the general commitment in published works and private correspondence is to the higher seriousness.[9] Such temperamental attributes, not usually associated with the behavior of the young, lend a distinctive flavor to the cluster of ideas that comprised the particular "youth ideology."

The imbuing of doctrinal postulates with the color of a collective sensibility is typified by the persistent efforts of the Restoration *jeunesse* to come to terms with the problematic heritage of Voltaire. As André Billaz demonstrates in his definitive work *Les Ecrivains romantiques et Voltaire*, the second-generation romantics accepted neither the demonic version disseminated by the reactionary partisans of throne and altar nor the revival of the Voltaire cult in liberal circles.[10] To the extent

---

[8] *Globe*, 18 May 1825. For Hugo, see below in this chapter. The reference to *méditation sérieuse* appears in the Profession de foi of the *Globe*. For Delacroix see, for example, Delacroix to A. Piron, 8 October 1819, in Eugène Delacroix, *Lettres intimes* (Paris, 1954), 88: "L'étude console de tout. Les livres sont de vrais amis. Leur conversation silencieuse est exempte de querelles et de divisions. . . . Combien les livres ne nous font-ils pas oublier de chagrin, par le spectacle des hommes vertueux livrés au malheur." See also André F. Carrion-Nisas, *La France Au Dix-Neuvième Siècle; ou, Coup d'oeil sur l'état présent des lumières, des richesses, de la morale et de la liberté* (Paris, 1821), 12: "La jeunesse actuelle est grave et laborieuse, en dépit de ceux qui aimeraient mieux la voir plus futile, au risque de la voir plus immorale."

[9] The comic spirit of a young Balzac was, I think, compatible with the "gravity" of the generation's self-image. Barbéris, *Balzac Et Le Mal du siècle*, 1:122–23; Billaz, *Les Ecrivains romantiques et Voltaire*, 2:912–13.

[10] Billaz, *Les Ecrivains romantiques et Voltaire*, 2:828–29, 1002–5, R. R. Ridgway, *Voltaire and Sensibility* (Montreal and London, 1973), 266–72.

that they shared the common conception of Voltaire as the philosophe par excellence, incarnation of the eighteenth century—"le système critique ... c'est Voltaire tout entier"—they assigned him an historically indispensable, but inevitably obsolescent, role.[11] "It is not in the century of Bonaparte," writes the young Hugo, "that one can continue Voltaire."[12] But this did not entail a categorical repudiation. Rémusat's recollection that they had accepted Voltaire's conclusions while rejecting "his arguments, his doctrines, his language," referred on the one hand to the great blows struck at obscurantism and intolerance, and on the other to the failure to grasp the essential nature and sources of the religious spirit.[13]

There is something more complex than ideological difference in Rémusat's evocation of the *language* of Voltaire, in his repudiation of a style of discourse that reflected an objectionable literary and moral sensibility. But even in this regard the attitude toward Voltaire is qualified in the attempt to distinguish him from his contemporary epigoni. Defending the "young friends of the country" (that is, himself and his associates) against the accusation of having been insufficiently anticlerical and therefore false to the spirit of Voltaire, Paul Dubois contrasts the mendacious and flippant pseudo-Voltairians with the master himself, who had spoken "with all the seriousness and candor of his sublime reason."[14] Victor Hugo, who spent his life trying to come to terms with Voltaire, drew the same distinction. However flawed, Voltaire's genius was infinitely superior to its "frivolous and fatal applications." In the passage where Hugo asserts that one cannot continue Voltaire in Bonaparte's century, he contrasts the flabby and impudent literature that celebrated Cardinal Dubois, flattered Pompadour, and "outraged our Joan of Arc" with the literature appropriate to a new era. The new literature "keeps in step with the times, but at a grave and measured pace; its character is serious, its voice is sonorous and melodious; it is, in a word, what the general opinion of a great nation should be after great calamities—sad, proud, and religious."[15]

To grasp the actual correlative for the generational critique of the travesties of the Enlightenment, one has only to note what passed for

[11] *Producteur*, 3 (1826): 35.

[12] *Muse française*, 2:301.

[13] Rémusat, *Mémoires*, 2:149.

[14] Dubois, *Fragments littéraires*, 1:240, originally published in the *Globe*, 21 October 1826.

[15] *Muse française*, 2:302–6.

wit in the columns of the *Mercure* or the *Pandore*, where aging prima donnas such as Jay and Jouy paraded the cult and appropriated the mantle of Voltaire. There was, however, a deeper and more subtle strain in the moral and intellectual sensibility alien to the new generation that offended them because it puzzled them. This temperament was incarnated in Stendhal. We have seen how much Stendhal's exchange with the Saint-Simonians at the *Producteur* has to do with sensibility as well as substance. Cerclet and Carrel taxed him for his shallow and flippant approach to serious issues, and he summed up the controversy with reference to *"mes plaisanteries,"* and *"vos obscurités prétentieuses."* The memoirs of Delécluze record that afternoon in his Sunday salon when Cerclet appeared with the prospectus of the *Producteur* in hand to introduce the gathering to the principles of political economy. Beyle "made a frightful face, took his hat, and departed to the sound of general laughter at his detestation of political economy." One suspects that the ostentatious departure dramatized not so much a horror of political economy as the resolution not to be bored.[16]

It is scarcely surprising to discover that the Saint-Simonians in their early "industrial" phase and Stendahl were incompatible, but even the young literary critics who sensed that the scourge of a sclerotic classicism more or less belonged in their camp did not quite know how to assimilate him. For example, the *Muse française* gave his book on Rossini a good review, qualified with reference to "all the bizarre and paradoxical ideas, all the inappropriate expressions, all the faulty and slovenly turns of phrase encountered in these two volumes."[17] To the editors of the *Globe*, who had praised and published him, he became an increasingly irritating enigma. The mutual ambivalence in the relationship between Stendhal and that articulate portion of the *jeunesse* he once described as "the hope of the country" traces the temperamental frontier between the most perceptive and open-minded members of the successive cohorts.[18]

Jean-Jacques Goblot's meticulous essay on Stendhal's relations with

---

[16] Delécluze, *Souvenirs de soixante années*, 265. Rudé, *Stendhal Et La Pensée de son temps*, 101, remarks that the anecdote scarcely constitutes proof of Stendhal's indifference to political economy and merely recorded, "une boutade, une simple plaisanterie de salon."

[17] *Muse française*, 1:329.

[18] This appeared in the *Paris Monthly Review*. I will cite the edition of Stendhal's English journalism in his *Courrier anglais*, ed. H. Martineau (Paris, 1935), 1:329.

Paul Dubois and the *Globe* surveys the history of a deteriorating relationship in which temperamental differences were more important than incompatible doctrines.[19] Not that doctrinal differences were negligible. This is especially apparent in Stendhal's assessment of Victor Cousin and his coterie.[20] He admired the theatrical presence and the eloquence that had made disciples "of all our young Parisians if they are neither parasites of the court nor dupes of Jesuit intrigues," but found the actual substance of Cousin's philosophy obscurantist to the point of unintelligibility. His young followers had enlisted in the campaign to domesticate German mysticism and to repudiate the scientific psychology of Condillac, Cabanis, and Destutt de Tracy.

Stendhal never tried to reconcile his pleasure in the bold assault on the religious, classicist, and liberal establishments mounted by the young intellectuals, with his sense of their essential fatuity. He had been published and praised by the staff of the *Globe*, had frequented their circle at the Delécluze salon, and had enjoyed their successful campaign against Jouy, Jay, and all that clever, superficial "queue de Voltaire." But "the disciples of M. Cousin" he caricatured as the Roundheads of the literary civil wars, puritanical and pedantic, publishers of a passably sensible but infinitely boring journal.[21] He predicted their future success as replacements for the *arrivistes* in place, and—unforgivably—found them faintly comical. Perhaps he exaggerated a bit in remembering that he had made "eight or ten mortal enemies" by his friendly suggestion that the *Globe* was a trifle pedantic and slightly lacking in wit, but there is no doubt that his brand of wit left resentments to fester in the sensitive skins of erstwhile allies in the cultural campaigns of the Restoration.[22]

Even as the *Globe* fired off Stendhal's *Nouveau Complot* against the Saint-Simonians, it could not resist a little sanctimony, deploring the author's tendency to ad hominem argument as well as "this petty aristocratic affectation that conceals a French commoner beneath a Ger-

[19] Jean-Jacques Goblot, "Paul-François Dubois, Stendhal et 'Le Globe,' " *Stendhal Club*, 54 (15 January 1971): 121–43.

[20] See Hoog, "Un Intercesseur du romantisme," 185, for citation of Stendhal's references to Cousin.

[21] *Courrier anglais*, 4:332–33; Jean-Jaques Goblot, "Stendhal, Chroniqueur dévoilé? Le *Courrier anglais* et *Le Globe*," *Stendhal Club*, 56 (15 July 1972): 335–48.

[22] Stendhal, *Memoirs of an Egoist*, trans. T. W. Earp (New York, 1958), 128.

man name and title."²³ The young moralists never could assimilate M. Beyle's transparent pseudonym. Years later Mignet, who had exchanged compliments with him in the 1820s, recalled that "Beyle had wit, but not enough to be simple and natural; he affected eccentricity, and was bizarre rather than original; furthermore his books were no more authentic than his name."²⁴

This was the characteristic reminiscence of aging critics when, to their astonishment, Stendhal's stock began to rise in the middle of the century. Rémusat remembered his "singular melange of affectation and cynicism, his alternately clever and vulgar paradoxes," and Paul Dubois, lifetime guardian of the *Globe*'s memorial flame, would describe the snide critic of that noble journal as "a professional wit of labored originality, preoccupied with spoiling and perverting his natural gifts in the hope of astonishing his interlocutors."²⁵ Like his younger contemporaries, Stendhal despised that travesty of Voltairian irony characterized by cruel and shallow persiflage, but his own ambiguous brand of irony as the enemy of cant eluded or disturbed them. Even his close friends, the young aficionados of *beylisme*—Mérimée, Duvergier de Hauranne, and Victor Jacquemont (1801)—mistook his ironic intention for its cynical mask.

To be fair to the cohort of Rémusat and Dubois, one must admit that they were not the only contemporaries who found it difficult to swallow the paradoxes of Henri Beyle. Stendhal's friend and coeval Etienne Delécluze (1781) never could decide whether his peculiar companion was more admirable than exasperating.²⁶ But, like Stendhal, Delécluze could not march to the music of the young intellectuals whom he befriended, entertained, and admired. For their guru, Victor Cousin, he felt nothing but contempt—"the most insufferable poseur whom I

---

²³ *Globe*, 17 December 1825, reprinted in Stendhal, *D'Un Nouveau Complot*, 48.

²⁴ Quoted in the *Divan* edition of Stendhal, *Correspondance* (Paris, 1934), 6:124. For the retrospective ambivalence of Stendhal's close friend Mérimée, see Baschet, *Du Romantisme au Second Empire*, 24–25.

²⁵ Rémusat, *Mémoires*, 2:141; Dubois, quoted in Goblot, "Dubois, Stendhal, et 'Le Globe,'" 122. Sainte-Beuve characteristically disparaged Delécluze for insufficient recognition of Stendhal's talent and Balzac for praising it too much. Sainte-Beuve, *Nouveaux lundis*, 3:110; *Causeries du lundi*, 9:337. As early as 1824, Delacroix thought that Stendhal was, "rude, arrogant when he is right, and often nonsensical." Eugène Delacroix, *The Journal of Eugène Delacroix*, trans. Walter Pach (New York, 1937), 59.

²⁶ See the chapter, with citation of key sources, "Stendhal chez Delécluze," in Baschet, *E.-J. Delécluze*, 126–58.

have ever met." He respected the ex-*normaliens* and the other stars of the *Globe* circle who ornamented his Sunday gatherings but found them pedantic and didactic to the point where he had to burst out of their suffocating atmosphere, uttering "asinine commonplaces in order to reassure ourselves that we had not been smothered by that cacophony of doctrinaire, pedantic jargon."[27]

The temperamental element that separated the serious and self-important children of the brand-new century from the cohort of Delécluze and Stendhal also distinguished them from their younger brothers, who were often assimilated into a "generation of 1830." The personal style of Paul Dubois or Charles Rémusat or Alfred de Vigny, or even Victor Hugo, is not that of Théophile Gautier (1811) or Petrus Borel (1809) or Philothée O'Neddy (1811). The generation of 1820 had no particular desire to outrage society or *épater la bourgeoisie*, no interest in establishing a separate identity by deviating from social norms or by adopting distinctive styles of dress and behavior.

The changes wrought in the behavior of the successive cohorts reflect changes in the nature of what they opposed. The cultural establishment defied by the flamboyant shock troops at the battle of *Hernani* wore the black uniform of the complacent bourgeoisie; the neoclassicism combated by the generation of 1820 was still clad in the spiritual clothing of the eighteenth century.

Perhaps I have overdrawn the image of a *jeunesse* that was prematurely old. Not all of them had assumed the posture of the dignitaries they expected to become. Paul Dubois distinguishes the *jeunes savants* (including himself) from a "less disciplined *jeunesse*, capricious students, fond of daydreams and the pleasure, passion, and tumult of the artistic, commercial, and worldly aspects of Paris society."[28] But these more unbuttoned types—protorepublicans in the circle around Joseph Guinard, Charles Thomas, and Godefroy Cavaignac—were deadly serious in their opposition to the established order. They were not concerned with offending the proprieties but with overthrowing the regime. Their alienation was expressed not in a cultural Bohemia but in the political arena. And among their coevals who stifled Delécluze in their instant seminars or undertook to regenerate humanity by the way of industrial statistics were those who also risked their lives in the flam-

---

[27] Delécluze, *Journal*, 226, 78, 118.
[28] Dubois, "Souvenirs inédits," *Revue bleue*, 10 (8 August 1908): 161.

boyant projects of the secret societies. The grave *jeunes savants*, the prophets of a *juste milieu*, the future fathers of the Saint-Simonian evangel, the successive *promotions* of student militants, the cadre of professional ex-students, the ambitious young lawyers, and the anonymous apprentices of commercial establishments had all been seized by that momentary "mania for conspiracy." In their Promethean, potentially suicidal commitment to the far-fetched conspiracies of the early twenties, they seem unlikely candidates for their future eminence in the *juste milieu* and appropriate subjects for Lewis Feuer's survey of rebellious youth movements whose messianic and self-destructive alienation expresses the "deauthorization" of their fathers' generation.[29]

I have treated the subjects of this work as a cohort, chronologically defined in the light of contemporary perceptions and collective behavior, that is, as situated in a succession of historical contexts rather than in the biological succession of parent and child. But it would overdo methodological purity to pretend that the relation between successive cohorts had nothing to do with specific fathers and sons. Feuer was not the first to suppose that the collective repudiation of an older generation had something to do with the relation of children to parents. The generation of 1820 certainly met Feuer's standard of having deauthorized "the older generation as a collective whole." I have tried to show that this is what unified them irrespective of other loyalties. Even when they stood, as they often did, in their parents' political or ideological camp, they made a point of asserting their independence of the claims of seniority, whether in ambiguous alliance with aging grandees in the Carbonari, in relation to the liberal establishment that edited the *Constitutionnel* or the royalists who controlled the Academy, or in a dismissal of the pretensions of the Doctrinaires to dominate the *Globe* or of Catholic dignitaries to indicate the limitations of an appropriate romanticism.

There is little evidence, however, that this particular conflict of generations was "founded," as Feuer puts it, on a conflict between fathers and sons. One can scarcely find the "primal source" of the alienation of this generation in "father hatred" if we are considering the hatred of actual fathers by specific sons, whereas there are many examples of filial deference and affection.

There is certainly evidence of conflict and tension, most often of a

---

[29] Lewis S. Feuer, *The Conflict of Generations* (New York, 1969).

classic, recurrent sort, notably over the choice of a career—young J. B.
Boussingault (1801) off to the new School of Mines despite his father's
qualms about a "dangerous and difficult" occupation, or Balzac nego-
tiating support for a trial period as a writer, or Hector Berlioz pursuing
a musical career in the teeth of parental opposition.[30] There are the familiar maternal admonitions. "Don't concern yourself with politics, . . .
earn the esteem of your superiors and all honorable persons, respect
and never contradict *les opinions*";[31] or, "Speak frankly to me my child,
. . . but guard your tongue before others; respect the opinions and sentiments of those who are overwrought in these dangerous times."[32]

But the sons' responses are almost always fond and deferential, and
their reminiscences almost always characterize their parents in terms
amounting to veneration. Emile Bary (1799), seventeen-year-old *rhétoricien* writes to ask his father's permission to form an intimate friendship with a classmate: "Although your claims to my loyalty are more
sacred in my eyes that those of Bréville [the chum], his are almost as
dear to me." Calculated to sweeten the old man? Perhaps, but in his
notebook, for his own eyes, Bary ponders, "Shouldn't I ask myself before taking any action, will this please my father?"[33] Bary was very
young then, and certainly *bien élevé*, and he would grow up along these
lines to become a thoroughly conventional schoolmaster. But more as-
sertive egos expressed a similar respect. At the age of twenty-two,
Michelet can still pose the question to himself, "At what age is it per-
missible to disobey one's father in order to undertake a just action?
When does one attain his moral maturity?"[34] Michelet is perhaps the
most striking example of a precocious child destined in his own, and

---

[30] J.-B. Boussingault, *Mémoires de J.-B. Boussingault* (Paris, 1892), 1:256; Barbéris,
Balzac Et Le Mal du siècle, 1:146; Hector Berlioz, *The Memoirs of Hector Berlioz*, trans.
David Cairns (London, 1969), 48–49. For a classical example of the conflict between a
Voltairian father and a romantic son, see George Brunet, Introduction to Lefèvre[-
Deumier], *Les Vespres de l'Abbaye du Val*, xliv. For another ambivalent relationship, see
Eugène Bonnemère, *Biographie des deux Bodins* (Angers, 1846), 48–49.

[31] Boussingault, *Mémoires*, 1:270. Boussingault's mother begged him to leave politics
out of letters to his father, who was already upset by the consequences of the June 1820
riots. "Ces jeunes étourdis," wrote his father, "ont porté, sans le prévoir, le deuil dans
le coeur de leurs pères." Ibid., 268. F.W.J. McCosh, *Boussingault. Chemist and Agriculturist* (Boston, 1984), 1–26.

[32] Mme. de Rémusat to Charles, April 1814, in Rémusat, *Correspondance*, 1:4.

[33] Bary, *Les Cahiers d'un rhétoricien de 1815*, 110, 176.

[34] Michelet, *Ecrits de jeunesse*, 98.

his parents', eyes to transcend his father's station. Aware from an early age of his potential superiority, Michelet retained a "veneration for that excellent man, cool in the face of danger, cheerful when threatened with misfortune, with an inexhaustible fund of kindness for those he loved."[35]

Even those with far more problematic family situations would express little overt hostility in their behavior or their reminiscences. The story of Victor Hugo's voyage from his mother's intransigent royalism to a reconciliation with the revolutionary general who was his father has often been told. Auguste Comte, who would eventually conclude that there must have been a cosmic discrepancy in the production of such a remarkable son by such an insignificant father, remained on reasonably good terms with his father and on loving terms with his mother before his first breakdown.[36]

Perhaps there was some deauthorization of fathers in the deification of mothers. This was a generation rich in model boys with formidable, angelic mothers. The frequent and deeply affectionate correspondence of Quinet with his mother, or Rémusat with his, or Vigny with his, suggests the unanswerable question of whether "mother" should be read as "father." Vigny was explicit—his mother played the masculine, and his father the soft, feminine, role in the family circle.[37] J. B. Boussingault's description of what a promising boy could expect from a sensitive mother could have been expressed at any time and place in the modern era, but it is certainly a common theme in our cohort's recollection. Boussingault concluded on the basis of his own experience that the right sort of mother adores her most gifted child even when the rest of the family, including the father, misunderstands him.[38]

Of course, not every mother gave her highly endowed, determined,

---

[35] Ibid., 212.

[36] Gouhier, *La Vie d'Auguste Comte*, 33.

[37] Vigny, *Mémoires*, 55. According to Kenneth Keniston, "Among both the alienated and the young radicals [of the 1960s], there is evidence of an unusually strong tie to the *mother* in early childhood." Kenneth Keniston, "Different Childhood Experiences of Radical and Alienated Youth," in Alexander Klein, ed., *Natural Enemies* (Philadelphia, 1969), 266.

[38] Boussingault, *Mémoires*, 1:150: "Les enfants un peu doués, laborieux, décidés (j'en avais donné des preuves), sont généralement adorés de leur mère, à moins que celle-ci ne soit une femme vulgaire. Le père, le reste de la famille peuvent ne pas les comprendre, les blâmer même sur la direction qu'ils ont prise, la mère intelligente ne s'y trompe jamais."

and hard-working son the warmth and admiration he deserved. In all of the memoirs, reminiscences, and anecdotes that I have seen, the bitterest expression of filial resentment is that of Adolphe Blanqui, the eminent older brother of the revolutionary. In his successful middle years he is still obsessed by the coldness and even hostility of his youthful, beautiful, frivolous, widowed mother: "This has consumed my entire life as if a slow and subtle poison had run through my veins."[39] None of this turned Adolphe Blanqui into a rebel. He shared his generation's attitudes, the shaping experience of his cohort in the imperial *lycée,* and the desperate scramble for occupational survival in the early Restoration years, but he did not conspire and never understood, "even in my youth, and while sharing the liberal illusions of my contemporaries, this continuous intervention of students in political affairs; how can one pursue serious studies under the influence of constant turbulence and of cabals where impudent braggarts masquerade as men of good will?"[40] Perhaps this was because he always loved his father. It was the younger son, the mother's favorite, who became the rebel.

As another example, Adolphe Thiers, who despised his father with good reason but loved his mother and venerated his grandmother, was a rather qualified Young Turk in the 1820s. He steered clear of the conspiracies and worked closely with the elder statesmen of the *Constitutionnel* and other opposition journals.[41]

One might milk something out of the fragmentary materials on family relationships of the most militant and imprudent leaders of the period of the conspiracies between 1820 and 1823 (Trélat, Buchez, Bazard, and the others),[42] but my reading of that evidence establishes no

[39] Blanqui, "Souvenirs d'un lycéen de 1814," *Revue de Paris,* 134 (1 May 1916): 110–11.

[40] Blanqui, "Souvenirs d'un étudiant sous la Restauration," *Revue de Paris,* 149 (1 November 1918): 168–69. Balzac is another who remembered his mother with bitter resentment.

[41] Thiers' father had deserted his family when Thiers was a child. For an example of the son's ferocious contempt when his father played the role of sponger, see "Thiers à son père, Paris 14 juillet 1832," published in Fernand Benoit, "Monsieur Thiers A La Conquête de Paris: Documents inédits (1821–1833)," *Correspondant,* 287 (1 June 1922): 817–19.

[42] Bazard was an illegitimate child. Buchez deeply loved his mother and apparently had ambivalent feelings toward his father. Isambert, *De la Charbonnerie au saint-simonisme,* 15–30.

correlation between the repudiation of specific fathers and the irrational political choices of their sons.

The point of dwelling on this issue is not to insist that Feuer's model fails to fit the case but to pose the problem of the discrepancy between the collective repudiation of the parents' generation and individual deference to particular parents. This is a significant and puzzling element in reimagining that generational *mentalité*, especially in light of the contempt for political and moral opportunists expressed by sons who might first have observed the sordid fluctuations of the *girouette* in the course of their fathers' careers.

Some fairly obvious repression-sublimation models, in the spirit of Feuer's unconscious origins of generational revolt, come to mind.[43] Unable to accept their contempt for their own fathers, the sons projected it onto the entire elder cohort—or something like that. Such explanations are usually circular. The absence of overt hostility suggests repression; the existence of the latent hostility is deduced from the assumed repression.

I can think of a single more or less documented example of sublimation of family conflicts into general conceptions of the contrast between cohorts. This is exposed in Charles Rémusat's dense and loving correspondence with his mother just at the point when his father was to negotiate the transition from dignitary of the Empire to functionary in the Bourbon administration and shortly before Charles was to launch his career as spokesman for a *jeunesse* untainted by the temptation of "gold and power" to which the older generation had succumbed. In his memoirs, Rémusat reproduces the entire text of a letter in which Mme. de Rémusat, sometime lady-in-waiting to the empress, chides her impetuous child for his scornful comments on Chateaubriand's literary crucifixion of his parents' former employer: He had no idea how much his father and mother had suffered under a regime they had continued to serve out of concern for his future. They had always been monarchists at heart. He would do well to guard his sardonic tongue and curb his contempt for a human species that could still produce such generous beings as the emperors of Russia and Austria and such well-intentioned men as "our princes." Years later, reflecting on this "touching and remarkable" letter, Rémusat recalled that he had not blamed his parents, who were forced to walk a fine line in cele-

---

[43] Feuer, *The Conflict of Generations*, 529.

brating the fall of the Empire without defaming it, but that he had never agreed with them.[44]

The obvious flaw in citing Rémusat to illustrate filial ambivalence is that his situation was unique. As he said, he went right from the *lycée* to this mother's salon. His parents were so consequentially committed to the service of his own ambitions, and he had such confidence in a personal future temporarily blighted by the ultraroyalism that also terminated his father's career, that it is difficult to characterize his coevals in the light of his example.

Without wishing to reject an interpretation in the absence of evidence, I find the accretion of particular examples of parent-child conflict less illuminating than reference to the collective experience of the objective, that is to say, the historical, situation of the age group. What they experienced in common was to be in just that place, at just that time, at a certain age. I share the conviction of Pierre Barbéris that, in this case at least, "History's great pulsations matter more than the secrets of the heart."[45] Or perhaps one might say that the generation's heart beat to history's pulsations. Eric Erikson's observation that cultural and historical change can prove "traumatic to identity formation: it can break up the inner consistency of a child's hierarchy of expectations" suggests the relation of the historical trauma of the collapse of the Empire to the expectations of the cohort emerging from adolescence at the moment of Napoleon's Götterdämmerung.[46] It was its chronological location that gave the cohort a collective identity as a historical generation as distinct from the solidarity that simply reflects a common position in the youthful stage of the life cycle. The experience of epochal transformations contributed to the historicist cast of a "total ideology" in Mannheim's sense of the fundamental concepts that are an outgrowth of a collective life.

The characterization of post-Enlightenment thought as "historicist" in some sense of the word is a commonplace.[47] Given the ubiquitous

---

[44] The letter is reproduced in Rémusat, *Correspondance*, cited above in note 31 and in his *Mémoires*, 1:144–46.

[45] Barbéris, *Balzac Et Le Mal du siècle*, 1:113.

[46] Eric H. Erikson, *Identity, Youth and Crisis* (New York, 1968), 159.

[47] I will define "historicism" as does Maurice Mandelbaum, *History, Man, and Reason*, 42: "historicism is the belief that an adequate understanding of the nature of any phenomenon and an adequate assessment of its value are to be gained through consid-

influence of intellectual systems grounded in a reading of the past, one can scarcely claim that a historicist temper of mind distinguished the Restoration intelligentsia from its older contemporaries in or out of France. What was distinctive was the way in which the generation of 1820 articulated its historical understanding as a particular "youth ideology" that, precisely as in Eisenstadt's definition, perceived youth as a distinctive human type bearing the indispensable values of the community and perceived the older generation as inadequate to new realities by the very fact of its seniority. This was the conviction that unified those who had grown up in the Empire's waning years, irrespective of their political loyalties or aesthetic preferences.[48]

Victor Cousin's appeal to the emerging generation as the last, best hope of the suffering nation, Jouffroy's eulogy for the predestined apostles of the new era, or the Saint-Simonians' summons to the *génération actuelle* to prepare the organization of the new social system, articulated the common conviction that a unique destiny was not the product of some inborn merit but of history, above all of the gigantic historical divide of the Revolution. They deserved no credit for having had the good fortune to inherit the Revolution without having made it, but because this legacy was received with spotless hands, "contemporary youth combined all of the attributes of a generation destined to establish the public weal on firm foundations."[49]

These were the sentiments of Carrion-Nisas, mouthpiece of the militant elements in the Paris faculties. When the generation spoke through Victor Hugo from the other side of the political and religious barricades, the loyalties were different but the self-image was the same: "A sweet and serious generation arises all around; full of memories and hope, it reclaims its future from the self-styled philosophers of the last century, who would like it to resume their past." Its spiritual purity enables it to forgive the crimes of its predecessors while repudiating atheism, anarchy, and the deadly heritage of the Revolution. It had returned to religion as the source of life; while the generations of antiquity had only demanded that their poets give them laws, contemporary youth required a new faith.[50]

---

ering it in terms of the place which it occupied and the role it played within the process of development."

[48] See the excellent treatment of this theme in Brown, "*The Generation of 1820*," 121–24.

[49] André F. Carrion-Nisas, *De la Jeunesse française* (Paris, 1820), 6.

[50] This piece was first published in the *Muse française*, 1:75–76. Even in his most roy-

The antiroyalist element among Hugo's educated coevals would, no doubt, have agreed that they constituted a sweet and serious generation in search of a faith but would have refused to repudiate the heritage of the Revolution. They were, wrote Charles Rémusat in 1818, "born of the Revolution" and steeped in its principles and consequences.[51] In a favorable review of a new law journal, Augustin Thierry took occasion to link the brilliant revival of legal studies to the rediscovery of the foundations laid by the Revolution beneath the ruins of the Empire:

> In the year 1814 the French Revolution suddenly awakened. Springing out of the morass of the Empire, liberal France reappeared, brilliant and young, like those cities discovered after centuries, intact under layers of lava. The spirit of a France reborn transformed the colorless and lifeless legal profession and the schools of law. In the last five years this new life has spawned a multitude of generous aspirations, distinguished creations, and national reputations. The dogma of sacred liberty has resounded in the courts and the classrooms; though often proscribed, it will never again surrender its terrain.[52]

One must not read such celebrations of the revolutionary legacy in Thierry or Rémusat as nostalgia for an obsolete revolutionary *politique*. The *esprit révolutionnaire* was not to be confounded with the *esprit né de la révolution*—what the former had undertaken, the latter was to consolidate.[53] The mission of the fathers was to destroy, that of the sons to conserve. And as Théodore Jouffroy had argued with great effect, the very nature of their accomplishments disqualified the surviving members of the revolutionary generation from occupying the ground they had cleared.

Such presumptions assumed the authority of historical laws. "Political revolutions," observed de Staël-Holstein, "like maladies of the human body, reach a limit that it is more or less possible to identify. This

---

alist phase, Hugo expressed a solidarity with his coevals. In January 1822 he wrote an imprudent letter to the mother of a childhood friend who was implicated in the Carbonari offering to hide him from the police. Hugo to Mme. Delon ca.2 January 1822, in Hugo, *Oeuvres*, 2:1323.

[51] Charles de Rémusat, "La Révolution française," *Passé et Présent* (Paris, 1847), 1:109.

[52] Thierry, *Dix Ans d'études historiques*, 496, first published in the *Censeur européen*, 1 May 1820.

[53] Rémusat, "La Révolution française," 109–11.

limit is the point at which the combatants who opened the struggle begin to retire from the field and at which a new generation begins to
replace them."[54] De Staël intended a critique of the exclusion of the
young from the political system. Ulysse Trélat would retrospectively
apply the same considerations to those who had tried to overthrow it.
The new era required a new generation. The young had been the first
to risk the overthrow of the *royauté-cosaque*. If some of the senior elements had not completely lost their nerve, they no longer displayed the
old dynamism.[55] Trélat arrived at these conclusions in the light of his
experience as a conspirator in the early 1820s. His experience as a
young doctor during the same period impelled him to deplore the "old
conviction that the genuine representatives of science ought to have
white hair," when, in fact, their years away from the living practice of
medicine in the hospital guaranteed the incompetence of venerable
doctors who still retained "public confidence as an acquired possession."[56]

Philippe Buchez, who collaborated with Trélat in political conspiracy and medical publication, gave these convictions a Saint-Simonian
twist. The appointment of doctors and other *savants* to the Academy of
Science stimulated the reflection that past a certain age academicians
ought to be made "honorary," and admitted to a legalized retirement
in order to make way for young minds full of energy and force: "Our
savants are far enough from readying themselves for the role of spiritual directors of society."[57]

As in the professions, so in the arts. The crop of literary works composed by *"jeunes gens, . . .* precocious writers, formed by the new century" was manifestly superior to the productions of a crabbed and prej-
udiced gerontocracy. That did not inhibit the graybeards from reading
moral lessons to a brave *jeunesse* whose pure voice "had never praised
anarchy or despotism, had never humiliated the unfortunate nor flattered the powerful, had never taken two oaths and would never sell
itself for money."[58] Thus J. J. Darmaing, ex-*normalien* and aspiring
journalist, damns the older generation, not only because it was hope-

[54] Auguste de Staël-Holstein, *Du Nombre et de l'âge des députés* (Paris, 1819), 58.

[55] Trélat, *Paris révolutionnaire*, 2:277.

[56] Ulysse Trélat, *De La Constitution du corps des médecins et de l'enseignement médical*
(Paris, 1828), 69–71.

[57] *Producteur*, 5 (1826): 102.

[58] J. J. Darmaing, *Le Surveillant politique et littéraire* (Paris, 1818), 71.

lessly rigid in its devotion to obsolete dogma but also because it had been shamefully flexible in its response to the temptations of power. Even the very best of those who had survived the heroic epoch of the Revolution were stained by the compromises required for survival or had become so disillusioned by the failure of grandiose ideals as to fall prey to the meretricious awards of the Empire. "We, on the other hand," affirms Charles Rémusat, "should be proof against false promises, prestige, or power."[59] This crucial contrast between the "clean hands" of an idealistic youth and the tainted past of aging *girouettes* was emphasized by young publicists in all the political camps, from the manifestos of the student agitators of 1820 to Victor Hugo's poetic lampoon of the political operator in the first issue of the *Conservateur littéraire*.[60]

The conviction of superior rectitude was a vital constituent of the generation's *mentalité*; the comtemplation of the political turncoat was, quite literally, part of its education. The students of 1814–1815 had been assembled in the courtyards of their *lycées* by teachers sporting white cockades where the tricolor had been pinned the day before and marched into chapels still echoing with imperial hosannas to celebrate a thanksgiving mass for the return of good King Louis XVIII.[61] They had been harangued at academic ceremonies by Fontanes, the grand master of the University and master of the grand eulogy, who switched

[59] Rémusat, "La Révolution française," 115–16.

[60] [Senemaud], *Détails historiques sur les événements de la première quinzaine de juin MDCCCXX, par M. Senemaud, élève de la Faculté de droit de Paris* (Paris, 1820), 8: "quel nom, selon les hommes sages, doit mériter une jeunesse dont les mains sont pures de sang, dont les années n'ont point été souillées, de qui le coeur n'est point noir et coupable, mais franc, sensible, généreux, et toujours ému aux noms sacrés de Patrie et d'Honneur?" Victor Hugo, "L'Enrôleur politique," *Conservateur littéraire*, 1 (December 1819), and his unpublished "Dialogue entre le drapeau et la girouette," in *Oeuvres*, 1:417–18. See also, among many other examples of this attitude, Saint-Valry in the *Muse française*, 2:343–44.

[61] See, for example, Blanqui, "Souvenirs d'un lycéen," 134 (1 May 1916): 115 (cited in chapter 2); Boussingault, *Mémoires*, 1:89. There is a similar description in the semi-fictionalized reminiscence of one of Jules Simon's old teachers, Simon, *Mémoires des autres*, 76: "Je vous laisse à penser ce qui nous arriva en 1815, nos transports au 20 mars, nos désespoirs au 8 juillet, et le parfait mépris que nous inspirèrent nos maîtres, qui passèrent trois fois d'un enthousiasme à un autre. Il nous semblait que nous n'avions plus affaire qu'à des comédiens, qui changeaient de costume et de rôle au moindre signe du régisseur."

from emperor to monarch without breaking oratorical stride.[62] They took up their literary careers in the patronizing presence of the Augers and Jouys, whose own careers had been ornamented by the instinct for the main chance and the mutual aggrandizement of the literary coterie.

The perception of checkered careers, however successful, gave young critics the courage to come to grips with old dignitaries. When the young poet Charles Loyson (1791) took his turn at confronting Benjamin Constant, he turned predictably to the liberal titan's past:

> You have presumed to eclipse the name of an obscure young man in the rays of your glory . . . but, after all, I am young, Sir, and you have been around for a long time. For a man who has navigated for twenty years through revolutionary chaos, the memory of the past should suggest more than one reef to avoid.[63]

Beyond the failure of the moral authority of a less than perfect older generation there was the more profound ideological failure. This was the inability to reconstruct. We have seen the immense appeal in Henri de Saint-Simon's or Victor Cousin's or Auguste Comte's promise to assuage the thirst for synthesis by the formulation of a new general doctrine. Occasionally, as when articulated by the young admirers of La-mennais, the indispensable synthesis was actually to be in the form of an *old* general doctrine, but it was more often assumed that the necessary concomitant of a new world was to be a new unifying ideology. This was the overriding aspiration not only of the Saint-Simonians but also of the enthusiastic public for Cousin's lectures and for Jouffroy's historical sketch of the destiny of dogmas, wherein the old revolutionary generation is to succumb, "not as adversaries of old dogmas . . . but as adversaries of all dogmas; they had conquered as enemies of everything false, but as they were unable to reveal the truth, the people were

---

[62] For vintage Fontanes, see Louis Fontanes, *Collection complète des discours de M. Fontanes* (Paris, 1821), especially his *discours* at the *distribution des prix* from *1809 to 1814*.

[63] Charles Loyson, *Oeuvres choisies* (Paris, 1869), 336, originally published in *Lettre à M. Benjamin Constant, l'un des rédacteurs de la 'Minerve'* (Paris, 1819). See Dubois, *Fragments littéraires*, 1:253–54, on the "liberal Jesuits" at the *Constitutionnel*: "il s'est formé depuis douze ans une génération d'hommmes qui, Dieu merci, n'a pas pris de lui [*Le Constitutionnel*] ses opinions. Nous appartenons à cette génération; et comme elle, nous n'avons ni odieux souvenirs, ni lâches transactions à cacher."

alienated from them by the need to believe and delivered them to the vengeance of their enemies."[64]

Thus, in the company of Comte, Cousin, and the Saint-Simonians, Jouffroy diagnoses the excess of skepticism and the critical spirit as the essential malady that it is the destiny of the new generation to cure. This mission, conceived in its broadest sense, as it usually was, was not merely to articulate a new faith but to create the ideological cement for the entire society. It was the task of the *génération nouvelle*, wrote Tanneguy-Duchâtel, to provide the new theories: "It is up to us to create the doctrines that should shape our moral, religious, political, and literary life, for those left to us by our fathers are sterile and shopworn."[65]

The conception of the integrating function of culture had its implication for art as well as philosophy and political economy. Numerous versions of Bonald's assertion that literature was the expression of society were cast in the form of ethical norms, and not only in the columns of the *Producteur*. In their review of the salon of 1824, Ferdinand Flocon (1800) and Marie Aycard (1794) remind young artists that "the real goal of their art to which they ought ceaselessly to strive is to instruct and to move. A moral or patriotic conception should guide their brushes if they wish to combine every distinction and conquer that double laurel of which Horace speaks: "Omne tulit punctum qui mescuit utile dulci" [He carries every point who combines the useful with the pleasant]."[66] The observation that art is a social product was transformed into the stipulation that art should have a social function— even in the *Muse française*, where Victor Hugo defines the novelist's goal as "to express a useful truth in an interesting tale."[67] Virtually no one in the generation of 1820, not even Victor Cousin, who used the phrase in the 1840s, was a partisan of *"l'art pour l'art,"* and this sharply separates them from their successors in the cohort of Théophile Gautier.[68] Cousin's great appeal to his Restoration audience lay precisely in

---

[64] Jouffroy, "Comment Les Dogmes finissent," in *Cahier Vert*, 75.

[65] *Globe*, 20 November 1824.

[66] Ferdinand Flocon and Marie Aycard, *Salon de 1824* (Paris, 1824), 4.

[67] *Muse française*, 1:29; Stenzel and Thoma, "Poésie et société dans la critique littéraire du *Globe*," 30; Max Milner, *Le Romantisme*, 202, cites passages in which Hugo affirms, "l'autosuffisance de l'art et la necessité de la soustraire aux exigences de l'utilité sociale et de la morale," which shows that Hugo was, on this as other subjects, inconsistent.

[68] Albert Cassagne, *La Théorie de l'art pour l'art en France* (Paris, 1906), 37–38.

that assimilation of beauty to truth and goodness, in that cosmic synthesis that was, presumably, to fill the void at the center of the generation's moral universe.[69]

The familiar descriptions of romantic individualism in the arts and of the aesthetics of cultural synthesis are reconciled in Max Milner's distinguished treatment of romanticism. Beneath the "multiplicity of tendencies," the affirmation of the creative ego, and the celebration of human diversity, Milner discerns "a sort of underlying purpose" that characterized the entire era. This was the search for a synthesis that might reestablish the fractured equilibrium between man and his universe. With wholesome resolution, the French romantics had reacted against feelings of isolation, helplessness, and absurdity induced by the experience of historical catastrophes and political disappointments.[70]

The criteria of synthesis, unity, and collective purpose were not, however, applied consistently or without qualification. The *Globe*'s polemic against Saint-Simonian dogmatism reflected another facet of the self-image of the contemporary *jeunesse*—the affirmation of libertarian values and the freedom from cultural conventions. At its most consistent, in the writings of Paul Dubois, the *Globe*'s liberalism was a set of deductions from its commitment to "*laissez faire, laissez passer*: that is the fundamental maxim of the nineteenth century. It is the remedy for all evil and the source of all improvement."[71]

From this rampart the *globistes* sallied forth to do battle, not only with the shopworn supporters of a narrow anticlericalism or a suffocating neoclassicism, but with the young heirs of Saint-Simon, who decried an excessive "liberty of conscience," or with the young acolytes of Lamennais on the *Mémorial catholique*, who had not the least intention of allowing truth and error equal time. They proudly accepted the designation of "protestant" applied by the *Mémorial* to their affirmations of autonomous judgment.[72]

---

[69] Cousin's Platonism and his belief that beauty was a manifestation of God's presence certainly distanced him from the sort of utilitarian aesthetic that was affirmed by the Saint-Simonians; Milner, *Le Romantisme*, 202. However, the assimilation of beauty to truth and goodness implies an ethical, and therefore a social, evaluation of art. See especially, Will, *Flumen Historicum*, 1–13.

[70] Milner, *Le Romantisme*, 205, 227.

[71] *Globe*, 5 November 1825.

[72] According to Ludovic Vitet, romanticism was "en deux mots, le protestantisme

But, as the polemicists of the *Mémorial* were able to demonstrate with shrewd citations from the columns of the *Globe*,[73] the conflict was within the liberal mind itself. The most dedicated libertarians would be unable to resolve the discrepancy between the pluralism of commitment to an unqualified liberty of opinion and the organicism of the demand for a new unifying social doctrine. Paul Dubois offered no comfort "to those who assumed that the positive beliefs of the future were at hand in this age of transition. Neither the doctrines of Lamennais nor the dogmas of industrialism were to become the religion of the century, whose character was not to have one [dogma] but to have one thousand."[74] This pluralist version of contemporary uncertainties cannot, in principle, be squared with Jouffroy's evocation of the new regenerating dogma or with the lectures of Victor Cousin that promised to transcend the critical spirit of the eighteenth century in a higher synthesis of all that was best in past thought. Cousin's lectures expose the very bones of the dilemma in formulations that present as solutions what are really statements of the problem, as in his commitment to reconstruct eternal beliefs out of contemporary materials and to arrive at unity by the route of the experimental method.[75]

Cousin's assertion that the experimental method will arrive at truths congruent with immanent Reason lays claim to the sort of authority asserted by Comte or the Saint-Simonians when they insist on the mathematical certainty of the propositions of a valid science of society. The positivists, in turn, were caught in their own version of the contradiction between a radical empiricism in the spirit of David Hume and the presumptions of a positivist metaphysics.[76] When Laurent's review of Cousin's philosophy in the *Producteur* proceeded from a critique of the philosopher's penchant for "ontological hypotheses" to a defense of sensationalist psychology, the editors hastened to insert a

---

dans les lettres et les arts." *Globe*, 2 April 1825, reprinted in Trahard, "Le Romantisme défini par 'le Globe,'" 21.

[73] *Mémorial catholique*, 4 (1825): 136–55; see F. A. Isambert, "Epoques critiques et époques organiques: Une contribution de Buchez à la théorie sociale des saint-simoniens," *Cahiers internationaux de sociologie*, 27 (July–December 1959): 137.

[74] Dubois, *Fragments littéraires*, 1:102, originally published in the *Globe*, 20 July 1825.

[75] Cousin, *Fragments philosophiques*, 1:82.

[76] Mandelbaum, *History, Man, and Reason*, 10–11, makes this distinction in contrasting the critical positivism of Huxley and Mach with the systematic positivism of Comte and Spencer.

footnote asserting the absolute neutrality of the journal on any question that did not bear in a practical way on the perfection of human society.[77] This epistemological chastity, the vow never to partake of pseudoproblems, did not inhibit the Saint-Simonians or Auguste Comte in their search for the historically inevitable, socially indispensable, logically irrefutable, grand general doctrine.

The tension between liberty and unity, pluralism and synthesis, was to be resolved by the authority of a uniquely privileged location in, and therefore access to, history. Edgar Quinet, who was eleven years of age at the Empire's fall, recalled that:

> the great invasions of 1814 and 1815 had left a wealth of impressions in my memory, images through which I perceived everything. My earliest education had been the collapse of a world. I was interested in everything in the past that suggested some resemblance to those immense upheavals that had been my first experience. Thanks to this analogy, a history which I could not have experienced was brought to life. The past became in many respects my turbulent present.[78]

Thus the collapse of the Empire rendered the past both problematic and accessible to its last cohort. Once engaged in the illumination of its present situation through reflection on the past, the generation of 1820 would not stop with the history of the Empire. It was impelled to situate its own era in some intelligible relationship to the entire course of those immense transformations that constituted the history of France from the destruction of the Old Regime to the Restoration of the Bourbon monarchy and then to rethink the historical thought of the previous century.

Moreover, the function of historical understanding was not merely to interpret the present in the light of the immediate past, but to ground the understanding of the human situation in the mastery of the history of humanity. In his prize-day speech to the students of Sainte-Barbe in 1825, Jules Michelet celebrated a historical pedagogy that en-

---

[77] *Producteur*, 4 (1826): 25.

[78] Quinet, *Histoire de mes idées*, 200–1. In a review of Thierry's *Histoire de la conquête d'Angleterre*, Lefèvre writes, "Quand un peuple commence à se reposer du fracas des guerres et des révolutions, les esprits ébranlés par le tableau des catastrophes récentes, deviennent plus curieux du passé." Jules Lefèvre[-Deumier], *Critique littéraire (1825–1845)* (Paris, 1896), 12–17.

abled young students to "relive" the long life of mankind, recapitulating, as it were, the education that God himself had bestowed on the human species.[79] "This effort at understanding the past," writes Pierre Barbéris, "is one of those which most clearly distinguishes the new generation from the imperial generation."[80] The widely expressed desire to emerge "from the profound ignorance of history in which the imperial University had kept its pupils,"[81] and in which the Restoration University intended to keep them,[82] was not to be gratified by the historical productions of previous generations. An adequate reconstruction of the past could only be compassed by those who enjoyed the perspective of a location in contemporary time.

It was this temporal location that enabled the new generation to understand the history of the Revolution better than could those who had made it. As Paul Dubois put it in his review of Thiers' *History of the French Revolution*, "our generation, that is to say, those men who date from the first years of this century, is the most appropriate for writing

[79] Michelet, "Discours sur l'unité de la science," in *Ecrits de jeunesse*, 295.

[80] Barbéris, *Balzac Et Le Mal du siècle*, 1:243; Brown, *"The Generation of 1820,"* 205–6. For a general treatment of Restoration historiography, see B. Reizov, *L'Historiographie romantique française, 1815–1830* (Moscow, 1962). See also Lionel Gossman, "Augustin Thierry and Liberal Historiography," *History and Theory*, 15 (1976): 3–83; Stanley Mellon, *The Political Uses of History* (Stanford, 1958); Shirley M. Gruner, "Political Historiography in Restoration France," *History and Theory*, 8 (1969): 346–65. For history under the Empire, see June Burton, *Napoleon and Clio: Historical Writing, Teaching and Thinking During the First Empire* (Durham, N.C., 1979).

[81] Dubois, *Fragments littéraires*, 2:203; for the similar recollections of Michelet, see Viallaneix, *La Voie royale*, 97, 111.

[82] Smithson, *Augustin Thierry*, 78–79. For a marvelous example of Bourbon pedagogy, see Taillefer's memorandum to history professors, *De Quelques Améliorations à introduire dans l'instruction publique*, 244–45. "Le professeur ne peut espérer d'être utile à ses élèves, qu'en se mettant toujours à leur portée. C'est pour eux et non pour lui qu'il doit faire sa Classe. Son objet étant de graver dans leur mémoire les principaux faits de l'Histoire, dont on n'acquiert la connaissance qu'imparfaitement et avec beaucoup de difficultés dans un âge plus avancé, il ne doit chercher d'autre source d'intérêt que la simple exposition des faits historiques et la liaison naturelle qu'ils ont entre eux: il devra surtout éviter tout ce qui pourrait appeler les Elèves dans le champ de la Politique et servir d'aliment aux discussions des Partis. Cet avertissement regarde particulièrement le Professeur chargé de l'Enseignement de l'Histoire moderne. Sans doute, il lui serait difficile, il ne conviendrait même pas de dérober à la jeunesse la connaissance de certains faits qui sont du domaine de l'Histoire; mais il doit s'abstenir de tout commentaire. C'est par la simplicité et la gravité de son récit qu'il éloignera les allusions et les fausses conséquences que l'inexpérience de la jeunesse pourrait en tirer."

the history of the Revolution." Those who had participated in the great
events could not view them with objectivity: "the *jeunesse*, on the contrary, do not have the passions of their fathers."[83] Dubois' point was not
only that his coevals were unbiased but that their own situation had
given them a taste for impartiality and sincerity of which Thiers' history was a virtually perfect expression. Thiers himself, in his introduction to the work, granted that the survivors still had something to contribute as sources: "Perhaps the moment when the participants have
passed away is the most appropriate for writing history. One can harvest their testimony without sharing all their passions."[84] To Thierry,
however, the superiority of the new breed of historians was not confined to the impartiality of nonparticipants. The historical location of
their cohort granted them a perspective denied to their predecessors.
Repeating a virtual commonplace, Thierry asserts:

> There is not one of us men of the nineteenth century who does
> not know more than Velly or Mably, or even than Voltaire him-
> self, regarding rebellions and conquests, the dismemberment of
> empires, the fall and restoration of dynasties, democratic revolu-
> tions, and counterrevolutionary reactions.[85]

By no means all of Thierry's coevals would accept his particular version of the content of a new history, but they agreed on their potential
superiority over the old historians. "I think in France and after the
French Revolution," said Auguste Comte, "while Herder thought in
Germany and before this energetic and admirable upheaval had so
brutally confronted theory with practice."[86]

Such views were not expressed merely to denigrate predecessors. In
his *"Considérations sur l'histoire,"* published in the *Producteur,* Bazard

---

[83] Dubois, *Fragments littéraires*, 1:46.

[84] Adolphe Thiers, *Histoire de la révolution française* (Brussels, 1845): 1:109.

[85] Thierry, Preface to "Lettres sur l'histoire de France," in *Dix Ans d'études historiques*, 3. In 1823 François Mignet remarked, "Nous sommes arrivés à l'âge mûr de
l'esprit humain, et l'histoire est peut-être la seule carrière qui lui reste à parcourir. On
possède aujourd'hui toutes les conditions pour y exceller: ses matériaux sont complets,
et on dirige mieux l'art des recherches. Nous savons nous transporter dans les moeurs
du temps, en concevoir l'esprit, en prendre la couleur; nous avons acquis cette univer-
salité des connaissances politiques et économiques nécessaires pour montrer l'ensemble
d'une société; enfin, placés au milieu de la plus grande des révolutions, nous avons un
précieux terme de comparaison pour toutes les autres." Quoted in Knibiehler, *Naissance des sciences humaines*, 104.

[86] Comte to Eichtal, 5 August 1824, in Comte, *Correspondance*, 1:107.

reminds those who "reproached historians of the eighteenth century for having envisaged events of the past with the ideas of their own time" that they could scarcely have done otherwise, which, in Saint-Simonian terms, was to say that in a prescientific era a scientific history was not possible.[87] Or, as Thierry put it, "One cannot, whatever his intellectual superiority, transcend the horizon of his century, and each new epoch gives to history new points of view and a particular form of expression."[88]

Such views are aspects of that broader historical relativism that, as in Cousin's treatment of philosophy through a history of philosophy and Saint-Simon's treatment of science through a history of science, asserted the conception of human development through historical stages in which patterns of culture have an integral relation to their particular eras. This approach was characteristically pushed to its extreme by Auguste Comte, who argued that "the institutions and the political ideas of a people in a given epoch must have been consonant with the degree of enlightenment of those people in that period. ... There is nothing absolute in this world, everything is relative."[89]

This affirmation of an extreme cultural relativism was allied to the conception of historical understanding as empathetic re-creation, to the celebration of "local color" in historical narrative, to the veneration of Walter Scott, and to that quest for the very quiddity of the texture of past lives.[90] It also informed a specific historiography, notably in the works of the so-called fatalist school of the historians of the French Revolution. The *thèse des circonstances* developed in the remarkable works of Mignet and Thiers was understood by contemporary partisans and critics as an argument from historical necessity—an implicit justification of inevitable events that carried humanity inexorably from stage to historic stage.[91]

But, if every stage in the history of civilization was immediate to

[87] *Producteur*, 4 (1826): 409.

[88] Augustin Thierry, *Histoire de la conquête de l'Angleterre par les normands* (Paris, 1825), 1:viii.

[89] Comte to Valat, 15 May 1818, in Comte, *Correspondance*, 1:37.

[90] On the significance of Walter Scott, see Bazard, "Considérations sur l'histoire," *Producteur*, 4 (1826): 394. See also, Reizov, *L'Historiographie romantique française*, 124, 160–64; Martyn Lyons, "The Audience for Romanticism: Walter Scott in France, 1815-51," *European History Quarterly*, 14 (January 1984): 21–46.

[91] Reizov, *L'Historiographie romantique française*, 353–449; Knibiehler, *Naissance des sciences humaines*, 118–82.

God, some stages were more immediate than others. The relativism of Restoration historiography was conceived of as compatible with the idea of progress. Maurice Mandelbaum has demonstrated how Comte's historicism managed to assimilate the conviction that the doctrines and institutions of a given period inevitably attain "the greatest perfection compatible with the corresponding civilization," to "a criterion of value which he assumed to be implicit within the historical process itself: the criterion of progressive development."[92] Since the development is progressive, the most recent stage must be the highest. Then, the contemporary understanding of the past is itself an historical product, validated with reference to the process that guaranteed its inevitability and its superiority. The concomitant of the emergent scientific or positive stage was a scientific history whose reading of the past was its own validation.[93]

This "historicism of the scientistic approach," often associated with Comte and the Saint-Simonians, was as much the property of the Cousinian circle or of Thierry.[94] The universal repudiation of the critical spirit, or the affirmation of the new organicism (or any of the attitudes associated with romanticism) did not inhibit the attempt to accrue the accumulated prestige of the physical sciences to a historicist metaphysics. The self-refuting dilemma of any consistent relativism was resolved through an interpretation of historical development that was authenticated with reference to the historical necessity of its location in a scientific era.

This question-begging appropriation of the past was brilliantly criticized from a Catholic perspective by the Baron d'Eckstein in a passage that reads like a critique of the Saint-Simonians but was actually directed against the "politique de l'éclectisme" that conceived of the "century" itself as incarnating a wisdom beyond that of the wisest individuals:

> In general, this sect characteristically attributes a great deal to the times, or what they refer to as the force of things. It is true that

[92] Mandelbaum, *History, Man, and Reason*, 65–66.

[93] As Mandelbaum remarks, this "teleological theme" was fundamental to major tendencies of nineteenth-century thought, notably in the works of Marx and Hegel; ibid., 68–71.

[94] F. A. Hayek, *The Counter-Revolution of Science: Studies in the Abuse of Reason* (Glencoe, Ill., 1955), 64–79.

the times are rich in experience; but that is not the way they understand it. They conceive of the times as sweeping the tide of human thought on toward an ocean of glory, where navigate, ensigns aloft, all of these self-designated missionaries of the present, and prophets of the future. In their opinion they themselves have been shaped by the century, and the wisdom of the age is worth more than their particular science, or rather their particular science is simply the reflection of the wisdom of the age. At the base of this humility there is an excess of pride. They proclaim themselves the organ of the era in order to substitute themselves for the era itself.[95]

Eckstein's critique anticipates a century of historicism. Although the version articulated during the first decade of the Restoration was not the exclusive property of a particular cohort, a reading of the past that forecast the emergence of a higher synthesis was especially appropriate to a youth ideology and to the conviction that *A une ère nouvelle, il fallait une génération neuve*—for a new era, a new generation.

Yet that confident affirmation contained a germ of anxiety. The history that had launched the new generation onto an "ocean of glory" had also cast it adrift on Musset's storm-wracked sea. In that uncharted limbo between past and future, the children of the new century (deftly shifted by Musset from sea to land) were uncertain whether they marched forward across the seedbed of the future or the ruins of the past.[96] The oft-repeated metaphors of "ruins" or "debris" delineate

---

[95] Ferdinand d'Eckstein, "Politique de l'éclectisme moderne," *Catholique*, 15 (1829): 320. In a similar but not identical critique, the sociologist Bennett Berger remarks on the attempt to write the history of one's own generation: "This is anticipatory socialization or other directedness of a peculiarly ghostly sort; oriented toward history, intellectuals collapse the historical process in their attempts to find their place in it; and by attempting to write the history of their time before it is actually made, intellectuals create the myth of their time." Bennett Berger, "How Long Is a Generation?" *British Journal of Sociology*, 11 (March 1960): 19.

[96] Musset, *Confession d'un enfant du siècle*, 8–9: "Trois éléments partageaient donc la vie qui s'offrait alors aux jeunes gens: derrière eux un passé à jamais détruit, s'agitant encore sur ses ruines, avec tous les fossiles des siècles de l'absolutisme; devant eux l'aurore d'un immense horizon, les premières clartés de l'avenir; et entre ces deux mondes . . . quelque chose de semblable à l'océan qui sépare le vieux continent de la jeune Amérique, je ne sais quoi de vague et de flottant, une mer houleuse et pleine de naufrages, traversée de temps en temps par quelque blanche voile lointaine ou par quelque navire

what Jacques Barzun has called the dominant problem of the Romantic era; the need "to create a new world on the ruins of the old."[97]

In fact, that virtually universal assumption was not precisely congruent with reality; that is to say, the year 1815 was not 1795. The Restoration regime did not occupy ruins but moved into a vast institutional complex vacated by Napoleon with, admittedly, some sections incomplete and others in a state of considerable disrepair. The metaphor of postrevolutionary ruins is most persuasive when applied to the intellectual debris of churches and philosophies. Daily life and the business of the state went on; what lay in ruins were the old verities and the old authorities as yet replaced—it seemed to many—by nothing.

The metaphor served the Restoration youth as a legitimation of future promise, which only they who had not produced the ruins could fulfill, and as a justification for their alienation from a contemporary order that denied them emotional anchorage in a system of beliefs. This sense of historical anomie, rhetorically embellished by young litterateurs nourished in actuality by a rich inheritance of social norms, has often been identified as the source of that epidemic disease peculiar to the young—the notorious *mal du siècle*. The essential symptom of this protean disorder was a pervasive melancholy for which there was no completely appropriate cause or cure, an "element of eternal dissatisfaction," as Barbéris puts it.[98] One of the problems it poses for our analysis is its persistence, as it infected several generations, at least three according to the best authorities.[99]

Our afflicted *jeunesse* are not the first of the line but might be con-

---

soufflant une lourde vapeur; le siècle présent, en un mot, qui sépare le passé de l'avenir, qui n'est ni l'un ni l'autre et qui ressemble à tous deux à la fois, et où l'on ne sait, à chaque pas qu'on fait, si l'on marche sur une semence ou sur un débris."

[97] Barzun, *Classic, Romantic and Modern*, 14. Robert Brown, "*The Generation of 1820*," 129, emphasizes the persistent use of the metaphor of the sea.

[98] Barbéris, *Balzac Et Le Mal du siècle*, 1:54. This is the most thorough and documented treatment of the problem for the period of the Restoration. Among many other relevant works, see Renée Canat, *Une Forme unique du mal du siècle: Du Sentiment de la solitude morale chez les romantiques et les parnassiens* (Paris, 1904); Paul Charpentier, *Une Maladie morale: Le Mal du siècle* (Paris, 1880); and Armand Hoog,"Who Invented the *Mal du siècle?*" *Yale French Studies*, 13 (Spring–Summer 1954): 42–51.

[99] Barberis, *Balzac Et Le Mal du siècle*, 1:55, takes issue with René Jasinski's designation of three generations of the *mal du siècle*, that of Chateaubriand's René, of Musset and Sainte-Beuve, and of Gautier, Flaubert, and Baudelaire. See Jasinski, *Histoire de la littérature française*, 2:199.

sidered the self-elected progeny of René, described, and disowned, in Chateaubriand's self-parody:

A family of Renés, poets and prose writers, has swarmed into being: we have heard nothing but mournful and desultory phrases; it has been a question of nothing but winds and storms, of unknown words directed to the clouds and the night. No scribbler fresh from college but has imagined himself the unhappiest of men; no babe of sixteen but has believed himself to have exhausted life and to be tormented by his genius, but has, in the abyss of his thoughts, abandoned himself to the "wave of his passions," struck his pale and disheveled brow, and astonished stupefied mankind with a misfortune of which he did not know the name, nor they either.[100]

Even when they disagreed with his politics, the intellectuals of the 1820s continued to read and admire Chateaubriand and to model themselves on René, on Sénancour's Obermann, on the Young Werther, or on Byron or a pastiche of Byron. They recognized themselves in Lamartine's narcissistic poesy and in the desperate fulminations of Sainte-Beuve's Joseph Delorme. "Our generation," Paul Dubois recalled, "had been fascinated by that perpetual self-absorption through which René, Adolphe, Obermann, and how many others had experienced an unhealthy, feverish arrogance, a sort of intellectual onanism in the weak, and the source of serious research and poetic inspiration in the strong."[101]

Dubois and his circle were at some pains to disassociate themselves from romantic excess, but like many of their coevals they indulged in occasional bouts of cosmic despair, inexplicable melancholia, *taedium vitae*, the satanic defiance of a world they never made, and so forth. The expression of the *mal du siècle* in prose and verse was coin of the

---

[100] François de Chateaubriand, *Mémoires d'outre-tombe* (Paris, 1948), 2:43–44. I have borrowed the translation by A. T. de Mattos, *The Memoirs of François René, vicomte de Chateaubriand* (New York, 1902), 2:182; cf. Carné, *Souvenirs*, 50: "la maladie de René était celle de presque toute la génération qui cherchait laborieusement sa voie dans la politique et dans les lettres."

[101] Dubois, *Cousin, Jouffroy, Damiron*, 116; Sainte-Beuve, *Portraits contemporains*, 1:179. The celebration of this sort of literature was not quite unanimous. Victor Cousin reportedly described Sénancour, Byron, and Lamennais as "polissons, degrés de néant." J. J. Ampère to Jules Bastide, 10 August 1820, in Ampère and Ampère, *Correspondance*, 1:169; G. Michaut, *Sénancour: Ses Amis et ses ennemis* (Paris, 1909).

literary realm. The fact that Louis Belmontet enjoyed the reputation of a Bonapartist and conspirator did not inhibit the *Muse française* from publishing a sample from his slim volume of verse, *Les Tristes*, in which a *jeune homme souffrant* is consumed with slow sorrow despite his youth, and "dreams, with tortured soul in this perverse world, of some better land."[102]

This sort of thing was not merely produced in print as a literary conceit. The correspondence of J. J. Ampère and his friends reads as if they were modeling themselves on a textbook chapter on the *mal du siècle*. Referring to an illness of their revered Victor Cousin, the nineteen-year-old Ampère writes to his chum Jules Bastide: "There are moments when it seems to me, as to Werther, that God had turned his face from me and delivered me to sorrow." At least there is some correlative here—Cousin was sick—but Ampère requires no particular stimulus: "Monday I would have written a satanic letter to you but I destroyed it. This excess of rage against destiny gave way to a profound disdain for everything, for the future and for myself." As their friend Albert Stapfer had remarked to him only the other evening, "there will always be something somber and disenchanted at the basis of our existence."[103]

Ampère was not the man to settle for a mild and transitory melancholic *crise* but contracted a classic case of hopeless love for an older woman, the gently heartless Mme. de Récamier.[104] A quite different sort, Charles de Rémusat, paused briefly, in his confident progress through the higher social and literary circles, at the feet of a married woman, passing a month of "sorrows and sweetness that only Jean-Jacques could have depicted" in the charming company of Mme. de Barante.[105]

Even Delacroix, amidst bursts of ferocious creativity, would strike the appropriate chord: "Try as one will, one always sees within oneself

[102] *Muse française*, 1:82. The poem is entitled "*L'Isolement.*"

[103] Ampère to Bastide, 3 June 1820; 10 November 1821; and (dated incorrectly, I believe) January 1825, in Ampère and Ampère, *Correspondance*, 1:159, 162, 169.

[104] Louis de Launay, *Un Amoureux de Madame Récamier. Le Journal de J. J. Ampère* (Paris, 1927).

[105] Rémusat, *Mémoires*, 2:73. Unrequited love even tempted the prudent Adolphe Blanqui to put a loaded pistol to his head "à la Werther," but, predictably, his sense of duty stayed his hand. "Souvenirs d'un étudiant sous la Restauration," 149 (1 November 1918): 171.

a gulf, an abyss that is never filled. One is always longing for something that never comes. There is always a sense of emptiness, never an abundance, a full draught of happiness."[106] Of course, the real world gave the young Delacroix plenty to be gloomy about—poverty, an unsympathetic older sister as a substitute for his deceased mother, and ill health. Paul Dubois, who suffered from a sort of spiritual malaise all his long life, had by the age of twenty-five lost a wife, a son, a father, and a brother.[107] Objective circumstances, including the problem of economic survival and the difficulties in commencing a career (to be discussed below) were the occasions of unaffected sorrows and authentic anxieties. But the letters of Delacroix illustrate a more basic modification of the image of an entire generation in the grip of a grand malaise. For every passage expressing ennui or a diffuse *angst*, there are twenty or thirty dealing with the problems of his art, the possibilities of advancing his career, warm and loving relations with his friends, hopes for amour, and enthusiasm about trips to Italy. And here Delacroix is representative, if on a gigantic scale, of his cohort.

This antithesis was expressed in theory as well as in practice. Charles Rémusat, sharing his coeval's admiration for Lamartine, will also criticize the *Méditations* as a hymn to skepticism and despair: "Man is not simply made to sing, speculate, and love to no effect. He is not here on earth as an outlaw who pines for his pardon; for life is not an exile but a harvest of deeds, a voyage of discovery."[108] As Milner, Barbéris, and other scholars have remarked, the French romantics, taken together, convey a powerful impression of vitality, pugnacity, and creative power that their genuine misfortunes and their pessimistic affectations could never repress.[109]

It has been argued that there were two temperaments, or perhaps two generational units, one romantic and melancholy, as represented by Vigny and Musset, the other liberal and optimistic, as exemplified

---

[106] Delacroix, *Correspondance générale*, 1:115. I have used the translation of Jean Stewart. *Eugène Delacroix, Selected Letters* (London, 1971), 97.

[107] Gerbod, *Paul-François Dubois*, 31.

[108] Rémusat, "La Révolution française," in *Passé et présent*, 1:240. See also Charles Coquerel, *Tableaux de l'histoire philosophique du christianisme; ou, Etudes de philosophie religieuse* (Paris, 1823), 345–53.

[109] Milner, *Le Romantisme*, 21; Barbéris, *Balzac Et Le Mal du siècle*, 1:88–89, quotes Quinet to the effect that the generation's despair had nothing to do with spleen or the *ennui de la vie* but represented rather "*une aveugle impatience de vivre.*"

by the dynamic types who edited the *Globe* or celebrated the emergence of the industrial era.[110] While one can identify individuals who specialized in one style or the other, I believe that most of our subjects were, like Delacroix, simultaneously prey to diffuse anxiety and intermittent despair, *and* possessed by immense ambitions and a sense of unlimited opportunity.

Paradoxically, the energy and the optimism were drawn from that perception of a heritage of historical catastrophe. The diffuse anxiety of De Musset's pale, ardent, neurotic generation, suspended between past and future, was the concomitant of its unprecedented opportunities. They struggled into maturity out of the wreck of the assumptions by which they had been raised, "hopeful but confused," Rémusat remembered, wondering what standards to follow and whether they were forever to be the victims of circumstance.[111] The anxiety that weighed upon the *jeunes gens* was understandable, wrote Léon Halévy, in the light of the moral and cultural void left by the cataclysmic course of events and their unrequited dreams of justice and beauty. But they had not been raised to the sound of battle in vain. Memories of that still-living past could not be sterile. They were "rich in thoughts beyond their years and capable of emotions and desires unknown to their fathers."[112] Virtually the words, too, of Darmaing: "The influence of the past and the spectacle of so many revolutions, of so many extraordinary events, has enlarged the sphere of thought for us and quickened the march of reason."[113] And even Jules Lefèvre, a true knight of mournful countenance and fashionable despair, believed that "This present generation is, so to speak, experienced at birth."[114] So we have

[110] See Brown, *"The Generation of 1820,"* 18. Erik Erikson writes of periods when the personal identity crisis reflects "anxieties aroused by symbolic dangers vaguely perceived as a consequence of the decay of existing ideologies; and, in the wake of disintegrating faith, the *dread* of an existential abyss devoid of spiritual meaning." Other periods "present a singular chance for a collective renewal which opens up unlimited identities for those who, by a combination of unruliness, giftedness, and competence, represent a new leadership, a new elite, and new types rising to dominance in a new people." Erik Erikson, *Life History and the Historical Moment* (New York, 1975), 21. I argue that these possibilities were experienced simultaneously by the *jeunesse* of the Restoration era.

[111] Rémusat, *Séance de l'Académie française*, 54.

[112] Saint-Simon, *Opinions littéraires, philosophiques et industrielles*, 12–13.

[113] *Surveillant politique et littéraire*, 71.

[114] Lefèvre[-Deumier], *Critique littéraire*, 41–42. Lefèvre rang all the changes on the

turned again to the historical moment as the matrix for the generational *mentalité*, to the equivocal promise of unbounded horizons glimpsed across ruins.

In a marvelously evocative, almost paradigmatic, passage, an anonymous reviewer for the *Tablettes universelles* spoke of the contradiction that obsessed the *générations actuelles*: "the importance of man and the insufficiency of his destiny on earth." The successive political trauma of the past thirty years had liberated thousands of individuals from the prison of social class and encouraged them to search for their own rights, interests, and place in the world. But this assertion of personal autonomy was accompanied by the poignant sense of the limits placed upon it, and like Milton's Satan beating his wings in vain in the empty immensity, the individual spirit "falls back on itself, fearful and skeptical of its destiny; it wonders why there should be this intensity of impressions in a being manifestly unable to acquire what the impressions demand, why the desires that so powerfully impel us to act depend on the hopeful fulfillment; it searches the outside world for a situation appropriate to its ambitions and exhausts itself fruitlessly in the effort to discover the meaning and end of human existence."[115]

This poignant sense of the discrepancy between great expectations and constricted opportunities has been given a quite specific content in interpretations that emphasize the generational experience of underemployment, a consequence of the production of an excess of educated men. I will refer to this interpretation as the "frustrated mobility thesis" and discuss it in the following chapters, first with regard to the process of socialization and formal education that instilled the expectation of magnificent destinies in a generation of *lauréats de concours* crowned in schoolboy competitions, and then through an examination of the actual careers available to young ambitions after the avenues of imperial glory had been closed off.

---

mal du siècle, including unrequited love and the temptations of suicide. See Lefèvre[-Deumier], *Les Vespres de l'Abbaye du Val*, xxvi–xl. P. L. Jacob, "Notice biographique," in Lefèvre[-Deumier], *Sir Lionel D'Arquenay*, viii–ix.

[115] *Tablettes universelles*, 17 July 1823.

CHAPTER 8

A Cohort of
Lauréats de Concours

"The memorable year [1815] when France almost
ceased to exist and there was no *concours général.*"
Léon Halévy: *F. Halévy: Sa Vie et ses oeuvres*

T he cohort that discovered its
identity in the first decade of the Restoration was, like the larger
society, deeply marked by its experience of the immediate past
and the transition from the imperial order. For those on the
threshold of maturity, the experience of transition had been coincident with the process of socialization. I have argued that it was
the experience of socialization in the public realm of school and
society, rather than any transformation of child-rearing practices
or family relationships, that reinforced the consciousness of a distinct generational identity. This interpretation will proceed from
its apparent contradiction—that the children of the new century
were educated according to the dominant practices of the old.

The Restoration youth had begun its formal education in the
new institutions of the imperial educational system, or in that system recently redecorated with the Bourbon lilies. The pedagogy
of both regimes was characterized by the obsessive discipline and
the classical culture of the prerevolutionary *collèges*. Whether
they were called to class by the beat of the imperial tambours or,
a few years later, to the tolling of church bells, the students were
educated in the tradition of eighteenth-, or indeed seventeenth-,
century belles-lettres and motivated by the competitive distinction of the academic *concours*. The establishment of the imperial
University began with the decree of 11 Floréal an X (1 May 1802),
which replaced the republican *écoles centrales* with the Napoleonic *lycées*, and culminated with the decree of 1811 in that immense, centralized, hierarchical, minutely regulated machine
that was to be proof against a century and a half of social change
and innumerable projects of reform. It was a salient practical

and symbolic representation of what the amalgam of postrevolutionary elites—Bonapartist and Bourbon—did not intend to inherit from the Revolution, a repudiation of the attempt to found a wholly secular, scientific, libertarian education appropriate to the sons of revolutionaries and a return to profoundly conservative cultural standards and methods of socialization.[1]

The important decree of 17 March 1808 allayed the often-expressed anxiety of bourgeois families with the article that enacted the "precepts of the Catholic religion" as the basis for the pedagogy of all the schools of the University. Daily prayers were decreed and an *aumônier* appointed for each *lycée*. But these reassuring gestures did not guarantee a Christian education. The intellectual temper of the schools would not derive from the scriptures but from the version of classical humanism taught in the eighteenth-century *collèges*. "Knowledge of the Latin language will always be the principal element of instruction," read the report of the imperial commission on the selection of books to be assigned in the school system.[2] Latin was the core of the curriculum, the list of classical authors virtually identical with those assigned to scholars in the Old Regime.

French masterpieces prescribed for the courses in rhetoric and belles-lettres featured Bossuet, La Bruyère, Mme. de Sévigné, the inevitable Boileau, Rousseau (not Jean-Jacques but Boileau's disciple, the lyric poet J. B. Rousseau), Voltaire's *Histoire de Charles XII* and *Henriade*, and for a (barely) living model, Delille's translation of the *Georgics* to be committed to memory.

The favorite exercise was the *version*, a translation from Latin to French, and the *thème*, a translation from French to Latin. The imperial commission had noted and rejected the familiar "ignorant and frivolous" criticisms that emphasized "the disgust and ennui that the

[1] Antoine-Augustin Cournot, *Des Institutions publiques en France* (Paris, 1864), 276–79; Alphonse Aulard, *Napoléon Ie Et Le Monopole universitaire* (Paris, 1911), 93–103; Clément Falucci, *L'Humanisme dans l'enseignement secondaire en France au XIXe siècle* (Toulon, 1939), 117–32, 158; Francisque Vial, *Trois Siècles de l'enseignement secondaire* (Paris, 1936), 155–70; Liard, *L'Enseignement supérieur*, 2:3–11; Françoise Mayeur, *Histoire générale de l'enseignement et de l'éducation en France* (Paris, 1981), 3:458–62. R. R. Palmer, *The School of the French Revolution* (Princeton, 1975), 205–7; Weill, *L'Histoire de l'enseignement secondaire*, 34–38.

[2] Université impériale, *Rapport de la commission nommé par arrêté du gouvernement du 27 frumaire an XI pour le choix des livres classiques des lycées, dans chaque classe de latin et dans celles de belles-lettres* (Fait et arrêté le 27 février an 9), 2.

thèmes usually elicit in the very young, but is it not true that arduous tasks are always the most fruitful?"[3]

The supreme achievement for the young scholar would be victory in the yearly competition, the *concours général*, which had its antecedents in the middle of the eighteenth century. In 1757, La Harpe had carried off the first prize for the Discours français with his rendition of *Un Senator exhorte Pompée à défendre Ciceron contre Clodius*: "Vous ignorez, sans doute, illustres Romains, l'état affreux de la patrie." In 1816 the prize went to Michelet's treatment of *Dion exilé fait un empereur*: "Vous marchez contre votre patrie, Ô Romains! Je ne vous reproche pas de vouloir venger votre empereur."[4]

The preservation of these antique procedures was not merely an expression of the conservative recoil from revolutionary innovation but of the cultural world view from the apex of the educational pyramid. Louis Fontanes, Napoleon's grand master of the University, was the archetype of those pedagogues who looked back into the seventeenth century for their literary models and to a sort of modified Jansenist pietism for their philosophic stance. The men who dominated the educational and cultural establishments under Bonaparte and under the Bourbons subscribed to the principle of the eternal verities as articulated on numerous occasions and with undiluted complacency by such spokesmen as Fontanes:

> The principles of belles-lettres are not subject to the same revolutions as are those of science: they are based on a model that never changes. . . . Instruction in these essentially eternal arts has long been subject to certain rules. . . . It would be ridiculous to cite the authority of Ptolemy or Epicurus for contemporary astronomy and physics, but the principles of Aristotle and Horace have not changed, orators and poets still apply them. . . . The true principles are trumpeted by the voice of twenty centuries.[5]

These are the very principles against which an entire generation of young philosophers and critics would rebel—the principles that placed the editors of the *Constitutionnel* or the *Minerve* and Bishop Frayssinous on one side of the literary barricades and the contributors to the

---

[3] Ibid., 7. See "La Culture scolaire" in Antoine Prost, *Histoire de l'enseignement en France, 1800–1967* (Paris, 1968), 52–55.

[4] D. P. Belin, ed., *Annales des concours généraux* (Paris, 1825), 1:143, 203.

[5] Université impériale, *Rapport de la commission*, 1–2.

Globe, the *Producteur*, and the *Muse française* on the other. As Durkheim observed, beneath the principles of neoclassic pedagogy lay a profoundly ahistoric conception of human nature "as some kind of eternal reality, immutable, unchanging, independent of time and space."[6] This conception was opposed by the virtually unanimous voice of a generation convinced of the historical contingency of culture and the contemporary necessity of its radical transformation.

The apparent repudiation of the University's dominant assumptions by its first *promotions* was one of those ironies savored by such a perceptive observer as Antoine Cournot, himself a product of the system. The founders of the imperial University had supposed that "it was still possible to dominate the century and direct society by means of a sound and wholesome education, that is to say, by an education of the sort that they themselves had received. . . . All of that was unintelligible to the new generations." Somehow those partisans of "*bonnes études* in the French and Latin taste of the two preceding centuries manufactured philosophers of the German and Scotch persuasion," and the attempt to train a cadre for the imperial military machine ended in the formation of "a generation of young liberals and *parlementaires*, in the modern sense of the word."[7]

Cournot voiced a common recollection of the unanticipated consequences of imperial pedagogy. "Subject to the discipline of the imperial *lycées*, our generation," recalled Paul Dubois, was "providentially prepared . . . for the great events that were to mature it, and for this revival of the pure and generous ideas of the Revolution." One of Dubois's fellow *normaliens* remarked on the fortunate aberration through which the greatest moral and intellectual liberty had coincided at the Ecole normale with the "most narrow and exclusive practical discipline." Guizot applied almost the same term in his observation that it was sometimes given to great despots to build better than they knew. Napoleon had not founded the University to train advocates of liberal principles, but by a fortunate oversight the quiet progress of philosophic and literary studies tempered the spirit of the emerging generation.[8]

[6] Emile Durkheim, *The Evolution of Educational Thought: Lectures on the Formation and Development of Secondary Education in France*, trans. Peter Collins (London, 1977), 273.

[7] Cournot, *Des Institutions publiques en France*, 277.

[8] Lair, "Les Souvenirs de M. Dubois" (1 December 1901), 310–11; Joseph-Daniel

But the ironies and contradictions implicit in the imperial educational system went deeper than the most promising members of the cohort raised in the system had perceived. In fact, the elite *promotions* of the new university never did completely renounce the values of its founders. They wanted to be free to discover the culture appropriate to the unprecedented conditions of the new era, but they would continue to apply the standards in which they had been trained. We have seen that the libertarians of the *Globe* or the romantics of the *Muse française* insisted on the preservation of the purity of the French tongue. The same people who repudiated a sterile neoclassicism during the Restoration would preside over an essentially traditional, formalistic literary curriculum under the next regime.

It is commonly asserted that the inculcation of an aristocratic *culture générale* continued to meet the ideological requirements of the upper bourgeoisie well into the nineteenth century. The mastery of standardized skills, which had served to ornament aristocratic pretensions with a mandarin veneer, was transformed, after the brief aberration of a revolutionary pedagogy, into the legitimation of nineteenth-century class distinctions.[9] A crucial element in this process was the revival of the competitive principle, which had especially characterized the pedagogy of the old Jesuit *collèges*, in the ubiquitous practice and pervasive ethic of the academic *concours*.[10]

The decree of 21 Vendémiaire an IX (13 October 1800) reestablishing the yearly prize contest—the *concours général*—for the Paris *écoles centrales* begins, "Considering that, in general, emulation is the soul of education ..." This simple affirmation concealed a conviction at the very heart of French pedagogy, and of French bourgeois culture, that

Guigniaut, *Notice historique sur la vie et les travaux de M. Augustin Thierry*, 5; François Guizot, *Trois Générations: 1789–1814–1840* (Paris, 1863), 90–91.

[9] Pascale Gruson, *L'Etât enseignant* (Paris, 1978), 50–54; Edmond Goblot, *La Barrière et le niveau* (Paris, 1967), 78–87; Roland Barthes, *Writing Degree Zero*, trans. Annette Lavers and Colin Smith (Boston, 1970), 56–59; Maurice Crubellier, *Histoire culturelle de la France, XIXe–XXe siècle* (Paris, 1974), 118–19. Among the several works of Pierre Bourdieu and associates that carry this theme into the twentieth century, see Pierre Bourdieu and Jean-Claude Passeron, *Reproduction in Education, Society and Culture*, trans. Richard Nice (Beverly Hills, 1972).

[10] Durkheim, *The Evolution of Educational Thought*, 260–62; Palmer, *The School of the French Revolution*, 21–22; Roger Chartier, Marie-Madeleine Compère, and Dominique Julia, *L'Education en France du XVIe au XVIIIe siècle* (Paris, 1976), 256–58.

was accepted with a peculiar intensity by the *promotions* recruited to fill in the spaces in the vast new architecture of the imperial University.

Like so many institutions set in place by Napoleon, the educational meritocracy was based on earlier precedents, reorganized, rationalized, centralized, and built on foundations calculated to last a century. The competitive element was not merely an ornament of this system but mortared into its very structure. In place of the Old Regime's distribution of privately endowed *bourses* for the talented poor, there was to be a national system of state scholarships awarded on the basis of an examination and a *concours*. The decree of 21 Prairial an XI (10 June 1803) establishing general regulations for the *lycées* stipulated in detail the distribution of prizes each trimester for each class and each *genre d'instruction*. The legal stipulations were rapidly assimilated, not only into the pedagogical, but into the ceremonial, life of the schools. Each *lycée* or *collège* would have its own public prize-day ceremony, complete with proud parents, boring speeches from academic dignitaries, and attendance by important officials. The emotional freight of these ceremonies is recalled in Adolphe Blanqui's bitter reminiscence of how his vain and beautiful young mother upstaged her talented son on prize day, and it is fictionally represented in Balzac's *Le Lys dans la vallée* when the hero's heartless parents do not even attend the ceremony.[11]

Prize competitions were not confined to the *collèges* or the *grandes écoles*. The School of Mines, the Conservatoire des arts et métiers, and the Ecoles d'art et métiers all had their finely graduated series of *concours*, their annual ceremonies, and their hierarchy of *lauréats*. In a sense, a student was defined as one eligible to sit for a *concours*. J. B. Boussingault, after winning a first in his class at the Ecole des mines at Saint-Etienne, did so well in chemistry as to be given the post of lab assistant. As he could no longer compete against students whose work he directed, he could not be considered a student in the fullest sense and was designated an *élève breveté*.[12]

The application of the term *concours* did not distinguish between a contest and an examination. Examinations for admission to a school were administered as competitions among a large number of applicants for a limited number of places. They were called *concours*, as were

[11] Adolphe Blanqui, "Souvenirs d'un lycéen de 1814," 102–3; Honoré de Balzac, *Le Lys dans la vallée* (Paris, 1966), 300.

[12] Boussingault, *Mémoires*, 1:220–21.

prize contests such as the yearly poetic competition set by the Académie française. The artistic concours for the Grand Prix de Rome encapsulated this ambiguity—the lauréat was not only the winner of an annual contest but the sole successful applicant for an academic position at the end of a course of studies.

When Bourdieu and Passeron identify the symbiosis of examination and *concours* in the classbound pedagogy of the Fifth Republic, they precisely describe the system that had been set in place by the end of the First Empire:

> In the French system, the concours is the fully realized form of the examination (which university practice always tends to treat as a competition) and the competition for the recruitment of secondary school teachers, the *agrégation*, constitutes, together with those advance recruitment competitions, the *Concours Général* and the *Ecole Normale Supérieure* entrance examination, the archetypal triad in which the University acknowledges its authentic self and of which all other competitions and examinations are but variously distant emanations and more or less deformed copies.[13]

Of that "archetypal triad," the *concours général* became the ceremonial expression of the national educational ideal.[14] The original contest between the best students from the *collèges* of the University of Paris dates from 1747. The *concours*, and the solemn ceremonies in which prizes were awarded for the best compositions in French and Latin, were terminated with the University, and much else, in 1793. But the revolution had not liquidated the conviction that emulation was the heart of education; in 1800 a contest was organized for the students of the Paris *écoles centrales*, and the classic *concours général* was reestablished with the founding of the four imperial *lycées* in 1805.

Thereafter, the annual prize day was staged as a great national ceremony attended by political and cultural luminaries. The opening *discours* in Latin was followed by an address, usually delivered by the grand master of the University and often the vehicle for a major policy

---

[13] Bourdieu and Passeron, *Reproduction in Education, Society and Culture*, 150.

[14] Nicolas-Rodolphe Taranne, *Notice historique sur le concours général entre les collèges de Paris* (Paris, 1847); Jacques Champion, "Le Concours général et son rôle dans la formation des élites universitaires au XIXe siècle," *Revue française de pédagogie*, 31 (April–June 1975): 71–82; and Champion, "Discours et idéologie: Le Concours général," *Pensée*, 188 (September–October 1976): 80–97.

statement or at least an encomium of the chief of state. The results of the competition were published in the national press, as they continue to be.[15] The annual *prix d'honneur* always went to the winner of the *concours* in Latin composition and carried with it formal exemption from university fees and a tacit exemption from military conscription, which was written into law under the Restoration.[16]

The *concours général* was the paradigm of the post-Napoleonic version of careers open to talents, and significant careers were, in fact, launched from the recognition granted a seventeen-year-old for the supreme mastery of mandarin skills. Victor Cousin was the archetype. In 1810 he not only won the *prix d'honneur* but took two other firsts and an honorable mention. In recognition of this epochal feat, the government waived the requirement of a substantial family income and offered him the post of *auditeur* in the *conseil d'état*. He turned this down to enter the first *promotion* of the Ecole normale, where he was welcomed as virtually the peer of his professors.

Many other names familiar as participants in the various associations, institutions, and personal networks that articulated the collective identity of the Restoration youth first appear in the public eye in the

[15] The significance of the *concours général* in the life of the University, indeed in the intellectual life of the country, is indicated by the list of members of the examining committee for science and mathematics in 1816: Cuvier, Lacroix, Biot, Poisson, and Gay-Lussac. Archives nationales, AJ[16] 881. The public interest in the *concours* is suggested by a *Tableau historique, chronologique des concours généraux* published by Adrien Jarry de Mancy (1796) in 1826, 1827, and 1828. On a large single sheet suitable for framing, Jarry de Mancy entered a chronological list of all the winners of the *prix d'honneur* and the official *orateurs* at the yearly ceremony, the names of the prize winners of the year of publication of the *Tableau* in the general *concours* and in the Paris *collèges*, and the complete text of the speech of the official *orateur* for that year. Adrien Jarry de Mancy, *Tableau historique, chronologique des concours généraux de l'Université, ancienne et nouvelle, depuis la fondation des concours jusqu'en 1825 inclusivement, suivi du tableau de la distribution des prix du concours général, et des distributions des prix des huit collèges de Paris et de Versailles en 1826* (Paris, s.d.).

[16] Awards proliferated for the yearly champion. When A. A. Cuvillier-Fleury (1802) took the 1819 *prix d'honneur*, his collège, Louis-le-Grand, awarded him a gold medal and the minister of the interior celebrated the "brilliant success" of this fortunate scholar with the presentation of the complete works of Bossuet—fifty volumes in eight. Lycée Louis-le-Grand, *Palmarès, 1810–1819* (Paris, s.d.). Reminiscing about the tragic year of 1815, Léon Halévy recalls it as "the memorable year when France almost ceased to exist and there was no *concours général.*" Léon Halévy, *F. Halévy: Sa Vie et ses oeuvres, récits et impressions personnelles, simples souvenirs* (Paris, 1862), 11.

yearly *palmarès*—the prize list—of the *lauréats de concours*. After Cousin there were the *normaliens*: Trognon, Guigniaut, Gérusez, Paulin, Viguier, and the school's only martyr, Jean-George Farcy, who fought and died in the July Days. The Saint-Simonian ranks would be ornamented by Olinde Rodrigues (who distinguished himself in physics and math), Léon Halévy, and Gustave d'Eichtal. The circle of J. J. Ampère and his friends comprised a coterie of *lauréats*, Ampère, Jules Bastide, Adrien Jussieu, and Albert Stapfer all appeared on the lists of successful competitors between 1816 and 1819. Others who were to make successful and often precocious careers in literature, law, and government included Casimir Delavigne and Eugène Scribe (1791), Michelet and Rémusat, Charles Magnin and Charles Renouard, Adolphe Crémieux (1796), Littré (1801), Fould (1800), Baroche, and Montalivet.[17] There was no better starting point for those who began without the advantages of wealth or birth, but no career filter was finer meshed.[18]

The triumphs of these teenage gladiators were closely marked and long remembered. Reflecting sadly on the career of a childhood friend become bitter antagonist, Paul Dubois looks back over forty years to recall that Pierre Leroux, who won a scholarship to the *lycée* at Rennes, had been a *lauréat* in the Paris *concours*. And, sure enough, there on the list of *lauréats* for 1809 is the twelve-year-old Pierre Leroux, runner-up in the *version latine* and the *thème*. Perhaps because of a certain "bizarrerie d'esprit" or the pressure of necessity, muses Dubois, the young Leroux did not pursue a liberal career like law or medicine or "some occupation appropriate to his talents," but apprenticed himself to a printer—going off the rails at an early age.[19]

The preoccupation with early distinction is not surprising in someone like Paul Dubois, whose life's texture would be woven into the institution that matriculated the brightest talents in successive cohorts of ambitious males. As a promising boy from the provinces, Dubois had been impressed and challenged by that "brilliant elite of the *lauréats de*

[17] Belin, *Annales des concours généraux*.

[18] The results of the *concours* also contributed to the careers of the *lauréats'* instructors. For example, Michelet was congratulated by his friend Poret for the fine record of his students at Sainte-Barbe: "Tu vois donc que le concours ne t'a fait tort dans l'esprit de personne." Henri Poret to Michelet, 20 August 1823, Bibliothèque historique de la Ville de Paris, Papiers Michelet, Correspondance, 18, A 4809.

[19] Papiers Dubois, AN 319 AP³, Dossier 1, 80–84.

concours" who dominated the first *promotions* of the Ecole normale.[20] During the early years of the school, students were recruited through recommendations of the inspectors general of the University, but it was already perceived as the summit of the hierarchy of academic competitions.

The Ecole never forgot its champions. The obituaries of old boys recently deceased, delivered at the annual meeting of the alumni association, are full of references to honors won for the *version* or the *thème* in titanic contests some thirty or forty years past. The same spirit of superiority that was guaranteed to last a lifetime would characterize those who had won the contest that had enlisted them in the ranks of the mathematical-scientific elite of the Ecole polytechnique.

The competitive principle was applied far beyond the confines of the *grandes écoles*. Michelet, for example, although not a *normalien*, competed successfully for the *agrégation*, prerequisite for a post in a *collège*. Thus, the teaching cadre was staffed through the *concours*, and this meant that the content of the discipline was defined by the personnel of the *jury d'agrégation*. Philosophy à la Laromiguière was no longer taught in the *lycées* of the July Monarchy after Cousin and his coterie assumed control of the competition.[21]

The Bourbon regime continued to staff the University according to the competitive principles laid down under the Empire, with the exception of the professorships of the faculties, which it withdrew from open competition in order to reserve the power of appointment to sensitive posts. This was a much-resented but minor modification of the role of the *concours* as the essential criterion for recruitment and promotion in the educational system and the professions.[22]

Prospects for a medical career were especially affected by success in public competition. Although the chairs of the medical faculties had been returned to the hands of the government (thus permitting the notorious purges of the Paris faculty), many of the major positions in the national medical establishment were still staffed by competitive ex-

---

[20] *Mémorial de l'association des anciens élèves de l'Ecole normale*, 56.

[21] Paul Gerbod, "L'Université et la philosophie de 1789 à nos jours," in *Actes du 95e Congrès national des sociétés savantes: Section d'histoire moderne et contemporaine, 1: Histoire de l'enseignement de 1610 à nos jours* (Paris, 1974), 260–63.

[22] The Restoration did, however, institute a *concours* for *agrégés* who were to be *suppléants* to the professors of the faculty. Jacques Léonard, "La Restauration et la profession médicale," *Historical Reflections*, 9 (Spring and Summer 1982): 75-77.

amination—notably teaching positions below the rank of professor and the highly valued *internat* and *externat* at the Paris hospitals, the centers of French medical education and the loci of professional prestige. Appointment to the *internat*, the "marshal's baton of a medical student," was the guarantee of a brilliant future.[23] The memoirs of the impresario, publisher, and all-purpose *arriviste*, Louis Véron (1798), begin with his entrance into a medical career marked by the milestones of successful competition for the *internat* and *externat* and disappointing failures in the special *concours* in anatomy, natural history, physics, and chemistry that left him with the conviction that he had enemies among the professors of the Faculty of Medicine.[24] The competition for key posts, such as the *internat*, and for various awards, prizes, medals, and honoraria contributed to what Jacques Léonard called the *fièvre des concours* that characterized the profession in the first half of the nineteenth century. In Paris major contests drew excited crowds of students, whose interest reflected ideological as well as professional preoccupations.[25]

The competitive principle was applied not only in the selection of a professional elite. The national cultural establishment embodied in the great royal academies—Sciences, Beaux-Arts, Belles-Lettres et inscriptions, and the Académie française—which comprised the Institut under the Restoration, carried out their traditional and legal obligations to set contests and award prizes for distinguished contributions to culture.[26] The most venerable and prestigious prize competition was the

---

[23] François-Louis Poumiès de la Siboutie, *Dr Poumiès de la Siboutie (1789–1863): Souvenirs d'un médecin de Paris* (Paris, 1910), 111.

[24] Louis Veron, *Mémoires d'un bourgeois de Paris* (Paris, 1856), 1:4–14.

[25] Among other medical competitions, Léonard lists: "Concours d'entrée à l'Ecole pratique; concours pour l'externat, puis pour l'internat des hôpitaux; concours pour les places de prospecteur, aide d'anatomie, chef des travaux anatomiques; concours pour tous les grades de la médecine militaire ou de la médecine navale; concours pour des postes de médecin ou de chirurgien adjoint de grand hôpital de province; concours pour le Bureau central des hôpitaux de Paris; concours pour l'agrégation de médecine, de chirurgie ou des sciences accessoires. . . ." Jacques Léonard, *Les Médecins de l'ouest au XIXe siècle* (Paris, 1978), 2:711–12.

[26] Léon Aucoc, ed., *L'Institut de France: Lois, Statuts et règlements concernant les anciennes académies et l'Institut de 1635 à 1889* (Paris, 1889). For the competitions set by the Academy of Sciences, see Elisabeth Crawford, "The Prize System of the Academy of Sciences, 1850–1914," in Robert Fox and George Weisz, eds., *The Organization of Science and Technology in France* (Cambridge, Eng., 1980), 283–87; Maurice Crosland,

concours first set by the Académie française in 1671, which crowned *lauréats* in poetry and oratory in alternate years. During the Restoration this grand national ceremony took place on the king's birthday.

Edmond Biré's debunking book on the young Victor Hugo devotes some ten pages to demonstrating that Hugo's feat in winning an honorable mention in the *concours* of 1817 at the age of fifteen was not as remarkable as had been supposed.[27] Biré's meagre point is that the judges actually tilted in favor of Hugo because of, not despite, his youth. For our purposes, the point is that the contest opened the avenue to recognition of obscure young talents. One of the two winners of the first prize that year was the nineteen-year-old all-around *lauréat* and future playwright J. X. Boniface, dit Saintine (1798). Casimir Delavigne, well on his way to literary distinction at the age of twenty-one, more or less stole the show with an unauthorized entry. The subject set for 1817, "Le Bonheur que procure l'étude dans toutes les situations de la vie," was treated by Delavigne as an issue for poetic debate rather than the object of eulogy in verse, and was therefore ruled *hors de concours*. His clever poem was, however, read to the distinguished audience and excerpted in the *Moniteur*.[28]

That glimmer of recognition granted Hugo for his precocious tour de force was the anticipation of the dawn that broke upon his successes in another contest at the mature literary age of seventeen. His odes "Le Rétablissement de la statue de Henri IV," and "Les Vierges de Verdun" were "crowned" by the Académie des jeux floraux of Toulouse at the annual floral games of 1819. The tradition of awarding jeweled flowers for the best submissions in various poetic genre, which, so the legend went, descended from the Middle Ages, was enthusiastically revived under the Restoration. When Hugo was awarded the golden lily for his ode on the "Statue de Henri IV," he joined the circle of *lauréats*—Soumet and the others—with whom he was to found the *Muse française*. Subsequently, the signal honor of membership in the Academy of Toulouse impelled Hugo to request the right of exemption from military conscription granted by law to the winners of the *prix d'honneur* in the *concours général* and the competitions set by the Insti-

---

"From Prizes to Grants in the Support of Scientific Research in France in the Nineteenth Century: The Montyon Legacy," *Minerva*, 16 (Autumn 1979): 355–80.

[27] Biré, *Victor Hugo Avant 1830*, 94–102.

[28] *Moniteur universel*, 29 August 1817.

tut. The head of the Adademy of Toulouse forwarded Hugo's request to the appropriate ministry, which granted it.[29]

Thus artistic merit was something more than its own reward. The poetry contest set by the Academy of Toulouse and the Académie française even provided opportunities for the recognition of talented women. The literary and artistic *concours* opened that small space in which an obscure young woman might become visible, begin to establish an autonomous identity, and take a step onto that avenue of mobility blocked off in so many other ways. Delphine Gay, whose beauty, youthful talent, and aggressive mother made her the star of the Paris literary salons at the age of nineteen, first came into view at a special competition set by the Académie française. "Scarcely seventeen years of age," as the *Moniteur* put it, she left an "indescribable impression" as she read her verses on the Charité des Soeurs de Saint-Camille during the plague of Barcelona.[30]

The institution of the *concours* ramified out through all the arts. Indeed, formal education in the arts consisted of a system of competitions culminating in the Grand Prix de Rome awarded to painters, sculptors, architects, musicians, and engravers by the Académie des beaux-arts. The various competitions through which one ascended to that supreme contest were administered by the sections of the Ecole des beaux arts, whose faculties functioned less as a teaching corps than as a board of judges. The architecture faculty did virtually no teaching, except for an occasional lecture, but presided over a series of *concours* through which a student advanced to the annual competition for the Prix de Rome. Private ateliers did the actual teaching, essentially to prepare the students for the official *concours*. The same procedure was followed to a considerable extent in the ateliers for the other arts.[31]

The narrow path that led through the ateliers and the Ecole and the

[29] Ségu, *L'Académie des jeux floraux*, 142–43.

[30] *Moniteur universel*, 26 August 1822. Delphine was not awarded the prize, because her poem did not fulfill all of the conditions set by the contest. For a sardonic description of the public performance of the Gays *mère et fille*, see Delécluze, *Journal*, 246–51.

[31] For the meticulous, detailed regulations of the various *concours*, see *Recueil des règlements, relatifs aux concours ouverts et aux grands prix décernés par l'Académie Royale des Beaux-Arts* (Paris, 1821); Harrison C. White and Cynthia White, *Canvases and Careers: Institutional Change in the French Painting World* (New York, 1965), 18–20; Richard Chafee, "The Teaching of Architecture at the Ecole des Beaux-Arts," in Arthur Drexler, ed., *The Architecture of the Ecole des Beaux-Arts* (New York, 1977), 77–97.

Académie to the lonely summit of the Prix de Rome was not the only road to public recognition. For painters, the broadest and most frequented avenue was by way of submission to the great Paris Salon. This institution also had its roots in the old regime. The first salon had been established in 1673 under the authority of the Royal Academy of Painting and Sculpture. During the Revolution there was an attempt at egalitarian reform when the National Assembly decreed that all artists, French and foreign, were equally free to exhibit their works at the Louvre. There was a characteristic revision, recodification, and rationalization of the exhibition under the Empire into a formal, highly organized *concours* stipulating the submission of works to a jury selected by the government. Admittedly, the mesh was coarse, as the jury was not concerned with the selection of the best works but the exclusion of those that were morally offensive, politically obnoxious, or irredeemably poor works of art. As is often told in the tales of the unrecognized genius of all of those great *refusés*, the system of selection became a system for the exclusion of unsettling and unconventional works. It also became the occasion for the awarding of individual prizes.[32]

In the institutionalization of the artistic *concours* we can still discern the tradition of artistic production for the rewards of patronage, but under Napoleon this was transformed into the attempt to infuse the vast imperial machine with that spirit of emulation expressed, for example, in the invention of the Legion of Honor and in the vast project of a system of decennial awards for supreme achievement in the arts, sciences, and useful activities. That particular expression of the patron as megalomaniac disappeared with its conceiver, but the Salon survived, along with the theory and practice of art as a competitive enterprise. We can observe the system celebrate itself in François Heim's well-received entry in the Salon of 1827, which portrays, on a grand historical scale, Charles X distributing the prizes at the Salon of 1824.

Reference to the best-known national prize competitions in the educational system, the professions, or the arts barely begins to describe the immense network of *concours* set by government organs, provincial academies, learned societies, and public-spirited individuals. One has only to open virtually at random the pages of the *Moniteur universel* to find the Société centrale de vaccine setting a prize for administering the greatest number of vaccinations, or the Royal Society of Prisons estab-

---

[32] François Benoit, *L'Art français sous la révolution et l'empire* (Paris, 1897), 228–39.

lishing awards for the best proposals for improving the organization of prisons and correcting the vicious propensities of prisoners, or the Medical Society of Marseilles awarding a gold medal for the best paper on the maladies of the uterus likely to be confused with cancer.[33] Most of these competitions were open to contestants of any age, but they often afforded the best opportunity for someone young and obscure to emerge from anonymity.

It was almost possible to parlay a contestant's skills into a permanent vocation. Anne Bignan (1795) exhibited at an early age, we are told, "a pronounced taste for literature and a marked vocation for a contestant's career." Launching that career with laurels in the *concours généraux* of 1814, Bignan went on to a triple crown in 1822: a first, and a second *mention*, in the poetic *concours* of the Académie française, and a *violette* in the *Jeux floraux*. Thereafter, his name appears on lists of *lauréats* in contests set by national and local societies from the Académie française (recognition in ten competitions between 1824 and 1848) to the Société d' émulation de Cambrai and the Société archéologique de Béziers—some thirty-five awards in twenty-five laurel-strewn years. By the time we arrive at the July Monarchy's second, and Bignan's fifth, decade we begin to suspect that prize winning was not a sufficient condition for a mature career. Perhaps, as his biographer conjectures, he was crushed under the weight of his crowns and unfairly dismissed as "a clever collegian, a perpetual *lauréat*, a sort of academic wandering Jew boasting a talent for ubiquity in the absence of poetic talent."[34]

While one could not fulfill a career through the prize contest, it certainly provided a launching pad. The precocious abilities that won Adolphe Thiers all of the prizes at the *collège royal* at Marseilles convinced his teachers that his talents would have been adequate to the great prize competitions at Paris—even for the *grand prix de lycée*.[35] Cheated of that chance by geography, Thiers could still invade Paris at the age of twenty-four armed with a law degree and additional credentials as twice winner of gold medals in essay competitions set by the Academy of Aix. His inseparable friend, François Mignet, also came up from the provinces bearing laurels, "crowned" by the Academy of

[33] *Moniteur universel*, 5, 6 August, 1819; 2–3 November 1817.

[34] Edmond Biré and Emile Grimaud, *Les Poètes lauréats de l'Académie française* (Paris, 1865), 2:11–22.

[35] *Bibliothèque nationale*, Nouvelles acquisitions françaises, 20601: Papiers Thiers, 1: Correspondance, 1830–1834.

Nîmes for his *éloge* of Charles VII and distinguished by the national
Académie des belles-lettres et inscriptions for a historical essay.[36]

Provincial laurels were no guarantee of success in that great *concours*
that was the contest for careers in the Paris arena. Institutionalized
contests were merely an aspect of the vast system of social competition
through which all careers were in principle, and in greatly qualified
practice, open to the talents liberated by the destruction of a world of
privileged orders. Thanks to the sacrificial scrimping of his mother and
sister, Balzac's Lucien Chardon (de Rubempré) receives the indispensable education at the collège d'Angoulême that inculcates the skills
and ambitions requisite for that first upward step. Impressed by his
scholarly and poetic distinction, the headmaster of his *collège* com-
mends him to the benevolent attention of the local gentry, and to the
fond attentions of Mme. de Bargeton, affording him the opportunity to
test his strength and try his luck against all the other young ambitions
concentrated in the Paris Grub Street.

Balzac's magnificent depiction of the sordid realities of the scramble
for success guides us through a labyrinth of lost illusions, but the one
illusion that the young competitors refused to discard was that of the
essential validity of the competitive principle, especially in the educational system.

The pedagogical competition was integrally related to the mastery
of literary-oratorical skills derived from models of classical rhetoric.
While criticizing the slavish imitation of the classical model,[37] the rising generation not only acquiesced in the meritocratic conception of
education but objected to dilution of the competitive ideal. The students from the medical school at Montpellier would join their professors in a petition requesting the reestablishment of the *concours* for
chairs in the medical faculty. Ulysse Trélat, distinguished by the award
of *internat* at the hospital at Charenton (a success that in no way mod-
erated his dedication to political conspiracy), proposed not only that the
concours be applied to all medical positions and for all occupations ful-
filling a public function, but advocated periodic examinations to keep
aging practitioners up to date— "Men age, science marches on." Théodore Jouffroy's progressive alienation from the Restoration University

---

[36] Knibiehler, *Naissance des sciences humaines*, 16–26.

[37] See, for example, Félix Bodin, *Diatribe contre l'art oratoire* (Paris, 1824); Carrion-
Nisas, *La France Au Dix-Neuvième Siècle*, 13–14.

ıs expressed in his denigration of the policy of appointment *sans concours* and dismissal *sans jugement*.[38]

According to Michel Foucault, "the examination is at the center of the procedures that constitute the individual as effect and object of power."[39] For the young aspirants to power at the beginning of the nineteenth century, the examination and the competitive system of which it was the centerpiece legitimated their refusal of deference to the authority of those temporarily charged with certifying their success.

That is why criticism of the ubiquitous *concours* is found in the other camp. Even key functionaries of the cultural establishment, such as Quatremère de Quincy (another stuffed target for youthful contempt in the gallery with Auger and Jouy), expressed grave reservations about the system they administered. Perpetual secretary of the Academie des beaux-arts, implacable adversary of deviations from the classical ideal, indefatigable polemicist on aesthetic issues, Quatremère took an active and invidious part in the administration of major artistic *concours*, while deploring the excess of the genre. In his patronizing *Eloge de Girodet*, he damned Bonaparte's regime for instituting

> this stupid monkey business of instruction through emulation as practiced in the schools, which at this time began to import into the world of mature abilities the petty procedures of the *concours*—prizes, medals, and scholastic triumphs, practices calculated to transform masters into schoolboys and their works into class assignments.

On this, as on other occasions, Quatremère was hissed by "unruly elements" (read students) in the audience.[40]

The *bien-pensant* pedagogue Taillefer, drafter of instructional manuals for the *collèges royaux*, deplored the erosion of deference in the self-

---

[38] *Archives parlementaires*, 2nd series, 27:717; Trélat, *De La Constitution du corps des médecins*, 59–61; Jouffroy, *Correspondance*, 283, 287.

[39] Michel Foucault, *Discipline and Punish: The Birth of the Prison*, trans. Alan Sheridan (New York, 1977), 184–92.

[40] Antoine-Chrysostôme Quatremère de Quincy, comp. *Recueil des notices historiques lues dans les séances publiques de l'Académie-Royale des Beaux-Arts à l'Institut, par M. Quatremère de Quincy-secrétaire perpétuel de cette académie* (Paris, 1834), 321–25. René Schneider, *Quatremère de Quincy Et Son Intervention dans les arts (1788–1830)* (Paris, 1910), 266.

esteem of the young *lauréat* and the tendency to flaunt a "deplorable taste for independence, whose germ is to be found in pride and to the correction of which education could not devote too much zeal."[41]

To some extent, distaste for an overemphasis on competitive distinction reflected specific political concerns, such as the intention to control faculty appointments, but in a broader sense it represented the regime's mistrust of all those forces that threatened to burst through the defenses of the precarious clerical-royalist cultural order. Restoration conservatives were not prepared to repudiate a system whose foundations had been laid down by the clerical orders of the Old Regime; indeed they contributed to its fulfillment in instituting the baccalaureate as a formal prerequisite for the awarding of a professional degree. Their occasional objection to the overemphasis on the *concours* was an example of the ambivalence with which they accepted the University and other problematic aspects of the imperial legacy. The royalist imagination could conceive of no viable substitute for a system that was partially incongruent with its essential spirit. This ambivalence contributed to the rising tension between an aspiring youth and a defensive establishment.

The socialization of the cohort that came of age in the first decade of the Restoration was therefore coincident with the development of a system of limited mobility through more or less meritocratic procedures that coopted talented members of the middle and lower middle classes into the strata of the notables. The standardization of these procedures in the educational system was only then taking shape as it freed itself from the constraints of the imperial military machine. We are now familiar with the extent to which social promotion through state-sponsored competition is really a form of co-optation in which those who set the standards for competitive success reproduce themselves. This relationship is usually hidden to those who expect to be successful in the competition, and they characteristically criticize it with reference to its violation of its own rules.

Generations of critics from Renan to Durkheim to Bourdieu have damned the system that rewarded oratorical skills and reinforced the tendency toward shallow abstraction and facile argument.[42] So too

[41] Taillefer, *De Quelques Améliorations à introduire dans l'instruction publique*, 356–57.

[42] Ernest Renan, "L'Instruction supérieure en France," published in *Questions con-*

would the first *promotions* of the imperial and Restoration University pose the ideal of a morally serious and rigorously scientific education against a sterile and shallow pedantry, but in many cases the self-confidence that allowed them to assume a precocious authority depended on their superior mastery of the standard skills. They confused the establishment of a regular system of recruitment, indoctrination, and cooptation through meritocratic procedures with a unique historical conjuncture in which the public recognition of individual talents was evidence of the historical superiority of a particular cohort. Thus personal expectations were reinforced by a sense of collective promise.

The reality could never be adequate to these personal and collective expectations, and the great discrepancy between the expectations and the opportunities contributed to the frustration, and therefore the resentment, that set the most ambitious and dynamic elements in the Restoration *jeunesse* against the established order. At least this is the argument of those who focus on the crucial significance for French, and European, society of an "excess of educated men."

temporaines in *Oeuvres* (Paris, 1947), 1:95; Durkheim, *The Evolution of Educational Thought*, 274–76. The critics are also cited by Pierre Bourdieu, "Systems of Education and Systems of Thought," in Earl Hopper, ed., *Readings in the Theory of Educational Systems* (London, 1971), 176–83. See also Pierre Bourdieu and Monique de Saint-Martin, "L'Excellence scolaire et les valeurs du système d'enseignement français," *Annales*, 25 (January–February 1970): 147–75.

CHAPTER 9

An Excess of Educated Men?

"I expect a great deal of the century."
Adolphe Thiers to E. Teulon, 16 April 1821

The most powerful evocation of the spirit of the cohort that sought its future in the "ruins" of post-Napoleonic France is in works of fiction. Julien Sorel, determined to "expose himself to a thousand deaths rather than fail to achieve success"; De Musset's pale, ardent, and neurotic generation, whose dreams of glory are answered with the admonition, "become priests"; and Balzac's hungry young provincials competing in the Paris arena like fifty thousand spiders in a pot are all tortured by the discrepancy between boundless ambition and constricted opportunity. These representations have been condensed into the definition of the *mal du siècle* as a "phenomenon of underemployment."[1]

This is an interpretation with a long history, encapsulated in the title of Leonore O'Boyle's article, "The Problem of an Excess of Educated Men in Western Europe, 1800–1850," and summed up in her observation that "too many men were educated for a small number of important and prestigious jobs so that some men had to be content with underemployment or with positions they considered below their capacities."[2] The presumption of economic cause and social effect implicit in that statement received its classic formulation in the 1840s, when Louis Philippe's prefect of the Seine warned him to beware of

the déclassés, the doctors without patients, the architects without buildings, the journalists without journals, the lawyers without clients, all the misunderstood, maladjusted, famished characters who, having found no seat at the ban-

[1] Barbéris, *Balzac Et Le Mal du siècle*, 1:79.
[2] Leonore O'Boyle, "The Problem of an Excess of Educated Men in Western Europe, 1800–1850." *Journal of Modern History*, 42 (December 1970): 471.

quet, try to overturn the table to get the plates. There are your makers of revolutions, your high-priests of anarchy, your buccaneers of insurrection.[3]

The explanatory power of this frustration-aggression hypothesis, especially when applied to the young, seems confirmed by the frequency of its application. This persuasive explanation for the alienation of an overeducated, underemployed *jeunesse* is so pat that it has been applied to every unruly generation from the insubordinate collegians of the seventeenth century to the demi-insurrectionists of May 1968. Cardinal Richelieu's concern with the excess number of colleges devoted to the production of déclassé malcontents is reproduced in yesterday's analysis of the militant alienation of the young and today's explanation for their passive alienation.[4]

To apply this interpretation to every cohort of discontented collegians since the seventeenth century is to reduce it to a generalization about the recurrent attributes of youth as a stage in the life cycle where to be young is to be predictably frustrated, aggressive, and underemployed. If the phenomenon is ubiquitous, it scarcely helps us to distinguish the restive generations of 1848 and 1968 from the pragmatic, acquiescent cohorts of the 1850s and 1950s.[5]

Yet one might grant this objection and still argue, as some of the best works on the period do, that the occupational situation of the ambitious youth of the Restoration was peculiarly frustrating and therefore an identifiable cause of collective alienation. In his synthesis of the history of the Restoration, Bertier de Sauvigny recapitulates the specific demographic and social circumstances that seem to support such an interpretation. In 1826, 67 percent of the French population was under the age of forty and thus legally prohibited from election to the Chamber of Deputies, and this at a time when to be forty was to have survived the threshold of old age. Only the oldest one-ninth of those alive in the

---

[3] Claude Philibert Barthelot de Rambuteau, *Memoirs of the Comte de Rambuteau*, trans. J. C. Brogan (London, 1908), 281.

[4] Gabriel Hanotaux, *Histoire du Cardinal de Richelieu* (Paris, 1893), 460–65. For a more recent example of the innumerable lamentations on the excess of the overeducated, see Louis Lévy-Garboua, "Les Demandes de l'étudiant ou les contradictions de l'université de masse," *Revue française de sociologie*, 17 (January–March 1976): 53–80.

[5] As O'Boyle herself observes, the overproduction of educated individuals "may well be a chronic one in any society with a large population and a relatively free market." O'Boyle, "The Problem of an Excess of Educated Men," 494.

mid-1820s had attained the age of twenty by 1789, that is, had fully experienced the immense trauma of the revolutionary era. The revolutionary cataclysm had cast very young men into leading positions in state and society—positions to which many of them had managed to cling throughout all the vicissitudes of the various revolutionary governments, the Napoleonic Consulate and Empire, and even the First and Second Restorations. Their jobs were also coveted by the famished royalist emigrés who righteously demanded compensation for all the years in the wilderness with their exiled king. Therefore, the normal attrition of age opened few positions to the young as unemployed royalists competed with politically vulnerable incumbents for the available openings. "Here," observes Bertier, "was the real *mal du siècle* from which the youth of 1830 suffered."[6]

And it was into this crowded market that the great career factory of the Napoleonic university system had just begun to spew out the first eager cohorts of the meritocracy—survivors of the fierce prize-day competitions and the entrance exams of the great professional schools, thoroughly educated in literature, philosophy, and the classics to care for nothing and to be good for nothing but careers in public administration and the liberal professions. Family investment in training for the desirable careers was substantial and pressures to realize the investment were intense, and in a more general sense there was that pervasive pressure on all those who had the least opportunity to risk an ascent through the tough but permeable layers of an ambiguously stratified society. One painful consequence of careers open to talent is that there is no excuse for failure. No one saw this more clearly than Balzac: "Nowadays, in inviting all its children to the same banquet, society arouses their ambitions in the very morning of life. It deprives youth of its charm and taints most of its generous sentiments with an admixture of calculation."[7]

A variant of the demographic approach has been presented by Marxists, who grant the significance of generational differences but insist that they should be understood as phenomena of social class. Over forty years ago, Louis Mazoyer argued that the unity of age groups is

[6] Guillaume de Bertier de Sauvigny, *The Bourbon Restoration*, trans. Lynn M. Case (Philadelphia, 1966), 238–40. For a contemporary conception of the relation of age differences to political behavior, see Charles Dupin, *Forces productives et commerciales de la France* (Paris, 1827), 1:111.

[7] Honoré de Balzac, *Illusions perdues* (Paris, 1961), 67.

never proof against the solvent of social antagonisms, but he granted that it was possible to identify age-related responses to specific socio-economic stimuli, and he did identify the occupational crisis—*crise des débouchés*—as a central event in the experience of French youth at the beginning of the nineteenth century.[8]

This theme is restated with polemical verve by Pierre Barbéris, who argues, as did Mazoyer, that "the notion of generation" is unintelligible unless related to its "social content." The notorious *mal du siècle* of Balzac's generation is to be understood as the alienation of a *jeunesse bourgeoise*, not in confrontation with political and clerical reaction but in response to an emerging social order that frustrated the very aspirations it evoked. Bourgeois society was simultaneously indoctrinating a young elite with a sense of its collective capacity and blocking its surge toward honorable careers by "overloading the tertiary sector." This was, in a sense, a consequence of the Revolution, which had permitted extraordinary possibilities of self-realization. But the barriers, briefly raised, had been lowered once more.[9]

This is a complex and detailed elaboration of Georg Lukács' evocation of the lost illusions of a youth that had come into the legacy of the "heroic age of the bourgeoisie" in an era dominated by the cash nexus: "It was the tragedy of a whole generation ... that bourgeois society would not let it realize the ideals that society itself had given them but forced them to shed their illusions to survive." Somewhat more concretely, Leonore O'Boyle observed that the principle of careers open to talent aroused extravagant hopes for personal advancement, encouraged by the educational system and focused on the state bureaucracy and the professions that could fully gratify them.[10] A more specific ver-

---

[8] Mazoyer, "Catégories d'âge et groupes sociaux," 385–423. See also Stenzel and Thoma, "Poésie et société dans la critique littéraire du *Globe*," 27–35.

[9] Barbéris, *Balzac Et Le Mal du siècle*, 1:75, 268. Cf. Leonore O'Boyle, "The Image of the Journalist in France, Germany, and England, 1815–1848," in Clive Emsley, ed., *Conflict and Stability in Europe* (London, 1979), 19: "What was new after 1815 was the conjunction, which was peculiar to France, of a relatively undeveloped economic system with the democratic and egalitarian tendencies inherited from the Revolution. The Revolution had sanctioned the goal of upward social mobility and rewarded the most aggressive personal ambitions. Comparable opportunities did not exist for the post-revolutionary generation." This essay first appeared in *Comparative Studies in Society and History*, 10 (1967–68): 290–317.

[10] Lukács, *Studies in European Realism*, 47–64; O'Boyle, "The Problem of an Excess of Educated Men," 493.

sion of this interpretation, focused on the Saint-Simonians, emphasizes the attractions the movement had for "marginal" men. Frank Manuel discusses the motives of the young Jewish intellectuals who came to the movement confused and bewildered by the revival of religious intolerance that had driven them from the University and closed off the new horizons opened by Napoleon. Robert Carlisle broadens the conception to include such marginal types as Enfantin and Bazard, illegitimate sons of unsuccessful fathers.[11] Many of the Saint-Simonians' coevals who also suffered from cosmic alienation and the thirst for a unifying faith might be situated in that margin. But the concept of marginality does not effectively distinguish an alienated from an integrated youth or characterize the motives that drove an ambitious young aristocrat like Rémusat or a consequential *arriviste* like Thiers.

There is, however, plenty of evidence of a generational malaise expressed as resentment against the older strata of the occupational pyramid. A classic expression of this attitude, whose title tells all, was *De la gérontocratie*, published by James Fazy in 1828. Its message was a diatribe against the political dominance of the old, who were sanctified by the constitutional provision that confined the destinies of France to "seven thousand or eight thousand asthmatic, gouty, paralytic eligible candidates with enfeebled faculties"—that is, to those older than forty and therefore eligible to stand for the Chamber of Deputies.[12]

Even more specific resentments were directed to the limitation of opportunities in the professions perceived as overcrowded. We have cited the complaint of Dr. Ulysse Trélat, sometime conspirator and a key figure in the network of young Paris activists, that "Today, all of the public functions are over-monopolized, the same men appear on nearly all the committees for reform, sanitation, manufacturing, *arts et métiers*, etc., and most of them have been in place since the Constituent Assembly or the Consulate." Naturally, what most concerned Dr. Trélat was his underpaid and overcrowded profession, dominated by greybeards long out of touch with scientific progress and prone to blunders

[11] Manuel, *The New World of Henri Saint-Simon*, 343–47; Carlisle, "The Birth of Technocracy," 453–55. For a qualification of the usual emphasis on the role of Jews in the early Saint-Simonian movement, see Ratcliffe, "Some Jewish Problems in the Early Careers of Emile and Isaac Pereire," 202.

[12] J. J. Fazy, *De La Gérontocratie; ou, Abus de la sagesse des vieillards dans le gouvernement de la France* (Paris, 1828), 5; see also, de Staël-Holstein, *Du Nombre et de l'âge des députés*.

that had to be rectified by dedicated young doctors whose professional competence had been enriched by the indispensable experience of service in the hospitals.[13]

The resentment against the sclerotic stratum at the top of the occupational pyramid was paralleled by the desperation of the search for a foothold at the bottom. "The necessity of choosing an occupation took me by the throat," Quinet recalled.[14] That necessity drove young men by the thousands to crowd into Paris, where the sanguine pursuit of success became a grim struggle for survival.

The familiar saga of the quest for a career is repeated in the memoirs of those who managed to attain the status of someone who writes memoirs: There is the first trip up from the provinces armed with letters of introduction to anyone with influence; the experience of penury and semistarvation; the acceptance of employment affording some marginal application of the redundant skills of a classical education, perhaps as an underpaid instructor in a small school or as a private tutor to the children of the rich; the competition for a chance to place a manuscript or to publish some brief review, very much as in the portrayal of the nether fringes of the French Grub Street in Balzac's *Illusions perdues*. The most fortunate, *lauréats de concours*, might start from the launching site of the Polytechnique or the Ecole normale, or even, if forced to accept a mundane job, might attend the lectures at the medical faculty or take one's *droit* as the first move toward self-propulsion into the professions.[15]

There is testimony, too, that not all opportunities were equally acceptable. "I want to become something," wrote the twenty-year-old J. J. Ampère to his distinguished father, repudiating a suggestion that he go into trade. "To go into business seemed impossible and antipathetic to me," remembered J. B. Boussingault, a shopkeeper's son who was to launch a career as a mining engineer. When Paul Dubois, victim of the purge of the University, disconsolately imagines marrying an

[13] Trélat, *De La Constitution du corps des médecins*, 59–61.

[14] Quinet, *Histoire de mes idées*, 248.

[15] There are such accounts in Adolphe Blanqui, "Souvenirs d'un étudiant sous la Restauration" 15 (15 October 1918): 776–96; Alexandre Dumas (1802), *Mes Mémoires* (Paris, 1954), 1:82–101; Hippolyte Auger (1796), *Mémoires*, 1–4, 39–42; Charles Paul de Kock (1793), *Mémoires de Ch. Paul de Kock* (Paris, 1873), 135; Auguste Jal (1795), *Souvenirs d'un homme de lettres (1795–1873)* (Paris, 1873), 42–48; Dora Weiner, *Raspail*, 54–55.

"ordinary" woman and setting up in a shop, his intimate friend Théodore Jouffroy responds with a horrified *"le repos d'une boutique! pour vous!"*—destiny has greater things in store. *"Le négoce* wasn't my thing," wrote Auguste Jal, who had been offered a position in his father's business after he had been expelled from midshipman's school for Bonapartist sympathies. So off to Paris he went, where he found a friend who wangled him a chance to review the *beaux-arts* for various journals. For Hippolyte Auger the position in a large shop seemed so little suited to "my self-development according to my abilities" that he seized the chance to enlist in Tsar Alexander's imperial guard.[16]

There is some discrepancy between all this and the cohort's self-image. As lit by the nostalgic glow of Charles Rémusat's recollections: "For the youth at that time, truth was everything, self-interest virtually nothing; the preoccupation with personal advancement, that *idée fixe* that is so assiduously instilled in well-bred youth, was an unthought of chimera in those days."[17] Thus the generation of Eugène Rastignac and Adolphe Thiers.[18]

Perhaps Rémusat was able to remember a youth exempt from careerism because his parents had been so energetically occupied with his personal advancement. While he dashed off courageous manifestos, his mother ran around to Guizot or Royer-Collard to make sure that his pieces would appear in the right place and at the right time and in a

[16] Ampère and Ampère, *Correspondance*, 1:132; Jouffroy, *Correspondance*, 321–24; Jal, *Souvenirs*, 41; Auger, *Mémoires*, 42; Boussingault, *Mémoires*, 1:102. See also Chasles, *Mémoires*, 1:73–74, who remembered how depressing to a youth raised on the classics was his father's suggestion that he be apprenticed "d'un métier manuel."

[17] Rémusat, "Théodore Jouffroy," in *Passé et présent*, 2:221. For a similar reminiscence, see Sylvestre de Sacy (1801), "Notice," in Ximenès Doudan, *Mélanges et lettres* (Paris, 1876) 1:viii. Boussingault, *Mémoires*, 1:102: "Si vous saviez, monsieur, combien nous étions peu préoccupés de ce qu'on appelle un avenir, une carrière, une fortune!"

[18] Thiers, the ideal type of the completely consequential careerist, made no attempt to varnish his motives. Characterizing the limited opportunities of a legal career in Aix, he writes, "Tout ça ne satisfait pas une âme inquiète qui voudrait voir du pays, des hommes, des évènements, des dangers, et arriver à la mort ou à de grands résultats. Je ne suis pas heureux, j'éprouve d'ardents besoins, et je suis pauvre. J'aimerais les femmes, la table, le vin, le jeu, et je n'ai point d'or." Thiers to Teulon, 3 July 1819, published in Franck Morin-Pons, "Thiers, avocat Aixois, 1818–1821," *Provence historique*, 9 (October-December 1959): 237. For the early career of someone who outdoes even Thiers in the precocious pursuit of honors and emoluments under Bonaparte and the Bourbons, see the depiction of the young Narcisse-Achille Salvandy (1795) in Louis Trenard, *Salvandy En Son Temps, 1795–1856* (Lille, 1968), 48–54.

manner that would not dangerously offend the authorities.[19] Rémusat's recollection of his disinterested coevals appeared, appropriately enough, in a memoir of Théodore Jouffroy, remembered as the very exemplar of the austere, selfless commitment to the life of the mind. There is a rather different flavor to Jouffroy's contemporary correspondence, especially during the period when he still had hopes of a brilliant university career under the patronage of Victor Cousin and Royer-Collard. "My letter is strictly business," he writes to Damiron in 1817. "Our position is sufficiently influential for us to begin to protect it. We need jobs, we need status; as we are human, we are ambitious, calculating, and cool." In other letters he counsels his somewhat less successful friends on how to handle Cousin, who dislikes ambitious people and who, above all, should never be contradicted, "that would be a poor way to succeed."[20]

None of this is cited to suggest that Jouffroy would use *any* means to succeed. He and his coterie were engaged in inventing techniques of social mobility, such as academic intrigue, appropriate to a new set of institutions, but they would not, as we shall see, submit to the requirements for professional success as stipulated by Bishop Frayssinous.[21] It is evident that Rémusat, Jouffroy, and their educated and semieducated male coevals, idealist or *arriviste*, did share a sense of immense personal and collective potential and resented the constriction of opportunities for the advancement of their expected careers.

The tension engendered by great expectations applied to small opportunities certainly bore bitter fruit. The plight of a friend engaged in a fruitless search for reputable employment tempted the young Auguste Comte to curse mankind:

> ... considering that an intelligent, able, and well-educated young man cannot, no matter how hard he tried, find a way to make a living, while so many idle ignoramuses sleep on their piles of

[19] See, for example, the letter of Rémusat's mother to his father, 30 June 1819, in Rémusat, *Correspondance*, 6:29–35.

[20] Jouffroy to Damiron, 5 May, 11 June 1817, in Jouffroy, *Correspondance*, 132–47. During the same period that other monument to *normalien* rectitude, Paul Dubois, was desperately petitioning his fellow Breton, the ultraroyalist minister of the interior the Comte de Corbière, to preserve his threatened career. This reference is in a letter, "Monsieur et cher ami," undated but almost certainly written in 1823 in AN 319 AP¹, Dossier 1.

[21] See below, pp. 257–58.

treasure. This painful situation gives food for thought: Would such a horrible abuse exist under a good government?[22]

Comte's complaint exemplifies what we have been taught by common sense and social science—that frustration breeds aggression—but what was the real source of the frustration felt by Comte's cohort? Such a question is suggested by Leonore O'Boyle's tentative qualification of her general thesis when she wonders whether the French educational system was in fact turning out enough educated men to fill the demand in the administration and public services.[23] The answer to this, and related questions, is to be sought in the actual demographic and occupational context at the relevant historical moment.

My approach to the answer proceeds from assumptions cogently stated in Norman Ryder's article on "The Cohort as a Concept in the Study of Social Change":

1. A cohort's size relative to the size of its neighbors is a persistent and compelling feature of its lifetime environment.
2. The experience of the cohort with employment and labor force status begins with the character of the employment market at the time of its entry.[24]

This is to suggest that the real question for new competitors in the job market is not what the chances are of climbing to the top of the ladder but how much space there is on the bottom rung. In fact, there was more space on the bottom rung, and there were more ladders available, during the first decade of the Restoration than there had been in the waning years of the Empire.

Indeed the Empire had itself provided some demographic space at the bottom of the Restoration ladder through the terrible erosion of young males during its disastrous later years. The calculations of Jacques Houdaille confirm the standard view that the years 1812 and 1813 were the most murderous. Houdaille estimates that those born after 1786 bore more than half of all the losses suffered by the French in the wars of the revolutionary-Napoleonic era and that over one-fourth of all deaths were concentrated in the cohort born between 1786

[22] Comte, *Correspondance générale*, 1:15.
[23] O'Boyle, "The Problem of an Excess of Educated Men," 490.
[24] Ryder, "The Cohort as a Concept in the Study of Social Change," 843–61.

and 1790. The consequences of Napoleon's wars are entered in the postimperial demographic pyramid.[25] The estimated size of the cohort of males aged twenty-five to twenty-nine in 1816, for example, exposes the erosion of the war years. Therefore, the succeeding cohort, our generation born in the 1790s, found somewhat fewer of its older brothers occupying the places to which it aspired.[26] On the other hand, the greater number in the younger cohort may have contributed to a sense of overcrowding and competition among coevals.

One canot make too much of this in either case, among other reasons because the 1817 Paris census reveals a smaller discrepancy between successive cohort sizes than do the national estimates.[27] Paris was the place where job candidates of every age were most likely to feel the competitive pinch, and there is no doubt of the perception there of overcrowding—*encombrement*—especially in the medical and legal

[25] Jacques Houdaille, "Le Problème des pertes de guerre," *Revue d'histoire moderne et contemporaine*, 17 (July–September 1970): 411–23; Jacques Dupaquier, "Problèmes démographiques de la France napoléonienne," *Annales historiques de la Révolution Française*, 199 (January–March 1970): 9–29.

[26] The age distribution of the male population (in thousands) was:

Age Groups (in years)	1806	1811	1816	1821
0–4		1836	1860	1906
5–9	1570	1510	1583	1635
10–14	1437	1490	1440	1510
15–19	1324	1384	1373	1398
20–24	1135	1090	1142	1313
25–29	1030	1068	990	1087
30–34	905	982	1002	943
35–39	860	848	930	950

Note: The Generation of 1820 is boxed; the Older cohort is in italic.

Source: Jean Bourgeois-Pichat, "Note sur l'evolution générale de la population française depuis le XVIIIe siècle," *Population*, 7 (1952): 322.

For our purposes, this merely indicates a more substantial erosion in the cohort aged 30–34 in 1821 than in the two succeeding cohorts that approximate our "generation of 1820." The former declined 36.3 percent between 1806 and 1811, the latter 20.1 percent. For a somewhat different analysis of the same data, see Allen, *Popular French Romanticism*, 86.

[27] The only systematic census recording ages before 1836 was that for Paris in 1817. Gilbert Chabrol de Volvic, *Recherches statistiques sur la Ville de Paris*, 2nd ed. (Paris, 1833), vol. 1, Table No. 4 (n.p.); see also Toussaint Loua, comp., *Atlas statistique de la population de Paris* (Paris, 1873), 18–19.

professions.[28] The comparison of cohort size is presented here to make the point that the usual citation of aggregate statistics on the proportion of young in the population sheds little light on the actual market for apprentices to the professions and the public administration. Ideally, the relationship to establish is that between the supply of, and the effective demand for, those fortunate enough to aspire to the genteel occupations.

There is no way to estimate the number of those trying to make some sort of living with the pen, but something can be said about changes in the supply of those who obtained the requisite training and certification to enter the professions. As in many other areas, the history of the professions under the Restoration is a continuation and fulfillment of Napoleonic innovations. Throughout Europe, the beginning of the nineteenth century saw the introduction of reforms calculated to systematize the legal definition of the professions, to require public certification to practice them, and to require formal schooling to obtain the certification. In France, the keystone of this system was mortared solidly in place in 1820 when the baccalaureate—a degree obtained by national examination—was required for entrance into the professional faculties and for access to all civil careers.

The "primordial social importance" of the decree of 13 September 1820 was immediately expressed in the increase in the number obtaining a *bachot*—from 2,297 in 1819 to 3,509 in 1820 and finally to 4,503 in 1821, the largest number for the entire period from 1815 to 1830. A total of 25,054 degrees were granted between 1821 and 1830, after the baccalaureate had become a professional *sine qua non*. For the period coincident with the early maturity of the generation of 1820 (that is from 1809, when the first *bachots* were granted, until 1825) there were 29,724 obtained by those who were to become doctors, lawyers, engineers, and administrators for an expanding population of some thirty million.[29]

Such figures offer only the crudest approximation of the effective

---

[28] O'Boyle, "The Problem of an Excess of Educated Men," 493: "It seems extremely probable that in Paris there was always an excess of talented young men relative to the immediate need for them, while no such surplus could be found in the provinces." See also Allen, *Popular French Romanticism*, 86; Mazoyer, "Catégories d'âge et groupes sociaux," 396–97; Léonard, *Les Médecins de l'ouest*, 2:530.

[29] J. B. Piobetta, *Le Baccalauréat* (Paris, 1938), 1–45; Paul Meuriot, *Le Baccalauréat: Son Evolution historique et statistique des origines (1808) à nos jours* (Nancy, 1919), 1–31.

supply of competitors for positions in the various fields. On the one hand, not everyone who obtained a baccalaureate went on into the professions or applied for a government job, and on the other, there were all sorts of unlicensed competitors for the paying clientele of the licensed professionals. The field of medicine, for example, was not only crowded with *officiers de santé* (paramedics confined to the practice of a sort of second-class medicine in a given department), but also with pharmacists, midwives, herbalists, faith healers, and assorted medical charlatans, all competing for the patient's franc.[30] Even in the light of such extracurricular competition, one might suppose that the yearly production of some 400 new doctors (or 750 lawyers) during the first decade of the Restoration would scarcely amount to an occupational glut in a country as large as France. But as Leonore O'Boyle observed, it is pointless to ask whether the number of trained men was adequate to the real need of the society.[31] The relevant question is not what society required in the way of medical treatment but what it afforded to graduates of medical schools or, rather, what they perceived to be the effective demand for their training and talents.

I have cited some of the ample evidence for the collective perception and resentment of occupational overcrowding. Scholars who introduce this sort of evidence usually pick their examples out of a rich selection of sources extending across the first four or five decades of the century, but that is precisely what makes it difficult to distinguish the historical significance of the frustration of the underemployed *jeunesse* of the early Restoration from that of the young bohemians of the 1830s or the revolutionaries of 1848. We need to narrow our focus to the specific circumstances in which the Restoration youth were socialized and commenced their careers, that is, to the period of transition from a rigidly authoritarian Empire to an equivocally constitutional monarchy. From that perspective we can discern not a contraction but a remarkable expansion of occupational opportunities for those with a secondary education or some presumption of literary skill. Granted, this increase of opportunity must be set off against what was lost through the con-

---

[30] Matthew Ramsey, "Medical Power and Popular Medicine: Illegal Healers in Nineteenth-Century France," *Journal of Social History*, 10 (June 1977): 560–87.

[31] O'Boyle, "The Problem of an Excess of Educated Men," 471; Jacques Léonard, "L'Exemple d'une catégorie socio-professionnelle au XIXe siècle, les médecins français," in *Ordres et classes: Colloque d'histoire sociale. Saint Cloud, 24-25 mai 1967* (Paris, 1973), 228–34.

traction of an imperial administration that had governed half of Europe and an army that had conquered it. Louis XVIII's first ministry cut 15,000 jobs from the government rolls. Undoubtedly there were many to mourn the chance to be apprenticed to the government of an Empire, but there is reason to doubt that all of the careers Napoleon had opened to young talents were as attractive at the time as they would appear in nostalgic retrospect.

By the end of the Empire, the most promising access to the upper reaches of the administration was by way of the post of *auditeur* to the *Conseil d'état*.[32] The number of these state apprenticeships dropped sharply under the Restoration, but even at its peak the recruitment of *auditeurs* provided an extremely narrow avenue of mobility. In the spirit of his policy of fusing governmental and social elites, Napoleon restricted eligibility for the post of *auditeur* to those with a law degree and an assured annual income of 6,000 francs. This confined career access to a far narrower economic stratum than that of the candidates eligible to compete for openings in the *grandes écoles*, an increasingly attractive alternative to enlistment in the army or even service in the administration of the disintegrating Empire.

We have seen that, in recognition of his brilliant performance in the *concours général* of 1810, Victor Cousin was offered the post of *auditeur* without having to satisfy the property qualification; he turned it down to enter the first promotion of the Ecole normale—a symbolic choice. Not only did Cousin's triumphs as super-laureate open a range of career possibilities, but they gained him exemption from military service, "a greatly appreciated favor during this period of incessant wars."[33] Here too he seems to incarnate the aspirations of his educated coevals. Of course, there is a certain truth in Stendhal's or de Musset's or Vigny's evocation of nostalgia for the heroic opportunities the Empire provided to those with the courage to march into the cannon's mouth and the luck to survive. But we are not really surprised to learn that many bright young men seemed to prefer the route of the new educational meritocracy, or other paths to preferment, rather than the road to Moscow.[34]

---

[32] Charles Durand, *Les Auditeurs du conseil d'état sous le Consulat et le Premier Empire*, Annales de la Faculté de droit d'Aix, new ser., no. 28 (Aix-en-Provence, 1937), 69–272.

[33] Barthélemy-Saint-Hilaire, *Victor Cousin*, 1:27.

[34] Paul de Kock resented Napoleon, "d'avoir contraint mon beau-père à m'acheter,

If, as I believe, the Restoration era provided more varied and more attractive career opportunities than had the Empire in its last frozen phase, what needs to be explained is the ubiquitous expression of youthful resentment against a stifling intellectual and occupational environment. This brings us back to the frustrated mobility hypothesis.

As an example of how occupational frustration engendered alienation, Pierre Barbéris cites the resentment of a *polytechnicien* at his demeaning first assignment, which was to surface roads. "There is," argues Barbéris, ". . . an underemployment of certain technical capacities, at least as far as quality is concerned."[35] While there is evidence that ambitious *polytechniciens* and *normaliens* were disappointed by subaltern assignments, it does not seem plausible that this sort of underemployment would alienate a significant proportion of a hand-picked elite, almost every one of whom could look forward to a substantial career in the field for which he had been trained.[36] Yet cells of the Carbonari were planted in the school, and throughout the Restoration it remained a *foyer d'agitation* in the eyes of the authorities, warranting severe reprisals.

With the fall of the Empire and the end of the wars, the rigid militarization of the school was mitigated by a regime that wished to retain the prestigious center of technical education. Internal discipline was somewhat loosened and an effort made to open the possibility of civilian employment to its graduates. On the other hand, the familiar dialectic of mistrust, agitation, and reprisal would guarantee the chronic disaffection of the successive *promotions* of Restoration *polytechniciens*. Under the aegis of the Duc d'Angoulême, the attempt to christianize

---

coup sur coup, deux hommes pour me remplacer comme soldat . . . les lauriers de Bellone n'étaient pas mon idéal." De Kock, *Mémoires*, 64–65.

[35] Barbéris, *Romantisme et politique*, 193.

[36] A. Fourcy, *Histoire de l'Ecole polytechnique* (Paris, 1828), 461–63, presents a listing of the current occupations of the early *promotions* of the school that demonstrates that virtually every graduate found appropriate employment. See also Terry Shinn, *Savoir scientifique et pouvoir social: L'Ecole polytechnique, 1794–1914* (Paris, 1980); Margaret Bradley, "Scientific Education for a New Society: The Ecole polytechnique, 1795–1830," *History of Education*, 5 (February 1976): 11–24; Terry Shinn, "La Profession d' ingénieur, 1750–1920," *Revue française de sociologie*, 19 (January–March 1978): 45–47, notes that most students came from privileged social strata, but Adeline Daumard, "Les Elèves de l'Ecole polytechnique de 1815 à 1848," *Revue d' histoire moderne et contemporaine*, 5 (July–September 1958): 229–31, points out that a substantial minority could look forward to a higher status than that of their parents.

and monarchize the school, entailing among other things a system of informers, stimulated the sort of defiance that led to the notorious suspension and purge of the *promotion* of Auguste Comte.[37] Comte's anger at the hypocrisy of the administration in allowing the expelled students to sit for a civil service exam that they could no longer hope to pass—victims of a stacked *concours*—exemplifies the tendency to assimilate career frustrations to the malignity of the regime. Similar attitudes would be expressed by Victor Cousin and the *normaliens*, whose brilliant expectations were blighted by the clericoroyalist "reform" of the University.

The optimism with which the first *promotions* of the Ecole normale had contemplated their prospects after 1815 seemed justified on both intellectual and practical grounds. They had pictured themselves as germinating the seeds of intellectual freedom beneath the imperial snows. Now, liberated from the "narrow intellectual discipline" of the Empire, the University was to fulfill its authentic goals with the indispensable collaboration of its newly minted cadres.

The appointment of Victor Cousin as lecturer in philosophy at the age of twenty-three was not only testimony to his precocious distinction but evidence of the scarcity of trained academic personnel. "He arrived at a time when there was a dearth of scholars," remarked his pupil and biographer, Jules Simon:

> Public education had come to a virtual halt during the terrible years; the few self-taught people were taken by the army or the administration. Everyone was regimented in one way or another. Michelet recollects that when he left college (that was four or five years after Cousin), publishers pounced on mere schoolboys to make them men of letters, *c'était le beau temps pour paraître*; one wasn't lost in the crowd.[38]

Le beau temps pour paraître—above all in the educational system, which had yet to fill in Napoleon's vast scaffolding with a corps of trained instructors. During the first five years of the Restoration, under the benevolent aegis of Royer-Collard, Cousin and a confident coterie of *normaliens* looked forward to filling the empty places, including the highest posts in the system. These hopes withered with the political

---

[37] Shinn, *Savoir scientifique et pouvoir social*, 31–32.
[38] Simon, *Victor Cousin*, 6.

accession of ultraroyalism, accompanied by the increasing clericalization of the University. By 1827, sixty-six of the eighty-eight professors
of philosophy at the *collèges royaux* were priests.

We saw in chapter 2 how the educational *politique* crowned by the
accession of Bishop Frayssinous and culminating in the termination of
the Ecole normale was perceived as an attack on the very principle of
a secular University. It was also experienced as the spiteful interruption
of promising careers. Decades later, old *normaliens* would recall how
they were thrown into the streets with the liquidation of the school and
the purges of the University in 1822.[39]

The reopening of the Ecole normale and the reinstitution of
Cousin's philosophy course in the last years of the Restoration were
welcomed as the fruit of the declining fortunes of ultraroyalism, but by
that time the younger academics had become profoundly disaffected
from the regime. The evolution of attitudes in the University would be
repeated *mutatis mutandis* in the other professions: an initial period of
optimism and a sense of expanding horizons succeeded by resentment
at petty harassment or outright repression, culminating in disenchantment and alienation.

The profession of law certainly supplied articulate recruits to the
forces of opposition to the monarchy, whether legal, legalistic, or ex-
tralegal. This hostility might well have been stimulated by the anxieties
of young *avocats* and *avoués* who discovered that a law degree was no
guarantee of professional or financial security. Restoration legislation
added to the increasing costs of the privilege of admission to the bar.
To be inscribed on the register of *avocats*, a young barrister would have
had to bear the expense of a secondary education in order to obtain the
baccalaureate that admitted him to law school. After paying for three
costly years of legal education, he entered the profession as *stagiaire*, a
probationary stage that effectively limited his opportunity to make a
living for another three years. If he aspired to the lucrative and prestigious right to plead before the Cour de Cassation, he had not only to
deposit a substantial *cautionnement* but was also required to purchase
or inherit the office from a previous occupant. It is unlikely that many
young lawyers were depressed by the expense at the distant eminence
of the Cour de Cassation, but a Restoration decree also imposed the

[39] For reminiscences of the effects of the temporary closing of the Ecole normale, see
the obituary notices in the *Mémorial de l'association des anciens élèves de l'Ecole normale.*

cautionnement—caution money—and granted the sale of office for all *avoués* and *notaires*.[40] The *cautionnement* that had been in effect under the Empire was raised substantially, and the tacit practice that amounted to the sale of offices was formally enacted in the legal right of *présentation*, an innovation widely criticized as a return to the bad old practices of the Old Regime.

The brilliant prospects opened up by these years of financial sacrifice and deferred gratification were etched with acid in Balzac's *Old Goriot* in Vautrin's portrait of a legal career for the young Rastignac:

> Does the Baron De Rastignac think of becoming an advocate? Oh, excellent! He must slave for ten years, live at the rate of a thousand francs a month, have a library and chambers, go into society, go down on his knees before a solicitor for briefs, sweep the floor of the Palais de Justice with his tongue. If this led to anything good I should not say no; but show me five advocates in Paris who earn more than fifty thousand francs a year at fifty! Bah! Sooner than shrivel my soul like that I would turn pirate. Moreover, where would you find the cash? That question is no joke.[41]

Without presuming to challenge Balzac's immense authority on the cash coordinates of survival in Restoration France, I wish to emphasize the specific historical situation of the legal profession as it emerged from the chilly climate of the Empire. It has often been remarked that Napoleon detested lawyers, that, for example, only one full-fledged *avocat* received a decoration under the Empire.[42] One can imagine with what resentment that was remembered. A more fundamental cause of professional resentment, however, was the law of 14 December 1810, which laid down the regulations for the organization and discipline of

[40] This was the Law of 28 April 1816. *Avoués* did not usually have the right to plead but performed functions analogous to those of a solicitor. *Notaires* had a monopoly on the authentication of legal documents and performed other financial functions, including money lending.

[41] Honoré de Balzac, *Old Goriot*, trans. M. A. Crawford (Harmondsworth, Eng., 1951), 128.

[42] A.M.J. Dupin, *Profession d'avocat* (Paris, 1830), 1:132: "Napoléon était extrêmement prévenu contre les avocats. Il détestait leur indépendance et leur esprit de controverse." Marie-Oscar Pinard, *Le Barreau au XIXe siècle* (Paris, 1864), 1:91–92; J. Gaudry, *Histoire du barreau de Paris depuis son origine jusqu'à 1830* (Paris, 1865), 1:511. Jules Fabre, *Le Barreau de Paris, 1810–1870* (Paris, 1895), 36, 55.

a national bar. This "fatal decree" imposed the authority of the state upon the self-government of the profession and restricted the right of legal argument by penalizing even implicit criticism of the regime. Despite the possibilities afforded by the expanding economy and a new system of laws, recruitment for the magistrature as well as to the bar stagnated under the Empire.

There seemed much to hope for in the transition from a state dominated by soldiers to a regime that presented itself "with the idea of law," that is, with a written constitution.[43] This was especially attractive to the young bar. Perhaps they had been seduced by military glory as *lycéens*, but now, recalled Odilon Barrot, they were inspired by the revival of libertarian ideals and felt more at home than did their seniors in handling the legal implications of representative institutions. "Thus," he concludes, "my youth, instead of being an obstacle to me, was an advantage."[44]

The young bar found it advantageous not only to work within the boundaries of the constitution, but also to work against it. One of the ironies so characteristic of the Bourbon regime lay in the opportunities it afforded to oppose it in court. In a generally critical account of the past decade written in 1830, A. J. Dupin granted that the order had never been more numerous: "The young bar had rivalled the old in its zeal; the many brilliant opportunities for distinction offered by political trials have been taken up with enthusiasm."[45]

This was an avenue of mobility scarcely available under the Empire, for distinguished careers were begun during the Restoration in the defense of opposition journalists, dissident organizations, and those accused of political conspiracy. Indeed, there were attorneys who helped to create their clientele by participating in conspiracies that they would subsequently defend in court. Conspiring was itself a form of social mobility, enabling obscure students to hobnob with Lafayette or the Marquis Voyer d'Argenson.

There is much more evidence of promising careers launched in op-

[43] Pinard, *Le Barreau au XIXe siècle*, 1:92: "Nulle part la Restauration ne fut accueillie comme au barreau." Dupin, *Profession d'avocat*, 1:134: "La restauration trouva les avocats favorablement disposés pour elle; elle se présentait à eux avec l'idée du droit."

[44] Odilon Barrot, *Mémoires posthumes de Odilon Barrot* (Paris, 1875), 1:43.

[45] Dupin, *Profession d'avocat*, 1:139; Pierre Jacomet, *Le Palais sous la Restauration, 1815–1830* (Paris, 1922).

position to the regime than of opposition produced by frustrated careers. To take a few examples:

Félix Barthe (1795), admitted to the bar in 1817, delivers the graveside oration for the student-martyr Lallemand, whose military "assassins" he attempts to bring to justice, simultaneously conspires with the Carbonari and defends them in court, then assumes an active role in the legal opposition to the Bourbon state, well on his way to the post of prosecutor of young conspirators as minister of justice under the next regime.

Chaix d'Est Ange (1800), full-fledged lawyer at the age of seventeen, launches his phenomenally precocious career as counsel for defendants in the August 1820 Conspiracy and the trials of the Carbonari.

Adolphe Crémieux (1796), distinguishes himself at Nîmes as an aggressive defender of Protestants, Jews, and victims of the White Terror; by 1823 has built a flourishing practice in the Midi.

Jules Dufaure (1798), doctor of law in 1820, admitted as *stagiaire* at Bordeaux after having taken his oath before the Paris bar, within a year or so enjoys a substantial reputation as an effective defender of liberal causes and opposition journals.[46]

These vignettes are not intended to suggest that the penchant of young lawyers for the political opposition was strictly opportunistic. The Bourbon government made its characteristic contribution in policies that progressively alienated the entire profession. Predictably, the story of the legal profession's disenchantment with the Restoration began in the schools, where there was a considerable variation in the degree of student provocation and the intensity of official reprisals. The Grenoble faculty was suspended in response to riots amounting to a near insurrection. In Rennes, as we have seen, a most trivial incident was exploited as an excuse to expel any suspect students and to replace permissive, that is, moderate or liberal, professors with ultraroyalists. The Bavoux affair not only resulted in a humiliating defeat for the government in the courts but cemented the combative solidarity of student groups in and out of the Faculty of Law.

After the student-led political riots of June 1820, the government promulgated a series of regulations for the faculties of law and medi-

---

[46] For biographical information on all these individuals, see the *Dictionnaire de biographie française* (Paris, 1933–) and Robert and Cougny, *Dictionnaire des parlementaires français*. See also S. Posener, *Adolphe Crémieux* (Paris, 1933–34); Roger Allou and Charles Chenu, *Barreau de Paris: Grands Avocats du siècle* (Paris, 1894).

cine severely penalizing anything remotely resembling insubordination within the schools and subjecting extracurricular misbehavior to academic discipline irrespective of the action of the public authorities and the courts. These decrees, stigmatized as an unconstitutional violation of equality before the law in a journal edited by young lawyers, breathed the conviction that the students were factious by nature and potential enemies of the realm.[47]

When these assumptions were confirmed by further "disorders" in 1822, the temporary suspension of the Paris faculty was followed by a decree that reorganized the curriculum, dropping such unsettling innovations as the chairs in legal history and political economy so that students would receive only "positive and useful instruction" and would be shielded from courses that "might give the young an excuse to raise dangerous questions."[48] The various restrictions and prohibitions conceived by the authorities as legitimate measures of self-defense were perceived by the young legal community as the reinstitution of creeping despotism.

The entire legal community was bitterly disappointed when the crown finally introduced its long-awaited revision of the detested Napoleonic laws on the organization of the profession. The royal ordinance of 20 November 1822, celebrated by the Minister of Justice as a repudiation of imperial tyranny, was evaluated by the legal profession as more objectionable than its predecessor. In a pamphlet hurried into publication a month after the promulgation of the decree, the twenty-two-year-old Alfred Daviel (1800) remarked that however much the regime deplored the old despotic system it never failed to apply it on propitious occasions. This was a conviction widely shared by young liberals, who had welcomed the constitutional monarchy primarily because it promised a mitigation of the despotism of the Empire. Daviel presumed to speak for the entire profession, but he reserved special an-

[47] "Réflexions sur L'Ordonnance du 5 juillet 1820 concernant les facultés de droit et de médecine" (signed: Delaplesse, avocat), *Journal général de législation et de jurisprudence*, 2 (1820): 223–32.

[48] The grand master of the University, Frayssinous, quoted in Madeleine Ventre-Denis, "La Première Chaire d'histoire du droit à la faculté de droit de Paris (1819–1822)," *Revue historique du droit français et étranger*, 45 (October–December 1975): 615, and "Sciences sociales et Université au XIXe siècle: Une tentative d'enseignement de l'économie politique à Paris sous la Restauration," *Revue historique*, 256 (October–December 1976): 338.

imus for the articles that reorganized the *stage*, the three-year novitiate preceding full induction into the profession. The new provisions prohibiting *stagiaires* from pleading a case until after the attested completion of two years of assiduous attendance at the court imposed the conclusion that youth was the major target of the law.[49] Daviel's mournful conclusion, "Hatred of youth seems characteristic of this era," may seem a trifle excessive with reference to the frustrated ambitions of lawyers under the age of twenty-two, but his complaint does bear on the regime's inability to mask its mistrust of articulate groups that were not amenable to *bien-pensant* discipline.

The practice of the medical profession did not tie it so directly to political issues, but its young practitioners did share many of the attitudes and experiences of the graduates of the law schools, especially in the Paris arena. They played an active part in the militant student movements of the capital, almost living up to Ackerknecht's somewhat exaggerated portrayal:

> The medical students of the 1820s in their majority hated the Bourbons, brought back by Cossacks and Prussians; hated their caste society, that would not accept them as equals; hated the Jesuits who again ran the Universities, and went to prison for the Carbonari, before they went on the barricades of 1830.[50]

To accept even this unqualified version of the disaffection of fledgling physicians is not necessarily to assert that medical students and young doctors stepped out of the ruins of the Empire dedicated to the destruction of the Bourbon dynasty. It is a commonplace to describe French medicine at the beginning of the nineteenth century as the most advanced in the world and to attribute this in some part to the rationalization of medical education and professional certification accomplished under Napoleon's reign. But during that reign, as Dora Weiner has observed, "the needs of strategy, administrative efficiency and economy gradually gained ascendence over humanitarian and medical considerations. . . . While one might attempt to portray Napoleon as a

[49] M. A. Daviel, *Examen de l'ordonnance du 20 novembre 1822, concernant l'ordre des avocats* (Paris, December 1822), 37–42.

[50] Erwin H. Ackerknecht, "Broussais, or a Forgotten Medical Revolution," *Bulletin of the History of Medicine*, 27 (July–August 1953): 339–40.

patron of science, one could not possibly depict him as encouraging medicine."[51]

The portrait of Napoleon as a patron of science has been rather defaced by L. Pearce Williams, who argues that despite Napoleon's assiduous self-promotion as a magnificent benefactor of science, his politics reduced the Ecole polytechnique from a great teaching center of mathematics and science to a training school for military technicians, tied scientific research to narrow military goals, and in general reflected the suspicion that the scientific case of mind was potentially subversive.[52] Like other occupations, science and medicine were shackled by the "narrow, militaristic, utilitarian outlook" of the Empire in its last frozen phase.[53]

The end of the wars liberated medicine from these constraints and opened a flourishing era as well as one of overcrowding and murderous competition, even though the number of doctors produced in the decade preceding the Restoration seems negligible in relation to the size of the population.[54] Young doctors complained of the dead weight of aged practitioners, the competition of the *officiers de santé*, and of their own low economic and social status compared to the other professions.[55]

[51] Dora B. Weiner, "French Doctors Face War, 1792–1815," in Charles K. Warner, ed., *From the Ancien Régime to the Popular Front: Essays in the History of Modern France in Honor of Shepard B. Clough* (New York, 1969), 56–57.

[52] L. Pearce Williams, "Science, Education and Napoleon I," *Isis*, 47 (December 1956): 369–82; Robert Fox, "Scientific Enterprise and the Patronage of Research in France, 1800–1870," *Minerva*, 11 (October 1973): 445–49.

[53] Erwin H. Ackerknecht, *Medicine at the Paris Hospital, 1794–1848* (Baltimore, 1967), 39.

[54] Between 1803, when the basic law on medical practice was passed, and 1813, the three medical faculties of Paris, Strasbourg, and Montpellier graduated some 207 doctors per year. This average was raised to 369 during the Restoration. Ministère de l'instruction publique, des beaux-arts et des cultes, *Enquêtes et documents relatifs à l'enseignement supérieur*, vol. 21, *Etat numérique des grades, 1795–1885* (Paris, 1886), 42–43.

[55] On the increasing cost of a medical education, see Jacques Léonard, *La Vie quotidienne du médecin de province au XIXe siècle* (Paris, 1977), 26. On the perception of overcrowding in the profession (*encombrement*), see S. Eymard, *Coup d'oeil critique sur la médecine française au XIXe siècle* (Paris, 1829), 43–44; George D. Sussman, "The Glut of Doctors in Mid-Nineteenth-Century France," *Comparative Studies in Society and History*, 19 (July 1977): 288–89; George Weisz, "The Politics of Medical Professionalization in France, 1845–1848," *Journal of Social History*, 12 (Fall 1976): 3–7. Oliver Faure, "Physicians in Lyon During the Nineteenth Century: An Extraordinary Social Success," *Journal of Social History*, 10 (June 1977): 511. Jan Ellen Goldstein, "French

Perhaps, as Jacques Léonard remarks, "this contrast between a highly ambitious ideal and bitter realities" helps to explain the ardor of the medical students during the revolution of 1830, but the young doctors most prominent among the activists of the early twenties were already pursuing promising careers.[56]

In the course of his indefatigable revolutionary agitation, Philippe Buchez carried on medical studies under the benign patronage of royalist physicians. After the collapse of the Carbonari and at the time of his entrance into the Saint-Simonian circle, he obtained his doctorate in medicine, edited a medical journal, and published a book on hygiene. The coauthor of that work, Ulysse Trélat—militant of militants—had turned down the post of surgeon-general in the royal dragoons and had successfully competed for an *internat* at the hospital of Charenton. Another possessor of the coveted post of *interne*, Guillier de la Touche (1800), was involved in the unsuccessful attempt to liberate the notorious four sergeants of La Rochelle from the Bicêtre. Dr. Etienne Bailly de Blois, who delivered the eulogy at Saint-Simon's grave and helped to found the *Producteur*, had received his medical degree in 1817 and had established a successful practice by the early 1820s. Alexandre Bertrand (1795), one of the Breton radicals associated with Leroux and Dubois, was expelled on political grounds from the Ecole polytechnique in 1815 and the Rennes law school in 1817, conspired with the Carbonari, and wrote for the *Globe*, all while managing to obtain a medical degree and produce a best-seller on somnambulism.[57]

Psychiatry in Social and Political Context: The Formation of a New Profession" (Ph.D. diss., Columbia University, 1978), 22.

[56] Jacques Léonard, "Les Etudes médicales en France entre 1815 et 1848," *Revue d'histoire moderne et contemporaine*, 12 (January–March 1966): 94.

[57] The *Dictionnaire de biographie française* outlines the careers of Buchez, Bertrand, and Bailly. There is material on Buchez, Guillier de la Touche, and Trélat in Robert and Cougny, *Dictionnaire des parlementaires français*; on Buchez and Trélat in Jean Maitron, comp., *Dictionnaire biographique du mouvement ouvrier français, Part 1, 1789–1864* (Paris, 1964–66). For Buchez, see also A. Ott, "Une notice sur la vie," in Buchez, *Traité de politique*, 1:viii–ix; Isambert, *De la Charbonnerie au saint-simonisme*, 34–44. For Trélat, see Goldstein, "French Psychiatry in Social and Political Context," 317; and René Semelaigne, *Les Pionniers de la psychiatrie française avant et après Pinel* (Paris, 1930), 1:202–21. Bailly is discussed in Manuel, *The New World of Henri Saint-Simon*, 329; and Gouhier, *La Jeunesse d'Auguste Comte*, 3:238–39. Bertrand's short life (he died in 1831) is described by Leroux in *L'Encyclopédie nouvelle*, 2:641–44, and in Papiers Dubois, AN 319 AP³, Dossier 1.

Occupational frustrations almost certainly had something to do with the ferment in the young medical community, but, once again, the regime made its contribution to the discontent, especially through politically and religiously tendentious appointments to desirable posts.[58] Above all, the regime revealed its mistrust of the Paris medical faculty as a *"foyer* of Bonapartism and revolutionary ideas."[59] An attempt by Louis XVIII's personal surgeon to put the school back in the Old Regime by reinstituting separate faculties of medicine and surgery was beaten off, but the critics of the faculty were given their opportunity in 1822 when medical students hissed the speaker who welcomed them to the new semester for expressing what seemed to be religious sentiments. The official response to this horrendous provocation was to decree the suspension and reorganization of the Faculté de médecine de Paris, in effect to purge all of the politically unreliable—that is, virtually all of the outstanding—members of the faculty and to replace them with a list of nonentities distinguished only by the presence of the great royalist physician Laennec. After the Revolution of 1830, the royalist appointees were fired and their predecessors reappointed.[60]

The purge of the medical faculty had its distant consequences in July 1830, recalled Louis Veron, who had been a medical student in the 1820s: "The government should have looked twice before injuring and arousing that medical universe; slanders and petty *coups d'état* make poor politics; one irritates his enemies without disarming them."[61]

Veron's paraphrase of Machiavelli's advice to tyrants applies with even greater relevance to the Restoration's relationship with the professions of journalism and *belles-lettres*, and indeed with all those who hoped to make a living by the pen. Here too we find a sharp contrast between the tightly constricted opportunities permitted under the Empire and those equivocally afforded by the Restoration, and here too the partial, intermittent, politically motivated frustration of the ambitions unleashed in response to the expanding opportunities.

The total number of works published constitutes a crude indicator

---

[58] Paul Delaunay, *Les Médecins: La Restauration et la Révolution de 1830* (Tours, 1932), 74; Ackerknecht, *Medicine at the Paris Hospital*, 184–85; Weiner, *Raspail*, 55–57, 76–77.

[59] Liard, *L'Enseignement supérieur*, 2:162–63.

[60] Corlieu, *Centenaire de la faculté de médecine*, 222–23; Delaunay, *Les Médecins*, 48–49; Ackerknecht, *Medicine at the Paris Hospital*, 40; Léonard, "Les Etudes médicales en France entre 1815 et 1848," 88, and "La Restauration et la profession médicale," 75–77.

[61] Veron, *Mémoires*, 1:49.

of the transformation of the market for literary skills. In 1812, 4,648 printed works exclusive of periodicals were published within the boundaries of the great Empire, among them quite a few by Italian, German, or Dutch citizens of Napoleon's regime. In 1825, in the confines of the eighty-six departments of Restoration France, there were 7,542 publications. The contrast was much more striking with regard to periodicals—238 titles under the Empire and 2,278 under the Restoration.[62] Comparing the books listed in the *Bibliographie de l'Empire français* for 1813 and those in the *Bibliographie de la France* in 1825, I find 3,749 listed for the former date and 7,605 for the latter.

The consequences for Restoration careers are not self-evident. In *Popular French Romanticism*, James S. Allen emphasizes the relative youth of published authors of "romantic genres" under the Restoration.[63] But information on the actual age structure of Restoration authorship says nothing about the relation between the demand for, and the supply of, potential authors. There was a manifest expansion of the market for literary talent after 1815, but the magnet of the Paris literary market almost certainly attracted a far greater number of young competitors for a foothold in the world of letters than the market could actually absorb.

Once again, Balzac's *Lost Illusions* seems a persuasive re-creation of a saturated market, of that *crise des débouchés* for an excess of educated or half-educated men, and in the case of literature, women too. So one must grant considerable force to the standard emphasis on the alienating effect of the discrepancy between unlimited expectations and finite opportunities. It is also true, however, that with regard to this as to other avenues of mobility, the Restoration took on itself the onus of the partial, inconsistent, and irritating closing of the avenues that it had opened.

Under the Empire, the system of tight control, censorship, and prior restraint was applied to the publication of books as well as to the periodical press. The decree of 5 February 1810 reduced the number of licensed printers in Paris to sixty. All publications were listed with a Di-

---

[62] Sauvigny, *The Bourbon Restoration*, 329. Barbéris, *Balzac Et Le Mal du siècle*, 1:710, graphs the substantial rise in the number of pages printed between 1812 and 1825. He draws his data from Pierre A.N.B. Daru, *Notions statistiques sur la librairie pour servir à la discussion des lois sur la presse* (Paris, 1827), which draws its data from the annual *Bibliographie de la France* (dating from November 1811).

[63] Allen, *Popular French Romanticism*, 82–86; see also Robert Escarpit, *Sociology of Literature*, trans. Ernest Pick (Plainesville, Ohio, 1965), 26–29.

rector General of printing and publication or with the departmental prefect, and any publication that tended to subvert the duties of subjects toward their sovereign and state was subject to criminal procedure.

As we shall see, the Restoration regime was never inhibited by a strict construction of Article 8 of the *Charte*, which affirmed freedom of expression, but its earliest legislation did exempt all works of more than twenty pages from censorship. Publishers flourished and the book trade boomed. The opening out of intellectual horizons is manifest in the disproportionate growth in the number of historical publications. A useful base for comparison might be the years 1812 and 1813, the last two years before the imperial debacle that lists of the *Bibliographie de la France* were published. A comparison of the number of works labeled "history" published in 1812 and 1813 with that in 1824 and 1825 reveals a percentage increase five times greater than the increase of the total of all publications and greater than that of any other category, including theology, belles-lettres, and science.[64]

The increase in the number of works specifically on the history of France, which speaks most directly to my point, was fivefold.[65] This development represents not only the often-cited flowering of the his-

---

[64] The total of all works published in 1824 and 1825 (6,974 + 7,542 = 14,516) represented an increase of 40.3 percent over the total published in 1812 and 1813 (4,648 + 4,017 = 8,665). The number of works labeled "history" in 1824 and 1825 (1,336 + 1,324 = 2,660) topped the totals of 1812 and 1813 (405 + 408 = 813) by 216 percent. The data is compiled in Daru, *Notices statistiques sur la librairie*.

[65] Daru organizes the history categories as follows:

History Category	No. Works			
	1812	1813	1824	1825
Géographie	37	47	44	55
Voyages	58	61	109	119
Chronologie	9	3	7	7
Antiquités, moeurs, coutumes, etc.	13	15	54	39
Histoire universelle	22	18	12	18
Histoire sacrée et ecclésiastique	25	32	82	91
Histoire ancienne, grecque, romaine et du Bas-Empire	35	48	29	45
Histoire moderne des differents peuples	35	33	103	139
Histoire de France	61	60	359	387
Biographie	106	88	213	281
Politique et polémique	4	3	324	143
Total	405	408	1,336	1,324

torical imagination in the Restoration era, but also the political liberation of historical subject matter and the introduction of historical subjects that provided the stuff of literary careers. The French Revolution, a politically sensitive but not completely forbidden topic, became the favorite subject for young authors—most notably for Thiers and Mignet, who founded their reputation on works inconceivable under the previous regime.

However, the turn to the right after the assassination of the Duc de Berry impelled ultraroyalist courts to unearth a decree dating from 1723 that levied a fine for the publication of books without a *brevet*—a publisher's license—and lifted the *brevet* from publishers who distributed works deemed dangerous by the police.[66] This did not amount to the reimposition of the unqualified controls of the imperial censor. We know, for example, that Sautelet, a publisher engaged in a great many dissident and illegal activities, was given a clean bill of health by the *police de la librairie*.[67] But it did entail a continuous, frustrating, inhibiting, and harassing treatment of publishers and authors by an anxious establishment.[68]

A similar dialectic developed in the realm of the theatre, which provided many possibilities for novice talents to make some marginal mark. According to the *Globe*, the "little" theatres—the theatres of the boulevard—which were more or less "liberated from Aristotle's yoke," offered young authors a more prompt and easy way of earning money "than did the theatres devoted to the classical repertory." Perhaps, as the author of another piece on the same subject remarked, this easy remuneration stifled the germ of real talent in those encouraged to work too rapidly in *genres secondaires*.[69]

Whatever their threat to real talent, the *genres secondaires* (the vaudevilles, comedies, and melodramas), which were insatiable consumers of scripts because of their popularity with a wide public, provided that in-

---

[66] Charléty, "L'Avènement d'une génération nouvelle," 183.

[67] The dossier, Sautelet (Auguste) in AN F[18] 1824.

[68] Barbéris, *Balzac Et Le Mal du siècle*, 1:710: "Retraits de brevets, saisies, signalés par les spécialistes, sont un autre aspect de cette 'trahison' des 'espoirs' de 1815 qui est à la base du désenchantement romantique." This is to concede something to the effect of royalist politics as well as bourgeois economics.

[69] *Globe*, 15 February, 9 April 1825; see also Michel Hennin, *Des Théâtres et de leur organisation légale* (Paris, 1819), 34: "les jeunes auteurs s'éloignent des scènes privilégiées, et composent pour les théâtres où ils peuvent trouver concurrence d'acheteurs de leur marchandise; ils font des mélodrames et des vaudevilles."

dispensable space on the bottom rung of the theatrical business. That was the way, for example, that Alexandre Dumas obtained a foothold, or at least a toehold, in the world of letters. He would recall his anonymous but lucrative collaboration on a *pièce de circonstance*, one of those facile, trivial verse comedies cranked out for the mass market, as "the point of departure for the hundred plays that I have probably produced."[70]

The market for theatrical ephemera was much wider than that afforded under the Empire, whose characteristic policy of centralization and rigid control culminated in a decree that fixed the maximum number of Paris theatres at eight, and indicated the genre appropriate to each theatre of the boulevards. After 1814, when the Parisian theatre turned with its usual facility from the glorification of the emperor to a celebration of the legitimate line, it really had something to celebrate. The imperial decrees were suspended and theatres of every sort were allowed to open.[71] As a crude indicator of the opportunities available to apprentice playwrights, I have compared the plays listed in Charles Wicks' *The Parisian Stage* for the years 1823 to 1825 to those staged in the late Empire, 1811 to 1813. There were 655 all told in the second period, a considerable increase over the 433 that were seen under the Empire. More to the point is the comparison in the genre of the vaudeville. Only 45 were permitted by the imperial censorship, compared to over 300 ephemeral pieces in the mid-Restoration years.[72]

However, as we have come to expect, what the Restoration gave with one hand it more or less took away with the other. The system of imperial censorship was preserved. Indeed it was enforced by some of the same individuals who had done the job for the Emperor. While the Restoration censors could not impose the Empire's iron control over the much more varied, active, and freer theatrical world, they still had the authority to pass on every play, admitting it, rejecting it, or editing

---

[70] Dumas, *Mes Mémoires*, 2:389–90. The comedy or *vaudeville* was *La Chasse et l'amour*, performed at the Gymnase in 1825.

[71] Maurice Albert, *Les Théâtres des boulevards (1789–1848)* (Paris, 1902), 201–312; Charles-Marc Des Granges, *La Comédie et les moeurs sous la Restauration et la Monarchie de Juillet (1815–1848)* (Paris, 1904), 35–67; Claude Gével and Jean Rabot, "La Censure théâtrale sous la Restauration," *Revue de Paris*, 120 (November–December 1913): 339–62; Jean-Marie Thomasseau, "Le Mélodrame et la censure sous le Premier Empire et la Restauration," *Revue des sciences humaines*, 162 (April–June 1976): 171–82.

[72] Charles B. Wicks, *The Parisian Stage*, Part 1: *1800–1815*, Part 2: *1816–1830* (University, Ala., 1950–79).

it line by line in the light of the preoccupations of an anxious regime. The censors struck out anything that hinted at disrespect for royalty in general at any time or place, excessive celebrations of liberty (as in the dramatization of the independence struggles of the Swiss or the Greeks), all direct allusions to the Revolution or the emperor, all references to current events that were even remotely critical of the established order, all potentially negative references to dignitaries (social, religious, political, or administrative), and virtually all references to the clerical orders, whether positive or negative. The policy was also designed to shelter "the morals" of the audience and to preserve the proprieties. No suicides were to be portrayed and no corpses shown in public view. *Plaisanteries grivoises*—smutty jokes—were unsystematically excised. Imagine the frustration of some future historian, the *Globe* observed, attempting to reconstruct the French past from the record of the contemporary theatre. "The censors have done such a superb job that no trace of us will remain to satisfy the curiosity of our successors."[73]

The censorship constituted a piecemeal caricature of the political mentality and the cultural anxieties of the Restoration regime.[74] It was less thorough but more niggling than that of the Empire, pettily oppressive, increasingly harsh after the wave of censorship legislation in 1822, inconsistently enforced, and ultimately evaded. Above all, the tacit or blatant representations of the emperor in the pseudoclassical dramas and the melodramas could not be extirpated by the vigilance of the panel of literary hacks who executed the policy. Here, once again, the Bourbon government simultaneously afforded an ambitious youth opportunities for expression and motives for opposition.

The vitality of the popular theatre not only provided a market for untried literary talents but greatly expanded that for facile journalism. There was an immense literature of theatrical criticism—reviews of plays, advertising disguised as criticism, vignettes of popular performers, and so forth. How such opportunities could be parlayed into something like a literary career is exemplified by Balzac's Lucien de Rubempré, who seizes the chance to dash off a clever review of a play that sets him on the path of venal literary success and moral corruption.

Much like Balzac's fictional Lucien, Auguste Jal came to Paris after

---

[73] *Globe*, 7 December 1824.

[74] I have borrowed this insight from Claude Gével and Jean Rabot, "La censure théâtrale sous la Restauration," 343.

his expulsion from the royal naval academy in search of a genteel career. Although not equipped with literary or artistic credentials, Jal accepted the offer of an acquaintance (in this case not to review drama, but the *beaux-arts*) and then, in rapid succession, produced works on various artistic salons and a dictionary of the theatre and became an editor of the *Miroir des spectacles*—the rather improbable beginning of what became a long and incredibly prolific, if utterly undistinguished, career in belles-lettres.[75]

While the market for ephemera provided the widest possibilities, what is best remembered are those journals of opinion published and edited by a galaxy of brilliant writers under the age of thirty-five. The most influential and significant as a self-identified spokesman for the new generation was, of course, the *Globe*. We will not go over that ground again, nor reexplore the territory covered in the earlier description of the *Producteur* and the *Muse française*. There were other, less memorable examples, of course, not all dedicated to a critique of the established order. The brothers Hugo, comprising an editorial board barely out of its teens, had made a marked impression, at least on the friends of throne and altar, with the publication of the *Conservateur littéraire* in 1819. The *Mémorial catholique*, expressly dedicated to the defense of the faith, first appeared in 1824 under the direction of two twenty-seven-year-old acolytes of Lamennais. One of the most successful of the specialized journals, the *Gazette des Tribunaux*, was founded in 1824 by J. J. Darmaing, who had already floated an ephemeral sheet in 1818 at the age of twenty-four. Charles Coquerel was twenty-two when he began his career as a spokesman for French Protestantism with the publication of the *Annales protestantes*.

Such possibilities had not been available under the Empire. Napoleon's detestation of an unregulated press had been fixed in legislation that restricted the number of journals designated as "political" to four in Paris and one in each department. As they operated under the authority of the Minister of Police, we might think of their contributors as literary functionaries. The Restoration explicitly repudiated such restrictions. According to the Charte, all Frenchmen had the right "to publish and to have printed their opinions, while conforming with the laws that are necessary to restrain abuses of that liberty." The evident ambiguity of Article 8 would be expressed in the regime's relation to the press through its entire existence until its ultimate, unambiguous

[75] Jal, *Souvenirs*, 42–48.

resolution to stifle opposition journals through the coup d'état of July 1830.[76]

There never was a time when journalists enjoyed complete freedom from some sort of censorship or threat of prosecution for vaguely defined offenses, but there never was a time, either, when it was absolutely impossible to publish material offensive to the royal authorities.[77] As publishing houses, periodicals, pamphlet series, and short-lived quasi periodicals appeared and disappeared and were re-created under new names, with new editorial boards under old editors, it was possible for an obscure young journalist to pursue a hand-to-mouth existence as a contributor to established and ephemeral publications. And, as in the practice of law, it was probably easier to get a start as a voice of the opposition than as an apprentice to the royalist press.

Perhaps this is why the dominant spirit of the younger members of the Fourth Estate was antiestablishment. But the regime made its characteristic contribution in its relation to the Restoration press, which revealed that same dialectic of ambivalence, mistrust, defiance, and piecemeal reprisal that poisoned relations with the teaching corps and the professions. During the early years of Louis XVIII's reign, various forms of censorship irritated but never completely stifled the press. After the political accession of ultraroyalism in the 1820s, the government's increasingly repressive and devious policies—including an attempt to buy up all of the opposition journals—alienated not only young firebrands but also distinguished royalists such as Chateaubriand, thereby making a significant contribution to its own demise.[78]

[76] The most recent general history of the press under the Empire and the Restoration is Bellanger et al., *Histoire générale de la presse française*, 1:549–67; 2:27–99. A great deal of useful information is still to be found in Hatin, *Histoire politique et littéraire de la presse en France*, volumes 7 and 8. For the Empire, see André Cabanis, *La Presse sous le Consulat et l'Empire (1799–1814)* (Paris, 1975). For the Restoration, see Albert Cremieux, *La Censure en 1820 et 1821* (Abbeville, 1912); and above all Irene Collins, *The Government and the Newspaper Press in France, 1814–1881* (Oxford, 1959), 1–59; and Irene [Collins] Fozzard, "The Government and the Press in France, 1822 to 1827," 51–66.

[77] There were careers to be made in the offensive genre. After Auguste Barthélemy (1794) failed to strike oil with an ode on the coronation of Charles X, he crossed the poetic barricades and, with Joseph Méry, another facile versifier from Marseilles, tossed off a political satire, *La Villéliade*, which went through fourteen editions in 1826, in the midst of the ultraroyalist reaction. See especially Dumas, *Mes Mémoires*, 2:435–47, for their strikingly forgettable careers.

[78] Notably the *Tablettes universelles*, in which several of our subjects had invested their ambitions.

The press laws of 17 and 25 March 1825 incarnate the entire history of the Restoration's suicidal cultural *politique*. While they set aside censorship in the sense of prior restraint, they invented the crime of a tendency to threaten the public order or the respect due religion, the king, and the constitution. Violators were not to be tried by juries but brought before the bench of royal courts. As a negative intepretation of the "esprit" of a series of articles was sufficient cause to indict, the government initiated a number of successful prosecutions. But the king's magistrates did not prove to be completely reliable instruments (key cases ended in acquittals), and the guerilla war between the government and the press eventually damaged the regime far more than it inhibited the opposition. As Machiavelli tells us, "Men must either be caressed or annihilated; they will revenge themselves for small injuries, but cannot do so for great ones; the injury, therefore, that we do to a man must be such that we need not fear his vengeance."[79]

I have not intended to deny the significance of the pressure to succeed but rather to modify the frustrated mobility thesis by something like an old-fashioned political interpretation of the history of the Restoration. The application of political constraints to an unruly youth, especially in the schools, was experienced as the actual or potential frustration of career opportunities because of the integral relationship between educational accomplishments and licensing for the professions—to which the Restoration had applied the definitive decree in the imposition of the baccalaureate as a professional prerequisite. As well as repression and purges of the *grandes écoles* and the professional faculties, the sporadic suppression and manipulation of the press and the publishing enterprises threatened the fund of jobs for younger applicants and also cut those ties of patronage through which careers were initiated.

This is not simply to equate the political alienation of a future elite with occupational frustration. Many of those whose prospects were compromised in the light of political or ideological considerations could, after all, have met the requirement of an ultra *politique* or a clericalized University. Indeed, any fairly talented young person with the right credentials could expect a benign official interest in his early career. There were approaches to the bottom rungs of the career ladder other than through the standard success in the *concours* or through pre-

---

[79] Niccolò Machiavelli, *The Prince*, trans. Luigi Ricci (New York, 1940), 9.

cocious publication: a reputation for youthful piety; the recommenda-
tion of a family priest; or, best of all, a stint in the *chouannerie* or as a
volontaire royal in 1814 or 1815. Then, like A. F. Rio or Pierre Laurentie (1793), one could follow the path to Paris, armed with a letter perhaps, for the Vicomte de Lainé rather than Jacques Manuel, to be welcomed into the educational system, the royal administration, or the
editorial boards of such journals as the *Drapeau blanc* or *Quotidienne*,
and into the distinction of a lectureship in the *Société des bonnes lettres*,
precocious colleagues of Chateaubriand and the Comte de Serre. Like
Edouard Mennechet (1794), a laureate of the Académie française with
impeccable royalist credentials, one might accumulate an office in the
royal household at the age of twenty-three and the ribbon of the Légion
d'honneur at twenty-nine, or like Jacques Ancelot (1794) one could
craft an impeccable drama about Saint-Louis and win a substantial
pension, a title of nobility, and a place in the royal administration.[80]
And, of course, there were all sorts of opportunities for intelligent apprentices to the priesthood.[81]

But for someone of a different stripe, even someone as ambitious as
Théodore Jouffroy or the other members of Cousin's *normalien* coterie,
there came a point at which a "man of honor" could no longer contemplate remaining under the "terrible and shameful solidarity of the system of brutalization and servitude applied by the University."[82] In his
desperate attempt to preserve a position, Paul Dubois would appeal to
his fellow Breton, the ultraroyalist Comte de Corbière, and to the reactionary administrator Abbé Nicolle, but in the event Dubois never
could trim his sails to the prevailing climate of a university clerisy.[83]

[80] A. F. Rio, *Epilogue à l'art chrétien* (Freiburg im Bresgau, 1870), 1:168, 224–34. Sister Mary Camille Bowe, *François Rio: Sa place dans le renouveau catholique en Europe
(1797–1874)* (Paris, 1938), 29–48; Pierre Sébastien Laurentie, *Souvenirs inédits* (Paris,
1892), 35–44; Biré and Grimaud, *Les Poètes lauréats*, 1:256–60, *Dictionnaire de biographie française* 2:792–94. When it was performed in 1819, Ancelot's *Louis IX* was greeted
as the royalist answer to Casimir Delavigne's *Les Vespres siciliennes*. The dedication to
His Majesty Louis XVIII contained these lines: "Sous le règne de VOTRE MAJESTÉ il
m'était facile de retracer les vertus du père des Bourbons; et si mon ouvrage a obtenu
quelques applaudissements, je les dois sans doute au plaisir qu'ont éprouvé les Français, en retrouvant l'image du présent dans les souvenirs du passé."

[81] Among those who forged notable early careers as priests were Gerbet, Salinis,
Bautain, Henri Lacordaire (1802), and Félix Dupanloup (1802).

[82] Jouffroy to Dubois, 10 September 1822, in Jouffroy, *Correspondance*, 340.

[83] Gerbod, *Paul-François Dubois*, 40–41.

And Victor Cousin was notoriously unable to adapt his program of lectures to the requirements of a conservative ministry. Even Adolphe Thiers, driven by manic ambition, was canny enough, or perhaps principled enough, to resist the flattering offer of the Comte Villèle to transfer his journalistic talents from the *Constitutionnel* to the service of the regime.[84]

The Bourbon regime frustrated youthful aspiration, not because it wished to turn the clock back to 1789, but because it shared Napoleon's authoritarian mistrust of social groups that were articulate and unrestrained, though it lacked his ability to restrain them. The efforts of the monarchy, especially in its Ultraroyalist phase, to contain subversion and to discipline potential recruits to a disloyal opposition had the effect of making its own fears and suspicions into self-fulfilling prophecies. The rising generation would settle its hopes on the regime's demise.

[84] Henri Malo, *Thiers, 1797–1877* (Paris, 1932), 86–87, publishes long extracts from the correspondence, the originals of which are in the Bibliothèque nationale, Nouvelles acquisitions françaises, 20601.

CHAPTER 10

Lost Illusions:
Class and Generation Reconsidered

"Here, everything begins with money."
Honoré de Balzac, *Louis Lambert*

In his brilliant essay on "Lost Illusions," Georg Lukács quotes Balzac's condemnation of the Bourbon regime for its frustration of the energies born of the Revolution and the Napoleonic era:

> Nothing is such a condemnation of the slavery to which the Restoration has condemned our youth. The young men who did not know what to do with their strength, have harnessed it not only to journalism, political conspiracies, and the arts, but to strange excesses as well. . . . If they worked, they demanded power and pleasure; as artists, they desired treasure; as idlers, passionate excitement—be that as it may, they demanded a place for themselves and politics refused it to them.

This, says Lukács, was the tragedy of an entire generation, but the thrust of his essay is not to emphasize the repressive politics to which the quotation refers but the more basic transformation of culture through the cash nexus of emerging capitalism.[1] In Barbéris' expanded version of this theme, the conflict of generations takes place within the bourgeoisie. The specific political form of the alienation of the Restoration *jeunesse* is a transitory aberration: "The ultra-Restoration beginning with the Villèle ministry had masked the problem, had imposed the belief that the essential issue was still the struggle against the nobility and the clergy." That is, one might say that it had imparted a tem-

[1] Lukács, *Studies in European Realism*, 48–49. The quoted passage is in Balzac, *Illusions perdues*, 463. It is mistranslated in the English edition.

porary false consciousness to a bourgeois youth soon to locate the authentic source of its malaise in its own class.[2]

There is ample evidence for that sort of resentment, expressed in the cynical characterization of the literary marketplace by Balzac's fictional characters and by such contemporary voices as the *Globe*, whose raison d'être was to transcend a literary criticism that had become "une spéculation d'auteurs, et un commerce de librairie."[3] This condemnation of "the transformation of literature into a commodity"[4] is not, however, incompatible with Stenzel and Thoma's characterization of the *Globe* as an organ for the nascent ideology of a liberal bourgeoisie whose economic credo is argued in its columns.[5] Tanneguy-Duchâtel's essays on political economy in the *Globe*, or the brochures of Carrion-Nisas, or for that matter the economic writings of the Saint-Simonians for the *Producteur* comprised an up-to-date synopsis of bourgeois political economy.

The more or less implicit boundaries of the generation's approach to the economic order are suggested in the *Déclaration de principes de morale M...* drawn up in 1823 by a committee of the masonic lodge the *Amis de la vérité*. This was the front organization for the Carbonarist conspiracy, a node in the network of Paris activists, including Buchez, Dugied, and A. (probably Arnold) Scheffer, whose names appear among the signatories to the *Déclaration*. Proceeding from a familiar enumeration of human rights based on universal and self-evident natural law, the document affirms complete equality as indispensable for the enjoyment of rights. This egalitarianism, inherited from the Jacobin constitution of 1793, was balanced off by a negative and utilitarian conception of positive law, whose function was to "guarantee the *covenants* made by individuals or communities in the exercise of their rights."[6]

---

[2] Barbéris, *Balzac Et Le Mal du siècle*, 1:75–76. On page 450 and in an essay published after the above, Barbéris does grant the alienating effect of ultraroyalist policies that closed off the avenues opened at the fall of the Empire. Pierre Barbéris, "Structures et dynamiques du romantisme," in Pierre Abraham and Roland Desné, eds., *Histoire littéraire de la France* (Paris, 1976), 7:369–70.

[3] *Globe*, 14 September 1824.

[4] Lukács, *Studies in European Realism*, 49.

[5] Stenzel and Thoma, "Poésie et société dans la critique littéraire du *Globe*," 33–35.

[6] The *Déclaration de principes* is in the Papiers manuscrits de Buchez, Bibliothèque historique de la Ville de Paris. An abridged version was published in Flotard, *Paris*

An even more faithful reproduction of the clichés of Restoration liberalism can be found in Thierry's effusive review of Victor Cousin's course of lectures in 1819. Here, moral equality is celebrated as a natural right and the equal right to property is dismissed as a chimera.

> If we note with regret that among men who equally enjoy economic freedom some are wealthy and others impoverished, we should appeal to humanity, but not to justice, to lessen these unfortunate disparities. He who has been rendered destitute by the imbecility of his physical nature or by fate has no rights on our affluence, although we as human beings have an obligation to alleviate his misery.

And so forth, to the predictable, "It follows that natural law, which establishes the inviolability of persons, and civil law, which establishes the inviolability of possessions, are anterior, and therefore superior, to political laws."[7]

Perhaps this passage can be read as one more signpost on the highroad to the commanding heights of the July Monarchy's *juste milieu*, which Cousin, Thierry, and their friends and associates were to occupy so complacently, but I do not believe that the political economy of the Cousinians or any of the other young authors was merely a rationalization of a premature urge to assume their anticipated inheritance. In the most general sense, they shared a belief in the free market for talent and ideas that as Stenzel and Thoma point out in their essay on the *Globe*, they assimilated to the ideal of economic laissez-faire. Their celebration of "the magical results of liberty and competition" had quite specific content in the virtually universal commitment to the proliferation and rationalization of the academic, or any other, *concours*. Few of them were personally interested in the accumulation of industrial capital, but they all intended to capitalize their talents.

A commitment to the challenge and opportunities of the *concours* in particular, and the educational system in general, signified the beginning of the embourgeoisement of the Restoration aristocracy. This was apparent to contemporaries. As the question was put in the *Producteur*, "In place of training their children in hunting and the handling of

---

révolutionnaire, 2:454–57. I have borrowed the insights of the analysis of the document in Isambert, *De La Charbonnerie au saint-simonisme*, 127–29.

   [7] Thierry, *Dix Ans d'études historiques*, 207–9.

weapons, do they [the gentry] not send them off to study law and the exact sciences just as *the pères plébéiens?*"[8] The complete fusion of the upper classes had yet to be consummated, but it was anticipated by the social coalition that fraternized on the editorial board of the *Tablettes universelles* or the *Globe* or in the other ramifications of that dense network of the young intellectuals.

If we adopt the now-classic procedure of conflating those ambiguous and incommensurable socio-occupational designations—*propriétaire, maire, notaire, officier, homme d'affaires*, and so forth—into the categories constructed by Adeline Daumard and a succession of other social historians, we discover the unsurprising fact that most of the young talents who came to the attention of their contemporaries emerged from more or less privileged social strata (see Table 10.1).[9] The occupational profile of the fathers of 126 of our subjects is top-heavy with political and military careers founded in previous regimes. To a considerable extent, this book describes the scions of those with the means and inclination to guarantee their sons a head start in the privileged system of secondary education. The rest range down through the strata of French society to the upper edge of the *menu peuple*.

Social distinctions were not completely submerged in generational solidarity. This is implicit in Rémusat's patronizing reminiscences of Paul Dubois' lack of polish, or explicit in Dubois' or Michelet's or Jouffroy's proud affirmation of the modest antecedents that distinguished them from their coevals out of the aristocratic salons. Jouffroy is quoted as contrasting himself and his bourgeois comrades with the privileged world of Tanneguy-Duchâtel, Rémusat, and Duvergier de Hauranne: "Our aristocrats have never dreamed in a garret, have no idea of what stirs the heart of a young man who has to earn his keep and falls asleep

---

[8] *Producteur*, 2 (1826): 64.

[9] This literature proceeds from Adeline Daumard, "Une Référence pour l'étude des sociétés urbaines en France aux XVIIIe et XIXe siècles: Projet de code socio-professionnel," *Revue d'histoire moderne et contemporaine*, 10 (July–September 1968): 185–210. For an especially thoughtful discussion of the problems of making historical sense out of social and occupational designations, see John H. Weiss, *The Making of Technological Man: The Social Origins of French Engineering Education* (Cambridge, Mass., 1982), 248–56. I have not obtained detailed information on parental wealth, as did Weiss, or Terry Shinn for *l'Ecole polytechnique*, but simply group the 68 percent of my subjects for whom I obtained information on parental occupations in categories borrowed with minor qualifications from Daumard.

TABLE 10.1 THE OCCUPATIONS OF THE PARENTS OF 126 MEMBERS OF THE
GENERATION OF 1820

Occupation	No.	%
Officials		
High functionaries, military officers, and national politicians	33	26.2%
Middle functionaries, petty bureaucrats, and junior officials	18	14.3
Businessmen		
Industrialists, bankers, and large merchants	23	18.2
Small merchants	7	5.5
Members of the liberal professions	21	16.7
Artisans and shopkeepers	9	7.1
Domestics	2	1.6
Farmers	6	4.8
Miscellaneous	7	5.5
TOTAL	126	99.9%

to dream of the happiness that heaven has denied him."[10] But for all practical political or cultural purposes, these distinctions did not inhibit the friendship and collaboration of young intellectuals of diverse antecedents.

Not only were class distinctions temporarily obscured by the shared experience of location in a particular age group at a particular time and place but also by the experience of youth as a socially marginal category. This was especially the case when the father's occupation or status entailed no positive relation to the life chances of the child. At one time or another Thiers' father was a *propriétaire*, but he was a disreputable drifter who had abandoned his family. Adolphe Blanqui's father had been a *sous préfet* under the Empire, but the Empire was gone, the father had died, and the boy was penniless. Hortense Allart, Frédéric De George, J. T. Flotard, and several others were orphans too. But even those who enjoyed the consequential support of parents of substance had yet to realize the cash value in assured careers of the certificates awarded for academic skills and intellectual superiority. This is

[10] Quoted in Alexandre Estignard, *Portraits franc-comtois* (Paris, 1890), 3:271–72.

to suggest that under some circumstances age is a socioeconomic phenomenon, as Robert Bezucha has argued with regard to the social profile of the *gardes mobiles* during the revolution of 1848 when he observes that the simple alignment of the recruits along an occupational spectrum misses the point that they were relatively young and therefore economically marginal.[11]

In raising this issue I do not intend to confer some quasi-proletarian status on middle-class youth in the manner of the optimists of the 1960s who thought that because college students were being trained for the labor market they could be enlisted in the working class. Nor do I wish to press the analogy with Bezucha's *lumpenjugend* to the point of locating the Restoration *jeunesse* at the lower margin of the bourgeoisie or even of the professions. An impoverished *lycée* graduate such as Adolphe Blanqui, or a humbly born *agrégé* like Michelet, or an Alexandre Dumas clinging to the fringes of the theatrical profession, does not quite fit into the social strata occupied by a small shopkeeper, or an *officier de santé*, or even an unsuccessful provincial attorney. Theirs was the marginality of social ambiguity, of young men on the make who lived in a garret and scrabbled for sous while ornamenting high-class salons, dining with Royer-Collard, conspiring with Lafayette, publishing with Guizot—every future possible and none assured.

This uncertain potentiality is the common condition of the children of the well-to-do in the modern world, where parental wealth and status are less likely to be passed on as real property than as a privileged socialization, a passport to lucrative careers. Their marginality, in this sense, scarcely serves to distinguish the Restoration youth from succeeding cohorts, but there is a sense in which their identity as a generation was functionally related to the historical situation of certain social groups.

The sense of the term generation that distinguishes it from a regular stage in the life cycle entails the perception of a historically specific age-related identity usually affirmed by members of the relevant age group. Scott and Grasmick rightly assert that a "generational consciousness" is analogous to class consciousness in that it is a "potential source of group consciousness leading to collective action,"[12] but in historical

[11] Robert Bezucha, "The French Revolution of 1848," *Theory and Society*, 12 (July 1983): 469–84.

[12] Scott and Grasmick, "Generations and Group Consciousness," 191.

reality the generational phenomenon cannot be separated from the phenomenon of social class, because a certain sociohistorical location is the context for the experience and affirmation of a generational identity.

To get down to specific cases, fragmentary evidence on the coevals of the Restoration intelligentsia who occupied the lower social strata suggests that they experienced youth as a stage in their life cycle rather than as the prelude to the life of a historically distinct generation. Young artisans such as Agricol Perdiguier (1805) or Jules Vincard (1796) were separated from their elders during the Restoration years because they occupied a youthful life stage, engaged in behavior appropriate to that stage, and underwent an occupational and social apprenticeship to prepare them for the normal transition to maturity. To our hindsight, what the future dignitaries of the July Monarchy were undergoing was also an apprenticeship, but that was not how they saw it, and in fact the procedure through which upper-class children were to be trained and socialized for careers in the post-Napoleonic order had not been clearly worked out.

One thing was clear enough to them: the procedure had something to do with special merit. To a considerable extent, the young intellectuals of the Restoration confused the process of cooptation into the mature elites with a special historical election that validated their cohort's unique world-historical destiny. The *normaliens* did not see themselves simply as talented aspirants for future careers; Thiers, Mignet, and Thierry did not think of themselves as apprentice historians; Buchez and Trélat saw no reason to defer to the aging incompetents in the upper reaches of the medical profession; young lawyers, as Odilon Barrot remarked, were at home in a constitutional system for which their seniors had no precedent. Of course, significant exceptions spring to the eye, especially from the masthead of the established liberal journals where Thiessé or Philarète Chasles, or even Thiers, had more or less apprenticed themselves to the master craftsmen of the antiregime. For someone with eyes so cooly fixed on the main chance as Thiers, even this commitment was to be carefully qualified by keeping a foot in the camp of the self-elected seers of the society of the future. This dexterity is symbolized by his simultaneous contributions, under different pseudonyms, of reviews of the salon of 1824 to the *Globe* and the *Constitutionnel*.

This is not to say that the working class and peasant coevals of the "generation of 1820" did not share the experience of those immense and moving events that overturned the imperial order and brought back the Bourbons with the armies of the enemies of France. Jules Vincard's father got him a job in a munitions workshop in order to shield him from Napoleon's conscription.[13] Vincard and his friends who formed the *Sociétés chantantes* of the working-class *goguettes*, or Perdiguier and his journeyman chums were, like their educated coevals who conspired in the Carbonari, able to assimilate the nostalgia for imperial glories to the promise of a libertarian future. "I was a Bonapartist and at the same time I was a republican," says Perdiguier. "I confounded Napoleon with liberty. All of my comrades accepted the same logic." Perdiguier even contracted an authentic case of *mal du siècle*, if we can trust a reminiscence long after the event.[14] Nevertheless, if the comrades with whom Perdiguier sang, drank, and fought were roughly in the same cohort, his primary identity was with his *Devoir*—his fraternal order in the *compagnonnage*—and his expectation was to pass out of the journeyman stage at an appropriate moment into the next stage of life.

Under different circumstances, young members of the working class might constitute a generation in our sense, as perhaps they did in the 1830s, when a militant response to the social question might have divided the artisanate by a generation gap, but during the Restoration the gap is in the upper classes, where the experience of the imperial collapse took the form of the soiled reputation of parents and teachers, where success in academic competitions seemed to validate great expectations, and where the system of intergenerational patronage was briefly interrupted by an ultraroyalist *politique* that drove the most ambitious and talented youth back into their own cohort network. This mutual dependence was briefly experienced, not as a momentary expedient, but as a collective destiny.

[13] Jules Vincard, *Mémoires épisodiques d'un vieux chansonnier saint-simonien* (Paris, 1878), 13.

[14] Agricol Perdiguier, *Mémoires d'un compagnon* (Paris, 1964), 89, 117.

CHAPTER 11

A Conclusion and an Epilogue

"We cannot separate . . . the identity crisis in individual life and contemporary crises in historical development."

Erik H. Erikson, *Identity, Youth and Crisis*

I once taught in a survey course whose segments were labeled chronologically beginning with the traditional categories, the Ancient World, the Middle Ages, and the Renaissance. Somehow the chairman's imagination broke down at 1648, for from that point to circa 1954 the assigned category was The Age of Transition. And so it was. All ages are.

The trauma of growing up in an age of transition was scarcely confined to our French cohort even in its own era. The most relevant comparison is probably with the roughly identical age group in the contemporary German youth, notably those who formed the association of the *Burschenschaften*.[1] They too shared the sense of a world-historical mission for which their elders were inadequate. They too contrasted their stainless lives and selfless idealism with the shopworn and timeserving character of

[1] The fundamental work is the collection, Herman Haupt and Paul Wentzcke, ed., *Quellen und Darstellungen zur Geschichte der Burschenschaft und der deutschen Einheitsbewegung*, 17 vols. (Heidelberg, 1910–40). See also, Rolland Ray Lutz, "The German Revolutionary Student Movement," *Central European History*, 4 (September 1971): 215–41, and, "Father Jahn and His Teacher-Revolutionaries from the German Student Movement," On-Demand Supplement, *Journal of Modern History*, 48 (June 1976): 1–34; Gunther F. Eyck, "The Political Theories of German Academic Youth between 1815 and 1819," *Journal of Modern History*, 27 (March 1955): 27–38; Konrad H. Jarausch, "Sources of German Student Unrest," in Lawrence Stone, ed., *The University in Society* (Princeton, 1974), 2:533–69; Gary D. Stark, "The Ideology of the German *Burschenschaft* Generation," *European Studies Review*, 8 (July 1978): 323–48; Lenore O'Boyle, "Klassische Bildung und soziale Struktur in Deutschland zwischen 1800 und 1848," *Historische Zeitschrift*, 207 (December 1968): 584–608; Karl-Georg Faber, "Student und Politik in der ersten deutschen Burschenschaft," *Geschichte in Wissenschaft und Unterricht*, 21 (February 1970): 68–80.

the preceding generation, which had fallen so far short of its own ideals. They felt themselves adrift in a universe without landmarks and yearned for some higher synthesis that would guarantee an indispensable ideological and social coherence. They rejected those skeptical and materialist philosophies that had contributed to the moral void. Many of them exhibited the classic symptoms of the *mal du siècle* syndrome, and it is claimed that their *angst* owed something to fierce competition in a market crowded with an excess of educated men. As their aspirations were frustrated by the conservative forces that commanded political power, their alienation took the form of political opposition to the established order.

So it might be argued that the transitory age-related identities of the Restoration youth in both France and Germany were the identical products of the Revolution's dissolution of certainties and the trauma of the illusions created and lost in the *Götterdämmerung* of the great French Empire. However, these great events were experienced in different national contexts. The most obvious difference lay in the commitment of the militant German youth to national unification, a goal unnecessary and therefore unavailable to the French. Leaders of the German movement informed their sense of a unique national mission with the quality of revived Christian pietism—scarcely a preoccupation of the French intelligentsia even when it embraced Cousin's brand of transcendentalism. The religious tone of the German movement responded to the manner in which an idealistic youth was embedded in its social context. The piety of the *Burschenschaften* provided an ideological cement for heterogeneous groups and served to separate them from the mainstream of German academic youth in the *Landmannschaften*, the student fraternities dedicated to dueling, drinking, and wenching. So, too, the democratic populist flavor, completely absent from the French youth ideology, as well as the eccentric style of dress recalling the uniform of French Bohemia after 1830, were means of distinguishing the *Burschenschaften* from their less idealistic coevals.

Those who presumed to speak for their generation in France did not perceive the same problems. Not all of their educated, potentially articulate, coevals shared their views, but there was no rival for their self-election as the best and brightest of their cohorts. The militant German youth was swimming against the current. The French *lauréats de concours* were a bit impatient to come into their inheritance. In Germany the older order would implacably maintain itself against the quasi-revolutionary agitation of certain student groups. In France the activities of a self-conscious *jeunesse* took the form of participation in the national effort to define a new order.

The essential problem of all of those who entered public life in the postimperial era, including those committed to the restoration of the Bourbon dynasty, was not how to restore some old regime but how to transform the legacy of the Empire. It is commonplace to remark on the persistence of Napoleonic institutions, including the educational system. Those "ruins" universally perceived by an anxious youth were girt round with the solid edifice of the imperial administrative, institutional, and educational system. But things *had* changed in 1814, not only with regard to obvious symbols, loyalties, and constitutional arrangements, but also in relation to unfinished or provisional institutional structures and modes of behavior. From a certain perspective, imperial institutions were cast in bronze; from another, they had been, in a nation at war, necessarily provisional. The transition from a political and social system permanently organized for war to the real and imagined possibilities of a peacetime order instilled that exultant and apprehensive sense of infinite opportunity in those who were to find their maturity in the new world. That world was in process of definition, and it was this process that determined the unfortunate destiny of the Restoration regime.

The conflict over the construction and operation of a parliamentary system without French precedent was the narrow political expression of the inchoate effort to understand and to define what the postrevolutionary, postimperial society was to be and how it was to operate. For those with a personal future yet to make, the result of this effort would be coincident with their own destinies. Just as the system of representative government had to be invented in daily practice, so did procedures of elite training, apprenticeship, and mobility. Here, the insight of the sociologist Philip Abrams seems especially apposite:

> The more the overall configuration of a society leaves the mode of entry of new individuals open to negotiation the more likely it is that those individuals will put together a sense of themselves as being historically unlike their predecessors, will make something culturally or politically of their distinctiveness as youth.[2]

[2] Philip Abrams, *Historical Sociology* (Somerset, Eng., 1982), 256.

The mode of entry into the nineteenth-century social system was certainly open to negotiation, but it was not without precedent. There had been *concours* and a Grub Street under the Old Regime, but in a postrevolutionary society without legally privileged orders, the possibility of an ascent through semipermeable social strata was not only pursued with a ferocious dedication but felt as an immense pressure on self-esteem.

The mastery of the new rules of an old game was perceived as a matter of personal survival, and someone during those central Restoration years seemed to have changed the rules. In their obsession with the legacy of the Revolution, the ultraroyalists embraced the revolutionary precedent of the politicization of cultural relations and social arrangements. What the regime afforded by way of the Société des bonnes lettres and the benediction of the bishop of Hermopolis was felt to be more constricting and demeaning than the harshest constraints imposed on youthful aspirations by the imperial military machine.

Perhaps even more fundamental was the incompatibility of the conservative temperament with a "youth ideology" whose essential premise was the refusal of deference. We have seen how the spokesmen of the new generation took great pains to distance themselves from the dignitaries of the liberal opposition as well as from the fossils of clericoroyalism. The militant affirmation of the autonomy and prospective superiority of our providential cohort might provoke an irritated or patronizing response in the opposition establishment, but it found little difficulty in celebrating the promise of the *génération naissante*.[3] Where Constant and Lafayette were always happy to laud the future hope of the nation from the tribune of the Chamber, conservative deputies usually welcomed youthful petitioners with homilies on the proper place of the young in a well-ordered society. Benjamin Constant's "hope and glory of the fatherland" could measure the distance between their ambitions and their prospects under the current regime in the contemptuous comments of the Comte de Serre, or Joseph Fiévée, or even of their sometime guru Chateaubriand:

---

[3] Thus Benjamin Constant, often the target of young critics: "à aucune époque la génération naissante ne fut si avide de science, si consacrée à la recherche de tout ce qui est bon, de tout ce qui est beau. J'en prends à témoins tous ceux qui fréquentent les collèges; nos jeunes gens qui sont l'espoir, et qui seront la gloire de la patrie, n'ont de passion que celle de s'instruire, de plaisir que celui de chercher et de découvrir la vérité." *Archives parlementaires*, 2nd ser., 25:653–54; see also 27:717.

Our children are turning into little propagandists reasoning about government of right and government of fact, talking *nation et patrie*, disdaining their teachers, scorning their parents, treating religion as a prejudice and priests as imbeciles; they began by hanging themselves out of boredom, and have ended up rebelling in order not be be bored.[4]

In response to such attitudes, as well as on specifically political grounds, the most dynamic elements of the cohort entering its fourth decade increasingly located their aspirations in a permanent *fronde* against the established order. In alienating a substantial portion of the emerging elite, as in other regards, the Bourbon regime helped to produce its own gravediggers.

EPILOGUE: CONGEALED PRECOCITY AND THE PRISON OF THE LONGUE DURÉE

"Maturity does not always fulfill the promise of youth."
Victor Cousin, *Fragments littéraires*

An historian may legitimately conclude the history of a cohort when it no longer exhibits an age-based coherence, but the history of its members only ends with their lives. I do not intend to follow out the histories of the members of the cohort of 1820 past that moment when they manifested a historically significant coherence. Reflection on their separate destinies does, however, cast a retrospective light on the meaning

---

[4] *Conservateur*, 4 (1819): 132. The clever conservative publicist Fiévée thought that it required "toute la folie du siècle" for the Chamber of Deputies to receive a student petition. Law courts might just as well consider petitions from sons demanding that their fathers rehire discharged tutors. Ibid. Roughly the sentiments, too, of the Comte de Serre: "Et cependant ici, par le renversement le plus étrange de toutes idées et de tout ordre, les élèves eux-mêmes, cette jeunesse qui a tout à apprendre, et la science et la sagesse; cette jeunesse se présente devant les députés de la France, elle y vient audacieusement juger ses maîtres et les supérieurs de ses maîtres!" *Archives parlementaires*, 2nd ser., 25:655. The students *would* petition and the conservative deputies deliver the standard response: "Renverriez-vous au bureau de renseignements l'adresse des étudiants en droit? Pourriez-vous l'accueillir sans compromettre la dignité de la Chambre? Félicitons plutôt la jeunesse studieuse qui ne s'est point détournée de ses travaux pour manifester des craintes sur les sentiments de la Chambre des députés." Ibid., 26:31, or 27:717.

of their original identity. What might be thought of as an epilogue to
the history of the Restoration *jeunesse* is suggested by a question posed
in a piece on J. J. Ampère first published in 1868 by Sainte-Beuve in the
Revue des deux mondes. Citing Goethe's prediction of a brilliant future
for Ampère and the "thousands of men" who were to share his views,
Sainte-Beuve reflects on the actual fate of Ampère's generation, honored by a prophecy so disappointingly unfulfilled:

> What has become of those "thousands of men" who were to think
> as he? What has become of that novel, generous, and fertile tra-
> dition which, once established, was to persist and ramify for the
> honor of civilization and the liberated intellect? How few of those
> same young men, so early to mature and so brilliant when they
> first entered the world of letters, have accomplished their mission
> and fulfilled their promises![5]

Why, Sainte-Beuve mused, have even the most gifted "created nothing fully worthy of such proud beginnings . . . ?"

It is not surprising to find this question posed by Sainte-Beuve, who
had long since distanced himself from the nostalgic self-image of former mentors for whom the Revolution of 1830 w..s a glorious fulfillment and the coup d'état of 1851 a grotesque aberration. He had staked
out his ground a number of years before in a review of François Mignet's address in 1853 before the Academy of Moral and Political Sciences on the tenth anniversary of the death of Théodore Jouffroy. Mignet took that occasion to evoke the memory of the "fortunate
generation to which M. Jouffroy belonged, . . . a generation nourished
on the most wholesome doctrines and committed to the highest ideals,
which it never forsook during its time in power." True to its principles,
it had given France "the greatest well-being it had ever enjoyed, the
fullest liberty that had ever existed, the most moderate government
that it had ever known."[6]

This transparently veiled contrast with the current regime stimulated Sainte-Beuve, who had nailed his pennant to Louis Napoleon's
mast, to respond with characteristic deft malice. Mignet, he said, was a
fine historian when he stuck to his own last, but he had rather over-

[5] Sainte-Beuve, *Nouveaux lundis*, 13:206–7.
[6] François Mignet, "Notice historique sur la vie et les travaux de M. Jouffroy," 25
June 1853, *Mémoire de l'académie des sciences morales et politiques de l'Institut de France*
(Paris, 1855), 9:43, 63.

done the celebration of a generation to which he himself belonged—it was the familiar tendency, what might be called the weakness of Old Nestor, "to display ingenuously for the benefit of new generations the satisfaction of having belonged to a superior generation." But, after all, was not Mignet's generation responsible for much of what it currently deplored? When it came into possession of political authority it had dropped its commitment to letters and philosophy: "in effect, once at the top, this generation had pulled up the ideological ladder behind it."[7]

By 1853 Sainte-Beuve no longer cared to identify with what he thought of as a generation of losers, but to be fair to him one should note that even in 1833, when he treated Jouffroy and "the generation that had entered maturity during the storms of 1814 and 1815" with respect amounting almost to deference, he did remark on a discrepancy between its aspirations and its accomplishments. When it fought its way to the heights in 1830, it looked down not upon a land of milk and honey, but a sterile plain. "It had become apparent to those who had hoped for better things that it would not be this generation, so promising and so prone to self-praise, that would reach the promised land."[8]

Sainte-Beuve was not the last observer to emphasize the discrepancy between the generation's vainglorious expectations and its qualified accomplishments. In 1858, for example, a distinguished voice of the succeeding cohort, Ernest Renan, began his evaluation of the philosophic stature of Victor Cousin with such an assessment:

Nearly every generation as it comes into existence begins by an exaggerated evaluation of its strengths and of the destiny it feels called upon to fulfill. . . . The generation that preceded ours, the one that was launched in 1815 and attained maturity in 1830, carried with it virtually limitless aspirations. . . . To a man, it saw itself called to a task of renewal, and as if humanity was to be reborn with it, it was confident that it could inaugurate in its century a new literature, a new philosophy, a new history, and a new art. It has not delivered all that it had promised; it had promised the infinite; it has not renewed the human spirit; this is a more difficult task than was at first believed.[9]

[7] Sainte-Beuve, *Causeries du lundi*, 8:301–2.
[8] Sainte-Beuve, *Portraits littéraires*, 1:298–99.
[9] Renan, "M. Cousin," 55.

Twenty years later, Thureau-Dangin's volume on the Restoration liberals makes somewhat the same point. Thureau-Dangin quotes the passage from Sainte-Beuve's 1833 piece and goes on to remark that if the prospective generation's prospects seemed disappointing in 1833, how might one evaluate its accomplishments after the catastrophes of 1848, 1851, 1870, and 1871?[10]

The question is still occasionally posed. In one of his richly documented contributions on the personnel of the *Globe*, Jean-Jacques Goblot again refers to Sainte-Beuve's characterization of the "enigma" of these fine but not completely fruitful intellects.[11] This enigma had to do with the question of the disappointing destiny of the generation of 1820, but perhaps that question is *mal posée*. It does seem odd to characterize a cohort distinguished by such names as Balzac, Hugo, Comte, Thierry, Vigny, Thiers, Delacroix, and many others as a failure. As Henri Peyre remarked, and as Renan granted in his evaluation of the older cohort, they towered above their immediate predecessors and successors. The very interest one finds in the networks of obscure young intellectuals and activists who conferred and conspired together in the 1820s owes a great deal to their subsequent distinction. The investigation of those hare-brained attempts to overthrow the Restoration monarchy by a mixed bag of immature militants yields the names of Buchez, Bazard, Leroux, Carrel, Thierry, Jouffroy, Cousin, Raspail, Dubois, and the Cavaignacs.

Yet the question of collective failure in the face of so many individual successes is inescapable because it was anticipated by the generation's tendency to characterize itself in the light of a world-historical destiny. Its self-assigned role was to create that new general doctrine that was to be the indispensable agent of the transition to some future order. This never came to pass. Despite the brilliance of individual careers, the attributes that distinguished them from their predecessors did not "endure and transform culture"; their turn on the historical stage was not a turning point; their brilliant talents and fierce ambitions blended into a continuum that simply assimilated them into the larger society.[12]

[10] Thureau-Dangin, *Le Parti libéral*, 262–63.

[11] Goblot, " 'Le Globe' en 1827," 487–88. Goblot is quoting Sainte-Beuve, *Portraits littéraires*, 1:300.

[12] This concept is borrowed from Philip Abrams, "Rites de Passage," *Journal of Contemporary History*, 5 (1970): 183.

One obvious, and early, answer to the question of unfulfilled promise refers to selling out, first advanced by members of the generation who saw their coevals complacently acquire the perquisites of the July Monarchy. To the handful of republicans, *purs et durs*, the progress of their old comrades from the secret societies into the Orleanist establishment was the betrayal of those shared ideals that were the hope of the nineteenth century. Thus, Ulysse Trélat, still on the barricades in the 1830s, would mourn the transformation of Félix Barthe from liberty's most eloquent voice at the grave of the martyred Lallemand and the trials of the Carbonari to its executioner as minister of the July Monarchy's version of political justice.[13]

One man's treason is another's maturity. No doubt the alienation of a great many Restoration *arrivistes* was assuaged by what they obtained from Louis Philippe. Others waited somewhat longer to arrive. For Trélat, the barricades had shifted somewhat by June 1848, when he was the minister who liquidated the National Workshops.

Others continued to keep the faith. Pierre Leroux created a virtual subgenre of embarrassing reminiscence. His favorite target was Victor Cousin, but he also took occasion to recall all of those "bureaucrats, heads of the University, ambassadors, and magistrates" who had launched themselves from "that modest journal, the *Globe*, originally founded by us in 1825."[14] Leroux believed that merely to republish Jouffroy's *Comment Les Dogmes finissent* was to make a devastating comment on how much the Restoration intelligentsia, including Jouffroy, had betrayed its origins.

From the perspective of an additional century and a half, Leroux's premise—that Jouffroy's essay represented great promise betrayed—is not self-evident. Nor is it evident that the failure of eclecticism, or the unfulfilled promise of the *Globe*'s brilliant board of editors, was the result of trimming, timidity, the easy triumphs of the platform, or the

---

[13] Trélat, *Paris révolutionnaire*, 2:307–8: "Barthe, Barthe, n'étiez-vous donc qu'un habile comédien ou qu'un ambitieux, cupide quand vous excitiez autour de vous de si généreux sentiments; ou bien, après avoir eu la conviction et le dévoûment qui animaient vos amis, n'êtes-vous plus, à l'heure qu'il est, qu'un instrument dont on se sert pour martyriser la sainte liberté?"

[14] Leroux, *De La Mutilation d'un écrit posthume de Théodore Jouffroy*, 130–31. This passage, along with the text of Jouffroy's *Comment Les Dogmes finissent*, had originally been published in the *Revue indépendante* (November 1841). Leroux had also elaborated these themes in *Réfutation de l'éclectisme*.

dissipation of energies in the shallow channels of journalism, if such interpretations assume that there was some powerful philosophic core that might have been the source of a regenerating ethos.[15]

Of course, the focus on the eclectics—on Cousin or his extended circle—is far too narrow. The *normalien* network that purveyed eclectic philosophy or dominated the columns of the *Globe* tended to identify its generation with itself, and that tendency has been reflected in retrospective commentaries that equate the failures of the generation with the flaws of eclecticism. Leroux would taunt the eclectics for their failure to fill their ideological vessel with some substantial content, in contrast, he thought, to the Saint-Simonians. Yet the Saint-Simonians, despite the long-term ramifications of their influential ideas, did not provide that integrating ideology that was to master the unprecedented requirements of an emerging era and provide the cement for a new social order. New ideas purveyed by the Cousinians or the Saint-Simonians or Comte or Enfantin or Leroux, or Victor Hugo and his circle, never did amount to that. Why this was the case is suggested by F. A. Isambert's observation that the new generation had still "to define its positions in the intellectual universe of its predecessors." This is, in a way, to describe a universal experience characterized by Quentin Skinner: "The nature and limits of the normative vocabulary available at any given time will also help to determine ways in which particular questions come to be singled out and discussed."[16]

This observation has a particular point with regard to the Restoration intellectuals who thought that they were about to invent a new vocabulary and who would have claimed the paternity of a new paradigm if history had given them, too, the chance to misapply Thomas Kuhn's conception. Taine, among others, had long since exposed that illusion: "One is not his father's son with impunity; while contradicting him,

---

[15] Charles de Rémusat ascribed the disappointing performance of his generation to the experience of the constraints of the Restoration era, which rendered its best spirits "circumspects, prudents, défiants du succès." Rémusat, *Mémoires*, 5:276. The tendency to substitute public oratory for deep thought or original research is remarked by Taine and others. Robert Fox attributes the falling off of French science in part to this development. Fox, "Scientific Enterprise and the Patronage of Research in France 1800–1870," 452–59; Jacques Goblot views the declining powers of the *Globe* literati as a consequence of the creative erosion induced by the practice of journalism. Goblot, " 'Le Globe' en 1827," 488.

[16] Isambert, *De La Charbonnerie au saint-simonisme*, 63; Quentin Skinner, *The Foundations of Modern Political Thought* (Cambridge, Eng., 1978), 1:xi.

one reproduces him." The 1820s cohort disparaged the *philosophes* of 1760 and imitated them.[17] Oddly enough, François de Corcelle, who had been a faithful junior member of the cohort, saw this too, and as early as 1830:

> For a long time it has been a commonplace to pretend that the revolutionaries of '89 have destroyed everything while building nothing. Their ideas have been characterized as false or incomplete by the Doctrinaires and the Saint Simonians. It would be interesting, nevertheless, to establish just what these modern publicists have borrowed and what they have added. ... Our technique is reduced to concealing our borrowings under the appearance of novelty by means of a sort of grammatical facade derived from poetry and journalism.[18]

I have not intended to cite these correct insights to the point of contradicting the argument of this book. Its subjects *were* different in discernible ways from the older contemporaries, but not in ways that fundamentally transformed French culture. The differences that gave them a transitory significant identity were the product of certain circumstances; as the circumstances changed, their unity dissolved into the larger society.

This was scarcely a unique experience. To the extent that the distinctive qualities of the children of the century were the attributes of youth—reckless idealism, solidarity, overweening arrogance laced with insecurity, and so forth—they would erode with age. This is to grant a certain authority to a life-stage approach, but the life stage of the Restoration youth took on a historically specific form, a form that might be described as congealed precocity. The early distinction of salient individuals created the self-image of their generation that their subsequent performances would not confirm.

There would be many members of the cohort, especially in its younger strata, whose future would far outshine the eventual reputations of those who had once been its brightest stars. Théodore Jouffroy now figures in the footnotes of specialists, while the contributions of Augustin Cournot continue to engage generations of scholarship. Camille Corot, a year younger than Ary Scheffer, was still an appren-

---

[17] Taine, *Les Philosophes classiques*, 297.
[18] Corcelle, *Documens pour servir à l'histoire des conspirations*, 80–81.

tice when Scheffer was the young lion of the salons of 1824 and 1827. In 1825, when Casimir Delavigne was installed as one of the forty immortals in the Académie française at the age of thirty-two, Honoré de Balzac was contemplating the wreckage of his first attempt at a literary career. These contrasts are not cited simply to evoke the turn of fortune's wheel but to suggest that the talents that seemed best to forecast the generation's happy destiny would somehow never ripen into a fulfillment of the early promise.

The unintended irony of Victor Cousin's observation that "Maturity does not always fulfill the promise of youth" would be apparent to anyone familiar with the balance sheet of his career. In this as in so many other ways, Cousin seemed his generation's exemplar. The precocious flowering of a remarkable talent, followed by an apparently substantial success that somehow fell short of early expectations, and then the diminution of reputation down into the limbo of the intellectual history of the second-rate, was an orbit traced by many of the young comets of the 1820s, including the most promising members of Cousin's *normalien* coterie. There is a line in the capsule biography of Cousin in the *Dictionnaire de biographie française* that might be the epitaph for the entire generation: "He was eminently the philosopher of his time. That is why he did not transcend it."[19]

We find virtually the same phrasing in the balance struck by the sympathetic biographer of Ary Scheffer: "Ary Scheffer was in effect intimately mixed with the life of his time. He didn't transcend it, as had Delacroix; he personified it."[20] Tightly enmeshed in a dense network of personal relations, a member of the early Saint-Simonian circle, an admirer of Victor Cousin, a conspirator in the Carbonari, a frequenter of the Delécluze salon, Scheffer was perfectly at home with that segment of the cohort that would come into its own under the July Monarchy. And with his close companions in the Orleanist cultural elite, he would eventually suffer the contempt of the keenest spirits of the next generation. In Baudelaire's review of the salon of 1846, Scheffer is dismissed as an ape of sentiment who soils canvas.[21] In devastating contrast to Delacroix, of course.

[19] *Dictionnaire de biographie française*, 9:1071.
[20] Marthe Kolb, *Ary Scheffer Et Son Temps, 1785–1858* (Paris, 1937), 8.
[21] Charles Baudelaire, *Art in Paris, 1845–1862*, trans. Jonathan Mayne (Greenwich, Conn., 1965), 39, 97–99. The old crowd continued to cherish one of their own. See, for

Delacroix, who, with Hugo, is the giant exception to the history of phenomenal precocity unfulfilled, was defended by some of the younger critics, notably Thiers, against the fulminations of the reactionaries, but most of them felt more comfortable with Scheffer.[22] Even Thiers, rightly credited with the courageous recognition of Delacroix's genius in his reviews of the salon of 1824, mixed praise with a rather patronizing comment on the excess of an *esprit de système* in the *Massacre at Scios*. Thiers characterized Scheffer as the painter in the *jeune école* "who combines in the most natural manner composition, expression, and style, the three qualities most essential for historical painting."[23] In 1826 in the *Globe*, Vitet criticized Delacroix for exaggerating his weaknesses while disguising his good qualities and compared Ary Scheffer to Lamartine.[24]

No doubt the critics of the *Globe* were more open to the innovative power of Delacroix than were their older contemporaries. I have cited Dubois' remarkable comparison of Delacroix and Hugo, in which he rates creative energy higher than submission to aesthetic proprieties. The contrast between the contemporary and subsequent reputations of Delacroix and Scheffer is paralleled by that of Victor Hugo and Casimir Delavigne.

Delavigne was another infant prodigy.[25] At eighteen he wrote a dithyramb on the birth of the king of Rome that won the praise of the emperor himself and a job in the tax office. Within a few years he burst

example, Ludovic Vitet, "Peintres modernes de la France: Ary Scheffer," *Revue des deux mondes*, 17 (1 October 1858): 481–516.

[22] For a discussion of the contemporary evaluations of Delacroix and Scheffer, see Léon Rosenthal, *La Peinture romantique* (Paris, 1900), 94–109; David Wakefield, "Stendhal and Delécluze at the *Salon* of 1824," in F. Haskell, A. Levi, and R. Shackleton, eds., *The Artist and the Writer in France* (Oxford, 1974), 76–85; Pontus Grate, "La Critique d'art et la bataille romantique," *Gazette des beaux-arts*, 2 (1959): 129–48, and *Deux Critiques d'art de l'époque romantique: Gustave Planche et Théophile Thoré* (Stockholm, 1959), 1–34.

[23] *Globe*, 28 September, 2 October 1824. Thiers describes Scheffer's *La Jeune accouchée* as conveying, "le plus touchant de tous les sentiments humains, le sentiment de la maternité surmontant les affreuses douleurs de l'enfantement. Ce petit tableau est un poème digne de Bernardin de Saint-Pierre." Ibid., 16 October 1824.

[24] Ibid., 3 June, 2 September 1826.

[25] A useful edition of the early Casimir Delavigne is *Oeuvres complètes* (Paris, 1836). See Sainte-Beuve, *Portraits contemporains*, 5:169–92, 469–86. Marcelle Fauchier-Delavigne, *Casimir Delavigne intime* (Paris, 1907); Ferdinand Vuacheux, *Casimir Delavigne: Etude biographique et littéraire* (Le Havre, 1893).

out of the security of the administrative bureau with the smashing success of *Les Messeniennes*. This collection of poems was published in 1815 as a lament for the martyred heroes of Waterloo, a paean of pride in the past and hope for the future of the fatherland. These verses— which, to borrow George Boas' comment on Victor Cousin's philosophy, leave one dazed by their banality—were perfectly tailored to the historical moment. Such poems and a succession of almost equally successful verse dramas on historical themes brought Delavigne into the Académie française at the age of thirty-two and made him the nonpareil poet and playwright of the early Restoration, even after Hugo's brilliant star flashed into the literary galaxy.

In 1833, when Delavigne's star had begun to wane, the *National* could still write that "the reputation of M. Delavigne has far surpassed that of the author of *Hernani*: today it still retains popularity . . . that M. V. Hugo never had and will never have." At that date this was already probably a minority view, although we find Jules Lefèvre, Hugo's old friend and associate on the *Muse française* and beneficiary of his kind reviews of mediocre verse, expressing a preference for one verse of Casimir Delavigne over an entire ode of Victor Hugo.[26]

In his florid address welcoming Sainte-Beuve as Delavigne's replacement in the Académie française, Hugo himself recalled how the somber silence of a humiliated nation was broken by "an unknown voice speaking to every soul with a sympathetic accent full of faith in the country and of reverence for our heroes." Within this standard panegyric to the immortal who had passed away the year before, and even more in Sainte-Beuve's ritual eulogy at the same session, one can discern the waning of a literary eminence.[27]

As in so many other cases, Sainte-Beuve's successive evaluations trace out the orbit of a contemporary reputation. At the age of eighteen, Sainte-Beuve was "mad for Delavigne, a rare spirit whose qualities would shield him from the envy that merit always elicited." The critic soon freed himself from that uncharacteristic frame of mind. On subsequent appropriate occasions, such as the reception at the Académie française, he mixes a certain amount of praise of Delavigne with subtle

---

[26] *National*, 26 May 1833; Jules Lefèvre[-Deumier], *Sir Lionel Darquenay* (Paris, 1884), 1:xiv.

[27] For Hugo's address, see Hugo, *Oeuvres complètes*, 7:71–80; for Sainte-Beuve, see his *Portraits contemporains*, 5:169–92.

denigration of an art whose success lay in its ability to meet the shifting demands of successive publics.[28]

This was to be roughly the received opinion, to the extent that anyone *had* an opinion of Delavigne. Pairing him with another one of those adequate but eventually undistinguished talents from the Restoration generation, the contributor to the *Grande Encyclopédie* of the 1870s would evoke "average qualities and therefore those most accessible to the crowd [that] have granted to Casimir Delavigne and [the painter] Paul Delaroche (1797) a transitory fame. At the cost of efforts and struggles of a different nature, Victor Hugo and Eugène Delacroix have conquered a permanent glory."[29] From there, total eclipse. In that erudite and detailed two-volume treatment of Balzac and the children of the century by Pierre Barbéris, there are three references to Delavigne.

Contemplating Delavigne's career before the last word had been said, Alexandre Dumas concluded that to judge his friend and rival one had to situate him historically. Delavigne belonged to the epoch marked by the bitter hostility between the poets of the eighteenth century and the new school of the nineteenth, who were separated by "a ravine filled up by the volleys of five coalitions" and the bodies of a million men torn from their generation. Like Soumet, Delavigne was just old enough to have flung a bridge across that ravine, but in his role as an intermediary between "the old school and the new" lay Delavigne's weakness, exemplified by his reluctance to break out of the limits of the classical theatre.[30]

What had once been praised as Delavigne's technical virtuosity would eventually be damned as a sort of eclectic flabbiness. This was the eclecticism of which Ary Scheffer was Baudelaire's "disastrous example," and this was the eclecticism that characterized the philosophy

[28] Sainte-Beuve to Alexandre Auguste Adam, 5 May 1822, in Charles Sainte-Beuve, *Correspondance générale* (Paris, 1935), 1:38. As early as 1829 Sainte-Beuve characterized Delavigne as "ce pauvre diable, qui a vidé son sac et qui ne fait plus que de l'eau claire, cherche de tous côtés à se ravitailler. Comme la ballade *fleurit* maintenant, il a laissé les *Messeniennes* et le voilà qui fait des ballades sur l'Italie; c'est ainsi qu'en tête de sa *tragédie* de *Marino*, il va inscrire en grosses lettres *mélodrame*; tout cela, romantisme à l'écorce, absence de conviction poétique." Sainte-Beuve to Louis Jules Loudierre, 23 April 1820, ibid., 128.

[29] *La Grande Encyclopédie* (Paris, n.d.), 13:1172–73.

[30] Dumas, *Mes Mémoires*, 2:261–62.

of Cousin and his circles, as well as the paintings of Scheffer and the
verse of Delavigne.[31] They owed their precocious triumphs, not to a selection of the best of past creations, but to a composite of what best appealed to contemporary temperament.

It has been said that "the man who marries the spirit of his own age
is likely to be a widower in the next."[32] In this case, perhaps it would
be better to say that the tight identification with the transitory spirit of
the age was not an authentic challenge to the general course of French
culture but an expression of it. The self-elected spokesmen for the generation of 1820 had failed to break out of the prison of the cultural *longue durée*. They were not destined to regenerate French society but to
merge with it.

[31] Baudelaire, *Art in Paris*, 97–98: "Eclecticism has at all periods and places held itself
superior to past doctrines, coming last on to the scene, it finds the remotest horizons
already open to it; but this *impartiality* only goes to prove the impotence of the eclectics.
. . . M. Ary Scheffer is a disastrous example of this method—if an absence of method
can so be called."

[32] Dean Inge quoted in Berger, "How Long Is a Generation?" 23n.

Appendix A

183 Members of the "Generation of 1820," as They Were Entered on a Two-Dimensional Matrix. (See appendix B)

		Date of Birth			Date of Birth
1	Allart, Hortense	1801	20	Belloc, Louise Swantin	1796
2	Alletz, Pierre-Edouard	1798	21	Belmontet, Louis	1798
3	Allier, Joseph	1794	22	Berlioz, Louis Hector	1803
4	Ampère, Jean-Jacques	1800	23	Bertrand, Alexandre	1795
5	Ancelot, Jacques A. F. P.	1794	24	Beslay, Charles	1795
6	Arago, Etienne Vincent	1802	25	Beugnot, Arthur-Auguste	1797
7	Artaud, Nicolas	1794	26	Bignan, Anne	1795
8	Aycard, Marie	1794	27	Blanqui, Adolphe	1798
9	Auger, Hippolyte	1796	28	Bodin, Félix	1795
10	Bailly, Etienne Marin	1796	29	Boinvilliers, Eloi-Ernest	1799
11	Balzac, Honoré de	1799	30	Boniface, Joseph-Xavier, dit Saintine	1798
12	Baroche, Pierre Jules	1802	31	Bonjour, Casimir	1795
13	Barthe, Félix	1795	33	Bouillet, Nicolas	1798
14	Barthélemy, Auguste Marseille	1794	32	Boulay de la Meurthe, Henri Georges	1797
15	Bary, Emile	1799			
16	Bastide, Jules	1800	34	Boussingault, Jean-Baptiste	1801
17	Baude, Jean-Jacques	1792			
18	Bautain, Abbé Louis	1796	35	Buchez, Benjamin-Philippe	1796
19	Bazard, Saint-Amand	1791			

36	Burnouf, Eugène	1801
37	Cahaigne, Louis Joseph	1796
38	Cariol, Gilbert-Antoine-Jules	1798
39	Carnot, Hippolyte	1801
40	Carnot, Nicolas-Léonard-Sadi	1796
41	Carré, Paul-François-Emile	1800
42	Carrel, Armand	1800
43	Carrion-Nisas, André-François-Victoire-Henri	1794
44	Cavaignac, Eugène	1802
45	Cavaignac, Godefroy	1801
46	Cavé, Hygin Auguste	1794
47	Cerclet, Antoine	1797
48	Chaix D'Est Ange, Louis Albert	1800
49	Chasles, Philarète	1798
50	Comte, Isidore Auguste	1798
51	Coquerel, Charles Augustin	1797
52	Corcelle, (fils) François de	1802
53	Corot, Camille	1796
54	Coste, Jacques	1798
55	Cournot, Antoine-Augustin	1801
56	Cousin, Victor	1792
57	Crémieux, Adolphe	1796
58	Cuvillier-Fleury, Alfred-Auguste	1802
59	Dalloz, Désiré	1795
60	Damiron, Jean-Philibert	1794

61	Darmaing, Jean-Jérôme-Achille	1794
62	Daviel, Alfred	1800
63	Degeorge, Frédéric	1797
64	Delacroix, Eugène	1798
65	Delaroche, Paul	1797
66	Delavigne, Jean-François Casimir	1793
67	Delcasso, Laurent-Pierre	1797
68	Deschamps, Emile	1791
69	Desclozeaux, Ernest	1803
70	Desloges, Marcelin	1799
71	Didot, Hyacinthe	1794
72	Dittmer, Adolphe	1795
73	Doudan, Ximenès	1800
74	Dubochet, Jacques-Julien	1798
75	Dubois, Paul-François	1793
76	Duchâtel, Charles-Marie Tanneguy	1802
77	Dufaure, Jules	1798
78	Dugied, Pierre	1798
79	Duhamel, Jean-Marie-Constant	1797
80	Dumas, Alexandre	1802
81	Dumon, Pierre Sylvain	1797
82	Dupanloup, Félix	1802
83	Dupont de Bussac, J. F.	1803
84	Duvergier, Jean-B.-M.	1792
85	Duvergier de Hauranne, Prosper-Léon	1798
86	Enfantin, Prosper	1796
87	Farcy, Jean-Georges	1800

88	Fazy, James	1794		115	Jussieu, Adrien	1797
89	Feuillet de Conches,			116	Jussieu, Alexis	1802
	Jean-Sébastien	1798		117	Kock, Paul de	1793
90	Flocon, Ferdinand	1800		118	Lachevardière,	
91	Flotard, J. T.	1797			Alexandre de	?
92	Fould, Achille	1800		119	Lacordaire, Henri	1802
93	Fresnel, Fulgence	1795		120	Larauza, Jean-Louis	1793
94	Garnier, Adolphe	1801		121	Laurent de	
95	Gay, Delphine	1804			l'Ardèche, P. M.	1793
96	Gerbet, Olympe-			122	Laurentie, Pierre-	
	Philippe	1798			Sébastien	1793
97	Gérusez, Eugène-			123	Lefèvre-Deumier,	
	Nicolas	1799			Jules	1797
98	Girardin, Saint-Marc	1801		124	Lerminier, Jean-	
99	Gondinet, Adolphe	?			Louis-Eugène	1803
100	Guigniaut, Joseph-			125	Leroux, Pierre	1797
	Daniel	1794		126	Limpérani, Joseph-	
101	Guillier de la				Antoine	1798
	Touche, Camille			127	Littré, Emile	1801
	Henri	1800		128	Loyson, Charles	1791
102	Guinard, Joseph-			129	Magnin, Charles	1793
	Auguste	1799		130	Mahul, Alphonse-	
103	Guizard, Louis-				Joseph	1795
	Marie-A.	1797		131	Marchais, André	1800
104	Hachette, Louis-			132	Marrast, Armand	1801
	Christophe-			133	Mennechet, Edouard	1794
	François	1800		134	Mérimée, Prosper	1803
105	Halévy, Léon	1802		135	Méry, Joseph	1798
106	Hugo, Abel	1798		136	Michelet, Jules	1798
107	Hugo, Eugène	1800		137	Mignet, François	1796
108	Hugo, Victor	1802		138	Montalivet, Marthe-	
109	Isambert, François-				Camille,	
	André	1792			Bachasson,	
110	Jacquemont, Victor	1801			Comte de	1801
111	Jal, Auguste	1795		139	Morel, Edmond	1798
112	Jarry de Mancy,			140	Pance, Benjamin	1800
	Adrien	1796		141	Paravey, Charles-	
113	Joubert, Nicolas	?			Joseph	1801
114	Jouffroy, Théodore	1796		142	Patin, Guy	1793

143	Paulin, J. B.	1796	161	Salveton, Frédéric	1801
144	Péclet, Léon-Claude-		162	Sautelet, Auguste	1800
	Eugène	1793	163	Scheffer, Arnold	1796
145	Pereire, Jacob-Emile	1800	164	Scheffer, Ary	1795
146	Perreau, Emile-Jean-		165	Scheffer, Henry	1798
	Baptiste	1798	166	Senemaud, Edmond	?
147	Pons, Charles Pierre		167	Senty, Ambroise	1803
	Gaspard de	1798	168	Sigaud (Sigaux,	
148	Quinet, Edgar	1803		Sigond), Claude-	
149	Raspail, François-			François-Adolphe	?
	Vincent	1794	169	Stapfer, Albert	1802
150	Rémusat, Charles	1797	170	Stapfer, Charles	1799
151	Renouard, Charles-		171	Tastu, Amable	1795
	Augustin	1794	172	Thierry, Amédée	1797
152	Rio, A. F.	1797	173	Thierry, Augustin	1795
153	Rodrigues, Olinde	1795	174	Thiers, Adolphe	1797
154	Rouen, Pierre-		175	Thiessé, Léon	1793
	Isidore	1796	176	Thomas, Charles	?
155	Roulin, Désiré	1796	177	Trélat, Ulysse	1795
156	Sacy, Ustazade		178	Trognon, Auguste	1795
	Sylvestre de	1801	179	Véron, Louis	1798
157	Sainte-Beuve,		180	Vigny, Alfred de	1797
	Charles-Augustin	1804	181	Viguier, Epagomène	1793
158	Saint-Valry,		182	Vitet, Ludovic	1802
	Adolphe de	1796	183	Baradère, J. M.	1793
159	Salinas, Antoine de	1798			
160	Salvandy, Narcisse-				
	Achille de	1795			

Appendix B

A Sociogram of the Generational Network

The following figures are representations of the network of personal relationships of 183 members of the "generation of 1820."[1] They are not intended to convey a statistical argument but to function as a visual metaphor. The sociogram was derived from a two-dimensional matrix on which the presence or absence of a known contact of each individual with every other individual was indicated. The evidence for these relationships was drawn from common membership in such organizations as the Ecole normale, the Ecole polytechnique, masonic lodges, secret societies, and the four Paris *lycées*;[2] from appearance in informal groupings, such as the Victor Cousin circle and the Delécluze salon; and from anecdotal information on individual contacts at dinners, salons, and so forth. Obviously, many instances of personal relationships were not recorded or have not been unearthed by me. Fuller information, however, could only increase the density of the recorded network and thus strengthen the thrust of my interpretation.

To construct a visual representation of these data, Professor Gregory A. Caldeira of the Department of Political Science of the University of Iowa used the multidimensional scaling routine in *SOCK: A Sociometric Analysis System*.[3] The major criterion for selecting the configu-

[1] These figures were prepared with the assistance of the Graphics Unit of the University of Iowa Audiovisual Center. Figure 1 represents the 183-member network, in which each individual is identified by the number assigned on the list in appendix A—for example, Victor Cousin is 56.

[2] It seemed reasonable to assume that students at the Ecole normale between 1810 and 1820 would have had some contact even if there were six or seven years separating their dates of matriculation. This assumption was somewhat stretched to cover the Carbonari, organized in a pyramid of supposedly secret cells, but actually dependent on the interaction of the young Parisian militants who were members of our generation. For the four Paris *lycées*, I assumed that students enrolled in a span of four years would have been acquainted.

[3] Richard D. Alba and Myron P. Gutman, *SOCK: Sociometric Analysis System* (unpublished manual, Bureau of Applied Social Research, Columbia University, September 1974).

ration produced by this technique was ease of interpretation. The resulting sociogram is a two-dimensional representation of the relationships among the individuals in the network.[4]

The location of each individual has been plotted against the two axes, which have no substantive significance but are computational devices by means of which the individual is placed on the grid. The two coordinates that situate an individual are summary measures of the "distance" from every other individual. "Distance" is to be understood as a measure for each pair of individuals of the number of relationships they both have with each of the other individuals.[5] This does not refer to the intensity or significance of a given relationship—the brothers Hugo are fairly well-dispersed—but to common connections. In figure B.2, for example, the close juxtaposition of the black rectangles representing Godefroi Cavaignac, Joseph Guinard, and Charles Thomas is not the product of their long association as schoolboys at Sainte-Barbe, as conspirators in the Carbonari, or as unreconstructed republicans under the July Monarchy, but of their common connections with so many other members of the network.

The satisfying cluster of the Carbonari in figure B.6 reflects not only the fact that they were all connected with each other through common membership, but also that they shared other personal associations. What might be thought of as the *normalien/Globe* conspiratorial contingent is grouped around Cousin and Dubois at the bottom of the Carbonari cluster, while the future Saint-Simonians, such as Buchez and Bazard, are somewhat off to the right, closer to the other editors of the *Producteur*. (See figure B.7 for the staffs of and contributors to the *Globe*, the *Producteur*, and the *Muse française*.)

In figure B.7, the handful of royalist romantics who edited the *Muse française* cluster together, apart from their coevals, with Victor Hugo off at the top of the sociogram as an apparent outlier. Actually, Hugo is pulled up and to the left, as it were, toward his fellow alumni of the collège Louis-le-Grand. The "clustering" as conveyed by the computer is, therefore, a visual representation of patterns of actual relationships.

---

[4] For a more detailed discussion of multidimensional scaling, see Joseph B. Kruskal, "Multidimensional Scaling: A Numerical Method," *Journal of Psychometrica*, 29 (1964): 1–37; and Joseph B. Kruskal and Myron Wish, *Multidimensional Scaling* (Beverly Hills, 1978).

[5] On the concept and computation of "distance," see Kruskal and Wish, *Multidimensional Scaling*, 14–23.

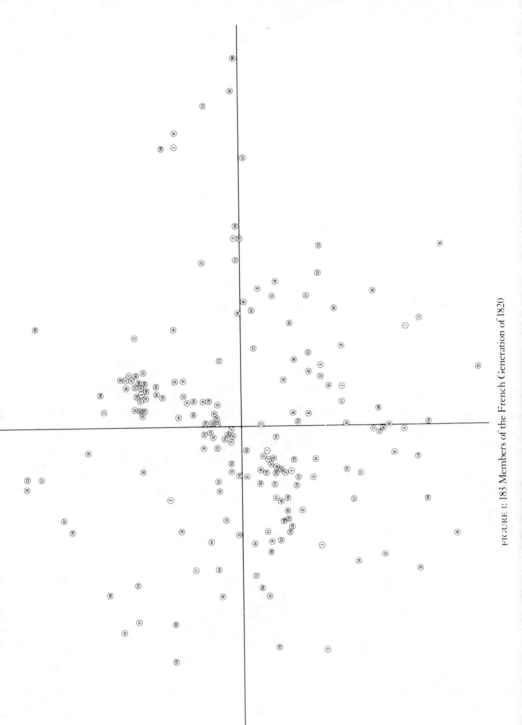

FIGURE 1: 183 Members of the French Generation of 1820

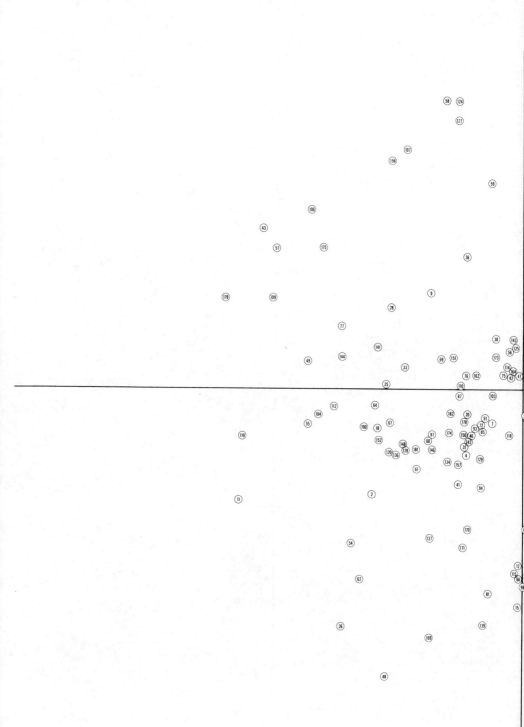

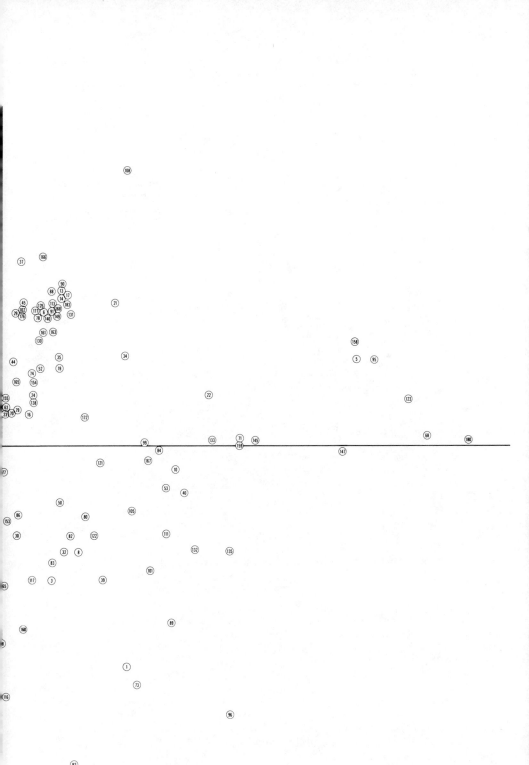

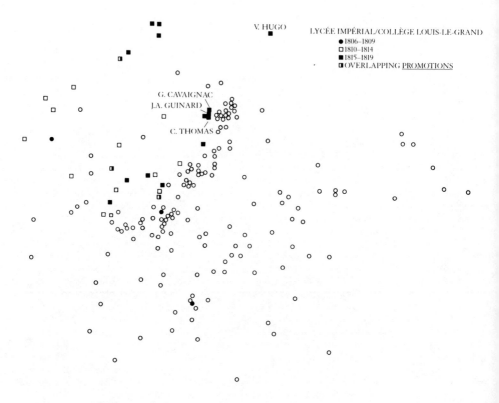

FIGURE 2: Students at the Lycée Impérial/Collège Louis-le-Grand

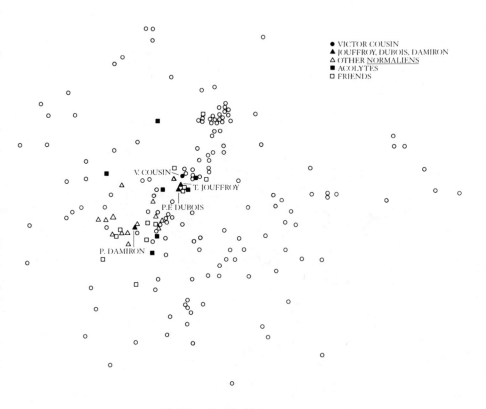

FIGURE 3: The Victor Cousin Circle

FIGURE 4: The Ramifications of Auguste Comte's Wedding Party

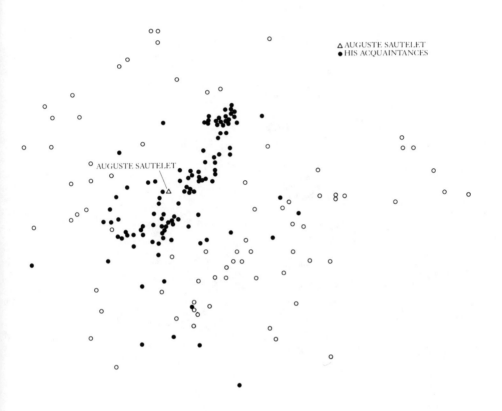

FIGURE 5: The Network of Auguste Sautelet

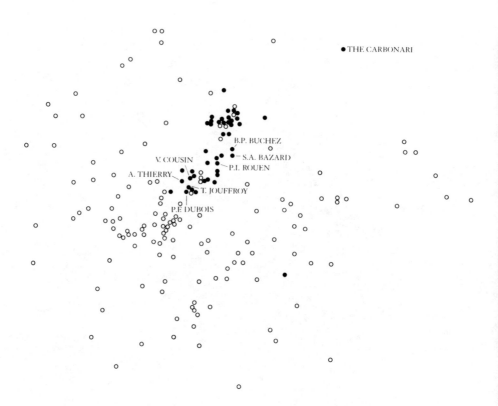

FIGURE 6: Members of the Carbonari

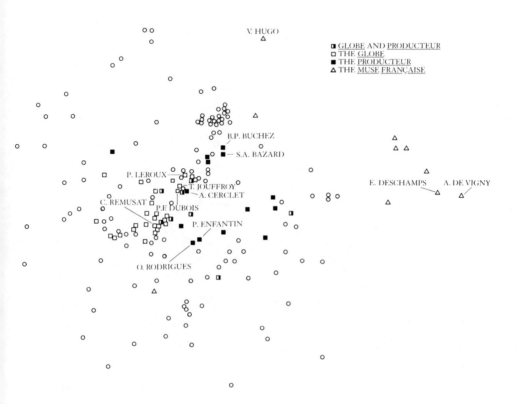

FIGURE 7: Staff and Contributors to the <u>Globe</u>, the <u>Producteur</u>, and the <u>Muse Française</u>

Bibliography

Manuscript Sources: Official Documents

Archives Nationales
Série F⁷: Police générale
    Considerable material on student unrest, especially in F⁷ 6693.
Série F¹⁷: Instruction publique
    Circulaires du grand maître de l'Université. F¹⁷ 1458.
    Facultés de droit: troubles et désordres 1817–1839. F¹⁷ 2105, F¹⁷ 2106.
    Dossiers d'élèves, 1786–1822. F¹⁷ 4155.
    Concours général et concours académiques. F¹⁷ 7234.
    Dossiers des anciens fonctionnaires des enseignements primaire, secondaire, et supérieur, XIXᵉ siècle. F¹⁷ 20492 (Victor Cousin), F¹⁷ 20638 (Paul-François Dubois).
Série F¹⁸: Imprimerie et librairie
    Déclarations des imprimeurs de Paris, 1817–1834. F¹⁸ 89.
    Imprimeurs, libraires et lithographes, Paris 1815–1870. F¹⁸ 1784, F¹⁸ 1824.
Série BB³⁰: Cabinet du Ministre de la Justice. BB³⁰ 192.
Série AJ¹⁶: Académie de Paris
    Concours général. AJ¹⁶ 881.

Manuscript Sources: Private Papers

Archives Nationales
    Archives privées
        Papiers Paul-François Dubois. 319 AP¹⁻³
Bibliothèque Nationale
    Fonds Franc-Maçonnerie. FM² 39 (Amis de la vérité), FM² 35 (Amis de l'Armorique).
    Nouvelles acquisitions françaises. 24378: Papiers Havet.
    Nouvelles acquisitions françaises. 24605: Correspondance et manuscrits du Comte Henri de Saint-Simon.
    Nouvelles acquisitions françaises. 20601: Papiers Thiers.
Bibliothèque Thiers
    Papiers Baroche. TMss 967.
    Thiers, Correspondance. TMss 24, 25.
    Fonds Thiers. TMss 557.

Bibliothèque historique de la Ville de Paris
    Correspondance Anglès-Mounier. MS 810.
    Papiers Buchez.
    Papiers Michelet.
Bibliothèque de l'Arsenal
    Fonds Enfantin.
Bibliothèque Victor Cousin à la Sorbonne
    Victor Cousin Manuscrits.
Bibliothèque historique de la Ville de Grenoble
    Papiers Joseph Rey. Fonds T3938, T3939, T3940.
Bibliothèque de Besançon
    Lettres de Théodore Jouffroy à Charles Weiss.
Archives du Musée Arbaud (Aix-en-Provence)
    Lettres de Thiers à divers. Dossier 4072 A².

Manuscript Sources: Unpublished Theses

Brown, Robert. "The Generation of 1820 During the Bourbon Restoration in France: A Biographical and Intellectual Portrait of the First Wave, 1814–1824" (Ph.D. diss., Duke University, 1979).
Goldstein, Jan Ellen. "French Psychiatry in Social and Political Context: The Formation of a New Profession" (Ph.D. diss., Columbia University, 1978).

Journals

Ami de la religion et du roi
Aristarque française
Catholique
Censeur européen
Conservateur
Conservateur littéraire
Constitutionnel
Courrier français
Globe
Journal des débats
Journal général de législation et de jurisprudence
Mémorial catholique
Mercure du dix-neuvième siècle
Minerve française
Moniteur universel
National
Pandore
Patriote des Alpes
Producteur
Surveillant politique et littéraire
Tablettes universelles

Printed Sources

Abraham, Pierre, and Roland Desné, eds. *Histoire littéraire de la France*. 12 vols. Paris, 1976.

————. *Manuel d'histoire littéraire de la France.* 6 vols. Paris, 1965–82.

Abrams, Philip. *Historical Sociology.* Somerset, Eng., 1982.

————. "Rites de Passage," *Journal of Contemporary History,* 5 (1970): 175–90.

[Académie royale des beaux-arts]. *Recueil des règlements relatifs aux concours ouverts et aux grands prix décernés par l'Académie Royale des Beaux-Arts.* Paris, s.d.

Ackerknecht, Erwin H. "Broussais, or a Forgotten Medical Revolution," *Bulletin of the History of Medicine,* 27 (July–August 1953): 320–43.

————. *Medicine at the Paris Hospital, 1794–1848.* Baltimore, 1967.

Albert, Maurice. *Les Théâtres des boulevards (1789–1848).* Paris, 1902.

Alem, J. P. *Enfantin: Le Prophète aux sept visages.* Paris, 1964.

Alfaric, Prosper. *Laromiguière Et Son Ecole.* Paris, 1929.

Allemagne, Henri-René d'. *Prosper Enfantin Et Les Grandes Entreprises du XIXe siècle.* Paris, 1935.

————. *Les Saint-Simoniens.* Paris, 1930.

Allen, James S. *Popular French Romanticism: Authors, Readers, and Books in the 19th Century.* Syracuse, 1981.

————. "Y-a-t-il en France une génération romantique de 1830?" *Romantisme,* 28–29 (1980): 102–18.

Allison, John M. S. *Thiers and the French Monarchy.* Hamden, Conn., 1968.

Allou, Roger, and Charles Chenu, *Barreau de Paris: Grands Avocats du siècle.* Paris, 1894.

Ampère, André-Marie, and Jean-Jacques Ampère. *Correspondance et souvenirs (De 1805 à 1864).* 2 vols. Paris, 1875.

Ancelot, Jacques A.P.F. *Louis IX.* Paris, 1819.

Ancelot, Virginie. *Un Salon de Paris de 1824 à 1864.* Paris, 1866.

Anderson, Robert D. *Education in France, 1848–1870.* Oxford, 1975.

————. "New Light on French Secondary Education in the Nineteenth Century," *Social History,* 7 (May 1982): 147–65.

Archives parlementaires de 1787 à 1860. 2nd ser.

Ariès, Philippe. *Centuries of Childhood,* trans. Robert Baldick. New York, 1962.

Armengaud, André. "Charles Rémusat, poète méconnu," in *La France au XIXe siècle: Etudes historiques. Mélanges offerts à Charles Hippolyte Pouthas.* Paris, 1973.

Arrigon, L. J. *Les Débuts littéraires d'Honoré de Balzac.* Paris, 1924.

Artaud, Nicolas. *Fragments pour servir à l'histoire de la comédie antique.* Paris, 1863.

Aucoc, Léon, ed. *L'Institut de France: Lois, statuts et règlements concernant les anciennes académies et l'Institut de 1635 à 1889.* Paris, 1889.

Auger, Hippolyte. *Mémoires d'Auger (1810–1859).* Paris, 1891.

[Auger, Louis Simon]. *Discours sur le romantisme prononcé dans la séance an-*

nuelle des quatre académies du 24 avril 1824, par M. Auger de l'Académie française. Paris, 1824.

Aulard, Alphonse. *Napoléon Ie Et Le Monopole universitaire.* Paris, 1911.

Bailly, Etienne-Marin. *Discours prononcé sur la tombe de M. Henri Saint-Simon par le Docteur E. M. Bailly de Blois.* Blois, 1825.

Baker, Keith Michael. *Condorcet: From Natural Philosophy to Social Mathematics.* Chicago, 1975.

Bakunin, Jack. *Pierre Leroux and the Rebirth of Democratic Socialism, 1797–1848.* New York, 1976.

Ballin, A. G. *Renseignements statistiques sur Paris et les départements.* Rouen, 1823.

Balzac, Honoré de. *Correspondance.* 5 vols. Paris, 1960–69.

———. *Illusions perdues.* Paris, 1961.

———. *Louis Lambert.* Paris, 1968.

———. *Le Lys dans la vallée.* Paris, 1966.

———. *La Peau de chagrin.* Paris, 1967.

———. *Le Père Goriot.* Paris, 1971.

———. *Old Goriot,* trans. M. A. Crawford. Harmondsworth, Eng., 1951.

———. *La Rabouilleuse.* Paris, 1966.

———. *Sténie; Ou, Les Erreurs philosophiques,* ed. A. Prioult. Paris, 1936.

———. *Un Début dans la vie.* Geneva, 1950.

Barante, Prosper de. *La Vie politique de M. Royer-Collard.* 2 vols. Paris, 1861.

———. *Souvenirs du Baron de Barante.* 8 vols. Paris, 1890–1901.

Barbéris, Pierre. *Aux sources De Balzac. Les Romans de jeunesse.* Paris, 1965.

———. *Balzac Et Le Mal du siècle.* 2 vols. Paris, 1970.

———. *Lectures du réel.* Paris, 1973.

———. *Le Monde de Balzac.* Paris, 1973.

———. "Mal du siècle, ou d'un romantisme de droite à un romantisme de gauche," in *Romantisme et politique, 1815–1851.* Colloque de l'Ecole normale supérieure de Saint-Cloud, 1966. Paris, 1969.

Barnes, John A. "Network Analysis: Orienting Notion, Rigorous Technique or Substantive Field of Study?" in P. W. Holland and S. Leinhardt, eds., *Perspectives in Social Network Research.* New York, 1979.

Barrère, Jean-Bertrand. *Victor Hugo: L'Homme et l'oeuvre.* Paris, 1952.

Barrot, Odilon. *Mémoires posthumes de Odilon Barrot.* 4 vols. Paris, 1875.

Barthélemy, Auguste, and Joseph Méry. *La Villéliade.* Paris, 1826.

Barthélemy-Saint-Hilaire, Jules. *M. Victor Cousin: Sa Vie et sa correspondance.* 3 vols. Paris, 1895.

Barthes, Roland. *Writing Degree Zero,* trans. Annette Lavers and Colin Smith. Boston, 1970.

[Bary, Emile-Louis-François]. *Les Cahiers d'un rhétoricien de 1815.* Paris, 1890.

Barzun, Jacques. *Classic, Romantic and Modern.* Boston, 1961.

Baschet, Robert. *E.-J. Delécluze: Témoin de son temps, 1781–1863.* Paris, 1942.

———. *Du Romantisme au Second Empire: Mérimée (1803–1870).* Paris, 1958.

Baudelaire, Charles. *Art in Paris, 1845–1862,* trans. Jonathan Mayne. Greenwich, Conn., 1965.

Beffort, A. *Alexandre Soumet: Sa Vie et ses oeuvres.* Luxembourg, 1908.

Belin, D. P., ed. *Annales des concours généraux.* 4 vols. Paris, 1825.

Bellanger, Claude, et al. *Histoire générale de la presse française.* 5 vols. Paris, 1969.

Bénichou, Paul. *Le Sacre de l'écrivain, 1750–1830.* Paris, 1973.

Benoit, Fernand. "Monsieur Thiers A La Conquête de Paris: Documents inédits (1821–1833)," *Correspondant,* 287 (1 June 1922): 786–819.

Benoit, François. *L'Art français sous la révolution et l'empire.* Paris, 1897.

Berger, Bennett. "How Long Is a Generation?" *British Journal of Sociology,* 11 (March 1960): 10–23.

Berlioz, Hector. *Lettres intimes.* 2nd ed. Paris, 1882.

———. *The Memoirs of Hector Berlioz,* trans. David Cairns. London, 1969.

Beslay, Charles. *Mes Souvenirs.* Paris, 1873.

Bezucha, Robert. "The French Revolution of 1848," *Theory and Society,* 12 (July 1983): 469–84.

Billaz, André. *Les Ecrivains romantiques et Voltaire: Essai sur Voltaire et le romantisme en France.* 2 vols. Lille, 1974.

Biographie des femmes auteurs contemporaines françaises, comp. Alfred de Montferand. Paris, 1836.

Biré, Edmond. *Victor Hugo Avant 1830.* 2nd ed. Paris, 1883.

Biré, Edmond, and Emile Grimaud. *Les Poètes lauréats de l'Académie française.* 2 vols. Paris, 1864–65.

Birnberg, J. " 'D'Un Nouveau Complot contre les industriels': Pamphlet possible ou impossible?" in O. Schellekens, ed., *Stendhal, le Saint-Simonisme et les industriels: Stendhal et la Belgique.* Brussels, 1979.

Blanqui, Adolphe. "Souvenirs d'un lycéen de 1814," *Revue de Paris,* 133 (15 April 1916): 847–65; 134 (1 May 1916): 97–117.

———. "Souvenirs d'un étudiant sous la Restauration," *Revue de Paris,* 148 (15 October 1918): 776–96; 149 (1 November 1918): 158–76.

Bloch, Marc. *The Historian's Craft,* trans. Peter Putnam. New York, 1953.

Boas, George. *French Philosophies of the Romantic Period.* Baltimore, 1925.

Bodin, Félix. *Diatribe contre l'art oratoire.* Paris, 1824.

———. *Résumé de l'histoire de France jusqu'à nos jours, suivi de principes et moralités politiques applicables à l'histoire.* Paris, 1823.

Boissevain, J., and J. C. Mitchell, eds. *Network Analysis: Studies in Human Interaction.* The Hague, 1973.

Bonnemère, Eugène. *Biographie des deux Bodins.* Angers, 1846.

Bourdieu, Pierre. "Systems of Education and Systems of Thought," in Earl Hopper, ed., *Readings in the Theory of Educational Systems.* London, 1971.

Bourdieu, Pierre, and Jean-Claude Passeron. *Reproduction in Education, Society and Culture*, trans. Richard Nice. Beverly Hills, 1972.

Bourdieu, Pierre, and Monique de Saint-Martin. "L'Excellence scolaire et les valeurs du système d'enseignement français," *Annales*, 25 (January–February 1970): 147–75.

Bourgeois-Pichat, Jean. "Note sur l'évolution générale de la population française depuis le XVIIIe siècle," *Population*, 7 (1952): 319–29.

Boussingault, J.-B. *Mémoires de J.-B. Boussingault.* 5 vols. Paris, 1892.

Bouthol, G. *Les Mentalités.* Paris, 1971.

Bowe, Sister Mary Camille. *François Rio: Sa place dans le renouveau catholique en Europe (1797–1874).* Paris, 1938.

Bradley, Margaret. "Scientific Education for a New Society: The Ecole polytechnique, 1795–1830," *History of Education*, 5 (February 1976): 11–24.

Braudel, Fernand. *The Mediterranean and the Mediterranean World in the Age of Philip II*, trans. S. Reynolds. 2 vols. New York, 1972.

Bray, René. *Chronologie du romantisme (1804–1830).* Paris, 1932.

Brehier, Emile. *The History of Philosophy.* Volume 6, *The Nineteenth Century: Period of Systems, 1800–1850*, trans. Joseph Thomas. Chicago, 1968.

Bruneau, Charles. "La Génération de 1820," in Ferdinand Brunot, ed., *Histoire de la langue française des origines à nos jours.* Vol. 12. Paris, 1968.

Buchez, Philippe-J. B. *Traité de politique et de science morale.* 2 vols. Paris, 1866.

Buisson, Ferdinand. *Nouveau Dictionnaire de pédagogie et d'instruction primaire.* Paris, 1911.

Burnand, Robert. *La Vie quotidienne en France sous la Restauration.* Paris, 1943.

Burt, Ronald S. *Toward a Structural Theory of Action: Network Models of Social Structure, Perception and Action.* New York, 1982.

Burt, Ronald S., Michael J. Minor, et al. *Applied Network Analysis: A Methodological Introduction.* Beverly Hills, 1983.

Burton, June. *Napoleon and Clio: Historical Writing, Teaching and Thinking During the First Empire.* Durham, N.C., 1979.

Cabanis, André. *La Presse sous le Consulat et l'Empire (1799–1814).* Paris, 1975.

Canat, René. *Une Forme unique du mal du siècle: Du Sentiment de la solitude morale chez les romantiques et les parnassiens.* Paris, 1904.

Canivez, André. *Jules Lagneau: Professeur de philosophie.* 2 vols. Paris, 1965.

Cariol, J. *L'Ecole de droit de Paris au 2 juillet 1819, par plusieurs élèves de cette école. Signé: J. Cariol, président de la commission des élèves.* Paris, 1819.

Carlisle, Robert B. "The Birth of Technocracy: Science, Society and Saint-Simonians," *Journal of the History of Ideas*, 35 (July–September 1974): 445–64.

———. "Saint-Simonian Radicalism: A Definition and a Direction," *French Historical Studies*, 5 (Fall 1968): 430–45.

Carné, Louis Joseph Marie, Comte de. *Souvenirs de ma jeunesse au temps de la Restauration*. Paris, 1873.

Carnot, Hippolyte. "Résumé général de la doctrine saint-simonienne fait en 1831," *Revue socialiste*, 17 (March 1893): 311–25.

———. "Sur le Saint-Simonisme," *Académie des sciences morales et politiques, compte rendu*, 128 (1887): 122–55.

Carrel, Armand. "Un Mort volontaire," *Revue de Paris* (June 1830): 210–16.

———. *Oeuvres politiques et littéraires*. 5 vols. Paris, 1857–59.

Carrion-Nisas, André F. *La France Au Dix-Neuvième Siècle; ou, Coup d'oeil sur l'état présent des lumières, des richesses, de la morale et de la liberté*. Paris, 1821.

———. *De la Jeunesse française*. Paris, 1820.

———. *Principes d'économie politique*. Paris, 1825.

Cassagne, Albert. *La Théorie de l'art pour l'art en France*. Paris, 1906.

Castellane, Esprit Victor E. B., Comte de. *Journal du maréchal de Castellane, 1804–1862*. 5 vols. Paris, 1895–97.

Cecconi, O. "La 'Restauration' intellectuelle," in Pierre Abraham and Roland Desné, eds., *Histoire littéraire de la France, 1794–1830*. Vol. 7. Paris, 1976.

Le Centenaire de l'Ecole normale. Paris, 1895.

Centenaire du lycée Condorcet, 1804–1904. Livre d'Or. Paris, 1904.

Chabrol de Volvic, Gilbert, comp. *Recherches statistiques sur la Ville de Paris*. 2nd ed. 4 vols. Paris, 1833.

Chafee, Richard. "The Teaching of Architecture at the Ecole des Beaux-Arts," in Arthur Drexler, ed., *The Architecture of the Ecole des Beaux-Arts*. New York, 1977.

Chambon, F. "L'Ecole normale en 1816–1818," *Revue internationale de l'enseignement*, 54 (1907): 320–25.

Champion, Jacques. "Le Concours général et son rôle dans la formation des élites universitaires au XIXe siècle," *Revue française de pédagogie*, 31 (April–June 1975): 71–82.

———. "Discours et idéologie: Le Concours général," *Pensée*, 188 (September–October 1976): 80–97.

Charléty, Sébastien. "L'Avènement d'une génération nouvelle," in *Histoire de France contemporaine depuis la Révolution jusqu'à la paix de 1919*. Vol. 4, *La Restauration*, ed. E. Lavisse. Paris, 1921.

———. *Histoire du saint-simonisme (1825–1864)*. Paris, 1931.

Charlton, D. G. *Secular Religions in France, 1815–1870*. London, 1963.

Charpentier, Paul. *Une Maladie morale: Le Mal du siècle*. Paris, 1880.

Chartier, Roger, Marie-Madeleine Compère, and Dominique Julia. *L'Education en France du XVIe au XVIIIe siècle*. Paris, 1976.

Chasles, Philarète. *Les Hommes et les moeurs au XIXe siècle.* Paris, 1850.

———. *Mémoires.* 2nd ed., 2 vols. Paris, 1876–77.

Chateaubriand, François de. *The Memoirs of François René, vicomte de Chateaubriand,* trans. A. T. de Mattos. 6 vols. New York, 1902.

———. *Mémoires d'outre-tombe.* 4 vols. Paris, 1948.

———. "Mémoires sur S.A.R. Mgr Le Duc de Berry," in *Oeuvres complètes,* vol. 9. Paris, 1869.

Chauvin, Victor. *Histoire des lycées et collèges de Paris.* Paris, 1866.

Chinard, Gilbert, ed. *The Letters of Lafayette and Jefferson.* Baltimore, 1929.

Clifford-Vaughan, M. "Some French Concepts of Elites," *British Journal of Sociology,* 11 (December 1960): 316–31.

Collins, Irene. *The Government and the Newspaper Press in France, 1814–1881.* Oxford, 1959.

Comte, Auguste. *Correspondance générale,* ed. Paul E. de Berridô Carneiro and Pierre Arnaud. Vol. 1, *1814–1840.* Paris, 1973.

———. *Ecrits de jeunesse, 1816–1828.* Paris, 1970.

Comte, Charles. *Traité de législation; ou, L'Exposition des lois générales.* 2nd ed. Paris, 1835.

Cooper, Barbara T. "Mérimée's Romantic Theater: The Present State of Scholarship," *Nineteenth-Century French Studies,* 6 (Fall–Winter 1977–78): 72–81.

Coquerel, Charles. *Tableau de l'histoire philosophique du christianisme; ou, Etudes de philosophie religieuse.* Paris, 1823.

Corcelles, François de. *Documens pour servir à l'histoire des conspirations des partis et des sectes.* Paris, 1831.

Corlieu, A. *Centenaire de la faculté de médecine de Paris (1794–1894).* Paris, 1896.

Corniez, Jean-Louis. *Jules Michelet: Un Aspect de la pensée religieuse au XIXe siècle.* Geneva, 1955.

Coser, Lewis. "Publishers as Gatekeepers of Ideas," *Annals of the American Academy of Political and Social Science,* 421 (September 1975): 14–22.

Cournot, Antoine-Augustin. *Des Institutions publiques en France.* Paris, 1864.

———. *Souvenirs.* Paris, 1913.

Cousin, Victor. *Cours de l'histoire de la philosophie moderne.* 5 vols. Paris, 1846.

———. *Discours prononcé à l'ouverture de cours de l'histoire de la philosophie, le 13 décembre 1815.* Paris, 1816.

———. *Fragments philosophiques.* 3rd ed. 2 vols. Paris, 1838.

Crawford, Elisabeth. "The Prize System of the Academy of Sciences, 1850–1914," in Robert Fox and George Weisz, eds., *The Organization of Science and Technology in France.* Cambridge, Eng., 1980.

Cremieux, Albert. *La Censure en 1820 et 1821.* Abbeville, 1912.

Crosland, Maurice. "The French Academy of Sciences in the Nineteenth Century," *Minerva*, 16 (Spring 1978): 73–102.

———. "From Prizes to Grants in the Support of Scientific Research in France in the Nineteenth Century: The Montyon Legacy," *Minerva*, 16 (Autumn 1979): 355–80.

———. *The Society of Arcueil*. Cambridge, Mass., 1967.

Crubellier, Maurice. *Histoire culturelle de la France, XIXe–XXe siècle*. Paris, 1974.

Damiron, Philippe. *Discours prononcé à la faculté des lettres (Cours d'histoire de la philosophie moderne)*. Paris, 1845.

———. *Essai sur l'histoire de la philosophie en France au dix-neuvième siècle*. Paris, 1828.

———. *Souvenirs de vingt ans d'enseignement à la faculté des lettres de Paris*. Paris, 1859.

Dantès, Alfred Laungue, comp. *Dictionnaire biographique et bibliographique alphabétique et méthodique des hommes les plus remarquables dans les lettres, les sciences et les arts, chez tous les peuples, à toutes les époques*. Paris, 1875.

Daru, Pierre A.N.B. *Notions statistiques sur la librairie pour servir à la discussion des lois sur la presse*. Paris, 1827.

Daumard, Adeline. "Les Elèves de l'Ecole polytechnique de 1815 à 1848," *Revue d'histoire moderne et contemporaine*, 5 (July–September 1958): 226–34.

———. "Une Référence pour l'étude des sociétés urbaines en France aux XVIIIe et XIXe siècles: Projet de code socio-professionnel," *Revue d'histoire moderne et contemporaine*, 10 (July–September 1968): 185–210.

Daviel, M. A. *Examen de l'ordonnance du 20 novembre 1822, concernant l'ordre des avocats*. Paris, December 1822.

Dejob, Charles. *L'Instruction publique en France et en Italie au dix-neuvième siècle*. Paris, 1894.

Delacroix, Eugène. *Correspondance générale*. 5 vols. Paris, 1936.

———. *The Journal of Eugène Delacroix*, trans. Walter Pach. New York, 1937.

———. *Lettres intimes*. Paris, 1954.

———. *Selected Letters*, trans. Jean Stewart. London, 1971.

Delaunay, Paul. *Les Médecins: La Restauration et la Révolution de 1830*. Tours, 1932.

Delavigne, Casimir. *Discours prononcés dans la séance publique tenue par l'Académie française pour la réception de M. Casimir Delavigne, le 7 juillet 1825*. Paris, 1825.

———. *Oeuvres complètes*. Paris, 1836.

Delécluze, Etienne-Jean. *Journal de Delécluze, 1824–1828*. Paris, 1948.

———. *Souvenirs de soixante années*. Paris, 1862.

Denis, F. *Notice sur l'Ecole de notariat de Fontenoy-le-comte, 1802–1840*. Niort, France, 1913.

Deschamps, Emile. *Oeuvres complètes.* 6 vols. Paris, 1872–74.

Des Granges, Charles-Marc. *La Comédie et les moeurs sous la Restauration et la Monarchie de Juillet (1815–1848).* Paris, 1904.

————. *La Presse littéraire sous la Restauration, 1815–1830.* Paris, 1907.

Dictionnaire de biographie française. 16 vols. to date. Paris, 1933–.

Dictionnaire des lettres françaises. 5 vols. Paris, 1951–72.

Doré, P. *De la Nécessité et des moyens d'ouvrir de nouvelles carrières pour le placement des élèves de l'Ecole polytechnique.* Paris, 1830.

Doudan, Ximenès. "Lettres de jeunesse (1824–1828)," *Revue Bleue,* 50 (22 June 1912): 769–74.

————. *Mélanges et lettres.* 2 vols. Paris, 1876.

Dubois, Paul-François. *Cousin, Jouffroy, Damiron.* Paris, 1902.

————. *Fragments littéraires.* 2 vols. Paris, 1879.

————. "Souvenirs inédits," [published by Adolphe Lair], *Revue Bleue,* 5th ser., 8 (21 September–12 October 1907): 353–58, 385–88, 420–25, 455–58; 9 (8 February–30 May 1908): 167–68, 321–25, 551–52, 673–74; 10 (18 July–26 December 1908): 65–67, 161–63, 232–34, 300–3, 741–44, 805–9.

Dubois, Abbé Pierre. *Bio-Bibliographie de Victor Hugo de 1802 à 1825.* Paris, 1913.

Duby, Georges. "L'Histoire des mentalités," in *Encyclopédie de la pléiade: L'Histoire et ses méthodes.* Paris, 1961.

Dumas, Alexandre. *Mes Mémoires.* 5 vols. Paris, 1954–68.

————. *Souvenirs dramatiques.* 2 vols. Paris, 1868.

Dunn, John. "The Identity of the History of Ideas," *Philosophy,* 43 (April 1968): 85–104.

Dunoyer, Charles. *L'Industrie et la morale considérées dans leurs rapports avec la liberté.* Paris, 1825.

Dupaquier, Jacques. "Problèmes démographiques de la France napoléonienne," *Annales historiques de la Révolution Française,* 199 (January–March 1970): 9–29.

Dupin, André-Marie Jean Jacques. *Mémoires de M. Dupin.* 4 vols. Paris, 1861.

————. *Profession d'avocat.* 2 vols. Paris, 1830–32.

Dupin, Charles. *Forces productives et commerciales de la France.* 2 vols. Paris, 1827.

Dupont [de Bussac], J. F., and Victor Guichard. *Consultation ni jésuitique, ni gallicane, ni féodale, en réponse à la consultation rédigée par M. Dupin.* Paris, 1826.

Dupont-Ferrier, Gustave. *Du Collège de Clermont au lycée Louis-le-Grand.* 3 vols. Paris, 1922–25.

Durand, Charles. *Les Auditeurs de conseil d'état sous le Consulat et le Premier Empire.* Annales de la Faculté de droit d'Aix, new ser., no. 28. Aix-en-Provence, 1937.

Durkheim, Emile. *The Evolution of Educational Thought: Lectures on the Formation and Development of Secondary Education in France*, trans. Peter Collins. London, 1977.

Duvergier, Jean B., ed. *Collection complète des lois, décrets, ordonnances, règlements et avis du conseil d'état*. Paris, 1834–38.

Duvergier de Hauranne, Prosper. *Histoire du gouvernement parlementaire en France*. 10 vols. Paris, 1857–71.

Eisenstadt, S. N. "Archetypal Patterns of Youth," in Peter K. Manning and Marcello Truzzi, eds., *Youth and Sociology*, Englewood Cliffs, N. J., 1972.

———. *From Generation to Generation: Age Groups and Social Structure*. Glencoe, Ill., 1956.

Encyclopédie nouvelle. 8 vols. Paris, 1835–41.

Erikson, Erik H. *Identity, Youth and Crisis*. New York, 1968.

———. *Life History and the Historical Moment*. New York, 1975.

Escarpit, Robert. *Sociology of Literature*, trans. Ernest Pick. Plainesville, Ohio, 1965.

Esler, Anthony. *Generations in History*. Author's Copyright, 1982.

———. "Youth in Revolt: The French Generation of 1830," in Robert Bezucha, ed., *Modern European Social History*. Lexington, Ky., 1972.

Estignard, Alexandre. *Portraits franc-comtois*. 3 vols. Paris, 1890.

Eyck, Gunther F. "The Political Theories of German Academic Youth between 1815 and 1819," *Journal of Modern History*, 27 (March 1955): 27–38.

Eymard, S. *Coup d'oeil critique sur la médecine française au XIXe siècle*. Paris, 1829.

Faber, Karl-Georg. "Student und Politik in der ersten deutschen Burschenschaft," *Geschichte in Wissenschaft und Unterricht*, 21 (February 1970): 68–80.

Fabre, Jules. *Le Barreau de Paris, 1810–1870*. Paris, 1895.

Fabry, Jean-Baptiste-Germain. *Le Génie de la Révolution considéré dans l'éducation; ou, Mémoires pour servir à l'histoire de l'instruction publique, depuis 1789, jusqu'à nos jours*. 3 vols. Paris, 1817–18.

Falucci, Clément. *L'Humanisme dans l'enseignement secondaire en France au XIXe siècle*. Toulin, 1939.

Fauchier-Delavigne, Marcelle. *Casimir Delavigne intime*. Paris, 1907.

Faure, Olivier. "Physicians in Lyon During the Nineteenth Century: An Extraordinary Social Success," *Journal of Social History*, 10 (June 1977): 508–23.

Fazy, J. J. *De La Gérontocratie; ou, Abus de la sagesse des vieillards dans le gouvernement de la France*. Paris, 1828.

Febvre, Lucien. "Comment Reconstituer La Vie affective d'autrefois? La Sensibilité et l'histoire," in *Combats pour l'histoire*. Paris, 1953.

Febvre, Lucien. "Générations," in Bulletin du centre international de synthèse. Section de synthèse historique, no. 7, published in *Revue de synthèse historique*, 47 (1929): 41–42.

Feuer, Lewis S. *The Conflict of Generations*. New York, 1969.

Feuillet de Conches, F. S. *Souvenirs de première jeunesse d'un curieux septuagénaire: Fin du premier Empire et commencement de la Restauration*. Vichy, 1877.

Flocon, Ferdinand, and Marie Aycard. *Salon de 1824*. Paris, 1824.

Flotard, J. T., Secrétaire général de la Mairie de Paris. *Aux Electeurs du département de la Seine, 24 mai 1849*. Paris, 1849.

Fontanes, Louis. *Collection complète des discours de M. Fontanes*. Paris, 1821.

Fortin, André. *Frédéric Degeorge*. Lille, 1964.

Foucault, Michel. *Discipline and Punish: The Birth of the Prison*, trans. Alan Sheridan. New York, 1977.

Fourcy, A. *Histoire de l'Ecole polytechnique*. Paris, 1828.

Fox, Robert. "Scientific Enterprise and the Patronage of Research in France, 1800–1870," *Minerva*, 11 (October 1973): 442–73.

Fozzard, Irene [Collins]. "The Government and the Press in France, 1822 to 1827," *English Historical Review*, 66 (January 1971): 51–66.

La France au XIXe siècle: Etudes historiques. Mélanges offerts à Charles Hyppolite Pouthas. Paris, 1973.

Gallaher, John G. *The Students of Paris and the Revolution of 1848*. Carbondale, Ill., 1980.

Garnier, Adrien. *Frayssinous: Son Rôle dans l'université sous la Restauration (1822–1828)*. Paris, 1925.

Gaudry, J. *Histoire du barreau de Paris depuis son origine jusqu'à 1830*. 2 vols. Paris, 1865.

Gerbod, Paul. *La Condition universitaire en France au XIXe siècle*. Paris, 1965.

―――. "Note sur la condition matérielle et morale de l'étudiant français," *Revue française de sociologie*, 21 (April–June 1980): 251–58.

―――. *Paul-François Dubois: Universitaire, journaliste et homme politique, 1793–1874*. Paris, 1967.

―――. "L'Université et la philosophie de 1789 à nos jours," in *Actes du 95e Congrès national des sociétés savantes. Section d'histoire moderne et contemporaine, 1: Histoire de l'enseignement de 1610 à nos jours*. Paris, 1974.

―――. "La Vie universitaire à Paris de 1820 à 1830," *Revue d'histoire moderne et contemporaine*, 13 (January–March 1966): 5–48.

Géruzez, Eugène. *Mélanges et pensées*. Paris, 1866.

Gével, Claude, and Jean Rabot. "La Censure théâtrale sous la Restauration," *Revue de Paris*, 120 (November–December 1913): 339–62.

Gillis, John R. *Youth and History*. New York, 1974.

Gilman, Stephen. "A Generation of *conversos*," *Romance Philology*, 33 (August 1979): 87–101.

Girard, Henri. *Un Bourgeois dilettante à l'époque romantique: Emile Deschamps, 1791–1871*. Paris, 1921.

Girardet, Raoul. "De La Conception de génération à la notion de contemporanéité," *Revue d'histoire moderne et contemporaine*, 30 (April–June 1983): 257–70.

Goblot, Edmond. *La Barrière et le niveau*. Paris, 1967.

Goblot, Jean-Jacques. "Un 'Mystérieux Rédacteur' du 'Globe': Marcelin Desloges," *Revue d'histoire littéraire de la France*, 85 (March–April 1985): 234–47.

———. *Aux Origines du socialisme français: Pierre Leroux et ses premiers écrits*. Lyon, 1977.

———. " 'Le Globe' en 1827. Lettres inédites de Damiron et de Dubois," *Revue d'histoire littéraire de la France*, 72 (May–June 1972): 482–506.

———. "Paul-François Dubois, Stendhal et 'Le Globe,' " *Stendhal Club*, 54 (15 January 1972): 121–43.

———. "Stendhal, Chroniqueur dévoilé? *Le Courrier anglais* et *Le Globe*," *Stendhal Club*, 56 (15 July 1972): 335–48.

———. "Stendhal, Jouffroy et la philosophie," *Stendhal Club*, 58 (15 January 1973): 133–46.

Godlewski, Henri. "L'Etudiant en médecine Philippe Buchez, fondateur du carbonarisme français," *Bulletin de la société française d'histoire de la médecine*, 31 (February 1937): 43–48.

Goldstein, Dora S. "Official Philosophies in Modern France: The Example of Victor Cousin," *Journal of Social History*, 1 (Spring 1968): 259–79.

Gossman, Lionel. "Augustin Thierry and Liberal Historiography," *History and Theory*, 15 (1976): 3–83.

Gouhier, Henri. *La Jeunesse d'Auguste Comte*. 3 vols. Paris, 1933–41.

———. *La Vie d'Auguste Comte*. Paris, 1965.

La Grande Encyclopédie: Inventaire raisonné des sciences, des lettres et des arts. 31 vols. Paris, 1886–1902.

Grate, Pontus. "La Critique d'art et la bataille romantique," *Gazette des beaux-arts*, 2 (1959): 129–48.

———. *Deux Critiques d'art de l'époque romantique: Gustave Planche et Théophile Thoré*. Stockholm, 1959.

Gruner, Shirley M. "Political Historiography in Restoration France," *History and Theory*, 8 (1969): 346–65.

Gruson, Pascale. *L'Etat enseignant*. Paris, 1978.

Guépin, Ange. *Philosophie du socialisme*. Paris, 1850.

Guigniaut, Joseph Daniel. *Institut impérial de la France: Notice historique sur la vie et les travaux de M. Augustin Thierry*. Paris, 1863.

Guiraud, Alexandre. *Oeuvres*. 4 vols. Paris, 1845.

Guizot, F. A. *Du Gouvernement de la France depuis la Restauration*. 3rd ed. Paris, 1820.

Guizot, François. *Mémoires pour servir à l'histoire de mon temps*. 8 vols. Paris, 1858.

———. *Trois Générations: 1789–1814–1840*. Paris, 1863.

Gunnell, Doris. *Sutton Sharpe et ses amis français*. Paris, 1925.

Guyon, Bernard. *La Pensée politique et sociale de Balzac*. Paris, 1947.

Halévy, Léon. *F. Halévy: Sa Vie et ses oeuvres, récits et impressions personnelles, simples souvenirs*. Paris, 1862.

———. "Souvenirs de Saint-Simon," *France littéraire*, 1 (March 1832): 521–46.

Hanotaux, Gabriel. *Histoire du Cardinal de Richelieu*. Paris, 1893.

Harpaz, Ephraim. *L'Ecole libérale sous la Restauration: Le "Mercure" et la "Minerve," 1817–1820*. Geneva, 1968.

Hatin, Eugène. *Histoire politique et littéraire de la presse en France*. 8 vols. Paris, 1859–61.

Haupt, Herman, and Paul Wentzcke, eds. *Quellen und Darstellungen zur Geschichte der Burschenschaft und der deutschen Einheitsbewegung*. 17 vols. Heidelberg, 1910–40.

Haussez, Charles d'. *Mémoires du Baron Haussez*. Paris, 1896.

Hayek, F. A. *The Counter-Revolution of Science: Studies in the Abuse of Reason*. Glencoe, Ill., 1955.

Hennin, Michel. *Des Théâtres et de leur organisation légale*. Paris, 1819.

Henri, Robert. "Napoléon et la justice," *Revue de Paris*, 164 (1 May 1921): 72–93.

Holland, P. W., and S. Leinhardt, eds. *Perspectives on Social Network Research*. New York, 1979.

Honour, Hugh. *Romanticism*. New York, 1979.

Hoog, Armand. "Un Intercesseur du romantisme: Victor Cousin vu par Stendhal," *Revue des sciences humaines*, new ser., 62–63 (April–September 1951): 184–200.

———. "Who Invented the *Mal du siècle?*" *Yale French Studies*, 13 (Spring–Summer 1954): 42–51.

Horkheimer, Max. *The Eclipse of Reason*. New York, 1947.

Houdaille, Jacques. "Le Problème des pertes de guerre," *Revue d'histoire moderne et contemporaine*, 17 (July–September 1970): 411–23.

Howarth, W. D., *Sublime and Grotesque: A Study of French Romantic Drama*. London, 1975.

Hugo, Adèle. *Victor Hugo raconté par un témoin de sa vie*, in Victor Hugo, *Oeuvres complètes*, ed. Jean Massin. Vols. 1 and 2. Paris, 1967–70.

Hugo, Victor. *Oeuvres complètes*, ed. Jean Massin. 18 vols. Paris, 1967–70.

Huizinga, Johan. *Men and Ideas*. New York, 1965.

Hutton, Patrick H. "The History of Mentalités: The New Map of Cultural History," *History and Theory*, 20 (1981): 237–59.

Iggers, George G. *The Cult of Authority: The Political Philosophy of the Saint-Simonians, A Chapter in the Intellectual History of Totalitarianism*. The Hague, 1958.

Isambert, F. A. *De La Charbonnerie au saint-simonisme: Etude sur la jeunesse de Buchez*. Paris, 1966.

———. "Epoques critiques et époques organiques: Une Contribution de Buchez à la théorie sociale des saint-simoniens," *Cahiers internationaux de sociologie*, 27 (July–December 1959): 131–52.

———. *Politique, religion et science de l'homme chez Philippe Buchez (1786–1865)*. Paris, 1967.

Jacob, P. L. "Notice biographique," in Jules Lefèvre-Deumier. *Sir Lionel D'Arquenay*. Vol. 1. Paris, 1884.

Jacomet, Pierre. *Le Palais sous la Restauration, 1815–1830*. Paris, 1922.

Jacquemont, Victor. *Letters to Achille Chaper*, ed. J. F. Marshall. Philadelphia 1960.

Jaeger, Hans. "Generations in History: Reflections on a Controversial Concept," *History and Theory*, 24 (1985): 273–92.

Jal, Auguste. *L'Artiste et le philosophe, entretiens critiques sur le salon de 1824, recueillis et publiés par A. Jal*. Paris, 1824.

———. *Souvenirs d'un homme de lettres (1795–1873)*. Paris, 1873.

Janet, Paul. "Le Globe de la Restauration et Paul-François Dubois," *Revue des deux mondes*, 34 (1 August 1879): 481–512.

———. *Victor Cousin et son oeuvre*. Paris, 1885.

Jarausch, Konrad H. "Sources of German Student Unrest," in Lawrence Stone, ed., *The University in Society*. Princeton, 1974.

Jasinski, René. *Histoire de la littérature française*. 2 vols. Paris, 1966.

Jensen, Christian A. E. *L'Evolution du romantisme: L'Année 1826*. Geneva, 1959.

Joravsky, David. "The Construction of the Stalinist Psyche," in Sheila Fitzpatrick, ed., *Cultural Revolution in Russia, 1928–1931*, Bloomington, Ind., 1984.

Jouffroy, Théodore. *Le Cahier vert*. Paris, 1924.

———. *Correspondance de Théodore Jouffroy, publiée avec une étude sur Jouffroy par Adolphe Lair*. Paris, 1901.

———. *Mélanges philosophiques*. Paris, 1833.

———. *Nouveaux mélanges philosophiques*. 3rd ed. Paris, 1872.

———. *Oeuvres complètes de Thomas Reid*. Paris, 1836.

Jouy, Etienne. *L'Hermite de la Chaussée d'Antin; ou, Observations sur les moeurs et les usages au commencement du XIXe siècle*. 2nd ed. Paris, 1813.

Kadushin, Charles. "Networks and Circles in the Production of Culture," *American Behavioral Scientist*, 19 (July–August 1976): 769–84.

Keniston, Kenneth. "Different Childhood Experiences of Radical and Alienated Youth," in Alexander Klein, ed., *Natural Enemies*. Philadelphia, 1969.

———. *Youth and Dissent*. New York, 1971.

———. "Youth: A 'New' Stage of Life," *American Scholar*, 39 (Autumn 1970): 631–54.

Keylor, William. *Academy and Community: The Founding of the French Historical Profession*. Cambridge, Mass., 1975.

Klein, Alexander. *Natural Enemies: Youth and the Clash of Generations*. Philadelphia, 1969.

Knibiehler, Yvonne. *Naissance des sciences humaines: Mignet et l'histoire philosophique au XIXe siècle*. Paris, 1973.

Knoke, D., and J. H. Kuklinski. *Network Analysis*. Beverly Hills, 1982.

Kock, Charles Paul de. *Mémoires de Ch. Paul de Kock*. Paris, 1873.

Kolb, Marthe. *Ary Scheffer Et Son Temps, 1785–1858*. Paris, 1937.

Kriegel, Annie. "Generational Difference: The History of an Idea," *Daedalus*, 107 (Fall 1978): 23–38.

Kruskal, Joseph B. "Multidimensional Scaling: A Numerical Method," *Journal of Psychometrica*, 29 (1964): 1–37.

Kruskal, Joseph B., and Myron Wish. *Multidimensional Scaling*. Beverly Hills, 1978.

Lacassagne, Jean-Pierre. "De la Charbonnerie au socialisme: L'Itinéraire politique de Pierre Leroux," *Revue des travaux de l'Académie des sciences morales et politiques* (2ᵉ semestre, 1971): 189–206.

Lafayette, Gilbert de. *Mémoires, correspondance et manuscrits du général La Fayette, publiés par sa famille*. 6 vols. Paris, 1837–38.

Lair, Adolphe. " 'Le Globe': Sa fondation—sa rédaction—son influence: D'Après Des Documents inédits," *Séance et travaux de l'Académie des sciences morales et politiques*, 161 (May 1904): 570–98.

———. "Les Souvenirs de M. Dubois," *Quinzaine*, 43 (1 November 1901): 74–87.

———. "Un Maître de Sainte-Beuve," *Correspondant*, 199 (1900): 317–26.

Lammenais, Félicité de. *Correspondance inédite entre Lamennais et le Baron Vitrolles*. Paris, 1886.

———. *Oeuvres inédites*, ed. A. Bleuze. 2 vols. Paris, 1866.

[Lamennais, Félicité de.?] *Quelques réflexions sur l'Ecole polytechnique*. Paris, 1816.

Laumann, Edward O., Peter V. Marsden, and David Perenky. "The Boundary Specification Problem in Network Analysis," in Ronald S. Burt, Michael J. Minor, et al. *Applied Network Analysis: A Methodological Introduction*. Beverly Hills, 1983.

Launay, Louis de. *Un Amoureux de Madame Récamier: Le Journal de J. J. Ampère*. Paris, 1927.

Laurent, P. M. *Résumé de l'histoire et de la philosophie*. Paris, 1826.

Laurentie, Pierre Sébastien. *Souvenirs inédits*. Paris, 1892.

Lefèvre[-Deumier], Jules. *Critique littéraire (1825–1845)*. Paris, 1896.

———. *Sir Lionel D'Arquenay*. Paris, 1884.

———. *Le Parricide, poème: suivi d'autres poésies*. Paris, 1823.

———. *Les Vespres de l'Abbaye du Val*. Paris, 1924.

Le Goff, Jacques. "Les Mentalités," in Jacques Le Goff and Pierre Nora, eds., *Faire De L'Histoire*. Vol. 3. Paris, 1974.

Lehmann, A. G. *Sainte-Beuve*. Oxford, 1962.

Leinhardt, Samuel, ed. *Social Networks: A Developing Paradigm*. New York, 1977.

Léonard, Jacques. "L'Exemple d'une catégorie socio-professionnelle au XIXe siècle, les médecins français," in *Ordres et classes: Colloque d'histoire sociale*. Saint-Cloud, 24–25 May 1967. No. 31, ch. 9. Paris, 1973.

———. "La Restauration et la profession médicale," *Historical Reflections*, 9 (Spring and Summer 1982): 69–81.

———. *La Vie quotidienne du médecin de province au XIXe siècle*. Paris, 1977.

———. "Les Etudes médicales en France entre 1815 et 1848," *Revue d'histoire moderne et contemporaine*, 12 (January–March 1966): 87–94.

———. *Les Médecins de l'ouest au XIXe siècle*. 3 vols. Paris, 1978.

Lerminier, Eugène. *Lettres philosophiques adressées à un Berlinois*. Paris, 1832.

Leroux, Pierre. *De la Mutilation d'un écrit posthume de Théodore Jouffroy avec une lettre à l'Académie des sciences morales et un appendice pour faire suite à la réfutation de l'éclectisme*. Paris, 1843.

———. *Réfutation de l'éclectisme*. Paris, 1839.

———. "D'Une Nouvelle Typographie," *Revue indépendante*, 6 (25 January 1843): 262–91.

Lévy-Bruhl, Lucien. *History of Modern Philosophy in France*. Chicago, 1899.

Lévy-Garboua, Louis. "Les Demandes de l'étudiant ou les contradictions de l'université de masse," *Revue française de sociologie*, 17 (January–March 1976): 53–80.

Le Yaouanc, Moïse. "Balzac au lycée Charlemagne," *L'Année balzacienne* (1962).

Liard, Louis. *L'Enseignement supérieur en France*. 2 vols. Paris, 1888–94.

Loua, Toussaint, comp. *Atlas statistique de la population de Paris*. Paris, 1873.

Loyson, Charles. *Lettre à M. Benjamin Constant, l'un des rédacteurs de la "Minerve."* Paris, 1819.

———. *Oeuvres choisies*. Paris, 1869.

Lukács, Georg. *Studies in European Realism*, trans. Edith Bone. London, 1950.

Lutz, Rolland Ray. "Father Jahn and His Teacher-Revolutionaries from the German Student Movement," On-Demand Supplement, *Journal of Modern History*, 48 (June 1976): 1–34.

———. "The German Revolutionary Student Movement," *Central European History*, 4 (September 1971): 215–41.

Lycée Louis-le-Grand. *Palmarès, 1810–1819*. Paris, s.d.

Lyons, Marty. "The Audience for Romanticism: Walter Scott in France, 1815–51," *European History Quarterly*, 14 (January 1984): 21–46.

McCosh, F.W.J. *Boussingault: Chemist and Agriculturist*. Boston, 1984.

Machiavelli, Niccolò. *The Prince and the Discourse*, trans. Luigi Ricci. New York, 1940.

Mahul, Alphonse. "Souvenirs d'un collégien du temps de l'Empire," *Revue des langues romanes*, 37 (1894): 506–20, 566–70; 38 (1895): 84–92, 135–45.

Maitron, Jean, comp. *Dictionnaire biographique du mouvement ouvrier français*. Part 1, *1789–1864*. Paris, 1964–66.

Malo, Henri. *Thiers, 1797–1877*. Paris, 1932.

Jarry de Mancy, Adrien. *Tableau historique, chronologique des concours généraux de l'Université, ancienne et nouvelle, depuis la fondation des concours jusqu'en 1825 inclusivement, suivi du tableau de la distribution des prix du concours général, et des distributions des prix des huit collèges de Paris et de Versailles en 1826*. Paris, s.d.

Mandelbaum, Maurice. *History, Man, and Reason*. Baltimore, 1971.

Mandrou, Robert. "L'Histoire des mentalités," under the entry "Histoire" in the *Encyclopaedia Universalis*. Vol. 8. Paris, 1968.

Mannheim, Karl. *Essays on Sociology and Social Psychology*. London, 1969.

———. *Ideology and Utopia*. New York, 1955.

———. "The Problem of Generations," in *Essays in the Sociology of Knowledge*. London, 1959.

Manuel, Frank E. *The New World of Henri Saint-Simon*. Cambridge, Mass., 1956.

———. *The Prophets of Paris*. Cambridge, Mass., 1962.

Maréchal, Christian. "Auguste Comte, Andrieux, La Mennais et l'Ecole polytechnique," *Correspondant*, 282 (25 February 1921): 628–56.

Marielle, M.C.-P. *Répertoire de l'école impériale polytechnique*. Paris, 1855.

Marrast, Armand. *Examen critique du cours de philosophie de M. Cousin (leçon par leçon)*. Paris, 1828.

Marsan, Jules. *La Bataille romantique*. Paris, 1912.

Marsan, Jules, ed. *Le Conservateur littéraire, 1819–1821*. 4 vols. Paris, 1922–26, 1935–38.

———. *La Muse française*. 2 vols. Paris, 1907.

Marsden, P. V., and N. Lin. *Social Structure and Network Analysis*. Beverly Hills, 1982.

Martineau, Henri, ed. *Cent soixante-quatorze lettres à Stendhal (1810–1842)*. 2 vols. Paris, 1947.

Martineau, Henri, comp. *Petit Dictionnaire stendhalien*. Paris, 1948.

Massin, Jean. "La Fin de la 'Muse française' et la mort de l'enfant sublime," in Victor Hugo, *Oeuvres*, ed. Jean Massin. Vol. 2. Paris, 1967.

Maurain, Jean. *Un Bourgeois français au XIXe siècle: Baroche, ministre de Napoléon III*. Paris, 1936.

Mauricet, J. J. *Souvenirs d'un vieux collègien*. Vienna, 1876.

Mayeur, Françoise. *De La Révolution à l'école républicaine* vol. 3 of *Histoire générale de l'enseignement et de l'éducation en France*, ed. Louis-Henri Parias. Paris, 1981.

Mazoyer, Louis. "Catégories d'âge et groupes sociaux: Les Jeunes Générations françaises de 1830," *Annales*, 10 (September 1938): 385–423.

Mellon, Stanley. *The Political Uses of History*. Stanford, 1958.

Mémorial de l'association des anciens élèves de l'Ecole normale, 1846–1876. Versailles, 1877.

Mentré, François. *Les Générations sociales*. Paris, 1920.

Mérimée, Prosper. *Correspondance générale*, ed. Maurice Parturier. 17 vols. Paris, 1941–64.

———. *Oeuvres complètes de Prosper Mérimée*, ed. Pierre Trahard et Edouard Champion. 12 vols. Paris, 1927.

Mes Idées sur l'ordre des avocats: Par un licencié en droit qui n'a pas encore prêté serment. Paris, 1822.

Meuriot, Paul. *Le Baccalauréat: Son Evolution historique et statistique des origines (1808) à nos jours*. Nancy, 1919.

Michaud, Joseph François, comp. *Biographie universelle*. 45 vols. Paris, 1854.

Michaut, Gustave. *Sainte-Beuve Avant Les "Lundis."* Paris, 1903.

———. *Sénancour: Ses Amis et ses ennemis*. Paris, 1909.

Michelet, Jules. *Ecrits de jeunesse*. Paris, 1959.

———. *Journal*. 2 vols. Paris, 1959–62.

———. *Oeuvres complètes*. Vols. 1–9, 16, 21. Paris, 1971–82.

Mignet, François. *Histoire de la Révolution française depuis 1789 jusqu'en 1814*. 2 vols. Paris, 1824.

———. *Institut Impérial de France. Notice historique sur la vie et les travaux de M. Victor Cousin*. Paris, 1869.

———. "Notice historique sur la vie et les travaux de M. Jouffroy," 25 June 1853, *Mémoire de l'académie des sciences morales et politiques de l'Institut de France*. Paris, 1855.

Milner, Max. *Le Romantisme*. Vol. 1, *1820–1843*. Paris, 1973.

Ministère de l'instruction publique, des beaux-arts et des cultes. *Enquêtes et documents relatifs à l'enseignement supérieur.* Vol. 21, *Etat numérique des grades, 1795–1885.* Paris, 1886.

Montalivet, Comte de. *Fragments et souvenirs.* 2 vols. Paris, 1899–1900.

Moody, Joseph. *French Education since Napoleon.* Syracuse, N.Y., 1978.

Moreau, Pierre. *Le Classicisme des romantiques.* Paris, 1932.

———. *Le Romantisme.* Paris, 1932.

Morin-Pons, Franck. "Thiers, avocat Aixois, 1818–1821," *Provence historique,* 9 (October–December 1959): 226–57.

Les Murailles révolutionnaires de 1848. 16th ed. 2 vols. Paris, 1868.

Musset, Alfred de. *La Confession d'un enfant du siècle: Oeuvres complètes en prose.* Paris, 1951.

Nettement, Alfred. *Histoire de la littérature française sous la Restauration.* 2 vols. Paris, 1874.

Nisard, Désiré. "Armand Carrel," *Revue des deux mondes,* 12 (1 October 1837): 5–54.

Nora, Pierre, ed. *Les Lieux de mémoire.* Vol. 1, *La République.* Paris, 1984.

O'Boyle, Leonore. "The Image of the Journalist in France, Germany, and England, 1815–1848," in Clive Emsley, ed., *Conflict and Stability in Europe.* London, 1979.

———. "Klassische Bildung und soziale Struktur in Deutschland zwischen 1800 und 1848," *Historische Zeitschrift,* 207 (December 1968): 584–608.

———. "The Problem of an Excess of Educated Men in Western Europe, 1800–1850," *Journal of Modern History,* 42 (December 1970): 471–95.

Odin, Alfred. *Genèse des grands hommes, gens de lettres français modernes.* Paris, 1895.

Ody, H. J. *Victor Cousin: Ein Lebensbild im deutsch-französischen Kulturraum.* Saarbrücken, 1953.

Ollé-Laprune, Léon. *Théodore Jouffroy.* Paris, 1899.

Orecchioni, Pierre. "Tentatives de restauration intellectuelle," in Pierre Abraham and Roland Desné, eds., *Manuel d'histoire littéraire de la France.* Vol. 4. Paris, 1972.

Palmer, R. R. *The School of the French Revolution.* Princeton, 1975.

Paris Révolutionnaire. 4 vols. Paris, 1833–34.

Pasquier, Etienne Denis. *Mémoires du Chancelier Pasquier.* 6 vols. Paris, 1896.

Patin, H.J.G. *Discours de M. S. de Sacy ... prononcé aux funérailles de M. V. Cousin le 24 janvier 1867, et discours de MM. de Parien et Patin.* Paris, 1867.

Peoples, Margaret H. "La Société des bonnes lettres (1821–1830)," *Smith College Studies in Modern Languages,* 5 (October 1923): 1–50.

Pépin, V. E. "Matériaux pour servir à la biographie d'Auguste Comte: Licenciement de l'Ecole polytechnique en avril 1816," *Revue positiviste internationale,* 7 (15 November 1909): 413–34.

Perdiguier, Agricol. *Mémoires d'un compagnon.* Paris, 1964.

Pereire, Alfred. *Autour de Saint-Simon*. Paris, 1912.

———. "Des Premiers rapports entre Saint-Simon et Auguste Comte d'après des documents originaux (1816–1819)," *Revue Historique*, 91 (1906): 57–98.

Peyre, Henri. *Les Générations littéraires*. Paris, 1948.

Picavet, François. *Les Idéologues*. Paris, 1891.

Pichois, Claude. *Philarète Chasles Et La Vie littéraire au temps du romantisme*. 2 vols. Paris, 1965.

———. "Pour Une Biographie d'Etienne Jouy," *Revue des sciences humaines*, 118 (April–June 1965): 227–52.

———. "Les Vrais Mémoires de Philarète Chasles," *Revue des sciences humaines*, 81 (January–March 1956): 71-97.

Picot, Georges. *Etudes d'histoire parlementaire*. Paris, 1883.

Pierrot, Roger. "Lettres inédites sur la révolution de 1848," *L'Année balzacienne* (1960): 43–63.

Pinard, Marie-Oscar. *Le Barreau au XIXe siècle*. 2 vols. Paris, 1864–65.

Piobetta, J. B. *Le Baccalauréat*. Paris, 1938.

Poirier, Jean. "Lycéens d'il y a cent ans," *Revue internationale de l'enseignement*, 67 (1914): 174–88.

———. "Lycéens impériaux (1814–1815)," *Revue de Paris*, 164 (15 May 1921): 380–401.

———. "L'Opinion publique et l'Université pendant la première Restauration," *La Révolution française*, 56 (March 1909): 234–70, 330–42.

———. "L'Université provisoire (1814–1821)," *Revue d'histoire moderne*, 1 (1926): 241–79; 2 (1927): 261–306.

Pommier, Jean. *Deux Etudes sur Jouffroy et son temps*. Paris, 1930.

Posener, S. *Adolphe Crémieux*. Paris, 1933–34.

Poumiès de la Siboutie, François-Louis. *Dr. Poumiès de la Siboutie (1789–1863): Souvenirs d'un médecin de Paris*. Paris, 1910.

Pouthas, Charles. *Essai critique sur les sources et la bibliographie de Guizot pendant la Restauration*. Paris, 1923.

———. *Guizot pendant la Restauration*. Paris, 1923.

[Proisy D'Eppe, César de]. *Dictionnaire des girouettes; ou, Nos Contemporains peints d'après eux-mêmes*. Paris, 1815.

Prost, Antoine. "La Culture scolaire," in *Histoire de l'enseignement en France, 1800–1967*. Paris, 1968.

Quatremère de Quincy, Antoine-Chrysostôme, comp. *Recueil des notices historiques lues dans les séances publiques de l'Académie-Royale des Beaux-Arts à l'Institut par M. Quatremère de Quincy—secrétaire perpétuel de cette académie*. Paris, 1834.

Quérard, J. M. *La France littéraire du dictionnaire bibliographique*. 12 vols. Paris, 1827–57.

Quicherat, Jules. *Histoire de Sainte-Barbe.* 3 vols. Paris, 1860–64.

Quinet, Edgar. *Correspondance de Edgar Quinet—Lettres à sa mère.* 2 vols. Paris, 1877.

———. *Histoire de mes idées.* Paris, 1878.

Raitt, A. W. *Prosper Mérimée.* New York, 1970.

Rambuteau, Claude Philibert Barthelot de. *Memoirs of the Comte de Rambuteau,* trans. J. C. Brogan, London, 1908.

Ramsey, Matthew. "Medical Power and Popular Medicine: Illegal Healers in Nineteenth-Century France," *Journal of Social History,* 10 (June 1977): 560–87.

Ratcliffe, Barry M. "Saint-Simonianism and Messianism: The Case of Gustave d'Eichtal," *French Historical Studies,* 9 (Spring 1976): 484–502.

———. "Some Jewish Problems in the Early Careers of Emile and Isaac Pereire," *Jewish Social Studies,* 34 (July 1972): 189–207.

———. "Les Pereire et le saint-simonisme," *Cahiers de l'Institut de science économique appliquée,* 5 (1971): 15–57.

Ravaisson, Félix. *La Philosophie en France au XIXe siècle.* Paris, 1904.

Recueil des règlements relatifs aux concours ouverts et aux grands prix décernés par l'Académie Royale des Beaux-Arts. Paris, 1821.

Reizov, B. *L'Historiographie romantique française, 1815–1830.* Moscow, 1962.

Rémusat, Charles de. *Correspondance de M. de Rémusat.* 6 vols. Paris, 1866.

———. *Essais de philosophie.* 2 vols. Paris, 1842.

———. *L'Habitation de Saint Domingue; ou, L'Insurrection,* ed. J. E. Derre. Paris, 1977.

———. *Mémoires de ma vie,* ed. 5 vols. Paris, 1958–67.

———. *Passé et Présent,* 2 vols. Paris, 1847.

———. *Séance de l'Académie française du 23 avril 1868. Discours de réception de Jules Favre. Réponse de M. De Rémusat.* Paris, 1868.

Renan, Ernest. "L'Instruction supérieure en France," in *Oeuvres.* Vol. 1. Paris, 1947.

———. "M. Cousin," in *Essais de morale et de critique,* in *Oeuvres complètes.* Vol. 2. Paris, 1947.

Reybaud, Louis. *Etudes sur les réformateurs contemporains; ou, Les Socialistes modernes.* 2 vols. Paris, 1864.

Richardson, Nicholas. *The French Prefectoral Corps, 1814–1830.* Cambridge, Eng., 1966.

Ridgway, R. S. *Voltaire and Sensibility.* Montreal and London, 1973.

Riley, Matilda White. "Aging and Cohort Succession: Interpretations and Misinterpretations," *Public Opinion Quarterly,* 37 (Spring 1973): 35–49.

———. "Aging, Social Change, and the Power of Ideas," *Daedalus,* 107 (Fall 1978): 39–52.

Rio, A. F. *Epilogue à l'art chrétien.* 2 vols. Freiburg im Bresgau, 1870.

------. *La Petite Chouannerie; ou, Histoire d'un collège breton sous l'Empire.* Paris, 1842.

Robert, Adolphe, and Gaston Cougny, comps. *Dictionnaire des parlementaires français.* 5 vols. Paris, 1889–90.

Rosenthal, Léon. *La Peinture romantique.* Paris, 1900.

Rouen, Pierre-Isidore. *Défense de M. Rouen devant le tribunal de police correctionelle de la Seine.* Paris, 1823.

Rudé, Fernand. *Stendhal Et La Pensée sociale de son temps.* Paris, 1967.

Ruppert, Johann. *Das Soziale System Bazards.* Würzburg, 1890.

Ryder, Norman R. "The Cohort as a Concept in the Study of Social Change," *American Sociological Review*, 30 (December 1965): 843–61.

Sacy, Silvestre de. *Variétés littéraires, morales et historiques.* 2 vols. Paris, 1858–59.

Sainte-Beuve, Charles-Augustin. *Causeries du lundi.* 15 vols. Paris, 1883.

------. *Correspondance générale.* 13 vols. Paris, 1935.

------. *Nouveaux lundis.* 13 vols. Paris, 1886–97.

------. *Portraits contemporains.* 5 vols. Paris, 1889–91.

------. *Portraits littéraires.* 3 vols. Paris, 1862–64.

------. *Premiers lundis.* 3 vols. Paris, 1882.

------. *Vie, poésies et pensées de Joseph Delorme.* Paris, 1956.

------. *Volupté.* Paris, 1912.

[Saint-Simon, Henri de]. *Oeuvres de Saint-Simon et d'Enfantin.* 47 vols. Paris, 1865–78.

Saint-Simon, Henri de. *Opinions littéraires, philosophiques et industrielles.* Paris, 1825.

Saint-Valry, Adolphe de. *Madame de Mably.* 2nd ed. Paris, 1838.

Sarrut, Germain, and B. Saint-Edme. *Biographie des hommes du jour.* Paris, 1836.

Sauvigny, Guillaume de Bertier de. *The Bourbon Restoration*, trans. Lynn M. Case. Philadelphia, 1966.

Schact, Richard. *Hegel and After.* Pittsburgh, 1975.

Scheffer, Arnold. *Considérations sur l'état actuel de l'Europe.* Paris, 1817.

------. *De l'Etat de la liberté en France.* Paris, 1818.

------. *Essais sur quatre grandes questions politiques.* Paris, 1817.

Schimberg, André. *Les Fragments philosophiques de Royer-Collard.* Paris, 1913.

Schmidtlein, Karl. "Saint-Amand Bazard: Ein Beitrag zur Entstehungsgeschichte des Sozialismus," *Schmollers Jahrbuch*, 46 (1922): 65–107.

Schneider, René. *Quatremère de Quincy Et Son Intervention dans les arts (1788–1830).* Paris, 1910.

Scott, Wilbur, and Harold Grasmick. "Generations and Group Consciousness: A Quantification of Mannheim's Analogy," *Youth and Society*, 11 (December 1979): 191–213.

Séché, Léon. *Le Cénacle de la "Muse française," 1823–1827.* Paris, 1909.

Ségu, Frédéric. *L'Académie des jeux floraux et le romantisme de 1818 à 1824.* Paris, 1935.

Semelaigne, René. *Les Pionniers de la psychiatrie française avant et après Pinel.* 2 vols. Paris, 1930.

[Senemaud, Edmond]. *Détails historiques sur les évènements de la première quinzaine de juin MDCCCXX, par M. Senemaud, élève de la Faculté de droit de Paris.* Paris, 1820.

[Serre, Pierre-François Hercule de]. *Correspondance du comte de Serre (1796–1824).* 6 vols. Paris, 1876–77.

Sève, Lucien. *Philosophie française contemporaine.* Paris, 1962.

Shinn, Terry. "La Profession d'ingénieur, 1750–1920," *Revue française de sociologie,* 19 (January–March 1978): 39–71.

———. *Savoir scientifique et pouvoir social: L'Ecole polytechnique, 1794–1914.* Paris, 1980.

Simmel, George. *The Web of Group Affiliations.* New York, 1955.

Simon, Jules. *Mémoires des autres.* Paris, 1890.

———. "Notice historique sur la vie et les travaux de M. De Rémusat," *Mémoires de l'Académie des sciences morales et politiques de l'Institut de France,* 14 (22 July 1883): 277–315.

———. *Victor Cousin.* 3rd ed. Paris, 1891.

Simon, Walter M. "History for Utopia: Saint-Simon and the Idea of Progress," *Journal of the History of Ideas,* 17 (June 1956): 311–31.

———. "The 'Two Cultures' in Nineteenth-Century France: Victor Cousin and Auguste Comte," *Journal of the History of Ideas,* 26 (January–March 1965): 45–58.

Skinner, Quentin. *The Foundations of Modern Political Thought.* Cambridge, Eng., 1978.

Smithson, Roulon Nephi. *Augustin Thierry: Social and Political Consciousness in the Evolution of a Historical Method.* Geneva, 1973.

Sommerville, C. John. *The Rise and Fall of Childhood.* Beverly Hills, 1982.

Spitzer, Alan B. "The Historical Problem of Generations," *American Historical Review,* 78 (December 1973): 1353–85.

———. *Old Hatreds and Young Hopes: The French Carbonari Against the Bourbon Restoration.* Cambridge, Mass., 1971.

———. "Victor Cousin and the French Generation of 1820," in Dora B. Weiner and William R. Keylor, eds., *From Parnassus: Essays in Honor of Jacques Barzun.* New York, 1976.

Spühler, Willy. *Der Saint-Simonismus: Lehre und Leben von Saint-Amand Bazard.* Zurich, 1926.

Spuller, Eugène. *Royer-Collard.* Paris, 1895.

Staël-Holstein, Auguste de. *Du Nombre et de l'âge des députés.* Paris, 1819.

Stark, Gary D. "The Ideology of the German *Burschenschaft* Generation." *European Studies Review*, 8 (July 1978): 323–48.

Stendhal, *Correspondance*, 10 vols. Paris, 1933–34.

———. *Courrier anglais*, ed. H. Martineau. 5 vols. Paris, 1935.

———. *D'un Nouveau Complot contre les industriels*. Nouvelle Bibliothèque Romantique, No. 3. Paris, 1972.

———. *Memoirs of an Egoist*, trans. T. W. Earp. New York, 1958.

———. *Racine et Shakespeare*, in *Oeuvres complètes*. 49 vols. Paris, 1970.

Stenzel, Helmut, and Heinz Thoma. "Poésie et société dans la critique littéraire du *Globe*," *Romantisme*, 39 (1983): 25–59.

Stone, S. Irving. "La Fin de la 'Muse française,' " *Revue d'histoire littéraire de la France*, 36 (1929): 270–77.

Sussman, George D. "The Glut of Doctors in Mid-Nineteenth-Century France," *Comparative Studies in Society and History*, 19 (July 1977): 287–304.

Szajkowski, Zosa. "The Jewish Saint-Simonians and Socialist Antisemites in France," *Jewish Social Studies*, 9 (January 1947): 33–60.

Taillefer, Louis Gabriel. *De Quelques Améliorations à introduire dans l'instruction publique*. Paris, 1824.

Taine, Hippolyte. *Les Philosophes classiques du XIXe siècle en France*. 7th ed. Paris, 1895.

Taranne, Nicolas-Rodolphe. *Notice historique sur le concours général entre les collèges de Paris*. Paris, 1847.

Thibaudet, Albert. "La Génération de 1820," in *Histoire de la littérature française*. Paris, 1936.

Thibert, Marguerite. *Le Rôle social de l'art d'après les saint-simoniens*. Paris, 1925.

Thierry, A. Augustin. "Histoire d'un Historien: Amédée Thierry 1797–1873," *Revue des deux mondes*, 46 (October 1928): 900–30.

Thierry, Augustin. *Augustin Thierry (1795–1856) d'après sa correspondance et ses papiers de famille*. Paris, 1922.

———. *Lettres sur l'histoire de France* [and] *Dix Ans d'études historiques*. Brussels, 1867.

———. *Histoire de la conquête de l'Angleterre par les normands*. Paris, 1825.

———. *L'Industrie*. Vol. 2 of *Oeuvres de Claude Henri de Saint-Simon*. Paris, 1966.

Thiers, Adolphe. *Histoire de la révolution française*. 2 vols. Brussels, 1845.

Thirion, André. *Revolutionaries without Revolution*. New York, 1975.

Thomas, P. Félix. *Pierre Leroux: Sa Vie, ses oeuvres, sa doctrine*. Paris, 1904.

Thomasseau, Jean-Marie. "Le Mélodrame et la censure sous le Premier Empire et la Restauration," *Revue des sciences humaines*, 162 (April–June 1976): 171–82.

Thureau-Dangin, Paul. *Le Parti libéral sous la Restauration*. Paris, 1888.

Tissot, Joseph. *Th. Jouffroy: Sa Vie et ses écrits*. Paris, 1875.

Tolédano, A.-D. *La Vie de famille sous la Restauration et la Monarchie de Juillet*. Paris, 1943.

Tolley, Bruce. "The 'Cénacle' of Balzac's *Illusions perdues*," *French Studies*, 15 (October 1961): 324–37.

Trahard, Pierre. *La Jeunesse de Prosper Mérimée*. 2 vols. Paris, 1925.

———. "Le Romantisme défini par 'le Globe,' " in Henri Girard, ed., *Etudes romantiques*. Paris, 1925.

Trélat, Ulysse. *De La Constitution du corps des médecins et de l'enseignement médical*. Paris, 1828.

Trénard, Louis. "L'Histoire des mentalités collectives: Les Livres—Bilan et perspectives," *Revue d'histoire moderne et contemporaine*, 15 (October-December 1968): 691–703.

———. *Salvandy En Son Temps, 1795–1856*. Lille, 1968.

Tyler, Robert. "Of Generations, Generation Gaps, and History," *Connecticut Review*, 5 (October 1971): 5–12.

Université impériale. *Rapport de la commission nommé par arrêté du gouvernement du 27 frumaire an XI pour le choix des livres classiques des lycées, dans chaque classe de latin et dans celles de belles-letttres* (Fait et arrêté le 27 février an 9).

Vacherot, M. E. "Notice biographique," in Paul-François Dubois, *Fragments littéraires*. 2 vols. Paris, 1879.

Vaulabelle, Achille de. *Histoire des deux Restaurations*. 4th ed. 8 vols. Paris, 1858.

Vaulthier, G. "Les Etudiants en droit en 1823," *Revue internationale de l'enseignement*, 63 (1912): 264–68.

Ventre-Denis, Madeleine. "La Première Chaire d'histoire du droit à la faculté de droit de Paris (1819–1822)," *Revue historique du droit français et étranger*, 45 (October-December 1975): 596–622.

———. "Sciences sociales et Université au XIXe siècle: Une tentative d'enseignement de l'économie politique à Paris sous la Restauration," *Revue historique*, 256 (October–December 1976): 321–42.

Venzac, Géraud. *Les Origines religieuses de Victor Hugo*. Paris, 1955.

———. *Les Premiers Maîtres de Victor Hugo*. Paris, 1955.

Vermeren, Patrice. "Une Politique de l'institution philosophique, ou de la tactique parlementaire en matière de religion et de philosophie: Edgar Quinet et Victor Cousin," *Corpus*, 1 (May 1985): 104–33.

Veron, Louis. *Mémoires d'un bourgeois de Paris*. 5 vols. Paris, 1856.

Vial, Francisque. *Trois Siècles de l'enseignement secondaire*. Paris, 1936.

Viallaneix, Paul. *La Voie royale*. Paris, 1971.

Viard, Jacques. "Leroux, 'Ouvrier typographe,' carbonaro et fondateur du *Globe*," *Romantisme*, 28 (1980): 239–54.

Viel-Castel, Louis de. *Histoire de la restauration*. 20 vols. Paris, 1865.

Vigny, Alfred de. *Correspondance d'Alfred de Vigny, 1816–1863*. Paris, 1905.

———. *Le Journal d'un poête*. Paris, 1913.

———. *Mémoires inédits d'Alfred de Vigny*, ed. Jean Sangnier. Paris, 1958.

———. *Oeuvres complètes: Correspondance, Première série (1816–1835)*. Paris, 1953.

Villèle, Joseph de. *Mémoires et correspondance du Comte de Villèle*. 5 vols. Paris, 1889.

Vincard, Jules. *Mémoires épisodiques d'un vieux chansonnier saint-simonien*. Paris, 1878.

Vitet, Ludovic. "Peintres modernes de la France: Ary Scheffer," *Revue des deux mondes*, 17 (1 October 1858): 481–516.

Vovelle, Michel. *Idéologie et mentalités*. Paris, 1982.

Vuacheux, Ferdinand. *Casimir Delavigne: Etude biographique et littéraire*. Le Havre, 1893.

Wakefield, David. "Stendhal and Delécluze at the *Salon* of 1824," in F. Haskell, A. Levi, and R. Shackleton, eds., *The Artist and the Writer in France*. Oxford, 1974.

Weill, Georges. *Histoire de l'enseignement secondaire en France (1802–1920)*. Paris, 1921.

———. *Histoire du parti républicain en France (1814–1870)*. Paris, 1928.

———. "Les Juifs et les saint-simoniens," *Revue des études juives*, 31 (1895): 261–80.

———. "Paul Dubois, Un Intellectuel Député," *Revue de synthèse historique*, 46 (December 1928): 66–100.

Weiner, Dora. *Raspail: Scientist and Reformer*. New York, 1968.

———. "French Doctors Face War, 1792–1815," in Charles K. Warner, ed., *From the Ancien Régime to the Popular Front: Essays in the History of Modern France in Honor of Shepard B. Clough*. New York, 1969.

Weinstein, Fred, and Gerald M. Platt. "The Coming Crisis in Psychohistory," *Journal of Modern History*, 47 (June 1975): 202–28.

Weiss, John H. *The Making of Technological Man: The Social Origins of French Engineering Education*. Cambridge, Mass., 1982.

Weisz, George. "The Politics of Medical Professionalization in France, 1845–1848," *Journal of Social History*, 12 (Fall 1976): 3–30.

White, Harrison C., and Cynthia White. *Canvases and Careers: Institutional Change in the French Painting World*. New York, 1965.

Wicks, Charles B. *The Parisian Stage*, Part 1: *1800–1815*, Part 2: *1816–1830*. University, Ala., 1950–79.

Wieclawik, Lucienne de. *Alphonse Rabbe Dans La Mêlée politique et littéraire de la Restauration*. Paris, 1963.

Will, Frederic. *Flumen Historicum: Victor Cousin's Aesthetic and Its Sources*. Chapel Hill, N.C., 1965.

Williams, L. Pearce. "Science, Education and Napoleon I," *Isis*, 47 (December 1956): 369–82.

Wohl, Robert. *The Generation of 1914*. Cambridge, Mass., 1979.

Wylie, Laurence W. *Saint-Marc Girardin, Bourgeois*. Syracuse, 1947.

Index

Library of Congress Cataloging-in-Publication Data

Spitzer, Alan B. (Alan Barrie), 1925–
 The French generation of 1820.

 Bibliography: p.
 Includes index.
  1. France—History—Restoration, 1814–1830.
 2. France—Intellectual life—19th century.
 3. Generations—France—History—19th century.
 4. France—Social conditions—19th century.
 I. Title.
 DC256.8.S66 1987   944.06   86-25471
 ISBN 0-691-05496-7 (alk. paper)